Wisconsin Obsolete Bank Notes and Scrip

By Chester L. Krause

Published by

700 E. State Street • Iola, WI 54990-0001
Telephone: 715/445-2214

Library of Congress Catalog Number: 93-80693
ISBN: 0-87341-300-8
Printed in the United States of America

Contents

Bank and Merchant Index

City Index

Introduction

In the Beginning

It is not known from where the designation "Wisconsin" came from, but we do know that reference to the Wisconsin glacier is made to the large sheet of ice that once covered the entire Midwest as well as mid-Canada.

By definition, "Wisconsin" means a large wide river. One of the great rivers that the glacier left was the Wisconsin River that rises on the border between Wisconsin and Michigan's Upper Peninsula at Lake Veau Desert and flows south and west to join the Mississippi River at Prairie du Chien. Before the white man arrived here and during his early influence, the Wisconsin River was the main north/south highway (waterway).

As one searches early history, you will find the spelling of the state name varied, i.e., Quisconsin and Wiskonsin.

Wisconsin began to take form when the United States acquired the Northwest Territory from Great Britain in 1783, as a result of the Revolutionary War. The Territory began its break-up when Ohio became a state in 1803, Indiana in 1815, Illinois in 1818 and Michigan in 1836. At that time, what remained of the Northwest Territory — what is now the states of Wisconsin, Iowa and Minnesota as well as those parts of North Dakota and South Dakota lying north of the Missouri River — became the Wisconsin Territory. Its capital was at Belmont, located about two miles north of the Village of Belmont in southwestern Wisconsin.

At that time, the main commerce was fur with its market in the eastern United States. Access to transporting these furs purchased from Indians was from Prairie du Chien up the Wisconsin River to Portage (about a mile of portage east to the Fox River flowing northeasterly), then to Lake Butte Des Morts, Lake Winnebago and down the lower Fox to Green Bay. Here John Jacob Astor had a trading post, as did other fur traders. Furs came to Green Bay via other routes as well. Green Bay was, by far, Wisconsin's most important trading center.

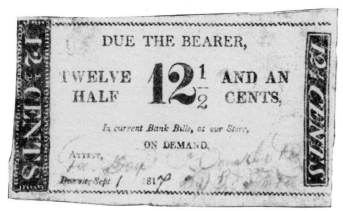

While much of the medium of exchange was barter, we find the earliest form of exchange was a piece of British currency dated 1814 and issued through Michilmackinac (Ft. Mackinaw), a cutline in Wis. Blue Book states it was the first paper money used in Wisconsin. The 1935 Wisconsin Blue Book illustrates a piece of scrip, dated 1914, printed for use in Wisconsin. There was also a piece

of scrip, dated 1817, issued by the city of Detroit with that city's name crossed out and "Green Bay" written in its place.

In *Wisconsin in 1833*, Lyman C. Draper wrote, "After several days rambling around through this section, we resumed our march toward Fort Winnebago. We found the whole Winnebago tribe of Indians encamped, I think, on the ground now occupied by Portage City (Ft. Winnebago). The settlement there consisted of those in the fort, and one man without, who kept a bakery for the accommodation of the garrison. The local currency used was common playing cards, cut in strips, issued by the baker with his name written on the back — every spot good for one shilling or a loaf of bread. If it was not quite a specie paying bank, bread — the staff of life — was always paid on demand."

Economy

Michigan plunged into statehood, and this very disastrous move had a serious ripple effect on the new territory of Wisconsin, which had little, if any, experience in governing, let alone setting up a new governing body.

On a national level, Andrew Jackson was elected president in 1828 and again in 1832. He had a single ambition, and that was not to renew the charter of the "United States Bank" of Philadelphia, a privately held fiscal agent of the United States. He was successful in doing so in 1836 when Martin Van Buren, his vice president, was elected president. As the money was withdrawn from the United States Bank (which did not lend money on real estate), it was deposited in many smaller state banks that *did* invest in real estate.

The result was that many loans were defaulted, and there was not enough money to either run the government or to conduct commerce.

In the case of Wisconsin, where fur in the New York market was Wisconsin's big source of revenue, the revenue practically dried up.

It should be noted here that by 1836, two new sources of income had emerged in the Territory. Lead was being mined in the southwestern part of the state. This had its outlet to the Mississippi River and downstream to St. Louis, where ammunition for the western frontier was being manufactured. Lumber was also beginning to fill a market niche; not to the degree it did twenty years later, but to some degree nonetheless. Northwestern and northern Wisconsin had huge stands of pine that had a ready market south to St. Louis and Chicago.

Wisconsin Territorial Currency

The Bank of Wisconsin, Green Bay had been chartered by the Michigan Territory, so it was grandfathered into the new Territory. Soon seven new charters were applied for. The Bank of Racine, The Bank of Iowa, Burlington and the Bank of Milwaukee all failed to raise capital to open their doors.

It should be noted, however, that the Bank of Milwaukee had several varieties of notes printed but never issued because of a feud that resulted in two rival board of directors. The Bank of Prairie du Chien and the State

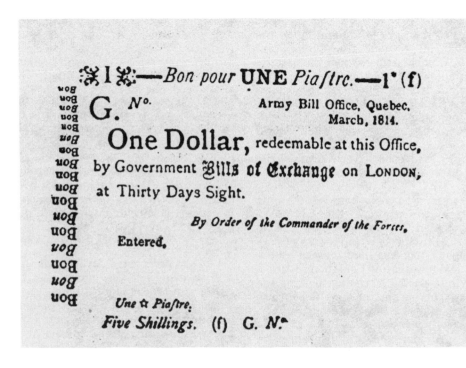

British currency dated 1814 and issued through Michilmackinac.

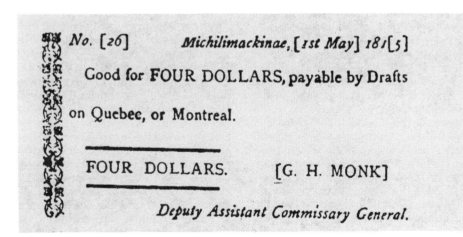

Bank of Wisconsin, Madison were turned down. Two banks were successful — the Bank of Mineral Point and the Miners Bank of Dubuque. No doubt the Mineral Point Bank was looked at favorably because it had the backing of James Doty, a familiar figure of the time who later became governor and a federal judge. In 1838, Iowa became a territory, and the Miners Bank came under new jurisdiction. Its backing originally was from St. Louis, as it was that city that was receiving the riches coming down the Mississippi.

These banks hardly had opened their doors when they were forced to dissolve because of the Hard Times (The Panic of 1837).

However, chartered bank currency was not the only currency to be used in the territory. The Fox River Hydraulic Company floated a group of certificates of deposits that did, for all intents and purposes, pass as money. But that company, too, was hard pressed by the Panic of 1837, and it had to withdraw from the practice.

In 1839, the territory passed legislation making the territory non-banking. This meant that one had to use specie (hard money) to transact business — a cumbersome and slow process for a market.

In 1839, the Wisconsin Marine & Fire Insurance Co., with George Smith from Chicago, backed by Scottish finances, opened its doors and issued certificates of deposits in Milwaukee. Its cashier was Alexander Mitchell, grandfather of Billy Mitchell. This bank, which never voluntarily closed its doors, later became the Marine Bank, which in recent years merged with Bank One. Several times there were great runs on the bank, but it always withstood them. It can be reasoned that that is why Milwaukee became the commercial center it is today rather than some other city on Wisconsin's east coastal area. It also reestablished Wisconsin's trust in banking.

Wisconsin first explored statehood in 1846, but it failed to agree on two points — whether there should be free banking, and which of three proposed canals should be dug: 1) about a six-mile ditch between Sturgeon Bay and Lake Michigan; 2) one from Milwaukee west to the Rock River that would allow traffic to St. Louis; or 3) the Fox and Wisconsin River — this included the lower Fox River from Green Bay to Lake Winnebago where several locks were required; also the damming of the lake to raise it thirty inches. The canal would continue up through Lake Butte Des Morts and up the upper Fox River to Portage (Ft. Winnebago), then to the Wisconsin River, the latter a mile distance. This canal would basically follow the trading routes of the Indians long before white men ever saw Wisconsin.

The first state constitution was rejected on September 27, 1847; the second one was ratified in April 1848. The conferees learned that without banks, outsiders with specie could control the state. Thus, the question of banking was put to the people in 1851, and it won.

As bank notes began to emerge in 1853, they were backed by eastern railroad bonds. At that time, the principal wealth of the country was held in Virginia. With the Panic of 1854 and again in 1858, plus the advent of the Civil War, the bonds securing state bank notes soon became less and less valuable, and on April 12, 1861 — with the firing on Ft. Sumter — they became worthless.

Canals, Railroads & Wheat

While there was great controversy over which of three different canals to build in Wisconsin, the only one that made any real sense was the Sturgeon Bay/Lake Michigan Canal, which was completed and still serves as a shortcut from Green Bay to the Great Lakes. The Fox and Wisconsin River Canal was eventually completed in the early 1870s, but by that time railroads had built branches to nearly every small community, and there was nothing to ship down the canal. The upper canal was short-lived, but the lower locks continued to operate until about 1990, in later years for recreational purposes only.

By the mid 1840s and early 1850s, Wisconsin had become the largest wheat-producing state in the union. (This was, of course, before the Great Plains opened up and Wisconsin found better use for its land.)

The need to get this product to market was very real. Unlike furs or lead, this market was either in Milwaukee or Chicago. A fierce battle between the two cities and most prestigious bank resulted.

Wisconsin's Early Bankers

It has been noted earlier that the Wisconsin Marine & Fire Insurance Co., under the leadership of George Smith and Alexander Mitchell, prospered during the 1840s, despite a law against banking. Under the free banking period after 1853, that company continued to prosper, becoming deeply rooted in railroads and grain shipments in and out of Milwaukee.

Another early banker of note was Cadwaller Washburn. He and his brother owned the Hallowell Bank of Hallowell, Maine, along with the Wisconsin Bank of Mineral Point. They also had agreements with the State Bank of Madison, as well as the Bank of Galena, Illinois, to pay out Hallowell notes in the Midwest and Mineral Point notes in Maine. While this scheme was not too successful, Washburn was a man of principle and did much to aid Wisconsin economy.

Bear in mind a large portion of the wheat-producing land was west of Milwaukee, reaching into northern Illinois as well as reaching northwest toward Minneapolis and westward to Prairie du Chien and LaCrosse.

Chicago had routes west of Chicago to Rockford and north to Madison, and had resources to greater capital. But through the wizardry of Alexander Mitchell and George Smith, Wisconsin was able to make headway west and northwest. Thus, Milwaukee became a port city for exporting grain as well as making beer. Evidence of this is seen in a bank at Sun Prairie and Whitewater, known as the Wheat Growers Bank and the Corn Exchange Bank of Waupun. In addition, there are ten Farmers Banks of the period, not the least of which is the Farmers & Millers Bank of Milwaukee, forerunner to the First Wisconsin National Bank of Milwaukee. Before the current merger craze, this bank was Wisconsin's largest.

The State Bank, organized in 1853 by Samuel Marshall, president, and Charles E. Ilsley, was located on Pinckney Street in Madison. This bank later closed, moving to Milwaukee in 1865 to become the Marshall & Ilsley Bank – more commonly known as M&I Bank. In 1993, M&I absorbed Valley Bank, becoming Wisconsin's largest banking institution.

Scrip

"Scrip" (not "script") is best defined as a substitute for paper money, much as a token is a substitute for a coin. The issuers are usually someone other than a bank, but scrip can be paid (redeemed) through a bank on certain occasions.

Perhaps the most common form of scrip is merchant scrip issued to buy produce from a customer, thus, the customer must return to his store for redemption. Lumber company scrip would be another common use. Here the scrip is paid to employees for redemption at the company store. (There were times when no other store was available.) In many cases, scrip is blank and is filled out by the issuer.

Unlike bank notes that were literally banned after 1865 (a ten percent fee was charged to reissue them), scrip contained in this catalog covers a period up to the turn of the century. After that, tokens were more in vogue to serve as a substitute for money.

Wild Cat Banks

The proper name for the notes in this catalog is "obsolete bank notes," as none are redeemable. They are often referred to as broken bank notes, as many of the banks that issued them went broke. The truth is that many of the notes were redeemed at par (or a percentage of par), either by themselves or by larger banks to restore people's trust in bank notes. Also listed in this book are notes that were never issued and, as a cataloger, we cannot definitely identify their existence, but rather suspect it. If a note has never been seen in circulated condition, it could very well be that no notes were ever placed in circulation. Or, in the process of planning a bank, sample notes were printed but the bank never opened its doors, and only the samples remained. In a couple of cases, descriptions of notes are known, but an example has never been seen.

In the case of Burlington W.T., no known notes exist, yet altered notes *do* exist. This seems to indicate the notes were never delivered to the bank, but rather were spirited out the back door.

We also have a case of the Wisconsin Miners Bank of Pekwecowa, which is nonexistent.

Hoards of Notes

Over the last twenty-five years, hoards of sheets of bank notes have come to light. They are sheets of the Wisconsin Bank of Green Bay, Wisconsin Territory in sheets of $1, $2, $3, and $5 as well as $5, $5, $5, and $10; also, the Summit Bank of Oconomowoc in sheets of $2 and $3, and the Bank of Watertown in sheets of $1, $2, $3, and $5, dated 1863 and printed by A B Co.

Rarity Scale

R 1 = over 200 notes printed; R 2 = 100 to 200; R 3 = 50 to 100; R 4 = 25 to 50; R 5 = 10-25; R 6 = 5 to 10; and R 7 = 1 to 5.

Bank Notes Numbering System

The presence of a lower-case letter suffix indicates a known or suspected variety. For example, a $1 bill for a certain bank might have three listings: G2, G2a and G2b. G2 could be for the version without an overprint, G2a for the same note with a red ONE overprint, and G2b for a blue ONE overprint. The fact that all three notes share the "G2" portion of the number shows they are closely related.

Scrip Numbering System

SC 1 = 5 cents; SC 2 = 10 cents; SC 5 = 25 cents; SC 6 = 50 cents; SC 7 = $1; SC 8 = $2; SC 9 = $3; SC 10 = $10; SC 13 = $50; SC 14 = $100; and SC 15 = $500.

Proof vs. Uncirculated

These two types are often confused and difficult to tell apart unless you have both types to compare. An uncirculated note is printed on bank note paper and has a gray cast to it. It also has a crisper sound when bent. Proof is printed on bond paper, is always whiter in color, tends to lay flatter and, in the case of a two-colored note, has greater contrast.

While both can have holes punched in the area where a signature normally is affixed, holes do not signify a proof note.

New notes with no signatures are often referred to as "remainders" or "unsigned."

Note Illustrations

Every effort has been made to illustrate every known note as the author feels a written description never adequately explains what can be illustrated.

Abbreviations

SENC	=	Surviving Examples Not Confirmed
A	=	Altered
S	=	Spurious
R	=	Raised
G	=	Genuine
SR	=	Scrip

Bibliography

There is no way a reference on early Wisconsin banking could be complete without referring to Krueger, i.e., Leonard Douglas Krueger and his book written in 1933: *History of Commercial Banking of Wisconsin*. The same could be said of Theodore A. Anderson's *A Century of Banking in Wisconsin*.

Banking in Frontier Iowa, 1836-1965 by Erling A. Erickson is a very good reference on the Miners Bank of Dubuque.

George Smith's *Money: The Story of the Wisconsin Marine & Fire Insurance Co.* is also a great reference.

In the case of this catalog, two gentlemen are owed a great debt. They are Ed Rochette, who visited the Wisconsin Historical Society in Madison and annotated Wismer's listings on Wisconsin Bank Notes as they appeared in *The Numismatist* from March to November 1936. Also, to Virgil Jackson, who photographed their collection.

That collection contains about 150 different sheets of notes, and we were fortunate to have photographed it some thirty years ago. It is not available to photograph today.

Two books were very helpful in locating otherwise lost towns: *Wisconsin Gazetteer 1853* and the *Wisconsin Post Office Handbook 1821-1971*, compiled by James B. Hale.

I would be remiss if I didn't recognize Jim Haxby, whose massive reference book, *Standard Catalog of United States Obsolete Bank Notes 1782-1866,* formed the basis of this book. We merely have made a few minor corrections to his listings. We also have added notes that were not covered, such as notes from private banks and scrip.

Thanks to William Pettit for supplying certain historical information.

I would also like to acknowledge the input of Jim Medd, Ron Calkins, Tom Fruit, John Wilson, Clayton High, Bob Branigan, Mark Anderson, Fred Markoff, and Eric Newman.

Abbreviations for Bank Note Engravers' Imprints

Abbreviation	Imprint
A	
AB&CDW	A.B.& C. Durand Wright & Co.
AB&CD&W	A.B.& C. Durand & Wright
ABN	American Bank Note Co.
ABNCo.mono.	American Bank Note Co. monogram
Adams	Dan. Adams, Nashville, TN
A&H	A&H
A&H	Aiken & Harrison
Argus	Argus
Arthur	W.H. Arthur & Co.
Austin	G.L. Austin
B	
B&D	Baker & Duyckink
B&E	Burton & Edmonds
B&G	Burton & Gurley
B&K	Brenker & Kessler
B&S	V. Balch & S. Stiles
BA	Baldwin, Adams & Co.
Bache	B.F. Bache, Philadelphia
Balch	V. Balch & Co.
VB	V. Balch
B&D	V. Balch C. Durand
Bald	Robt. L. Bald & Co.
Bald A	Bald, Adams & Co.
Baldwin	Baldwin & Co.
G.D. Baldwin	Geo. D. Baldwin
J.S. Baldwin	J.S. Baldwin
Bassett	W.H. Bassett
BB&C	Baldwin, Bald & Cousland
BBN	Boston Bank Note Co.
BC	Bald, Cousland & Co.
Bel	Bellows
BFC&M	B.F. Corlice & Macy NY
BG	Burton, Gurley & Co.
BG&E	Burton, Gurely & Edmonds
Bissell	F. Bissell
Blake	Blake & Co. NY
Blauvelt	A. Blauvelt
Bonar	I. Bonar
Bordentown	Bordentown Register
Bornemann	F.W. Bornemann
BN	Bornemann
BR	Balch, Rawdon & Co.
BS	Balch, Stiles & Co.
BSH&D	Bald, Spencer, Hufty & Danforth
BSW	Balch, Stiles, Wright & Co.
Bynon	Bynon & Co.
C	
C-M	B.F. Corlie & Macy, NY
C&M	B.F. Corlies & Macy, Statimers, NY
Carey	Matthew Carey
CBN	Cincinnati Bank Note Co.
CD	Casilear, Durand & Co.
CDB	Casilear, Durand, Burton & Co.
CDB&E	Casilear, Durand, Burton & Edmonds
CF	Cone, Freeman & Co., Baltimore
Child	Jno. V. Child
ConBN	Continental Bank Note Co.
CP	Courier Pr. (ess)
CP	Courier Press
Creed	Creed, sc.
D	
D&B	Day & Berger, NY
D&B	Doty & Bergen
D&Co.	Draper & Co.
D&H	Danforth & Hufty
D&M	Doolittle & Munson, Cincinnati
D&M	Doty & McFarland NY
D&W	Durand & Wright
Danforth	Danforth
Dane	W. Dane & Co.
DB	Danforth, Bald & Co.
DBS&H	Danforth, Bald, Spencer & Hufty
DdB	Durand, Baldwin & Co.
DH&M	Durand, Hammond & Mason
DnP	Danforth, Perkins & Co.
Doolittle	Amos Doolittle
Doolittle Doty	Doty
DP	Durand, Perkins & Co.
Draper	Draper
DrB	Draper, Bald & Co.
DrU	Draper, Underwood & Co.
DrW	Draper, Welch & Co.
DS&H	Danforth, Spencer & Hufty
DT	Draper, Toppan & Co.
DTL	Draper, Toppan, Longacre & Co.
DU	Danforth, Underwood & Co.
DUB&S	Draper, Underwood, Bald & Spencer
DUBS&H	Draper, Underwood, Bald, Spencer & Hufty
Durand	Durand & Co.
DW	Danforth, Wright & Co.
DWP	Daily Wisconsin Press, Milwaukee
E	
E&C	Evans & Cogswell
Eastern	Eastern Bank Note Co.
Ely	Chas. E. Ely, Philadelphia
Everdell	James Everdell, Broadway, New York
F	
FDU	Fairman, Draper, Underwood & Co.
G	
Gavit	Gavit & Co.
JG	J.E. Gavit & Co.
G.H.	Geo Hatch & Co.
H	
H&Co.	Hatch & Co. NY
H&D	Hufty & Danforth
H&L	Hoyer & Ludwig
H.S.	H. Seifort, Milwaukee
Haehnlen	Haehnlen, J. Lith., Philadelphia
Hamlin	Hamlin
WH	Wm. Hamlin
Hammond	Hammond & Co., St. Louis
Harris	Harris & Co.
J. Harris	James Harris
Harrison	Harrison
C.P. Harrison	C.P. Harrison
CPH	C.P.H.
C.P.Har.& Son	C.P. Harrison & Son
R.G. Harrison	R.G. Harrison
W. Harrison	W. Harrison
Hatch	Hatch & Co.
Hatseman	[K. or E.] Hatseman, New York
Haws & D	Haws & Dunkerley, Prs., Knoxville
Holyland	Holyland
Hoogland	Hoogland
Horton	Horton. Prov.
Hosford	Hosford & Co.
HP&C	Hall, Packard & Cushman
J	
JB	Jas. Barnet, Chicago
JDW	Jocelyn, Draper, Welch & Co.
Jewett	Jewett's print
JH	Jas. Harris & Co.

Abbreviation	Imprint
Jocelyn	Jocelyn (or Jocelin)
Jones	Jones

K

K&B	Keatinge & Ball
K&B	C. Kohlmann & Bros. Job Press
K&M	Kneass & Mason
K&R	Kendall & Russells
Kneass	W. Kneass
KY	Kneass, Young & Co.

L

L&R	Leney & Rollinson
Latham	Latham
Leg	R. Leggett
Lemet	L. Lemet, Albany
Leney	Leney & Co.
LL	L. Lysman, Milwaukee
Lowe	R. Lowe
LR	Looker, Reynolds & Co.
LR&M	Leney, Rollinson & Maverick

M

M&B	Merritt & Brown, NY
M&D	P. Maverick & Durand
M&H	Murray & Harrison
M&L	Maverick & Leney
M&T	Mason & Taylor
M&V	Murray & Vallance
Manouvrier	J. Manouvrier
PM	Peter Maverick
MD	P. Maverick, Durand & Co.
MD&F	Murray, Draper & Fairman
MDF	Murray, Draper, Fairman & Co.
MDFB	Murray, Draper, Fairman, Brewster & Co.
ML	Morgan, Lodge and Co. Print
ML&E	Milwaukee Litho & Engraving, Milwaukee
ML&E	Milwaukee Litho & Eng. Co.
ML&E. Co.	Milwaukee Litho & Engr. Co.
ML&R	Maverick, Leney & Rollison
MN	Milwaukee News Pr.
MNP	Milwaukee News Pr.
Murray	Murray
My&D	Murray & Draper

N

NBN	National Bank Note Co.
NEBN	New England Bank Note Co.
New England Co.	New England Co.
NI	No imprint present
NJ	N. & S.S. Jocelyn
NLI	National Lith. Institute, Chicago
NYBN	New York Bank Note Co.

O

Ormsby	W.L. Ormsby

P

P&B	Penniman & Bemis
P&H	Perkins & Heath [London, England]
P&W	Ed Percy Whites
Peabody	Peabody Ithaca NY
PL	The Pluger Litho Co., Milwaukee
Potter	P. & S. Potter, Printers, Poughkeepsie
PPSP	Perkins Patent Steel Plate
Price Current	Price Current, Print
PSSP	Patent Stereotype Steel Plate

R

R&B	Reed & Bissell
R&P	Reed & Pelton
R&S	Reed & Stiles
R. Rawdon	R. Rawdon, Albany
RC	Rawdon, Clark & Co., Albany
RD&B	Rawdon & Balch

Abbreviation	Imprint
Reed	A. Reed
RL&M	Rollinson, Leney & Maverick
Robertson	W.R. Robertson
Robinson	J. Robinson, printer
Rollison	Rollison & Co.
Rounds	S.P. Rounds, Chicago
RS	Reed, Stiles & Co.
RW	Rawdon, Wright & Co., New York
RW&H	Rawdon, Wright & Hatch
RWH	Rawdon, Wright, Hatch & Co.
RWH&E	Rawdon, Wright, Hatch & Edson

S

Sage	J. Sage & Sons
SBN	Southern Bank Note Co.
Sears	Sears Bros.
SH&D	Spencer, Hufty & Danforth
Snowden	Snowden
SS	Sage, Sons & Co. Buffalo, NY
SS&Co	Sage, Sons & Co. Buffalo, NY
SS&S	S. Stiles, Sherman & Smith
Steel	James W. Steel
Stiles	S. Stiles, New York

T

TC	Toppan, Carpenter & Co.
TCC	Toppan, carpenter, Casilear & Co.
Teubner	Geo. W. Teubner
ThC	Topham [sic], Carpenter & Co.
Throop	O.H. Throop, New York
Times	Times Press
TK&T	Tanner, Kearny & Tiebout
TM	Toppan, Maverick & Co.
CT	Chas. Toppan
T&C	Toppan & Co.
Torrey	Torrey, Sc. Nashville
TP	Terry, Pelton & Co.
TP	Tribune Print, Chicago
Tucker	W.E. Tucker & Co.

U

UBN	Union Bank Note Co.
UB&S	Underwood, Bald & Spencer
UBS&H	Underwood, Bald, Spencer & Hufty
Upham	S.C. Upham, Philadelphia

V

Vallance	J. Vallance
Valory	P.L. Valory, Petersburg, VA

W

W&H	Woodruff & Hammond
W&M	Woodruff & Mason
W&P	Wright & Prentiss
W&R	Willard & Rawdon
WB&H	Wellstood, Benson & Hanks
WBN	Western Bank Note Co.
WBN	Western Bank Note Co. Milwaukee
WBN&E	Western Bank Note & Engraving, Chicago
WE	Western Engraving, Chicago
WE& Co.	Western Engraving Co., Chicago
WH	Wellstood, Hanks & Co.
WHH&W	Wellstood, Hanks, Hay & Whiting
WH&W	Wellstood, Hay & Whiting
WH&W	Wellstood, Hay & Whiting, NY
Whiting	H. Whiting
Wilson	J. Wilson, Printer
WLSH	Wm. L.S. Harrison Engraver, NY
WT	Woodruff, Tucker & Co.
WW&L	Welden, Williams & Slick, Ft. Smith, Ark.

ALBANY

WI-5   BANK OF ALBANY, 1859-61

Capital $25,000. M. D. Miller, Pres., William Gould, cashier.
Fate: failed. 1861 notes redeemed at 73-3/4¢ in 1862. Outstanding circulation 1963 $821.

G2	$2	June 1, 1859 ABN. Capital: $25,000. No overprint.	R-7
G2a	$2	June 1, 1859 ABN. Same as above, except for overprint of red panel outlining a white TWO.	R-7
G2b	$2	September 1, 1860 ABN. Same as above, except for date and capital ($50,000).	R-7

G4	$3	June 1, 1859 ABN. Capital: $25,000. No overprint.	R-7
G4a	$3	June 1, 1859. ABN. Same as above, except for overprint of red panel outlining a white THREE.	R-7
G4b	$3	(September 1, 1860) ABN. Same as above, except for date and capital ($50,000).	R-7

Uncut Sheet

| X1 | $2, 3 ABN. G2, 4 | R-7 |

APPLETON

WI-10   BANK OF APPLETON, 1859-62

Capital $50,000. E. Hopkins Pres., R. D. Branch, cashier.
Failed 1861. Notes redeemed at 61-3/4¢ in 1862. Outstanding circulation 1863 $1,006.

G2	$1	___18__: (late 1850s) TC. R: Webster. No overprint.	R-7
G2a	$1	___18__: late 1850s TC. Same as above, except for red ONE overprint.	R-7

G4	$2	___18__: (late 1850s) TC. No overprint.	R-7
G4a	$2	___18__: late 1850s TC. Same as above, except for red TWO overprint.	R-7

G6	$3	___18__: (late 1850s) TC. No overprint.		R-7
G6a	$3	___18__: late 1850s TC. Same as above, except for red THREE overprint.	Remainder	R-7
			Signed Note	R-7

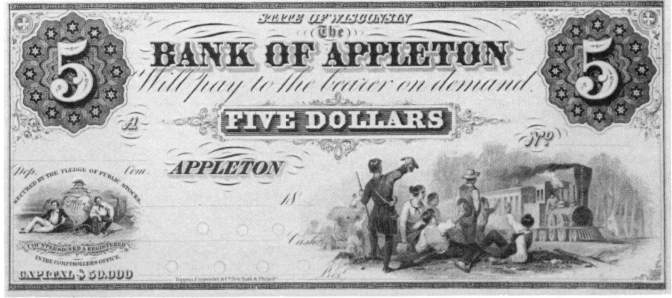

G8	$5	___18__: (late 1850s) TC. No overprint.	R-7
G8a	$5	___18__: late 1850s TC. Same as above, except for FIVE overprint.	R-7

Uncut Sheet

X1		$1, 2, 3, 5 TC. G2, 4, 6, 8	R-7

ASTOR

WI-13   **ASTOR, GREEN BAY, WISCONSIN TERRITORY 1836-48**

In 1835, Astor became what was roughly the South Ward (today the 4th Ward). The Astor House was located at the corner of Adams & Mason Streets. It was the trading post of John Jacob Astor of New York City.

SC 5 $.25   ___18__: RWH   R-5

SC 6 $.50   ___18__: RWH   R-6

SC 7 $1   ___18__: RWH   R-6

SC 8 $2   ___18__: RWH   R-6

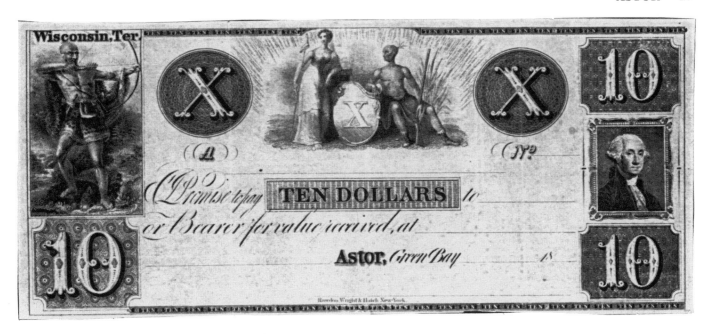

SC 10 $10   ___18__: RWH   R-6

SC 15 $50   ___18__: RWH - were printed in sheets of 4   R-6

Uncut Sheet

X1   A sheet of three $10s and one $50 exists.   R-7

AUBURNDALE

WI-16   **R CONNER COMPANY**

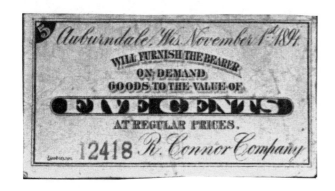 

SC 1   5¢   November 1, 1894   R-7

SC 2   10¢   November 1, 1894   R-7

HISTORY OF WOOD COUNTY
AUBURNDALE

The village of Auburndale was first settled by William St. Thomas, in April, 1871, when he built a claim shanty, and commenced to clear his land for cultivation. The first men to make improvements of a permanent and progressive character, were two brothers, John and Robert Connor, who came in May of the same year. The first dwelling at all resembling a house, was built by John Connor, in June. The Connors, being purchasers of a large amount of property in this section, drew up a plan of the village, and proceeded to lay it out. They also opened a general store. In 1872, the village was further improved by the erection of a saw-mill by Messrs. F. W. Kingsbury & Bro. This mill did a lively business until December, 1880, when it was completely destroyed by fire. Another saw-mill was erected in the Summer of 1874, by Messrs. Hoskins & Roe, who ran it until the Winter of 1876, when they sold it to R. Connor, who has owned and operated it ever since. In 1878 he built a planing mill, to run in connection with the saw mill. The average amount of lumber turned out from Connor's mill, per year, is 10,000,000 feet. R. Connor was obliged, on account of the great increase of business, to enlarge his store in 1874. In 1875 he erected upon the same site, a large frame building, putting in a large stock of goods. In 1877 he was again compelled to enlarge, this time building an addition to his new building. The line of the Wisconsin Central Railroad, passing through this region in September, 1871, made it a good point for the lumbering business, and the village has "boomed" ever since first settlement.

One of the first things attended to by the Connors Brothers, on their arrival at this place, was to petition the Post-office department, at Washington, to establish an office at this point, which was finally done in June, 1873, and Mr. John Connor appointed first Postmaster. He was succeeded, June 1874, by his brother, Robert Connor, who has remained in office ever since.

On the completion of the Wisconsin Central Road through the village, they erected a station and established a telegraph and express office.

In 1873, the first school was established, with a Miss Waters as first teacher, the school being held in a small house erected for the purpose. In 1876, this house was decided as being too small to accommodate the number of scholars living within the limits, and in 1877 another one was built, at a cost of $1,500.

The Presbyterian society was organized in 1875, and services were held in the school-house, and in the following year they erected a small church edifice. The first pastor in charge was the Rev. R. Fuller, who was succeeded by the present pastor L. F. Brickles.

The Catholic society was established in the village of Auburndale in 1876, and was under the pastorate of the Rev. Father Schuttlehoffer, of Marshfield, who held services here every two weeks. In 1879, they erected a church building at a cost $400, which was paid for by subscription.

There is a congregation of some seventy members of the German Lutheran Church, who hold their services in the new school-house, presided over by the Rev. John Schutte.

The first couple to be joined in the holy bonds of matrimony, were J. D. Vomb and Miss Mollie Johnson, on the twentieth day of March, 1875, at the official word of Justice Phelps. The first birth was Elizabeth, daughter of John Connor, in April, 1873. The first death was John Wilson, killed by the falling of a tree.

As the village grew in size and importance, the necessity for its incorporation became apparent, in order that such improvements might be made as would best advance its interests, improvements that the town would not consider. A preliminary meeting to take into consideration the subject of incorporation was held on the eleventh day of April, 1881. John Connor was made chairman of the meeting, and J. Lusk, secretary. At this meeting it was voted that a charter be applied for from the Circuit Court. A draft of application was made out, also a map of the village plat, to be embraced in the application. The application of the citizens was favorably considered by the court, and on the twenty-fourth day of May the village was duly incorporated. The first election for village officers being held on the twenty-fourth day of June, 1881, resulting in the choice of J. Connor, President; S. L. Smith, Joseph Austin, H. A. Bean, M. Cavenaugh, Louis Reynolds, and Jos. St. Thomas, Trustees; J. Lusk, Clerk; R. Connor, Treasurer; John R. Armeah, Marshal; L. Reynolds, Justice of the Peace, and J. Lusk, Police Justice.

The village of Auburndale is just ten years old, during which time it has grown very rapidly. Mr. Connor says: "When I came here, in 1871, I thought it the wildest looking place imaginable. There was nothing but marsh on that side of the railroad where the village now stands, and it was almost impossible to get through it. But, like everything else, it takes energy and time to build up a place, and while we do not boast of a handsome village with handsome residences, we do demand a little credit for our perserverance in making the village of Auburndale what it is. We have fine timber, good facilities for shipping it and any produce we have, either by railroad or by stage. Being near the Wisconsin River, we can send our produce into the pineries, where we can demand and get the best prices. Thus we have our choice of several markets. In 1871, there was one house built in what is now the village of Auburndale, now we have about thirty dwellings, five general stores, blacksmith shop, saw-mills where we turn out millions of feet of lumber per year, three organized churches and two church buildings, telegraph and express office, and a tavern."

Auburndale village is situated in town of same name, and is described as commencing at quarter post and running west on quarter line on Section 21, thence south on quarter line one mile to center of Section 28, thence east on quarter line two miles to center of Section 26, thence north on quarter line one mile to center of Section 23, thence west on quarter line one-half mile to the quarter post of place of beginning, containing an area of two miles, and sub-division southwest Section 23, south one-half Section 22, southeast one-quarter Section 21, northeast one-quarter Section 28, north one-half Section 27 and northwest one-quarter Section 26.

From *History of Northern Wisconsin*, 1881

AURORA

WI-15   NORTHERN WISCONSIN BANK, 1858-59

Capital $50,000. E. Wood, cashier. Liquidated July, 1860. Redeeming $1,655 worth of notes at par.

| G2a | $5 | July 1, 1857 WH&W. Tint: Red overall microlettering, counters, & outlined V V. Capital: $50,000. | R-7 |
| G2b | $5 | July 1, 1857 WH&W. As above, except for capital ($300,000). | — |

| G4a | $10 | July 1, 1857 WH&W. Tint: Red overall microlettering, counters, & outlined X. Capital: $50,000. | R-7 |
| G4b | $10 | July 1, 1857 WH&W. As above, except for capital ($300,000). | — |

Uncut Sheet

| X1 | | $5, 10 WH&W. G2a, 4a | R-7 |

BADGER MILLS

WI-18   **BADGER MILLS**

Badger Mills was located on the Chippewa River between Eau Claire and Chippewa Falls.

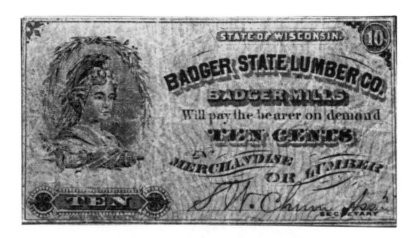

SC 2   10¢   Undated B/W ML&E.   R-7

Only the above notes have been seen however they were probably printed in a 5¢, 10¢, 25¢, 50¢, 1.00, 2.00, 5.00 sheet similar to other Lumber Co. scrip of the period. See Prairie Farm for example printed by Milwaukee Litho & Engr. Co.

BADGER MILLS

This place, on the Chippewa River, about six miles down the river from the Chippewa Falls, was formerly called the Blue Mills. The first mill built here was by Arthur McCann and J. C. Thomas, in 1843.

McCann had married Rosalie De Marie, and kept a public house at Dunnville, down the river. He was shot by a fellow by the name of Sawyer, who had been employed by McCann and Thomas in building the mill. Steve S. McCann took over his brother's interest in the mill. Mr. T. E. Randal subsequently owned the mill, or an interest in it, and his logs were all swept away in the freshet of 1847. The mill has one gang, one rotary, and a shingle-mill. The capacity is about 10,000,000 feet a year. There is a general merchandise store in the place, carried on by the company; a school house is used for stated Methodist preaching. There are about thirty families, and seventy-five men are employed by the company, making a total population of 175. There is a station on the railroad between Eau Claire and the Falls, near the village.

From *History of Northern Wisconsin*, 1881

BARABOO

WI-20   SAUK COUNTY BANK, 1857-65

Capital 1858 $50,000; 1863 $40,000. Simeon Mills, Pres., T. Thomas, cashier.
Succeeded by the Bank of Baraboo. Later Barbaboo National Bank.
The First National Bank of Baraboo was chartered January 31, 1873 and was placed in voluntary liquidation November 27, 1880. It issued $1 and $2 First Charter National Bank Notes and $5 and $10 Series of 1875 notes.

Genuine Notes, Raised Notes and Counterfeits

| G2a | $1 | ___18__; (1857-60) DW. Tint: brown lathework overall, counters, and panel of microlettering outlining white ONE. | Remainder | R-6 |
| G2c | $1 | April 1, 18__: 1860s (ABN). As above, except for date, probably imprint & change of tint color to light orange. | | — |

| G4a | $2 | ___18__: (1857-60) DW. Tint: brown lathework overall, counters, panel of microlettering & large white 2. | R-6 |

G4c $2   April 7, 18__: 1860s (ABN). As above, except for date, probably imprint & change of tint color to light orange.

G6a $3   ___18__: (1857-60) DW. Tint: Brown lathework overall, counter & panel of microlettering bearing THREE.   R-6

G6c $3   April 17, 18__: 1860s (ABN). As above, except for date, probably imprint & change of tint color to light orange.

G8a $5   ___18__: (1857-60) DW. Tint: Brown lathework overall, counters & panel of microlettering bearing FIVE.   R-6

G8c $5   April 7, 18__: 1860s (ABN). As above, except for date, probably imprint & change of tint color to light orange.

Uncut Sheet

X1 $1, 2, 3, 5 DW. G2a, 4a, 6a, 8a.   R-6

Altered, Spurious and Unattributed Non-Genuine Notes

N5 $5   (1850s-60) Unknown. NDA.

BEAVER DAM

WI-25   BANK OF BEAVER DAM, 1860-61

Capital $25,000. Charles Miller, Pres., J. R. Botsford, cashier.
Closed 1861. Redeemed notes at 57-1/2¢ in 1862. $320 outstanding circulation.

G2 $2   August 1, 1859 ABN   R-7

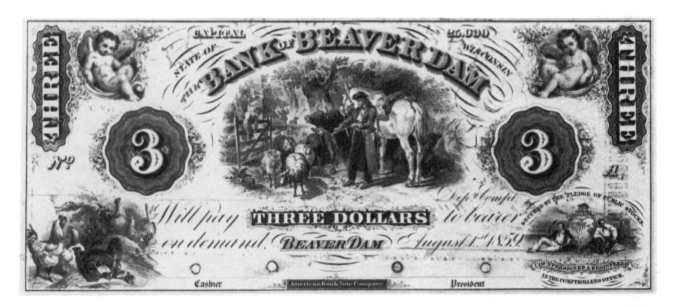

G4 $3   August 1, 1859 ABN   R-7

Uncut Sheet

X1 $2, 3 ABN. G2, 4   R-7

WI-30   CITY BANK OF BEAVER DAM, 1857-61

Capital $25,000. Daniel D. Read, Pres., B. G. Bloss, cashier.
Failed 1861. Notes redeemed at 80.5¢. Outstanding circulation $2,456.
The portrait on the bank's notes was that of the daughter of the bank's organizer Daniel D. Reed.

Genuine Notes, Raised Notes and Counterfeits

G2	$1	___18__: TC. C: daughter of the bank's organizer, Daniel D. Reed. No overprint.	R-7
G2a	$1	___18__: 1850s-60s TC. As above except for red ornate 1. 1 overprint.	R-6
R5	$5	___18__: late 1850s TC. Raised from $1, G2 or 2a. The bank issued no $5s.	
R6	$10	___18__: late 1850s TC. Raised from $1, G2 or 2a. The bank issued no $10s.	
R7	$20	___18__: late 1850s TC. Raised from $1, G2 or 2a. The bank issued no $20s.	

Uncut Sheet

| X1 | $1, 1, 1, 1 TC. G2, 2, 2, 2. | R-7 |

WI-32   FARMERS BANK OF BEAVER DAM

| SC 5 | 25¢ | R-7 |

WI-35   DODGE COUNTY BANK, 1855-62

Capital $50,000. S. L. Rose Pres., R. V. Bogert, cashier. July 2, 1866 circulation $23,400.
Failed 1862. Notes redeemed at 63.3¢.

| G2 | $1 | April 12, 1855 TC. No overprint. | R-7 |
| G2a | $1 | April 12, 1855 TC. As above, except for ornate red ONE overprint. | R-6 |

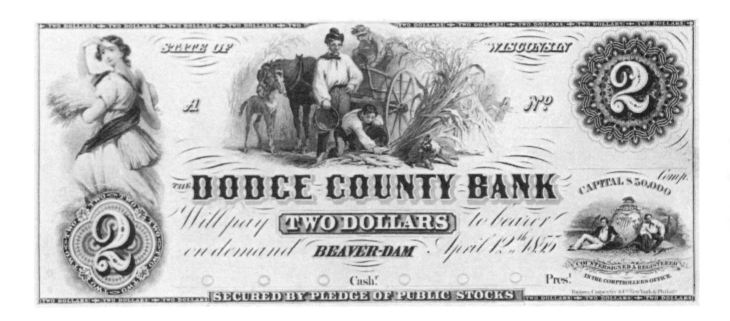

| G4 | $2 | April 12, 1855 TC. No overprint. | R-7 |
| G4a | $2 | April 12, 1855 TC. As above, except for ornate red TWO overprint. | |

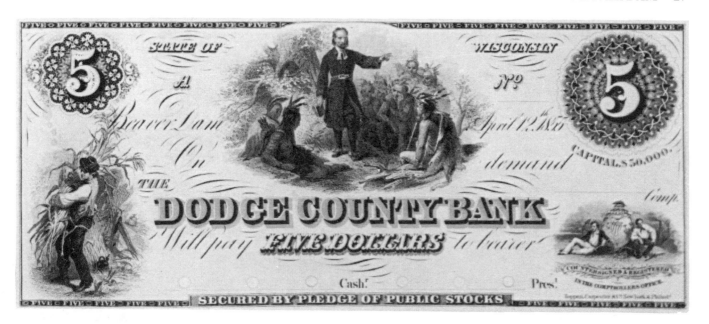

| G6 | $5 | April 12, 1855 TC. C: Eliot preaching to the Indians. No overprint. | R-7 |
| G6a | $5 | April 12, 1855 TC. As above, except for ornate red FIVE overprint. | |

Uncut Sheet

| X1 | | $1, 1, 2, 5 TC. G2a, 4a, 6a | R-7 |
| SC 5 | 25¢ | Undated | R-7 |

WI-40   FARMERS BANK, ca. 1863-65

Capital $50,000. Redeemed notes at par in 1865. Became the National Bank of Beaver Dam. Changed name to First National Bank 3220 in 1884. Liquidated 1904 to change name to Old National Bank. Became the National Bank of Beaver Dam in 1865. (S. S. Sherman, Pres., C. W. Whinfield, cashier.) It was succeeded by the First National Bank of Beaver Dam in 1884, and succeeded by The Old National Bank of Beaver Dam in 1904. All banks issued National Bank Notes.

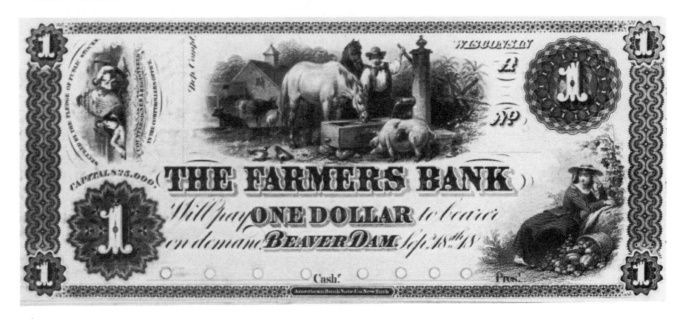

| G2 | $1 | ___18__:___ ABN. Same as G2a, except for lack of an overprint. | R-7 |
| G2a | $1 | ___18__: (1860s) ABN. As above, except for overprint of a red panel outlining a white ONE. | R-7 |

| G4 | $5 | ___18__:___ ABN. Same as G4a, except for lack of an overprint. | R-7 |
| G4a | $5 | ___18__: (1860s) ABN. As above, except for overprint of a red panel outlining a white FIVE. | R-7 |

Uncut Sheets

| X1 | $1, 5 ABN. G2,4. | R-7 |
| X2 | $1, 5 ABN. G2a, 4a. | R-7 |

WI-45   **MERCANTILE BANK, 1854-61**

Capital $50,000. E. C. Huntington, Pres., W. S. Huntington, cashier. Notes redeemed at 79-1/2¢ in 1862.
Outstanding circulation $1,796.
Failed 1861.

Later location: Lodi (moved in 1859).

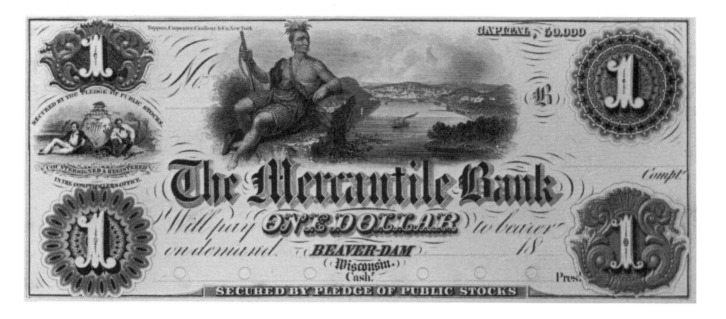

1-NOTES DATED AT BEAVER DAM

G2	$1	___18__:___ TCC. No overprint.	R-7
G2a	$1	___18__: 1850s TCC. As above, except for a red overprint.	

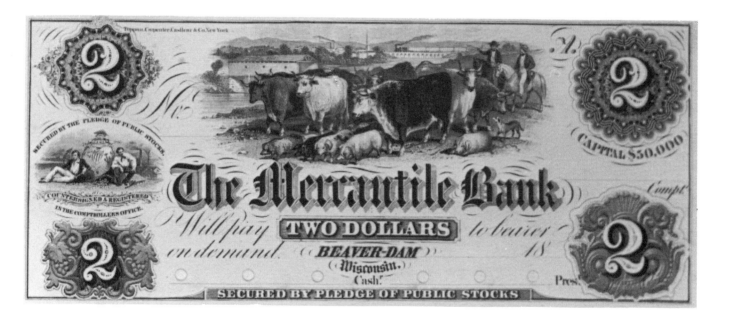

G4	$2	___18__:___ TCC. No overprint.	R-7
G4a	$2	___18__: 1850s TCC. As above, except for a red overprint.	

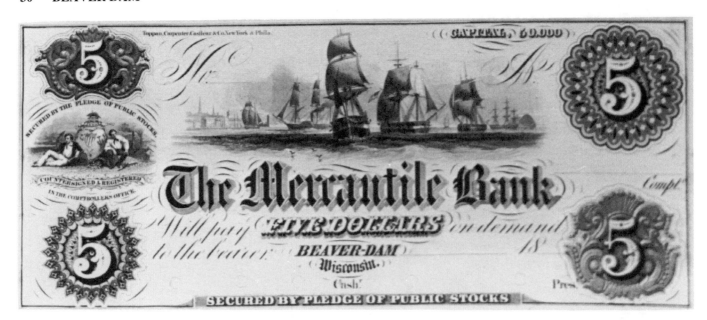

G6	$5	___18__:___ TCC. No overprint.	R-7
G6a	$5	___18__: 1850s TCC. As above, except for a red overprint.	

Uncut Sheet

X1		$1, 1, 3, 5 TCC. G2, 2, 4, 6	R-7

BELOIT

WI-50   BANK OF BELIOT, 1854-74

Capital July 1855 $36,000; Circulation $31,493. Geo. B. Sanderson, Pres., Louis C. Hyde, cashier. Succeeded by First National Bank #2163 in 1874. Voluntary liquidation 1887. Changed to L. C. Hyde & Brittain, later to L. C. Hyde & Brittain Bank.

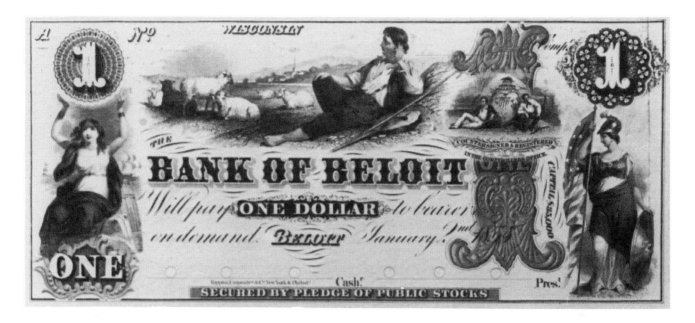

| G2 | $ | January 2, 1855 TC Capital: $35,000 | R-7 |
| G2a | $1 | January 2, 18565 TC Same as above, except for capital ($60,000) | R-7 |

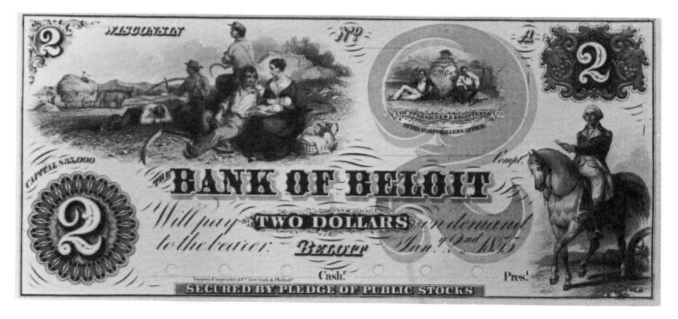

G4	$2	January 2, 1855 TC R: Washington. Capital: $35,000.	R-7
G4a	$2	January 2, 1855 TC Same as above, except for capital ($60,000).	R-6
G6	$3	January 2, 1855 TC Capital: $35,000.	R-7

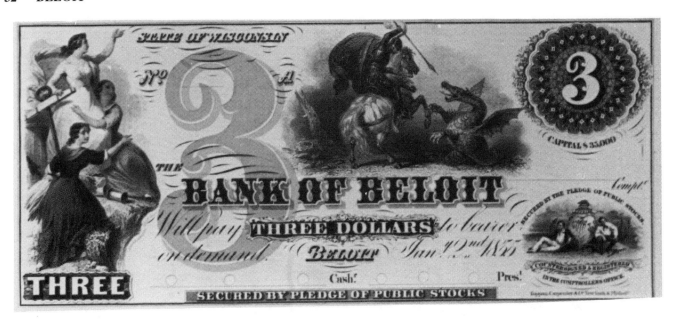

G6a $3   January 2, 1855 TC Same as above, except for capital   R-6
                 ($60,000).

G8 $5   January 2, 1855 TC Capital: $35,000.   R-7

G8a $5   January 2, 1855 TC Same as above, except for capital   R-7
                 ($60,000).

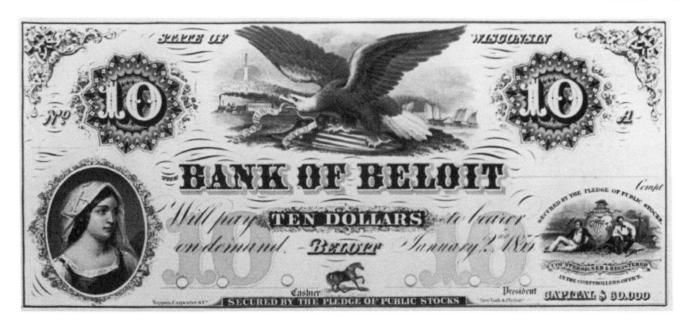

G10 $10   January 2, 1855 TC Capital: $60,000.   R-7

C10 $10   January 2, 1855 TC Photographic cft. of the above.   R-6

WI-55   BELOIT SAVINGS BANK, 1859-61

Capital $25,000. H. Pratt, Pres., J. J. Bushnell, cashier. Notes redeemed at 46-1/2¢ in 1862. Outstanding circulation 1863 $170. Closed 1861. The plate for this bank was originally prepared for the Oriental Bank, Warrensville, WI-815, then officially altered.

G2 $5   ___18__: (1859-61) BC, ABN   R-7

G4 $10   ___18__: (1859-61) BC, ABN   R7

Uncut sheet

X1 $5, 10, BC, ABN G2, 4   R-7

WI-60   **ROCK RIVER BANK, 1853-61**

1853 Capital $25,000. 1854 Capital $50,000. $47,272 in circulation July 3, 1854, J. M. Keep, Pres., A. L. Field, cashier. Notes redeemed at par 1861.
Failed 1861.

| G2 | $1 | ___18__: (1856-58) TCC. Capital: $500,000. No overprint. | R7 |
| G2b | $1 | January 1, 1859 ABN. As above, except for date, imprint, capital ($50,000), change in type style of city name to small capital letters and addition of red ONE overprint. | SENC |

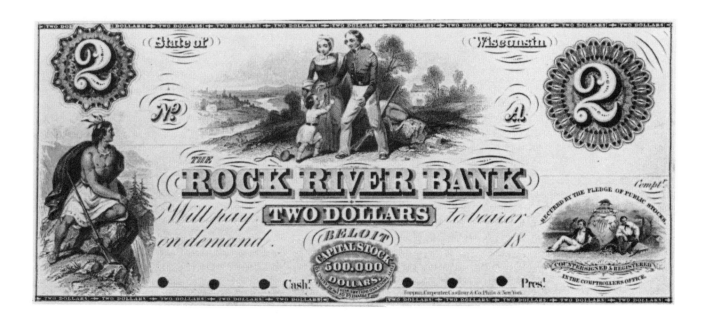

| G4 | $2 | ___18__: (1856-58) TCC. Capital: $500,000. No overprint. | R7 |
| G4b | $2 | January 1, 1859 ABN. As above, except for date, imprint, capital ($50,000) and addition of red TWO overprint. | R7 |

| G6 | $3 | ___18__: (1856-058) TCC. No overprint. | R7 |
| G6b | $3 | January 1, 1859 ABN. As above, except for date, imprint, capital ($50,000) and addition of red THREE overprint. | SENC |

G8	$5	___18__: (1856-58) TCC. No overprint.	R7
G8b	$5	January 1, 1859 ABN. As above, except for date, imprint, capital ($50,000) and addition of red FIVE overprint.	R7
R5	$5	___18__: 1850s TCC. Raised from $1. G2.	R7

Uncut Sheet

| X1 | | $1, 2, 3, 5 TCC G2, 4, 6, 8 | R-7 |

WI-65   **SOUTHERN BANK, 1859-61**

Capital $50,000. E. R. Wadsworth, Pres., E. W. Thompson, cashier.
Closed 1861. Notes redeemed at 70-1/2¢. Outstanding circulation $240.

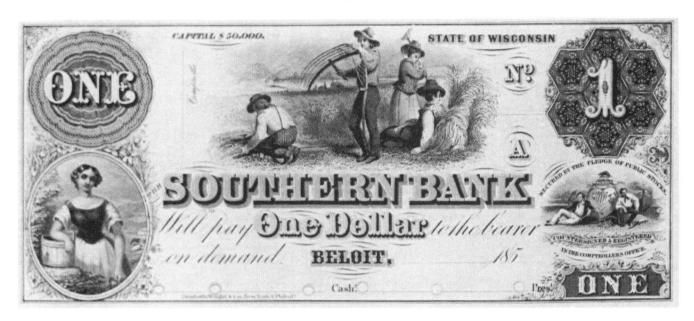

G2 $1   ___185_: 1850s DW.   R-7

G2a $1   September 1, 1860 ABN. As above, except for date,
                   imprint and addition of words "Dept. of" before
                   "Comptroller".

G4 $3   ___185_: (1850s) DW.   R-7

G4a $3   September 1, 1860 ABN. As above, except for date,
                   imprint & addition of words "Dept. of" before "Comp-
                   troller."

| G6 | $5 | ___185_: (1850s) DW. RC: "Red Jacket." | R-7 |

| G6a | $5 | September 1, 1860 ABN. As above except for date, imprint and addition of words "Dept. of" before "Comptroller." | |

| G8 | $10 | ___185_: (1850s) DW. | R-7 |

Uncut Sheet

| X1 | | $1, 3, 5, 10 DW. G2, 4, 6, 8 | R-7 |

1   5¢   (Handwritten Beloit Wisc. 1867) on orange cardboard.   R-7

While round cardboard due bills are not uncommon, they are to Wisconsin. Here we see an enterprising merchant merely altering a New York piece to meet his own needs without identifying his business.

BERLIN

WI-70   **ONEIDA BANK, 1858-62**

Capital $25,000, H. V. Kellogg, Pres., E. Kellogg, cashier.

Closed.

G2a $1   April 1, 1858 WH&W. Tint: Orange bank title & script   R-7
              ONE.

G4a $2   April 1, 1858 WH&W. Tint: Orange bank title & script   R-7
              TWO.

G6a $3   April 1, 1858 SH&W. Tint: Orange bank title & large   R-7
                     ornate 3.

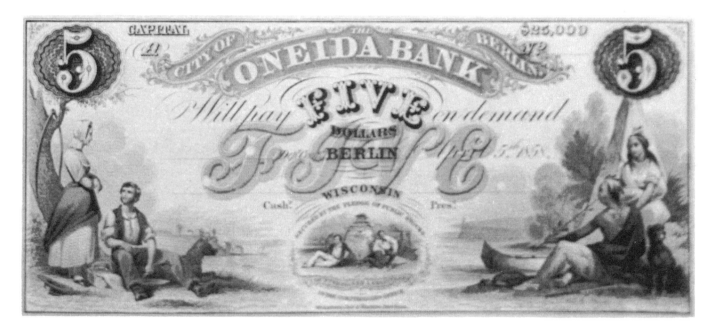

G8a $5   April 1, 1858 WH&W. Tint: Orange bank title and script   R-7
                     FIVE.

Uncut Sheet

X1 $1, 2, 3, 5, WH&W. G2a, 4a, 6a, 8a   R-7

WI-71   MARQUETTE COUNTY BANK, 1857

Capital $25,000. C. Cronkhite, Pres., D. B. Whitacre, cashier.
No further information is known on this bank.

BLACK RIVER FALLS

WI-73   BANK OF BLACK RIVER FALLS

A certificate of incorporation was issued but the bank never opened. (per Louis T. Hill, V.P. of the Bank of Sparta 1936.)

WI-75   CITIZENS BANK, ca. 1857-62

Later location: Oshkosh (moved ca. 1859).

Closed 1861.

1-NOTES DATED AT BLACK RIVER FALLS.

G2a	$1	?: (late 1850s) WH&W. C: steamboat, town in bkgd. L: 1/oval female portrait. R: 1/state arms. Tint: Color unknown, with outlined white ONE at lower ctr.	
G4a	$2	?: (late 1850s) WH&W. LC: state arms. RC: two men at work in saw mill. L: 2-1/2-length figure of woman. R:2/TWO. Tint: Color unknown, with outlined large white 2 at left ctr.	R-7

WI-80   **KANKAKEE BANK, 1857-58**

Capital $50,000. A. W. Mack, Pres., H. W. Harwood, cashier.
Closed, 1859, $445 of specie held in 1860 for the redemption of notes outstanding. Redemption expired
May 6, 1862.

Genuine Notes, Raised Notes and Counterfeits

G2a	$1	June 1, 1857 WH&W. Tint: Orange counter and microlettering overall.	R-7
C2a	$2	June 1, 1857 WH&W. Cft. of the above.	R-7

G4a	$2	June 1, 1857 WH&W. Tint: Orange counter and microlettering overall.	R-7

| G6a | $3 | June 1, 1857 WH&W. Tint: Orange counter microlettering overall and ornate 3. | R-7 |

| G8a | $5 | June 1, 1857 WH&W. Tint: Orange counters, microlettering overall, ornate V. V and panel at rt. | R-7 |
| R5 | $10 | June 1, 1857 WH&W. Raised from $1, G2a. The bank issued no $10s. | R-7 |

Uncut Sheet

| X1 | | $1, 2, 3, 5 WH&W. G2a, 4a, 6a, 8a | R-7 |

W1-82   **D.J. SPAULDING**

D. J. Spaulding was the largest lumber company that operated in the area south and east from the giant Knapp Stout & Co. of Menominie. It was also associated with the Wold Spaulding Lumber Co. who operated in central Wisconsin.

SC 7 $1   Deer undated. UKN Black with red serial number.   R-7

SC 7a $1   Undated/Wisconsin Seal. UKN Black with green   R-7
                    lathework.

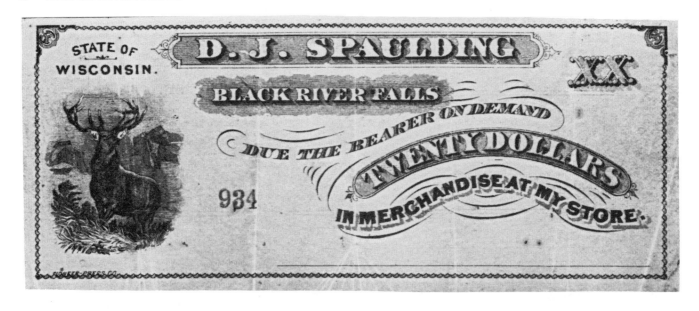

SC 11 $20   Deer undated. UKN Black with red serial number.   R-7

BOAZ

WI-83   **JAY BRIGGS**

SC 6   50¢   No.__ UKN Black on blue paper.   R-7

BOSCOBEL

WI-84   **MEYERS BROTHERS**

SC 7 $1.00   ___1874 NLI Black/green overprint.   R-7

BRINKERHOFF

WI-85   ST. CROIX RIVER BANK, 1858-62

Capital $150,000. Aaron Blank, Pres., Enoch Totten, cashier.
Later location: Grand Rapids (moved ca. 1860).

Probably issued notes only at Brinkerhoff. Failed.

G2 $5   ___18__: (1850s) WH&W.   R-7

G4 $10   ___18__: (1850s) WH&W.   R-7

Uncut Sheet

X1 $5, 10 WH&W. G2, 4   R-7

BURLINGTON

WI-90   FARMERS & MECHANICS BANK, ca. 1830-40s

Fate: probably failed.

G6	$5	___18__: (1830s-40s) B&G. C: woman holding cup in rt. hand, left arm resting on eagle.	SENC
G8	$10	___18__: (1830s-40s) B&G. C: Ceres reclining on sheaf, cattle in bkgd. L: woman stdg., pouring from goblet into cup. R: TEN on ornate die.	SENC
G10	$20	___18__: (1830s-40s) B&G. C: woman spinning. L: Hebe holding cup to eagle. R: Indian.	SENC
G12	$50	___18__: (1830s-40s) B&G. C: woman with one arm resting on anchor. L: woman with one foot resting on globe. R: stag.	SENC
G14	100	___18__: (1830s-40s) B&G. L: portrait of Washington. R: medallion head of Lafayette.	SENC

No known notes on this bank have ever been discovered. Haxby lists $5, 10, 20, and 50 notes on this bank that have been altered to read Philadelphia Pennsylvania, Morristown New Jersey and Steubensville Ohio. The $100 notes shown fit into that category. The top center vignette, Herb holding cup to eagle also appears on the $5 and 20 note.

MORRIS COUNTY BANK

Morristown, N.J.

Altered from Farmers & Mechanics Bank of Burlington, W.T.

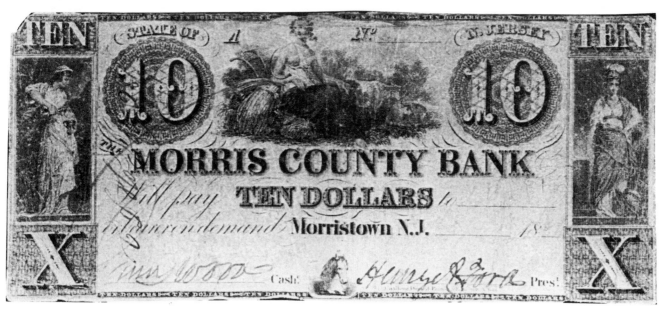

A10	$10a	___18__: 1830s-40s B&G C: 10; Ceres std. leaning on sheaves at left, two cows at rt.; 10. L: TEN/woman stdg. pouring from pitcher into cup/X. R: scrollwork panel with TEN, across. Altered from $10. Farmers & Mechanics Bank, Burlington, WI-90-GB.	R-7

A20 $50   ___18__: (1830s-40s) B&G C; woman with one arm rest-   R-7
                        ing on anchor. L: woman with one foot resting on
                        globe. R: stag. Altered from $50, Farmers & Mechan-
                        ics Bank, Burlington, WI-90-G12.

A30 $100   ___18__: (1830s-40s) B&G C: woman holding cup, right   R-7
                        arm resting on eagle. Portrait right.

BURLINGTON (WT)

WI-90   **FARMERS & MECHANICS, ca. 1830-40's**

Altered to Steubenville Ohio.

Altered, Spurious and Unattributed Non-Genuine Notes

A5	$5G	___18__: 1830s B&G C; woman holding cup in rt. hand, left arm resting on eagle. Altered from $5. Farmers & Mechanics Bank, Burlington, WI-90-G6.	R-7
A10	$10G	___18__: 1830s B&G C: 10; Ceres std. leaning on sheaves at left, two cows at rt.; 10. L: TEN/woman stdg. pouring from pitcher into cup/X. R: scrollwork panel with TEN, across. Altered from $10 Farmers & Mechanics Bank, Burlington, WI-90-G8.	R-7
A15	$50G	___18__: 1830s B&G C: woman with one arm resting on anchor. L: woman with one foot resting on globe. R: stag. Altered from $50, Farmers & Mechanics Bank, Burlington, WI-90-G12.	R-7
A20	$100G	___18__: 1830s B&G C: woman with left arm around eagle. L: portrait of Washington. R: medallion head of Lafayette. Altered from $100, Farmers & Mechanics Bank, Burlington, WI-90-G14.	R-7

All the above altered notes probably found their beginning in Burlington, Iowa, then part of Wisconsin Territory rather than what is now Burlington, Wisconsin.

CHILTON

WI-725   **SHAWANAW BANK, 1858-1865**

II - NOTES DATED AT CHILTON

This bank was founded at Shawanaw (Shawano) in 1858 and moved to Chilton, about 60 miles southeast. In 1863 it moved another 50 miles southeast to Sheboygan. Notes were issued at each location with the $1 & $2 issued at Chilton and the $5 & $10s at Shawanaw.

G6a $1   August 1, 1860 ABN. Tint: Green counter & panel. Capital: $50,000.   7

G8a $2   August 1, 1860 ABN. Tint: Green counter & panel. Capital: $50,000.   7

Uncut Sheet

X2 $1, 2 ABN, G6a, 8a   R-7

CHILTON

In January, 1845, Moses Stanton located on the site of the present city of Chilton, and in May his daughter Catherine was born. In 1846 he had a saw-mill and two years later a grist-mill in operation. His energy soon drew settlers to the spot. Frederick Sircher came in 1847, and Nicholas Chesboro in 1848. During this year also a number of industrious Irishmen, who had been employed in building the Sheboygan and Fond du Lac plank road, became residents of Chilton and increased its claims to be called a village. Through the influence of James Robinson, an honored citizen (since deceased), the town of Portland, afterwards Chilton, was organized, by special legislative act, in 1853. In December the county seat was fixed at Chilton, and every thing promised well for its continued growth. James Robinson, who had represented the county in the Legislature the previous Winter, was elected Chairman of the first Town Board, which convened at the hotel of Otto Schucht, on Sircher Street, April 21, 1853. Post-office conveniences had been enjoyed for two whole years, the first United States official in Chilton being L. Fields, Sr. Chilton certainly promised to be what it became, a thriving burg. Moses Stanton, its founder, lived here for over seventeen years, universally respected, and died in 1862. His wife still survives him.

Originally the village was called Stantonville, but in 1852 John Marygold, an Englishman, became proprietor of the place by purchase, and began to plat it. It was surveyed by A. Merrill in August of that year, and named "Chilington" by its owner, in remembrance of his native town. He sent a verbal message by one Patrick Donahoe, to have the change in name recorded at Stockbridge, the county seat. Such a burden upon his brain was too great for Patrick to carry, and before he arrived at his destination he eased it by dropping the middle syllable from Chil-(ing)-ton. "Chilton" was therefore recorded as the name of the new village.

Although by popular vote the county seat had been located at Chilton Center, about half a mile from the village, the citizens were not satisfied, but wanted a change made to Chilton itself. No buildings were erected for three years, although contracts had been let and the material for them was on the ground. In 1854 Harrison C. Hobart settled in Chilton in the practice of law. He took up the cause of Chilton vigorously, and chiefly by his and Mr. Stanton's efforts the change in location to the present court-house square was made, as previously stated. With this advantage gained, and some years afterwards the construction of the Milwaukee & Northern Railroad, Chilton left such rivals as New Holstein and Gravesville far behind.

The first child born in Chilton was the daughter of Moses Stanton (Catherine) in May, 1845; the first death his second daughter, Eliza, born in September, 1846, and died in January, 1848.

Miss Jane Scott taught the first school in the Summer of 1848. The first religious services were held in the same building by a missionary from the Stockbridge House.

In January, 1848, the first marriage ceremony occurred between Hugh Wilson, of Racine, and Miss Mary Hume.

The first Fourth-of-July oration was delivered by B. J. Sweet, then a law student in 1852.

Chilton is situated on the south branch of the Manitowoc River, and contains a population of 1,200, the prevailing nationality being German. Its people are industrious and thriving, a good general trade being carried on in addition to a variety of manufactures. The corporate limits of the city embrace a territory nearly two miles square.

By act of the Legislature the city was incorporated March 11, 1877. The charter was adopted by one majority on the twentieth of that month, the vote being 108 to 107. F. R. Gutheil was elected Mayor. The officers for 1881 are Mayor, Dr. D. La Count; Clerk, H. Arnold; Treasurer, William Rothmann. The city is divided into three wards.

Fire Department. — The Fire Department consisting of a hand-engine company and a hook-and-ladder company, was formed in 1875. The membership of both organizations is sixty. D. D. Ebert is Chief of the Department.

Schools. — In 1849 Moses Stanton erected a log building for a school house, on the land near where the post-office now stands. A frame building, on the site of the present district school-house, succeeded it. The two-story stone structure now occupied was erected in 1870. The value of the property is $5,000. The school (District No. 1) is divided into a Grammar Department (graded) and a High School. The Principal of the latter is J. E. Luce, and the former, J. O. Luce. Out of a total enrollment of 449, the attendance is 216. During the past Autumn the building has been renovated and improved. Its crowded condition, however, calls for an increase in accommodations.

Hotels. — The Chilton House was built in 1855 by J. C. Green. Mr. Vicking became the purchaser, and continued the same until 1867, when he sold it to Messrs. LaCount & Feind. F. W. Esser soon became the proprietor. In 1879, it was bought by E. Rossburg, its present proprietor.

The Central House, situated near the railroad station, was built by F. Reinboldt. It fell into Charles Koinke's hands the present owner.

The Wisconsin House. — Before 1875 the old buildings was occupied as a gent's furnishing store. It was remodeled the same year by Mr. Jackals for a hotel, and in 1876 sold to Joseph Bersch the present owner.

The Western House was built in 1874 by Menig & Goedertz. In 1875, Charles Menig became sole proprietor, as at present.

The American House was built in 1855 by Mr. Ortlieb. It was sold in 1875 to A. Mason, and to A. McHughe. J. D. Parker has been the owner since 1877.

Banks. — In 1859, Col. Bean established the Shawano Bank at Chilton. He turned the institution over to Meyer & Sprague in 1860. The bank suspended during the trying times of 1862. From that date up to January, 1875, the village was without a bank. Kersten Brothers then established the German Exchange Bank, which is still doing business under their management. Its capital is $7,600; resources $89,169.27.

CHIPPEWA FALLS

WI-130   TRADESMAN BANK

This bank of Eagle Lake moved to Chippewa Falls in 1859, but no notes are known as having been issued from this location.

WI-615   CLARK COUNTY BANK, 1859

Capital $150,000.
This bank moved from O'Neilsville (Neilsville) to Chippewa Falls in 1859 but no notes were issued from this location. No place of business or banking house is known.

WI-765   HOWARD BANK

This bank moved from Stiles about 200 miles to the east. As only Proof notes are known, it probably never issued notes.

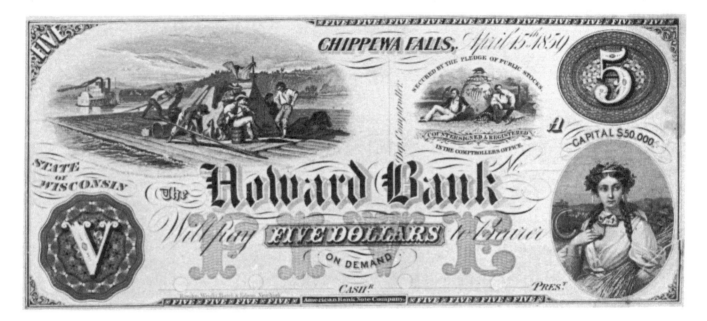

G6a	$5	April 15, 1859 ABN. Same as Stiles G2a, except for city & date.	R-7

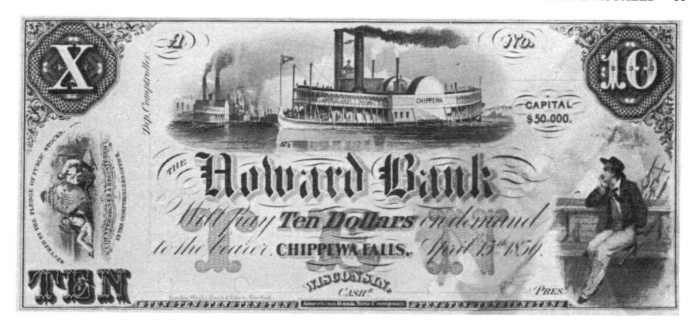

| G8a | $10 | April 15, 1859 ABN. Same as Stiles G4a, except for city & date. | R-7 |

Uncut Sheet

| X1 | | $5, 10 ABN. G6a, 8a | R-7 |

WI-767   **UNION BANK**

| | 5¢ | ND, 1860's period. Red tint/green back. Milwaukee Lith. & Eng. Co. | R-7 |

WI-2273   **UNION LUMBER CO.**

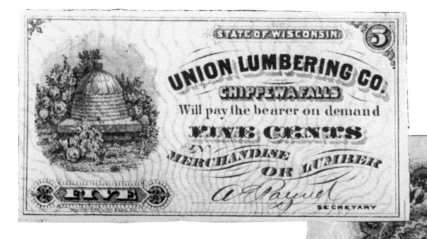

| SC 1 | 5¢ | Merchandise or Lumber | R-7 |

COLOMA

WI-94   COLOMA

SC 1a	6¢	Undated. Unknown.	R-7
SC 2	10¢	Undated. Unknown.	R-7
SC 2a	12¢	Undated. Unknown.	R-7

The issuer and date of the cardboard due bills is unknown, but as they are due "In Current Bank Bills" it suggests they were issued before 1865. They were intended to be numbered and signed by various issuers. As the specimens illustrated have been circulated, it would appear a single merchant issued them and was so well known there was no need to formalize the chit. Other denominations were probably issued, too.

COLUMBUS

WI-95   **BANK OF COLUMBUS, 1857-62**

Capital $50,000. Wm. L. Lewis, Pres., James C. Barnes, cashier. May 28, 1861. Circulation was $63,851. Closed 1862.

Genuine Notes, Raised Notes and Counterfeits

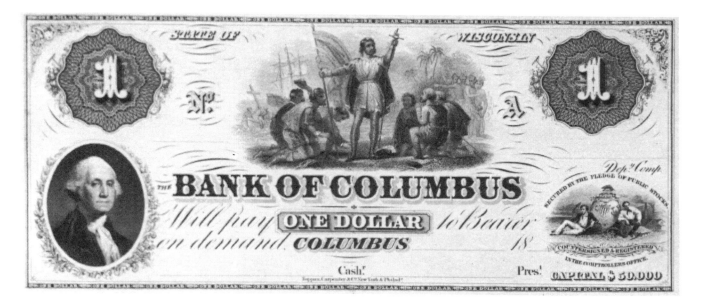

G2	$1	___18__: (1857) TC. C: landing of Columbus. L: Washington. Capital: $50,000.	R-6
G2a	$1	___18__: ca. late 1850s TC. As above, except for capital ($100,000).	—

Half note used as a half dollar, 50 cents.

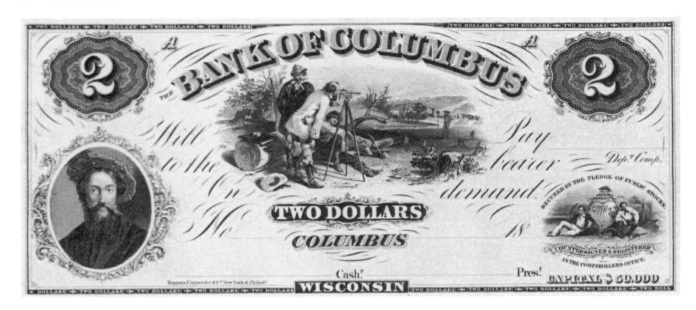

G4	$2	___18__: (1857) TC. L: Columbus. Capital: $50,000.	R-7
G4a	$2	___18__: ca. late 1850s TC. As above, except for capital ($100,000).	R-6
Ra	$3	___18__: late 1850s-60s TC. Raised from $1, G2 series.	R-7

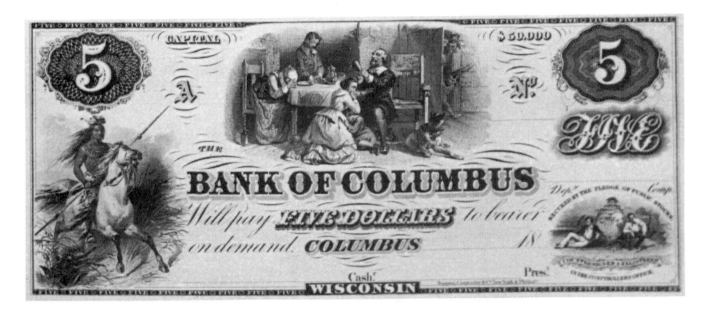

G6	$5	___18__: (1857) TC. Capital: $50,000.	R-7
C6	$5	___18__: late 1850s TC. Cft. of the above.	—
G6a	$5	___18__: ca. late 1850s TC. Same as G6, except for capital ($100,000).	—
R6	$5	___18__: late 1850s-60s TC. Raised from $1, G2 series.	—

R7 $5   ___18__: late 1850s-60s TC. Raised from $2, G4a.   R-7

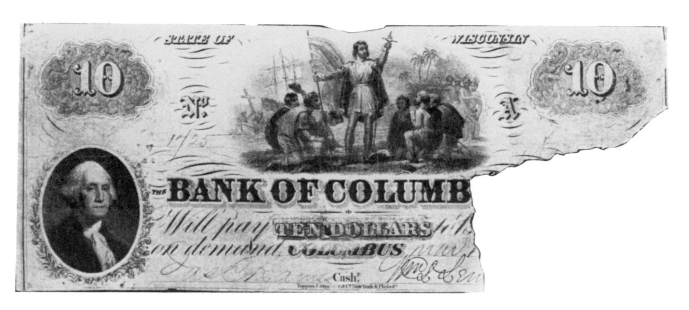

R8 $10   ___18__: late 1850s-60s TC. Raised from $1, G2 series.   R-7
                   The bank issued no $10s.

R9 $10   ___18__: late 1850s-60s TC. Raised from $2, G4 series.   —
                   The bank issued no $10s.

R10 $20   ___18__: late 1850s-60s TC. Raised from $2, G4 series.   —
                   The bank issued no $20.

Uncut Sheet

X1 $1, 2, 2, 5 TC. G2, 4, 4, 6   —

Records indicate that this bank failed in 1862. In 1863 the First National Bank of Columbus was chartered, charter #178.

Raised notes from this bank exist, which in addition to having been raised were messy pieces thus reducing the work required to raise the note's value. They represent some of few surviving raised notes of the period from Wisconsin.

WI-100   UNION BANK, 1861

J. R. Wheeler, Pres., A. G. Cook, cashier.
Became Farmers & Merchants Union Bank, one of Wisconsin's twenty-five oldest and strongest banks.

G2a $5   October 1, 1862 NBN. Tint: green frame, panels and   —
                          counters.

G4a $10   October 1, 1862 NBN. Tint: green counter, panels, etc.   R-7

Uncut Sheet

X1 $5, 10 NBN. G2a, 4a   R-7

CONTERELLE

WI-105   FARMERS BANK OF CHIPPEWA, 1858

Possibly never opened.

The $10 plate was officially altered to the Farmers Bank, Two Rivers, WI-800.

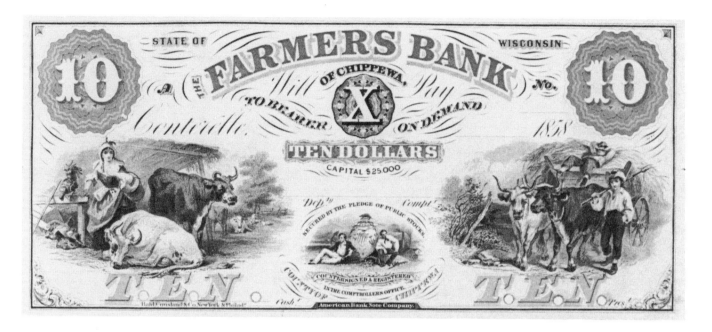

G8a $10   ___1858: BC, ABN. Tint: red counters & TEN TEN.   R-7

WI-810   LUMBERMAN'S BANK, 1858

Capital $200,000. E. Barnes, Pres., J. B. Kenere, cashier.
This bank was organized in 1858. It moved from Viroqua in 1858 and to Beloit in 1862 and became the
Second National Bank of Beloit in 1882.
Krueger indicates that in 1858 Conterelle was an unknown location.

II - NOTES DATED AT CONTERELLE

Genuine Notes, Raised Notes and Counterfeits

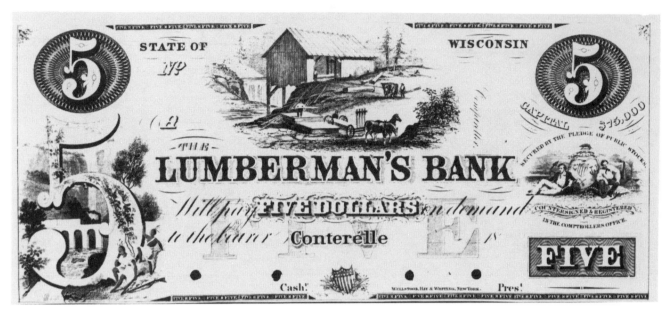

G6	$5	___18__: 1857 WH&W. Capital: $75,000.	R-6
G6a	$5	___18__: 1858 (WH&W). As above, except for capital ($200,000).	—
G6b	$5	___18__: 1859-61 (ABN). Same as G6a, except for capital ($150,000) and probably imprint.	—
C6	$5	___18__: 1850s WH&W. Cft. of G2, 6 or 6a.	—

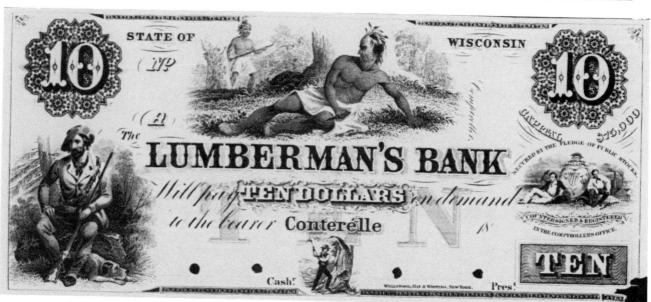

G8	$10	___18__: (1857) WH&W. C. Indian man reclining on ground holding knife, second Indian in rt. Bkgd. ("Death of King Philip"). Capital: $75,000.	—
G8a	$10	___18__: 1858 (WH&W). As above, except for capital ($200,000).	—
G8b	$10	___18__: 1859-61 (ABN). Same as G8a, except for capital ($150,000) and probably imprint.	—
C8	$10	___18__: 1850s WH&W. Cft. of G4, 8 or 8a.	—

Uncut Sheet

X1		$5, 10 WH&W. G6, 8	R-7

DELAVAN

WI-110   WALWORTH COUNTY BANK, 1855-65

Capital 1855 $50,000, 1863 $30,000. Wm. Callen, Pres., W. W. Desmore, cashier. Closed.

Genuine Notes, Raised Notes and Counterfeits

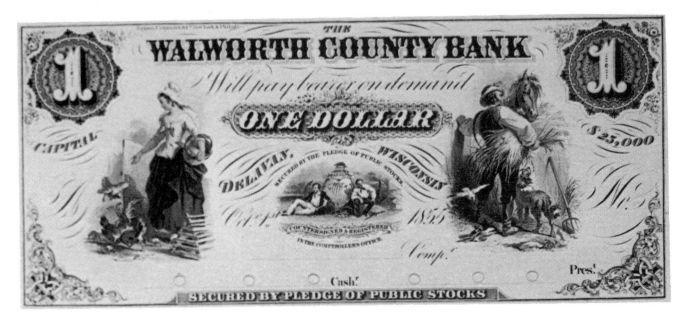

G2	$1	October 1, 1855 TC. Capital: $25,000. No overprint.	R-6
G2a	$1	October 1, 1855 TC. As above, except for red overprint	—
G2c	$1	October 1, 1855 TC. Same as G2a, except for capital ($50,000).	—

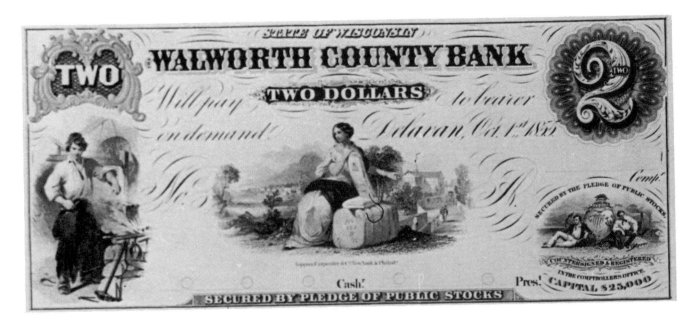

| G4 | $2 | October 1855 TC. Capital: $25,000. | R-6 |

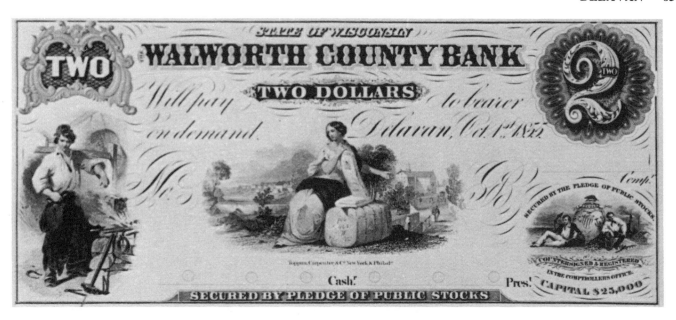

G4a	$2	October 1, 1855 TC. As above, except for red overprint.		—
G4C	$2	October 1, 1855 TC. Same as G4a, except for capital ($50,000).		—
G6	$5	October 1, 1855 TC. Capital: $25,000. No overprint.		R-6

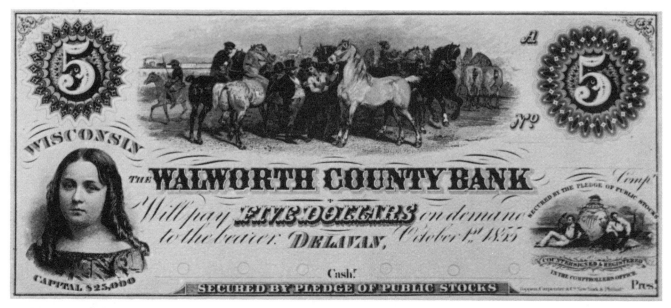

G6a	$5	October 1, 1855 TC. As above, except for red FIVE over-print.		—
G6c	$5	October 1, 1855 TC. Same as G6a, except for capital ($50,000).	Remainder	R-6
R6	$5	October 1, 1855 TC. Raised from $2, G4 series.		—
R8	$10	October 1, 1855 TC. Raised from $2, G4 series. The bank issued no $10s.		—
R10	$20	October 1, 1855 TC. Raised from $1, G2 series. The bank issued no $20s.		—
R12	$20	October 1, 1855 TC. Raised from $2, G4 series. The bank issued no $20s.		—

Uncut Sheet

| X1 | | 1, 2, 2, 5 TC G2, 4, 4, 6 | | R-6 |

DEPERE

WI-115   BROWN COUNTY BANK, 1856-60

Capital $25,000. George A. Lawton, Pres., John O. Roorback, cashier.
Closed prior to 1860. Specie held for redemption $2,062 until February 22, 1863.

Fate: closed.

G2 $1   ___18__: (1850s) RWH&E.   R-7

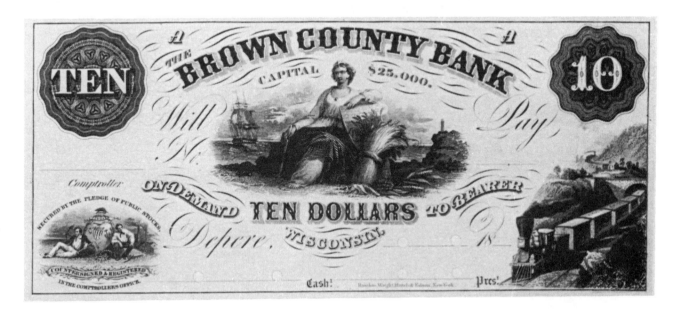

G4 $10   ___18__: RWH&E.   R-7

Uncut Sheet

X1 $1, 10 RWH&E. G2, 4   R-7

WI-119   **FOX RIVER HYDRAULIC COMPANY**

9          $3   Current Bank Funds. UNK.   R-7

The above piece of scrip is the earliest known draft on this company, dated August 10, 1837.

WI-120   **BANK OF FOX RIVER HYDRAULIC COMPANY, est. 1838**

Territorial bank.

As free banking laws were repealed in 1839, all bank notes including those of this private company were either redeemed or failed to circulate. As several of these notes remain it can be assumed the company failed to redeem all outstanding notes.

I-NOTES PAYABLE AT THE BANK IN DEPERE

G6 $5   ___18__: late 1830s DTL.   Remainder   R-5

           R: Clay.   Signed Note   R-5

G8 $10   ___18__: (late 1830s) DTL.   Remainder   R-5

G10 $20   ___18__: late 1830s DTL.   R-5

II-NOTES PAYABLE AT THE PHILADELPHIA LOAN COMPANY

G14 $1   April 1, 1839 DTL R: two allegorical women with harp.   R-7
                       Similar to G18, except for denomination.

G18 $5   April 1, 1839 DTL.   R-5

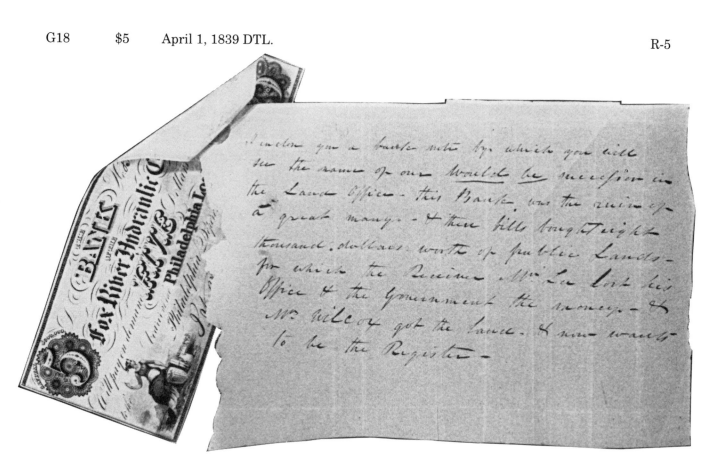

The above memo was attached via a wax seal to a Post note of the Bank of the Fox River Hydraulic Co. It reads as follows:

I enclose you a Bank Note by which you will see the name of our would be successor in the Land Office — this Bank was the ruin of a great many, and these bills bought eight thousand dollars worth of public lands for which the Receiver, Mr. Lee, lost his office, and the government the money. Mr. Wilcox got the land and now wants to be the Register.

Milwaukee Journal article

[E MILWAUKEE JOURNA

★ ★ Tuesday, October 31, 1961 ★ ★

A replica of Wisconsin's first bank, the Fox River bank of De Pere (Brown county) founded in 1836, has been started in Nelson Dewey state park in Cassville as part of Stonefield village.

1836 Style Bank Building Is Going Up at Stonefield

Journal Special Correspondence
Cassville, Wis.—Many attractive new banks have been built in Wisconsin recently, but the Wisconsin Bankers' association and State Historical Society of Wisconsin are building a real old one—of 1836 vintage.

The old bank is the latest project at Nelson Dewey state park's Stonefield village beside the Mississippi river here.

It will be a replica of Wisconsin's first bank—the Fox River bank of De Pere, founded in 1836. The original is still standing, but now is a private home.

Greek Style Planned

A foundation has been laid for the 26 by 34 foot replica. It will be of frame construction in a modified Greek style that was popular in the early 19th century, with wooden columns on each side of the front door.

Raymond S. Sivesind, supervisor of sites and markers for the historical society, and Robert A. Gehrke, a Ripon banker and society curator, are in charge of the project.

Wisconsin bankers have contributed all but $1,000 of the required $6,000. Many furnishings already have been gathered.

Last week, the State Bank of Lime Ridge, which is being remodeled, contributed s o m e barred cashier cages, a roll top desk and a 60 year old Oliver typewriter still in working condition.

Ledger books dating to 1878, a desk, counting trays, c o i n changers and a large pigeonhole desk have been d o n a t e d by Guerdon M. M a t t h e w s of Strong's bank, Dodgeville. The State Bank of Green Valley has contributed a coin changer and money tray used in the 1890's.

30 Buildings Planned

The replica bank will be one of a group of about 30 buildings fronting on a village square. Already in place are a school, general store, drugstore, barbershop and print shop.

The bank and some of the other new buildings will be opened to the public next summer.

Stonefield village is being restored to what a Wisconsin village would have looked like in the 1890's and earlier. The original village was laid out by Wisconsin's first governor, Nelson Dewey.

DESOTO

BLACK HAWK BRIDGE

SC 2   10¢   Iowa-Wisconsin Bridge Co.   R-7

SC 5   25¢   Iowa-Wisconsin Bridge Co.   R-7

SC 6   50¢   Iowa-Wisconsin Bridge Co.   R-7

$5.00 {NOT TRANSFERABLE}   COUPON
BOOK No. 10732

Date..19 ....

Received of the IOWA-WISCONSIN BRIDGE COMPANY,
One coupon book, value $5.00, for which I have today paid the
said Company the sum of $.................................

Auto No(s).................................... Signed....................................

Address....................................

— COUPON BOOK REGULATIONS —

1. The management reserves the right, by giving notice, to alter the sales
   discount on toll-coupon books.

2. Coupons will not be honored if detached from books.

3. Toll coupon books will be sold only if purchaser signs the receipt attached
   thereto, giving auto license number on car or cars, name and address.

4. Coupons good for one way only.   No coupons accepted in advance for
   return trip.

WELDON, WILLIAMS & LICK, FT. SMITH, ARK.

SC 10 $5.00   Iowa-Wisconsin Bridge Co. Booklet consisting of five 5¢,   R-7
                    ten 10¢, five 25¢ and five 50¢ coupons.

DOWNING

WI-127   **COOLIDGE BROS.**

SC 7 $1.00   Merchandise Coupon Black/red serial numbers.   R-7

DUBUQUE

WI-125   **MINERS BANK, 1837-38**

Territorial bank opened October 31, 1837. Became an Iowa Territorial bank of the same name (IA-5) when the Iowa Territory was split off from the Wisconsin Territory, 1838. It also issued notes after 1846 when Iowa became a state.

A. DEMAND NOTES

G2	$5	___18__: (1830s) RW&H		Remainder	R-5
G4	$10	___18__: (1830s) RW&H C: steamboat on river, wagon load of bales drawn by six horses: X. L: 10 / train, merchandise in foreground / 10. RL X / Ceres leaning on short column / TEN.		Remainder	R-5

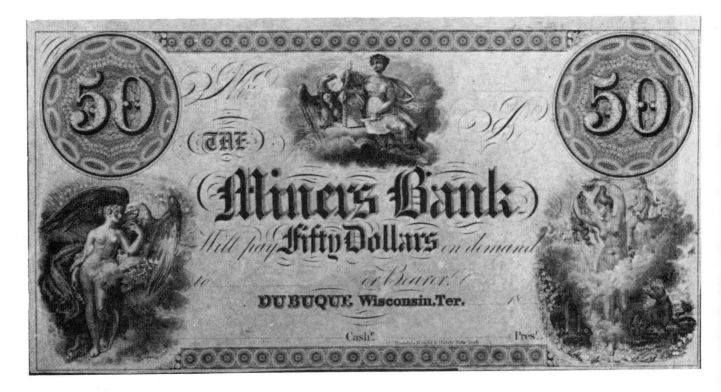

G8	$50	___18__: RW&H.	Remainder	R-7

G10 $100   ___18__: (1830s) RW&H.   Remainder   R-7

B. POST NOTES

G14 $5   ___18__: (1830s) RW&H.   Remainder   R-6

G16 $10   ___18__: (1830s) RW&H.   Remainder   R-6

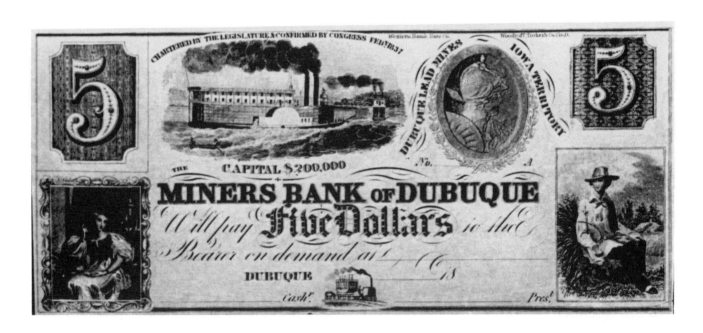

An Iowa Territorial note 1839.

An Iowa State note 1846.

G17 $20   ___18__: 1830 RW&R.   R-7

G18 $__   ___18__: (1830s) RW&H Denomination filled in by hand.   Remainder   R-7

Uncut Sheet

X1 $5, 10   RW&H. G14, 16   R-7

X2 $50,   RW&H. G8, 10, 18   R-7
       100

EAGLE LAKE

WI-130   **TRADESMENS BANK, 1858-61**

Capital $100,000. A. M. Brewer, cashier.
Later location: Chippewa Falls (moved in 1859).

William H. Marsten, Pres. No place of business was established in Chippewa Falls. Notes redeemed at 51¢ per dollar. $1,200 outstanding in 1863.
Notes were probably dated only at Eagle Lake. Failed. Krueger indicates the Eagle Lake was an unknown location in 1858.

G2	$5	___18__: DW. No overprint.		—
G2a	$5	___18__: (1858-61) DW. As above, except for red 5 5 overprint.	Remainder	R-6

G4	$10	___18__: DW. No overprint.	R-6
G4a	$10	___18__: (1858-61) DW. As above, except for large red 10 overprint. G4a.	R-6

Uncut Sheet

X1	$5, 10 DW. G2a, 4a	R-7

EAGLE POINT

WI-135   ARCTIC BANK, 1857-61

Capital $50,000. M. V. Hall, Pres., Isaac Plume, cashier.
Later location: Eau Claire (moved in 1858).

I-NOTES DATED AT EAGLE POINT

Eagle Point was described as being all of Portage County west of Range 5. This would be what today is Wood County.

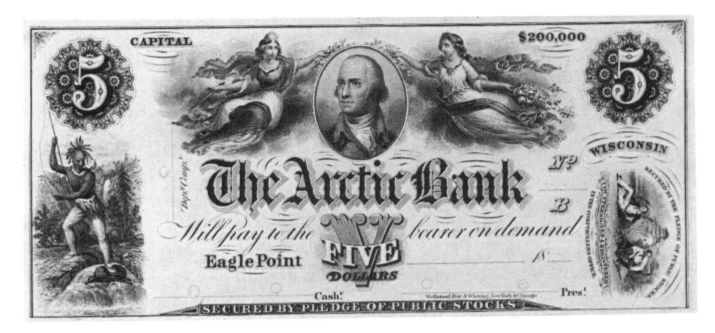

| G2 | $5 | ___18__: 1857 WH&W C: Washington. Same as G2a, except for capital ($50,000). | R-7 |
| G2a | $5 | ___18__: (1857-58) WH&W. Same as above, except for capital ($200,000). | R-7 |

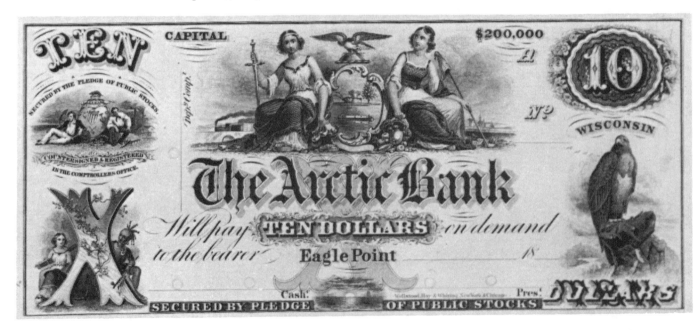

| G4 | $10 | ___18__: 1857 WH&W. Same as G4a, except for capital ($50,000). | R-7 |

| G4a | $10 | ___18__: (1857-58) WH&W. Same as above, except for capital ($200,000). | R-7 |

| G6 | $20 | ___18__: WH&W. Same as G6a, except for capital ($50,000). | R-7 |

| G6a | $20 | ___18__: (1857-58) WH&W. As above, except for capital ($200,000). | R-7 |

Altered, Spurious and Unattributed Non-Genuine Notes

| A5 | $5 | Various (1850s) DW. C: 1/2-length figures of farmer, sailor and mechanic. L: FIVE/oval state die, across. R: 5: 5/oval portrait of Pierce. Altered from $5 Bank of Washtenaw, Washtenaw, MI-50-G44 series. | R-7 |

| A10 | $5 | September 1, 1856 DW. C: whaling scene, men in boat in foreground, ship in rt. bkgd. L: 5/sailing ship, in circle. R: 5-1/2-length figure of sailor at ships wheel, in circle. Altered from $5 Commercial Bank of New Jersey, Perth Amboy, NJ-455-G44 series. | R-7 |

EAGLE RIVER

WI-140   **MARATHON COUNTY BANK, 1858-59**

Capital $60,000. C. Wheeler, cashier. $950 held to redeem a like amount of notes. Time of redemption expired May 17, 1862.
Fate: closed.

Genuine Notes, Raised Notes and Counterfeits

G2a $5   ___18__: (late 1850s) RWH&E. Tint: Overall green   R-7
                          lathework overall, with outlined white FIVE.

G4a $10   ___18__: (late 1850s) RWH&E. Tint: Overall green   R-7
                          lathework overall, with outlined white TEN.

Uncut Sheet

X1 $5, 10 RWH7E. G2a, 4a   R-7

Altered, Spurious and Unattributed Non-Genuine Notes

S5 $3   January 15, 18__; 1850s ABN. Overprint: brown THREE.   R-5
                        The bank issued no $3s.

S10 $10   January 15, 18__; 1850s ABN. Spurious design, but imi-   —
                        tates a rough verbal description of the genuine $10
                        noted (G4a) on this bank.

When a Wisconsinite thinks of Marathon County today, he immediately equates it to Wausau, Home of Employee Mutual Insurance Company. When he thinks of Eagle River he thinks of one of the great tourist areas encompassing a chain of beautiful lakes. Eagle River is about 75 miles north and a bit east of Wausau.

In 1858 the great northwoods of Wisconsin including Eagle River was being surveyed, thus it typifies a likely spot for a wildcat bank. Marathon County began in what is now Portage and Marathon County and extended north to the border of Michigan's upper peninsula.

It is doubtful if any genuine notes on the Marathon County Bank of Eagle River ever were circulated as only proof notes are known. The issuer of the spurious notes however must have seen proofs of the genuine notes as his look-alikes did follow a literal description.

A History of Logging in Vilas County 1856-1982 (including some personal reminiscences)

Walter Mayo

Retired Vilas County Forest Administrator

Before the Railroad

Early settlers came to the area about 1853; they were Bethuel Drapier and "Dutch Pete" Cramer. The first logging done in Vilas County was on the Eagle River chain of lakes in 1857 by the partnership of Fox & Helms. Fox built a good house prior to that time, approximately 1855, along the east shore of Eagle Lake. He cleared about two acres or more and planted potatoes and other garden vegetables with much success. (This was the site where the present Eagle Waters Resort is now located.) H. B. Polar operated a trading post on Yellow Birch Lake.

Fox's partner, Helms, previously had received a contract from Marathon County to build a road from Jenny (now Merrill) to the state line of Michigan. They followed an old Indian trail which was blazed through the woods by fur traders, also the old military trail, built during the Civil War, which had been used as an escape route for prisoners and slaves. The road was built just wide enough for a team of oxen. It extended from Wausau to Merrill, to Rhinelander, to Eagle River, then to Ontanogan, Michigan.

Fox and Helms brought ninety men and ten teams of oxen to start their logging operation. A young man by the name of John Curran, who had come to the area a year before, was their foreman. He was 19 years old and helped the man called "Dutch" Pete Cramer cut marsh hay along the Wisconsin River. Curran later settled in the Rhinelander area. Cramer built a home in the area. Curran and Cramer brought a canoe load of supplies to Eagle River from Merrill by way of the Wisconsin River a short time previously. They cut marsh hay to feed a team of oxen that belonged to a man by the name of Bonneville who had built a home at the mouth of the Deerskin River. This site was later to become a logging camp.

Helms started a bank called Marathon Bank which was also referred to as the "Kim-me-con", also the "She quan-agon" Bank. $50,000.00 of worthless notes were issued. Helms left the country before the defrauded loggers found out about this. There are a few of the three dollar bills that were issued that are still in the possession of some old time residents. They possibly are worth a small fortune now as collectors items.

EAU CLAIRE

WI-135   ARTIC BANK

Moved from Eagle Point in 1858.

Failed 1861.

II - NOTES DATED AT EAU CLAIRE

Genuine Notes, Raised Notes and Counterfeits

G8	$5	___18__: 1858-61 RH&W. Same as G2a, except for city.	R-7
G10	$10	___18__: 1858-61 WH&W. Same as G4a, except for city.	R-7
G12	$20	___18__: 1858-61 WH&W. Same as G6a, except for city.	R-7

Uncut Sheet

X1	$5, 5, 10, 20 WH&W. G2a, 2a, 4a, 6a	R-7

WI-145   BANK OF EAU CLAIRE, ca. 1858-62

Capital $50,000. C. M. Seley, cashier. Notes redeemed at 84¢ per dollar. 1863 circulation outstanding $1,202. Settled its affairs 1863.
Fate: failed.

Genuine Notes, Raised Notes and Counterfeits

G2	$1	___18__: ___ TC Capital: $50,000. No overprint.	R-7
G2a	$1	___18__: 1857 TC. As above, except for one ONE over-print.	R-7
G2b	$1	___18__: ca. 1858 (ABN) Same as G2, except for capital ($75,000) and probably imprint.	R-7
G2c	$1	___18__: ca 1858-62 ABN. Same as G2, except for imprint. Capital: $50,000.	R-7

G4	$2	___18__: TC Capital: $50,000. No overprint.	R-7
G4a	$2	___18__: 1857 TC. As above, except for red TWO overprint.	R-6
G4b	$2	___18__: 1858 (ABN). Same as G2, except for capital ($75,000) and probably imprint.	R-7
G4c	$2	___18__: ca. 1859-62 ABN. Same as G2, except for imprint. Capital: $50,000.	R-7
R5	$3	___18__: late 1850s TC. Raised from $1, G2 series. The bank issued no $3s.	R-7
R6	$5	___18__: late 1850s TC. Raised from $1, G2 series. The bank issued no $5s.	R-7
R7	$10	___18__: late 1850s TC. Raised from $1, G2 series. The bank issued no $10s.	R-7
R8	$20	___18__: late 1850s TC. Raised from $1, G2 series. The bank issued no $20s.	R-7

Uncut Sheet

X1		$1, 2 TC. G2, 4	R-7

WI-146   **CULVER & TARRANT**

SC 2	10¢	Undated. ML&E Front Black & Green, Back Brown	R-6
SC 5	25¢	Undated. ML&E Front Black & Green, Back Brown.	R-6
SC 6	50¢	Undated. ML&E Front Black & Green, Back Brown.	R-6

| SC 7 | $1.00 | Undated. ML&E Front Black & Green, Back Brown. | R-6 |

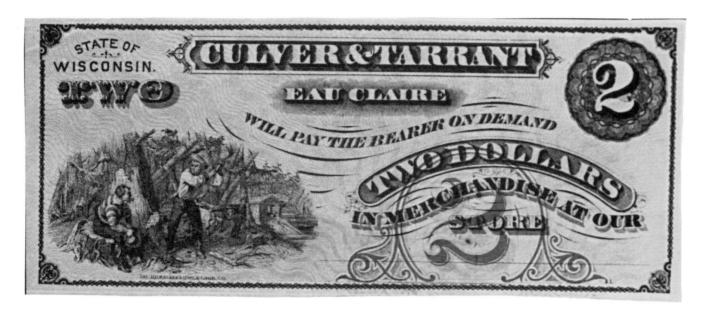

SC 8 $2.00   Undated. ML&E Front Black & Green, Back Brown.   R-6

SC 10 $5.00   Undated. ML&E Black/green overprint. Rev. lt. brown.   R-6

A sheet of these notes were cut several years ago thus examples of each denomination are available. See Knapp Stout & Company, Prairie Farm for sheet configuration.

WI-150   HALL & BROTHERS' BANK, 1858-61

Capital $50,000. B. F. Hall, Pres., D. R. Moore, cashier. Notes redeemed at 63¢ per dollar in 1862. Circulation outstanding 1863 $1,126.
Failed.

G2	$1	___18__: WH&W. Capital: $50,000. No overprint.	R-7
G2a	$1	___18__: 1857 WH&W. As above, except for red overprint.	R-7
G2b	$1	___18__: 1857-60s WH&W. As above, except for capital ($250,000).	R-7

G4	$2	___18__: WH&W. Capital: $50,000. No overprint.	R-7
G4a	$2	___18__: 1857 WH&W. As above, except for red overprint.	R-7
G4b	$2	___18__: 1857-50s WH&W. As above, except for capital ($250,000).	R-7

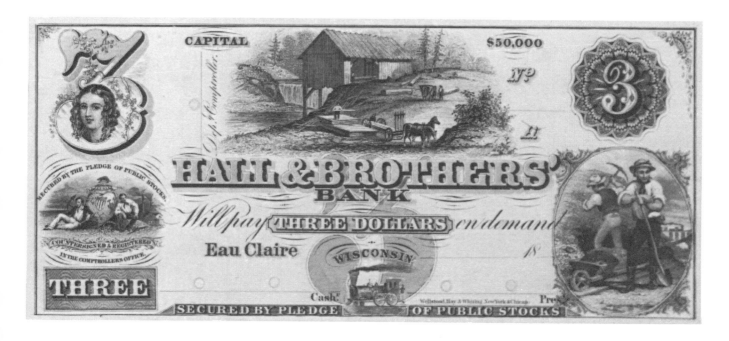

G8	$3	___18__: WH&W. Capital: $50,000. No overprint.	R-7
G6a	$3	___18__: 1857 WH&W. As above, except for red overprint	R-7
G6b	$3	___18__: 1857-60s WH&W. As above, except for capital ($250,000).	R-7

G8	$5	___18__: WH&W. No overprint.	R-7
G8a	$5	___18__: 1857 WH&W. As above, except for red 5 5 overprint.	R-7
G8b	$5	___18__: 1857-60s WH&W. As above, except for capital ($250,000).	R-7

Uncut Sheet

| X1 | | $1, 2, 3, 5 WH&W. G2, 4, 6, 8 | R-7 |

WII-152   **NORTH WESTERN LUMBER CO.**

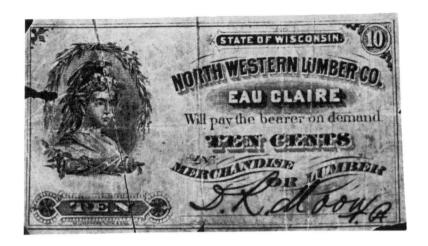

2	10¢	Undated. ML&E Black.	R-7
5	25¢	Undated. ML&E Black.	R-7
6	50¢	Undated. ML&E Black.	R-7
7	$1.00	Undated. ML&E Black/orange overprint, green rev.	R-7

| 8 | $2.00 | Undated. ML&E Black/orange overprint/green rev. | R-7 |
| 10 | $5.00 | Undated. ML&E Black/orange overprint/green rev. | R-7 |

While only a 10¢ and $2 note have been discovered on the Lumber Co. the author assumes the others were printed as the notes were typical of those of other lumber companies printed by the Milwaukee Litho & Engr. Co. See Prairie Farm for sheet configuration.

WI-155   **STATE STOCK BANK, 1858-61**

Capital $125,000. J. Sibley, Pres., H. O. Pratt, cashier. Outstanding circulation 1863 $6,483 redeemed at 95¢ per dollar.
Failed.

Genuine Notes, Raised Notes and Counterfeits.

G2a	$2	___18__: 1858 TC. Lower L: Cass Overprint: red TWO. "CAPITAL $25,000" printed in red.	R-6
G2b	$2	___18__: 1858 TC. As above, except for capital ($50,000), which is engraved.	R-7
G2c	$2	___18__: 1858 TC. Same as G2b, except for capital ($100,000).	R-7
G2d	$2	___18__: 1858 TC. Same as G2b, except for capital ($150,000).	R-7
G2a	$2	___18__: 1859 TC. ABNCo. mono. Same as G2b, except for imprint and capital ($175,000).	R-7
G2f	$2	___18__: 1859 TC. ABNCo. mono. Same as G2b, except for imprint and capital ($200,000).	R-7
G2g	$2	___18__: 1859 TC. ABNCo. mono. Same as G2b, except for imprint and capital ($250,000).	R-7
G2h	$2	___18__: 1859 TC. Same as G2b, except for capital ($275,000).	R-7
G4a	$3	___18__: 1858 TC. R: DeWitt Clinton. Overprint: red THREE. Same as G4h, except "CAPITAL $25,000" is printed in red.	R-7

G4b	$3	___18__: 1858 TC. As above, except for capital ($50,000), which is engraved.	R-7
G4c	$3	___18__: 1858 TC. Same as G4b, except for capital ($100,000).	R-7
G4d	$3	___18__: 1858 TC. Same as G4b, except for capital ($150,000).	R-7
G4e	$3	___18__: 1859 TC, ABNCo. mono. Same as G4b, except for imprint and capital ($175,000).	R-7
G4f	$3	___18__: 1859 TC. ABNCo. mono. Same as G4b, except for imprint and capital ($200,000).	R-7
G4g	$3	___18__: 1859 TC, ABNCo. mono. Same as G4b, except for imprint and capital ($250,000).	R-7
G4h	$3	___18__: 1850s TC Same as G4b, except for capital ($275,000).	R-6

Only the notes illustrated are known on this bank.

Altered, Spurious and Unattributed Non-Genuine Notes

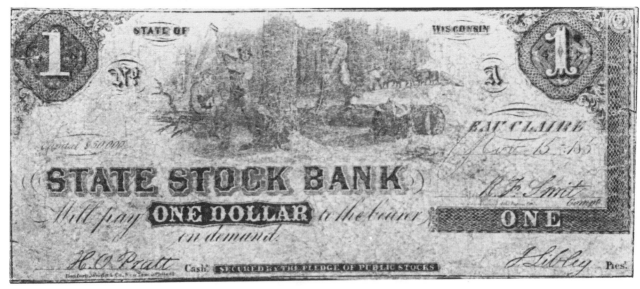

S5	$1	___18__: 1853 DW. Altered from a fraudulent plate, originally for a cft. $1 (IN-260-C2) on the State Stock Bank, Jamestown.	R-6

ELISIDE

WI-160   LABORER'S BANK, 1858-61

Capital $50,000. John Miller, Pres., E. C. Hall cashier (1859).
Later location: Markesan (town name changed).

Failed 1861. Notes redeemed at 87¢ per dollar. $570 outstanding in 1863.

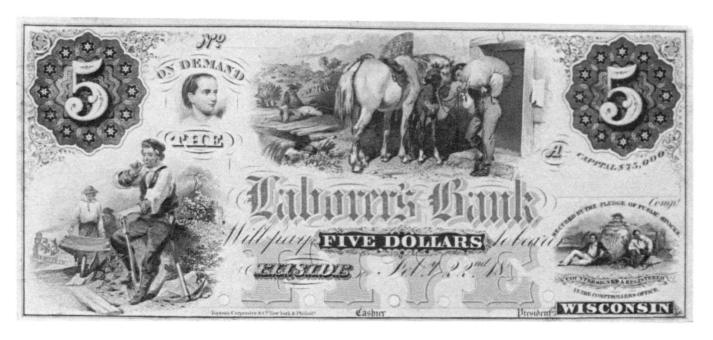

| G2a | $5 | February 22, 18__: (late 1850s) TC Tint: Red FIVE & bank title. | R-7 |

| G4a | $10 | February 22, 18__: (late 1850s) TC RC: Clay. Tint: Red TEN. | R-7 |

Uncut Sheet

| X1 | | $5, 10 TC. G2a, 4a | R-7 |

ELK HORN

WI-165   ELK HORN BANK, 1856-65

Capital $25,000. Legrand Rockwell, Pres., D. D. Spencer, cashier, 1856. J. L. Edwards, Pres., George C. Buckley, cashier, 1863.
Closed, became First National Bank of Elkhorn, 1865.

G2a $1   ___18__: (1856-60s) WH&W Overprint: red ONE.   R-7

G4a $2   ___18__: (1856-60s) WH&W Overprint: red TWO.   R-7

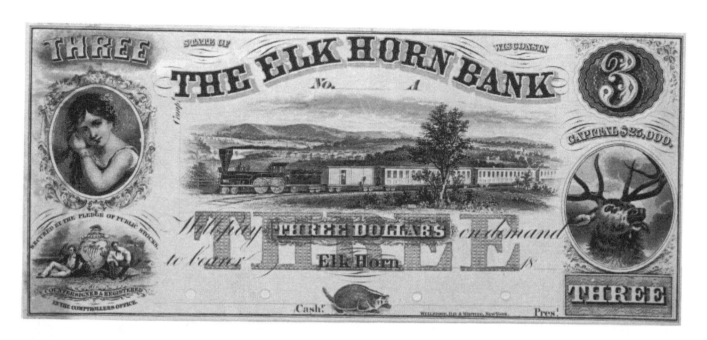

G6a	$3	___18__: (1856-60s) WH&W Overprint: red THREE.	R-7
R5	$5	___18__: 1850-60s WH&W. Raised from $1, G2a. The bank issued no $5s.	R-7
R6	$10	___18__: 1850s-60s WH&W. Raised from $1, G2a. The bank issued no $10s.	R-7
R7	$20	___18__: 1850s-60s WH&W. Raised from $1, G2a. The bank issued no $20s.	R-7

Uncut Sheet

| X1 | $1, 1, 2, 3 WH&W.G2a, 2a, 4a, 5a | R-7 |

WI-170   ROCKWELL & COMPANY'S BANK, 1859-65

Capital $25,000. L. C. Rockwell, Pres., L. R. Rockwell, cashier.
Fate unknown.

G2	$2	___18__: ___ ABN. L: Daniel Boone. No overprint.		R-7
G2a	$2	___18__: 1859-60 ABN. As above, except for overprint of a red panel outlining a white TWO.	Remainder Signed Note	R-6 R-7
G2c	$2	June 1, 1860 ABN. As above, except for date.		R-6

G4	$3	___18__: ___ ABN. No overprint.	R-7
G4a	$3	___18__: (1859) ABN. As above, except for red 3 overprint.	R-7
G4c	$3	June 1, 1860 ABN. As above, except for date.	R7

Uncut Sheets

X1	$2, 3 ABN. G2, 4	R-7
X2	$2c, 4c ABN. G2b, 4b	R-7

The above notes were designed to be cut, thus creating $1 notes (1/2 of $2) and 1/3 and 2/3 of a 3 ($1 and $2).

FOND DU LAC

WI-175   **EXCHANGE BANK, 1850s**

A non-existent bank, represented only by altered notes. The notes were intended to pass for those of the
Exchange Bank of Darling & Co., Fond du Lac, WI-180.

A5 $5   ___18__: 1850s DW. R: Kate Sevier. Altered from $5   R-6
                    Exchange Bank of Tennessee, Murfreesboro, TN-135-
                    G16.

WI-180   EXCHANGE BANK OF DARLING & COMPANY, 1856-68

Capital $50,000. Geo. McWilliams, Pres., K. A. Darling, cashier.
Failed. Stopped payments in 1868 with about $30,000 due depositors due to bad debts.

Genuine Notes, Raised Notes and Counterfeits

G2a	$1	___18__: (1850s) DW. Capital: $50,000. Overprint: red One.		R-6
G2b	$1	___18__: late 1850s DW. As above, except capital ($75,000).	Remainder Signed Note	R-6 —
G2c	$1	___18__: 1860s ABN. As above, except for imprint.		R-7

G4a	$2	___18__: (1850s) DW. Capital: $50,000. Overprint: red TWO.	R-6
G4b	$2	___18__: (late 1850s) DW. As above, except capital ($75,000).	R-7
G4c	$2	___18__: 1860s ABN. As above, except for imprint.	R-7

G6a	$3	___18__: (1850s) DW. Capital: $50,000. Overprint: red THREE.		R-6
G6b	$3	___18__: (late 1850s) DW. As above, except capital ($75,000).	Remainder	R-6
G6c	$3	___18__: 1860s ABN. As above, except for imprint.		R-7
R5	$3	___18__: 1863 ABN. Raised from $1, G2c.		R-6
R10	$5	___18__: 1850s DW. Raised from $2, G4a. The bank issued no $5s.		R-7

Uncut Sheet

X1	$1, 1, 2, 3 DW. G2a, 2a, 4a, 6a	R-7

Altered, Spurious and Unattributed Non-Genuine Notes

A5	$10	December 1, 1856 Ormsby. Altered from a spurious $10 (CT-150-S20) issue on the Exchange Bank, Hartford. The bank issued no $10s.	R-6

WI-185   FARMERS & MERCHANTS BANK, 1858-67

Capital $25,000. Samuel B. Amory, Pres., Robert A. Baker, cashier (1860-1863).
Closed 1867.

Genuine Notes, Raised Notes and Counterfeits

G2a	$1	___18__: (1860s) ABN. Tint: Red-orange titles, counters and ONE ONE.	R-7
G2b	$1	___18__: 1860s ABN. As above, except the tint is green.	R-7

G4a	$2	___18__: 1860s ABN. Tint: Red-orange title, counter and TWO TWO.	Proof-7
G4b	$2	___18__: 1860s ABN. As above, except the tint is green.	R-7
R5	$5	___18__: 1860s ABN. Raised from $1, G2a.	R-7
R10	$10	___18__: 1860s ABN. Raised from $2, G4a.	R-7

Uncut Sheet

X1	$1, 2 ABN. G2a, 4a.	R-7

***WI-190*   BANK OF FOND DU LAC, 1854-61**

Capital $25,000. W. J. Bell, Pres., A. G. Butler, cashier. Failed 1861, notes redeemed 1862 at 68-3/4¢ per dollar.

Genuine Notes, Raised Notes and Counterfeits

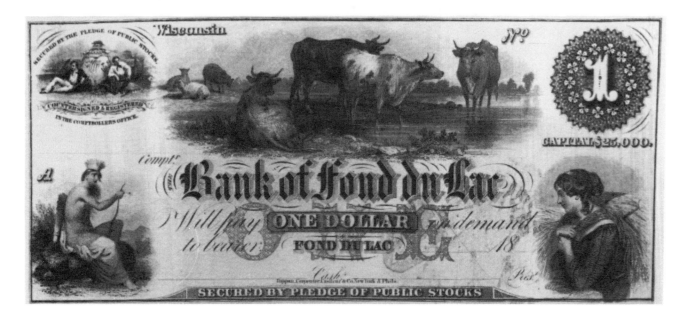

G2a	$1	___18__: (1850s) TCC. Capital: $25,000. Overprint: Ornate red ONE.	R-7
G2b	$1	___18__: 1857-61 TCC. As above, except capital ($50,000).	R-7

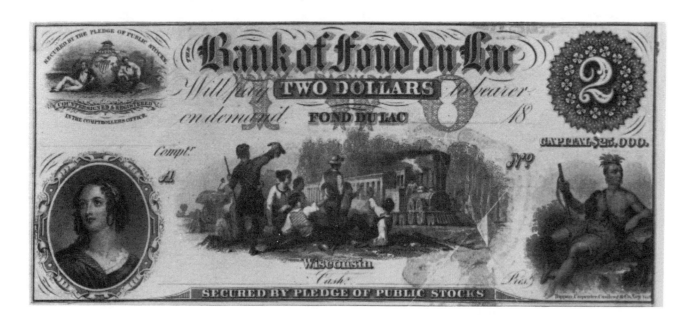

G4a	$2	___18__: (1850s) TCC. Capital: $25,000. Overprint: ornate red TWO.	R-7
G4b	$2	___18__: 1856-61 TCC. As above, except capital ($50,000).	R-7

G6a	$3	___18__: 1850s TCC. Capital: $25,000. Overprint: ornate red THREE.	R-6
G6b	$3	___18__: 1857-61 TCC. As above, except capital ($50,000).	R-7

G8a	$5	___18__: 1850s TCC. L: Daniel Boone. Capital: $25,000. Overprint: ornate red FIVE.	R-6
G8b	$5	___18__: 1857-61 TCC. As above, except capital ($50,000).	R-7

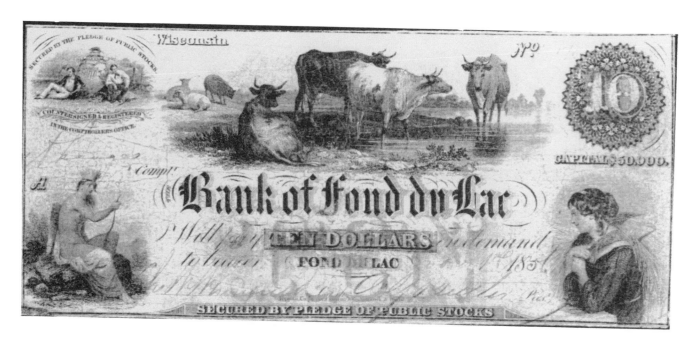

R5 $10   ___18__: 1850s TCC. Overprint: orange TEN. Capital   R-6
                $50,000. Raised from $1, G2b. The bank issued no
                $10s.

R6 $10   As above but G2, no overprint, capital $25,000.

Uncut Sheet

X1 $1, 2, 3, 5 TCC. G2a, 4a, 6a, 8a   R-7

WI-196   **CITY OF FOND DU LAC**

SC 1   5¢   October 16, 1862 Mendel. Black.   R-5

SC 2   10¢   October 16, 1862 Mendel. Black.   R-5

SC 5   25¢   October 16, 1862 Mendel. Black.   R-5

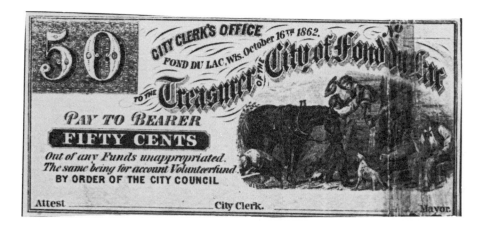

SC 6   50¢   October 16, 1862 Mendel. Black.   R-5

WI-198   I H CLUM & CO.

SC 1   5¢   ___18__: 1862. Black.   R-7

WI-195   BANK OF THE NORTH WEST, 1855-64

Capital $25,000. Benjamin F. Moore, Pres., Augustus C. Ruggles, cashier (1857). Edward Pier assumed President in 1863.

Became the First National Bank of Fond du Lac. Charter #555. In 1918 it absorbed the Fond du Lac National Bank #3665 and changed its name to First Fond du Lac National Bank.

G2	$1	___18__; TC. Capital: $25,000. No overprint.		R-7
G2b	$1	___18__: (1850s) TC. As above, except for capital ($50,000) and red 1 1 overprint.	Remainder	R-6
G2c	$1	___18__: (1858-60s) TC, ABNCo. mono. As above, except for imprint and shorter, wider is in the overprint.	Remainder	R-6

G4	$2	___18__: ___ TC. Capital: $25,000. No overprint.	R-7
G4b	$2	___18__: 1850s TC. As above, except for capital ($50,000) and red TWO overprint.	R-7
G4c	$2	___18__: 1858-60s TC, ABNCo. mono. As above, except for imprint mono.	R-6

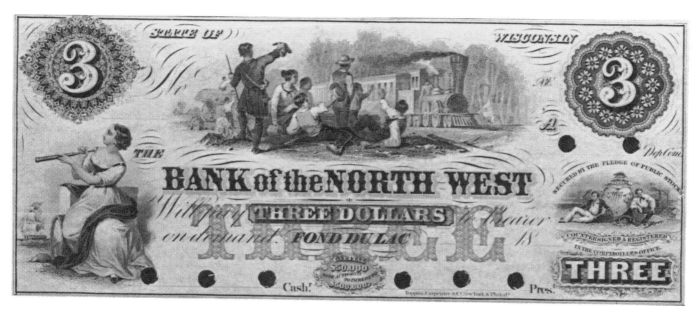

G6	$3	___18__: ____ TC. Capital: $25,000. No overprint.	R-7
G6b	$3	___18__: 1850s TC. As above, except for capital ($50,000) and red THREE overprint.	R-6
G6c	$3	___18__: 1858-60s. TC, ANBCo. mono. As above, except for imprint.	R-7

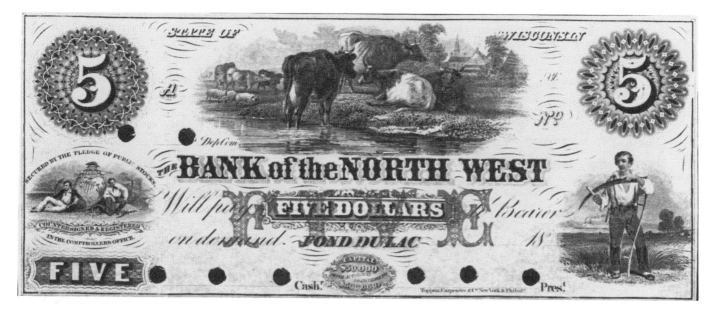

G8	$5	___18__: ____ TC. Capital: $25,000. No overprint.		R-7
G8b	$5	___18__: 1850s TC. As above, except for capital ($50,000) and red FIVE overprint.		R-7
G8c	$5	___18__: (1858-60s) TC, ABNCo. mono. As above, except for imprint.	Remainder	R-6

Uncut Sheets

| X1 | $1, 2, 3, 5 TC. G2, 4, 6, 8 | R-7 |

FORT ATKINSON

WI-200   KOSHKONONG BANK, 1859-61

Capital $25,000. J. D. Clapp, Pres., L. B. Coswell, cashier.
Failed. 1862 redeeming notes at 54-3/4¢ per dollar. $816 remained in circulation.

| G2a | $1 | January 15, 1859 ABN. Overprint: Red panel outlining a white ONE. | R-7 |

| G4a | $2 | January 15, 1859 ABN. Overprint: Red panel outlining a white TWO. | R-7 |

Uncut Sheet

| X1 | $1, 2 ABN. G2a, 4aa | R-7 |

WI-199   **THOMAS S. WRIGHT**

SC 6   50¢   May 7, 1861 Lipman. Black.   R-7

WI-202   **MORRISON, MANNING & CO.**

SC 6   50¢   July 1, 1862.   R-7

FOX LAKE

WI-205   BANK OF FOX LAKE, 1855-64

Capital $25,000. Wm. E. Smith, Pres., Wm. J. Dexter, cashier (1863).
Became the First National Bank of Fox Lake. Charter #426 in 1864. Liquidated Jan 14, 1890 voluntarily.

Genuine Notes, Raised Notes and Counterfeits

G2	$1	July 16, 1855 WHH&W. Capital: $25,000. Note the male portrait at the rt.	R-7
C2	$1	July 16, 1855 WHH&W. Cft. of the above.	R-7

G4	$1	July 1, 1857 WHH&W, ABNCo. mono. Capital: $50,000. Note the female portrait at the rt. No overprint.	R-6

G4b	$1	July 1, 1857 WHH&W, ABNCo. mono. As above, except for a red lazy 1 overprint.		R-6
G6	$2	July 1, 1857 WH&W. Capital: $50,000. No overprint.	Remainder	R-7

G8	$5	July 1, 1857 WH&W. Capital: $50,000. No overprint.	Remainder	R-6
R6	$10	Unknown, Raised from $1, G2 or 4. The bank issued no $10s.	Unknown	R-7

Uncut Sheets

X1		$1, 1 WHH&W. G2, 2	R-7
X2		$2, 5 WH&W. G6, 8	R-7

Altered, Spurious and Unattributed Non-Genuine Notes

N5	$5	(1850s) Unknown. L: Washington/large 5. Lower R: woman.	R-7

GEMEKON

WI-210   OSBORN BANK OF GEMEKON, 1858

Became the Osborn Bank of New London, WI-590.

Krueger indicates that this was an unknown location in 1858. Wisconsin Postal History indicates that Gemeken had a P.O. in Oconto County 1858-59. Its name changed to Kekkektagon in 1860 and continued as a P.O. until 1866.

| G2 | $5 | April 20, 1858 TC, ABNCo. mono. | R-7 |

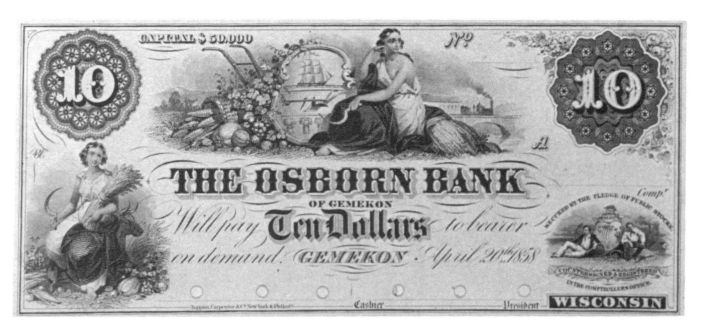

| G4 | $10 | April 20, 1858 TC, ABNCo. mono. | R-7 |

Uncut Sheet

| X1 | | $5, 10 TC, ABNCo. mono. G2, 4 | R-7 |

WI-215 **STATE SECURITY BANK, 1858-59**

Capital $100,000. C. H. Helmes, cashier.

Closed 1859. Agreed to have their notes redeemed at Milwaukee in New York Stock Exchange at 1/4, or at Madison at 3/8% below the current selling rates of exchange in Milwaukee, provided that no bank will be required to redeem at Milwaukee at less than 3/4, or at Madison at less than 5/8 of percent premium.

From November, 1858 *Bankers Magazine*

(In liquidation in 1859). $1,955 specie held in 1860, for redemption of notes amounting to $1,955. Time of redemption to May 17, 1862.

Fate: closed.

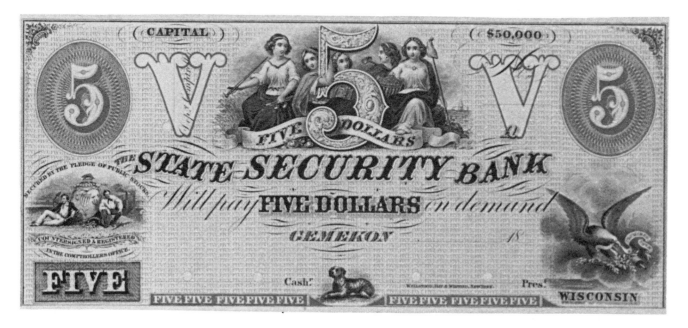

G2a	$5	___18__: (1858) WH&W. Tint: Red overall microlettering overall, counters & ornate V V. Capital: $50,000.	R-7
G2b	$5	___18__: 1858 WH&W. As above, except for capital ($100,000).	R-7
G2c	$5	___18__: 1858-59 WH&W. As above, except for capital ($200,000).	R-7

G4a	$10	___18__: (1858) WH&W. Tint: Red overall microlettering overall, counters & ornate X. Capital: $50,000.	R-7
G4b	$10	___18__: 1858 WH&W. As above, except for capital ($100,000).	R-7
G4c	$10	___18__: 1858 WH&W. As above, except for capital ($200,000).	R-7

Uncut Sheets

| X1 | | $5, 10 WH&W. G2a, 4a | R-7 |

GENEVA

WI-217   GENEVA HIGH SCHOOL BANK, 1870's

SC 2 $2   April 24, 1871. Will Pay Bearer $ ___ Dollars.   R-7
                      Black/Green.

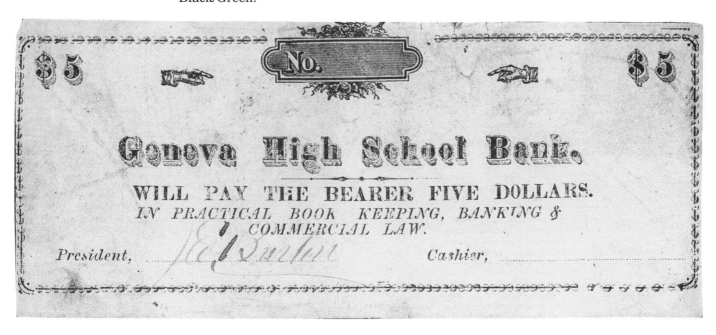

SC 9 $5   Undated. Black/Green.   R-7

SC 11 $10   April 20, 1871 Black/Green.   R-7

SC 12 $20   April 20, 1871 Black/Green.   R-7

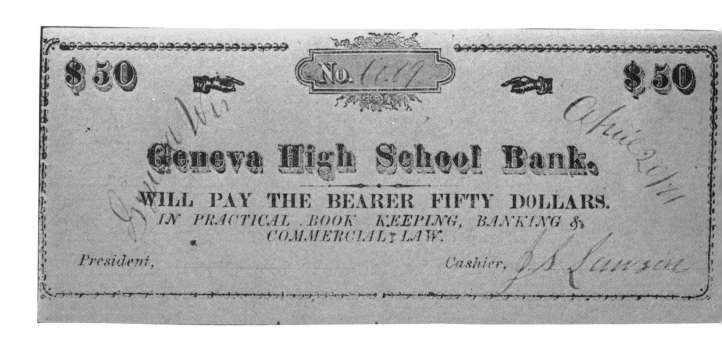

SC 13 $50   April 20, 1874 Black/Green.   R-7

SC 14 $100   April 20, 1871 Black/Green.   R-7

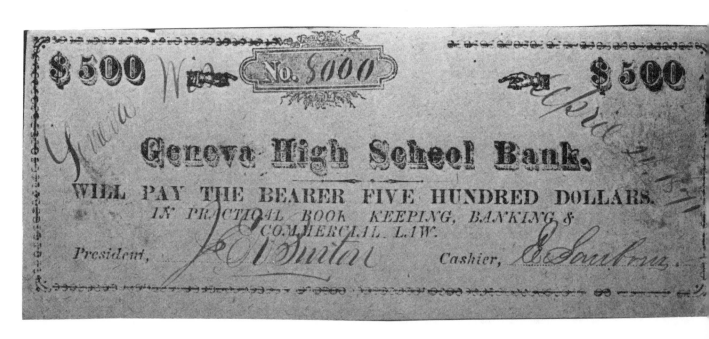

SC 15 $500   April 21, 1874 Black/Green.   R-7

GORDON

Gordon is located in Sauk County between Reedsburg and LaValle. It was a telegraph station on the C&NW RR. It was named after the RR president William W. Gordon.

WI-220   BANK OF MONEKA, 1858-61

Capital $75,000. J.H. Cole, Pres., J. Cole, cashier.
Later locations: Viroqua, Hustisford, Portage (moved in 1858 and twice in 1862).
Closed. Notes were probably dated only at Gordon & Hustisford.

1-NOTES DATED AT GORDON

G2a	$5	May 1, 1858 DW. Tint: Red lathework overall, with an outlined white FIVE DOLLARS.	R-7

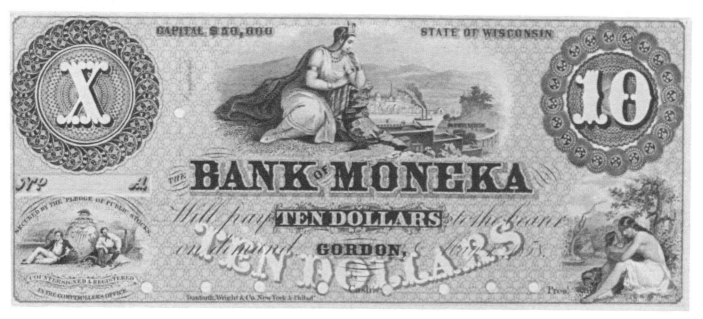

G4a	$10	May 1, 1858 DW. Tint: Red lathework overall, with an outlined white TEN DOLLARS.	R-7

Uncut Sheets

X1	$5, 10 DW. G2a, 4a	R-7

GRAND RAPIDS

WI-85   ST. CROIX RIVER BANK, 1857-62

Capital $100,000. J. M. Dickinson, Pres., W. W. Botkin, cashier. Failed 1861. Outstanding circulation $1,655. Redeemed notes at 75.5¢.
Moved from Brinkerhoff in the 1860s. Probably never issued notes from Grand Rapids. May even have changed its name. Grand Rapids merged in 1920 with a city on the east side of the Wisconsin River named Centralia. Thereafter the city was called Wisconsin Rapids. In part this solved a confusion with Michigan and Minnesota, each having a city named Grand Rapids.

WI-225   WOOD COUNTY BANK, 1859-61

Capital $25,000. George Paine, Pres., W. W. Botkin, cashier (1859).
Failed 1861. Notes redeemed at 77¢ per dollar. Outstanding circulation 1863 $1,381.

Genuine Notes, Raised Notes and Counterfeits

G2	$1	___18__: ABN. Capital: $25,000. No overprint.	R-7
G2a	$1	___18__: ABN. As above, except for overprint of a red panel outlining a white ONE.	R-7
G2b	$1	___18__: 1859-61 ABN. Same as G2a, except for capital ($50,000).	R-7
C2	$1	___18__: 1859-61 ABN. Photographic cft. of G2 series.	R-7
G4	$1	___18__:___ ABN. Capital: $25,000. No overprint.	R-7

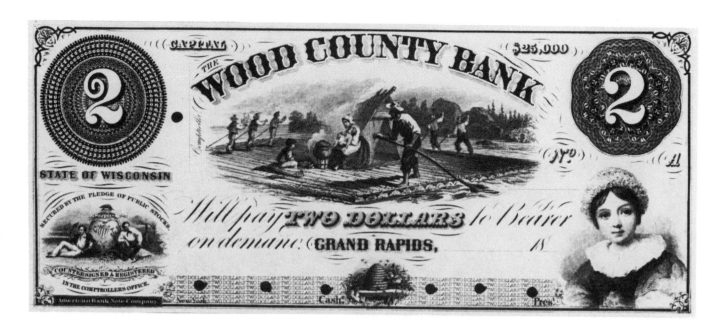

G4a	$2	___18__:___ ABN. As above, except for overprint of a red panel outlining a white TWO.	R-7
G4b	$2	___18__: 1859-61 ABN. As above, except for capital ($50,000).	R-7
R5	$10	___18__: 1859-61 ABN. Raised from $1, G2 series. The bank issued no $10s.	R-7

Uncut Sheet

| X1 | $1, 2 ABN. G2, 4 | R-7 |
| X2 | $1, 2 ABN. G2a, 4a | R-7 |

785   BANK OF NORTH AMERICA, 1859-61

Capital $100,000. T. M. Turley, Pres., H. M. Hunter, cashier.
Moved to Grand Rapids from Superior City but never issued notes from Grand Rapids.
Reportedly hailed from Grand Rapids, but whose president and cashier lived in Cook County, Illinois.
Closed 1861. Redeemed notes at 95.5¢ per dollar. Outstanding circulation 1863 $1,285.

GREEN BAY

WI-230   CITY BANK OF GREEN BAY, 1863-65

George A. Lawton, Pres., Conrad Kruger, cashier.
Became the City National Bank of Green Bay #1009. Chartered April 1865, liquidated November 1873, became The Kellog National Bank of Green Bay #2132.

G2a $1   February 2, 1863 NBN. Tint: Green frame, panel, etc.   R-7

G4a $5   February 2, 1863 NBN. Tint: Green frame, panel, etc.   R-7

Uncut Sheet

1X $1, 5 NBN. G2a, 4a   R-7

W-232   **BRANCH OF THE FARMERS JOINT STOCK BANKING COMPANY**

Upper Canada.
Office in Green Bay.

G2 $1   February 1, 1849.   R-7

G4 $2   February 1, 1849   R-7

G6 $5   February 1, 1894.   R-7

WI-235   FOX RIVER BANK, 1854-59

Capital $25,000. J. G. Lawton, Pres., F. Desnoyers, cashier.
Closed prior to 1860. Notes redeemed at 100¢ per dollar.

Genuine Notes, Raised Notes and Counterfeits

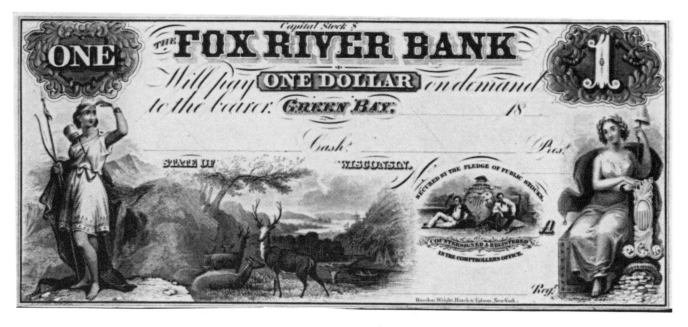

| G2 | $1 | ___18__: (1850s) RWH&E. "Capital Stock $___" at the top. | R-7 |
| G2b | $1 | ___18__: 1850s RWH&E. As above, except has "Capital $25,000 with authority to increase to $500,000" at the top. | R-6 |

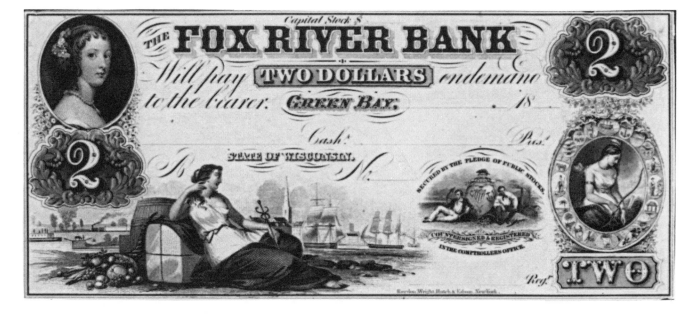

| G4 | $2 | ___18__: (1850s) RWH&E. "Capital Stock $___" at the top. | R-7 |
| G4b | $2 | ___18__: 1850s RWH&E. As above, except has "Capital $25,000 with authority to increase to $500,000" at the top. | R-6 |

| R2 | $3 | ___18__: (1850s) RWH&E. Raised from $1, G2. The bank issued no $3s. | R-7 |

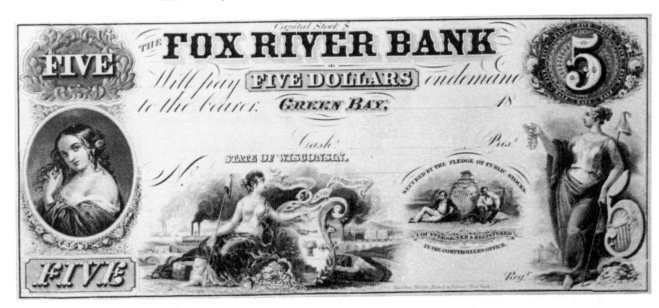

| G6 | $5 | ___18__: (1850s) RWH&E. "Capital Stock ___" at the top. | R-7 |

| G6b | $5 | ___18__: 1850s RWH&E. As above, except has "Capital $25,000 with authority to increase to $500,000" at the top. | R-6 |

| R4 | $5 | ___18__: 1850s RWH&E. Raised from $1, G2. | R-7 |

| R6 | $10 | ___18__: 1850s RWH&E. Raised from $1, G2. The bank issued no $10s. | R-7 |

| R8 | $10 | ___18__: 1850s RWH&E. Raised from $2, G4. The bank issued no $10s. | R-7 |

Uncut Sheet

| X1 | | $1, 1, 2, 5 RWH&E. G2, 2, 4, 6 | R-7 |

WI-240   BANK OF GREEN BAY, 1859-65

Capital $50,000. George Bowman, Pres., Henry Strong, cashier (1859). Strong assumed presidency in 1863 and M. D. Peak became cashier.

Became the First National Bank of Green Bay #874 in March 1865. Liquidated October 9, 1877 and became Strong's Bank.

Genuine Notes, Raised Notes and Counterfeits

G2	$1	___18__: (1859) ABN. Capital: $50,000. No overprint.		R-7
G2a	$1	___18__: 1859-60s ABN. As above, except for red ornate 1 overprint.		R-6
G2b	$1	September 1, 18_: 1860s ABN. Same as G2, except for date, capital ($75,000) and overprint of a large ornate green 1 and panel outlining a white ONE.		R-7
G2c	$1	September 1, 1862 ABN. Same as G2b, except for date & capital ($50,000).	Remainder	R-6

G4	$2	___18__: 1859 ABN. Capital: $50,000. No overprint.	R-6
G4a	$2	___18__: 1859-60s ABN. As above, except for red ornate TWO overprint.	R-6
G4b	$2	September 1, 18_: 1860s ABN. Same as G4, except for date, capital ($75,000) and overprint of a large ornate 2 and a green panel outlining a white TWO.	R-6
G4c	$2	September 1, 1862 ABN. Same as G4b, except for date and capital ($50,000).	R-6
R2	$3	___18__: 1859-60s ABN. Raised from $1, G2 series. The bank issued no $3s.	R-7
R3	$5	___18__: 1859-60s ABN. Raised from $1, G2 series. The bank issued no $5s.	R-7
R4	$10	___18__: 1859-60s ABN. Raised from $1, G2 series. The bank issued no $10s.	R-7

Uncut Sheets

| X1 | $1, 2 ABN. G2, 4 | R-7 |
| X2 | $1, 2 ABN. G2c, 4c | R-7 |

WI-246   GREEN BAY MINING CO. OF NEGAUNEE

While these notes appear as being issued at Green Bay, Wisconsin, they probably were issued at Negaunee, Michigan, site of the mine. They are very popular with Michigan collectors.

SC 7 $1   ___18__: ML&E. Brown/black front green reverse.   R-6

Reverse of all denominations.

SC 8 $2   ___18__: ML&E Brown/black front green reverse.   R-6

SC 9 $3   ___18__: ML&E Brown/black front green reverse.   R-6

SC 10 $5   ___18__: ML&E Brown/black front green reverse.   R-6

WI-260   **NORTHERN BANK**

Capital $50,000.
Established at Howard in 1854, moved across the river to Green Bay in 1862, closed in 1865.

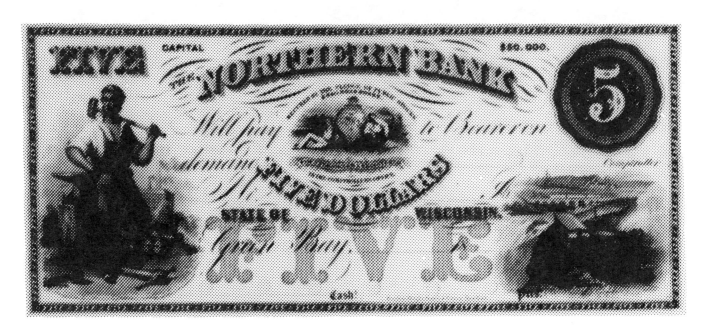

G18a $5   ___18__: (1860s) RWH&E. Same as G8, except for city   R-7
                       and red ornate FIVE overprint.

G20a $10   ___18__: (1860s) RWH&E. Same as G10, except for city   R-7
                       and red ornate TEN TEN overprint.

WI-245   BANK OF WISCONSIN, 1836-39

Territorial bank. Chartered in 1835 by Michigan Territory; Wisconsin Territory inherited the charter in 1836 when Wisconsin became a state. Charter repeated Mar. 11, 1839.

Failed.

G2	$1	___18__: 1830s RW&H.		Remainder	R-1
				Signed Note	R-3

G4	$2	___18__: 1830s RW&H.		Remainder	R-1
				Signed Note	R-3

G6 $3   ___18__: 1830s RW&H.   Remainder   R-1
                                                                Signed Note   R-3

G8 $5   ___18__: 1830s RW&H RC: Treaty of Prairie du Chien,   Remainder   R-1
                    1826.   Signed Note   R-3

G10 $10   ___18__: 1830s RW&H LC: Treaty of Prairie du Chien,   Remainder   R-1
                                  1825.   Signed Note   R-3

G12 $20   ___18__: 1830s RW&H RC: Treaty of Prairie du Chien,   Remainder   R-1
                                    1825.   Signed Note   R-3

| G14 | $50 | ___18__: 1830s RW&H LC: Treaty of Prairie du Chien, 1825. | R-6 |

Uncut Sheets

| X1 | $1, 1, 2, 3, RW&H. G2, 2, 4, 6 | R-1 |
| X2 | $5, 5, 5, 10 RW&H G8, 8, 8, 10 | R-3 |

**Vignette of the Treaty of
Prairie Du Chien 1825**

As the Bank Of Green Bay had been chartered by the Michigan Territory in 1835, the Wisconsin Territory inherited the Charter. Thus, this is Wisconsin's first bank. Two signitors were very familiar in territorial times, James Doty & Morgan L. Martin.

JAMES DUANE DOTY — Was born at Salem, Washington county, New York, in the year 1799. He received a common education, and then devoted himself to the study of law. In 1818, he removed to Detroit, in the territory of Michigan, where, in the following year, he was admitted to the bar. He early attracted attention, and, in 1820, accompanied Governor Cass on one of his extensive tours, and was present when the governor hauled down the British flag, displayed by the Chippewas on the American side of the straights of Mackinaw, despite their menaces. In the winter of 1821, while visiting Washington, Doty was admitted to the bar of the United States supreme court. A year later, upon the passage of the act forming Northern Michigan into a judicial district, he was selected by President Monroe to occupy the bench. This district embraced the counties of Michilimackinac, Brown, and Crawford, comprising more than one-half of the present state of Michigan, all of Wisconsin, and that part of Minnesota east of the Mississippi. Courts were to be organized at the Sault Ste. Mary, Green Bay, and Prairie du Chien. In the fall of 1823, Judge Doty, with his wife - he had recently married a daughter of General Collins, of Oneida county, New York - removed to Prairie du Chien for the purpose of entering upon his duties; but, the following spring, established his home in Green Bay. During this year, the organization of the courts was completed, and thereafter he held his terms with strict regularity until 1832, when he was succeeded by Judge Irwin. Thus relieved

of official duties, he made repeated tours over the then unsettled territory, became thoroughly acquainted with its natural resources, and contributed not a little toward obtaining the good-will of the Indian tribes toward the government. In 1831-2, he was one of the commissioners who surveyed the United States military roads from Green Bay to Chicago and Prairie du Chien. In 1834, he was elected to the territorial council of Michigan, in which he served two years with distinction. In that body he introduced the proposition for the formation of a state government and the separate territorial organization of Wisconsin, which prevailed in 1836. Meanwhile, at the Green Bay land sales of 1835-6, he was intrusted with large sums of money for investment in eligible locations, and many flourishing villages now stand on sites of his selection. He was chiefly instrumental, at the Belmont session of the Wisconsin legislature, although not a member, in securing the location of the seat of government at the Four Lakes, now Madison. In 1838, he was elected delegate in congress from Wisconsin territory serving until 1841. He became governor by appointment from President Tyler, in September, 1841, which office he held until June, 1844, being the second territorial governor of Wisconsin. He was a member of the first convention chosen to draft a state constitution in 1846. He was elected to congress from the third or Green Bay district, in 1848, and re-elected in 1850. At the close of his term in 1853, he retired to private life. His last residence in Wisconsin was at Menasha, on Doty's island of Lake Winnebago. In 1861, he was appointed superintendent of Indian affairs by President Lincoln, and subsequently governor of Utah, holding this position until his death, which occurred June 13, 1865. He was emphatically one of the most eminent pioneers of Wisconsin, and his important public services entitle him to lasting honor.

MORGAN L. MARTIN — The subject of this sketch was born at Martinsburg, Lewis county, New York, on the thirty-first of March, 1805. He was the son of Walter Martin and Sarah *nee* Turner. His birthplace was named in honor of his father, on whose land the city was built.

Morgan L. soon developed a taste for study, and at an earlier age than usual, completed the common-school course. He forthwith matriculated in Hamilton College, and, in 1824, at the age of nineteen, having graduated, he bade adieu to his Alma Mater. The law suited best the inclination of his mind, and, accordingly, he entered the office of Collins & Parish, of Lowville, New York, where he pursued legal studies for two years. At the end of this time, he removed to Detroit, Michigan, where he continued the study of law in the office of H. S. Cole, and was admitted to the bar in 1827. Thus prepared, with a thorough education, the inspiration of youth, and a fund of energy, he started for Wisconsin. On the twentieth of May, 1827, he landed at Green Bay. He soon became the legal adviser for the place. In July, 1833, he visited the mouth of Milwaukee river, and found there Solomon and Peter Juneau's cabins. In September of the same year he again visited this point, and entered into a verbal contract with Solomon for the undivided half of his claim. Subsequently, he obtained Peter's claim, and the "floating" rights of William Powell, Asa Sherman and others. By this means he and Juneau held possession of all that part of the city now east of the Milwaukee river. He, with Juneau, made out the first plat of the city, and put it on record in July, 1835. To Morgan L. Martin belongs the honor of founding the city of Milwaukee. His connections with the place were directly with reference to making it the site of a metropolis; whereas, Juneau dreamed of nothing beyond his trading post and a collection of frail cabins. Together, they realized immense sums from the sale of these lands. They expended money freely in public improvements. Out of this investment he realized a handsome fortune. In 1851, he became identified with the Fox river improvement, and gave it his attention until 1858. In this enterprise he lost much of his property, but preserved his integrity.

At the opening of the war in 1861, he entered the United States service as paymaster. He remained in that position until 1865, when he resigned and returned to his home at Green Bay, where he resumed his legal practice.

Aside from the regular duties of his profession, Mr. Martin has occupied many places of trust and confidence. In 1831 he was chosen to the territorial legislature of Michigan, and served in that body until Michigan became a state. After the organization of Wisconsin territory, he served in her assembly from 1838 to 1844, when he resigned. In the following year he was elected to congress, and remained there during one term. He was president of the constitutional convention of Wisconsin, in 1848. He was a member of the state legislature during the sessions of 1855, 1858, 1859 and 1874. After the latter date, he positively withdrew from politics. In 1875 he was chosen county judge for Brown county, in which capacity he still remains. He has grown up side by side with the state from her infancy, intimately connected with her prosperity, and a strong contestant for her political honor. Morgan L. Martin was married July 25, 1837, to Miss Elizabeth Smith, daughter of Colonel Melancthon, of Pittsburgh, New York, and sister of Rear-Admiral Smith, of the United States navy. He has a family of two sons and two daughters.

Biographies from *Historical Atlas of Wisconsin*, 1878.

GREEN LAKE

WI-246   MECHANICS BANK, 1859-61

Capital $25,000. E. B. Smith, Pres., E. T. Martin, cashier. Failed 1861. Notes redeemed at 62-1/4¢ per dollar in 1862. Circulation outstanding 1863 $370. The bank was established solely for the purpose of issuing notes.

IMPORTANT NOTE! No note of this bank has ever been reported!

HANCHETTVILLE

WI-248   HANCHETTVILLE BANK

Renamed Marshall.

SC 6   50¢   DWP. Black/red.   R-7

HILLSDALE

WI-250   **KOKOMO BANK, 1857-59**

Renamed Mooney's Mills in 1884 Barron County.

Later location: Whitewater (moved in 1858). Failed.

1-NOTES DATED AT HILLSDALE

G4a $5   May 25, 1857 DW. Tint: Red-brown lathework overall   R-7
                   with script FIVE FIVE, both across.

G6a $10   May 25, 1857 DW. Tint: Red-brown lathework overall   R-7
                   with script TEN TEN, both across.

As only Proof notes are known, it is possible none were ever placed in circulation.

HORICON

WI-255   BANK OF HORICON, 1859-61

Capital $25,000. Outstanding circulation 1863 $852. Redeemed at 60¢.
Failed.

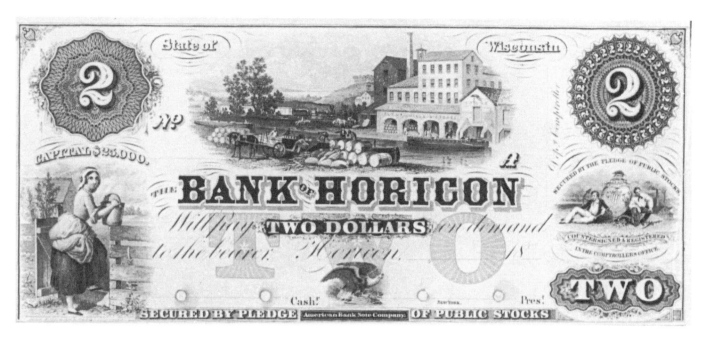

| G2a | $2 | ___18__: 1859 ABN. Capital: $25,000. Overprint: Red TWO. | R-7 |
| G2b | $2 | ___18__: 1859-61 ABN. As above, except for capital ($50,000). | R-7 |

| G4a | $3 | ___18__; (1859) ABN. Capital: $25,000. Overprint: Red THREE. | R-7 |
| G4b | $3 | ___18__: 1859-61 ABN. As above, except for capital ($50,000). | R-7 |

Uncut Sheet

| X1 | | $2, 3 ABN. G2a, 4a | R-7 |

WI-226   HORICON MILLS

SC 5   25¢   Undated (70's). Black/red I.L. L. Lipman, Milwaukee.   R-7

HOWARD

WI-260   NORTHERN BANK, 1855-62

Capital $50,000. U. H. Peak, Pres., Robt. Chappell, cashier (1862).
Later location: Green Bay (moved in 1862). Closed.

Genuine Notes, Raised Notes and Counterfeits

| G2 | $1 | ___18__: (1850s) RWH&E. No overprint. | R-7 |
| G2a | $1 | ___18__ (1850s) RWH&E. As above, except for red overprint. | R-7 |

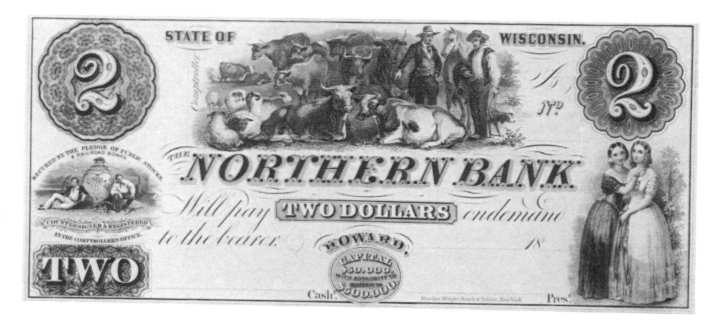

| G4 | $2 | ___18__: (1850s) RWH&E. No overprint. | R-7 |
| G4a | $2 | ___18__: (1850s) RWH&E. As above, except for red overprint. | R-7 |

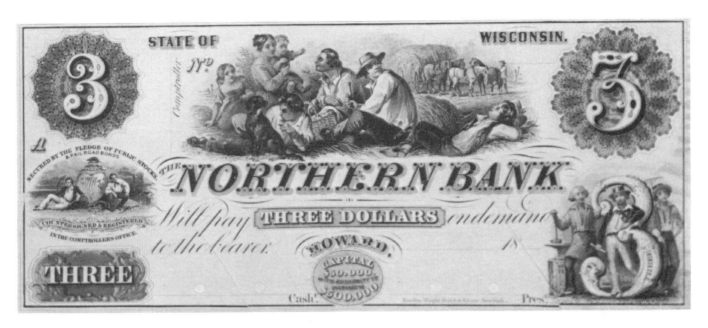

| G6 | $3 | ___18__: (1850s) RWH&E. No overprint. | R-7 |
| G6a | $3 | ___18__: (1850s) RWH&E. As above, except for red over-print. | R-7 |

G8	$5	___18__: 1850s RWH&E. No overprint.	R-7
G8a	$5	___18__: 1850s RWH&E. As above, except for red over-print.	R-6
R5	$5	___18__: 1850s RWH&E. Raised from $1, G2.	R-7
G10	$10	___18__: 1850s RWH&E. Similar to G20a.	R-7
R6	$10	___18__: 1850s RWH&E. Raised from $1, G2.	R-7
R7	$20	___18__: 1850s RWH&E. Raised from $1, G2. The bank issued no $20s.	R-7

Uncut Sheet

| X1 | | $1, 1, 2, 3 RWH&E. G2, 2, 4, 6 | R-7 |

HUDSON

WI-273 **CITY OF HUDSON, ___18__**

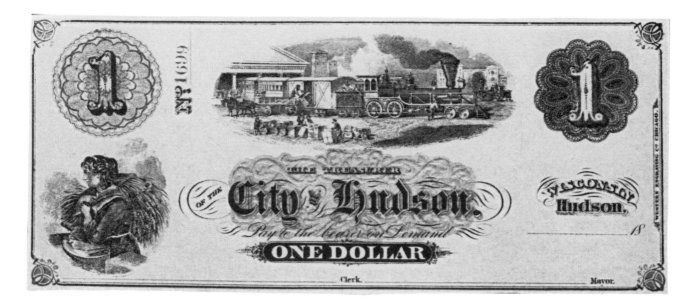

SC 7 $1   Green/Black. Red serial numbers. WE.   R-3

SC 8 $2   Green/Black. Red serial numbers. WE.   R-3

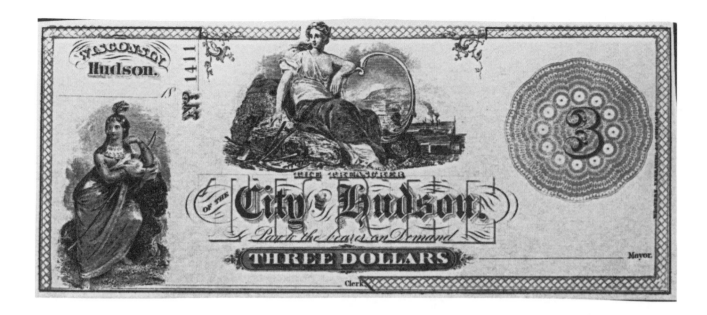

SC 9 $3   Green/Black. Red serial numbers. WE.   R-3

SC 10 $5   Green/Black. Red serial numbers. WE.   R-5

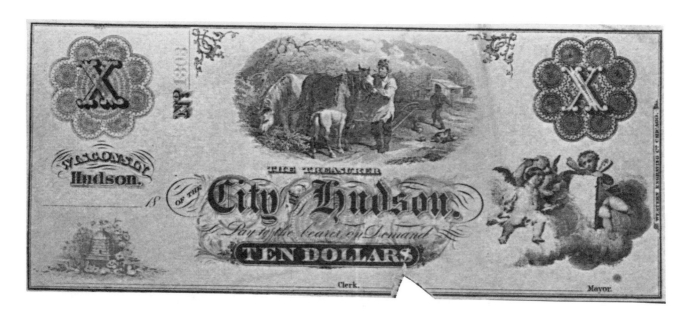

SC 11 $10   Green/Black. Red serial numbers.   R-7

WI-265   **FARMERS BANK AT HUDSON, 1857-58**

Capital $50,000. Otis Hoyt, Pres., C. E. Derter, cashier.
Closed. $471 of specie held in 1860 for redemption of notes totaling $471. Time of redemption May 6, 1862.

Genuine Notes, Raised Notes and Counterfeits

G2a $1   ___18__: 1857-58 DW. Tint: Red-brown frame, lathework   R-7
                     overall and microlettering outlining a white ONE.

G4a $2   ___18__: (1857-58) DW. Tint: Red-brown frame,   R-7
                     lathework overall and microlettering outlining a
                     white TWO.

| G6a | $3 | ___18__: (1857-58) DW. Tint: Red-brown end panel, lathework overall and microlettering. | R-7 |

| G8a | $5 | ___18__: (1857-58) DW. Tint: Red-brown end panel, lathework overall and microlettering. | R-7 |
| R5 | $10 | ___18__: 1857-58 DW. Raised from $1, G2a. The bank issued no $10s. | R-7 |

Uncut Sheet

| X1 | | $1, 2, 3, 5 DW. G2a, 4a, 6a, 8a | R-7 |

Altered, Spurious and Unattributed Non-Genuine Notes

| A5 | $5 | August 6, 1855 None (TC). Upper C: Franklin. Overprint: Red ornate VV. Altered from $5 Farmers Bank, Wickford. RI-565-G8a. I. | R-7 |
| A10 | $10 | ___18__: 1855 None (TC). C: man in white shirt stdg. over boy gathering corn, horse-drawn wagon in bkgd. L: 10/allegorical woman stdg. & Justice std., flanking shield bearing anchor. R: 10/portrait of girl with ringlets. Overprint: Red ornate X X. Altered from $10 Farmers Bank, Wickford, RI-565-G10a. | R-7 |

WI-270   HUDSON CITY BANK, 1856-62

Capital $25,000. M. S. Gibson, Pres., J. O. Henning, cashier (1856).
Closed 1862.

Genuine Notes, Raised Notes and Counterfeits

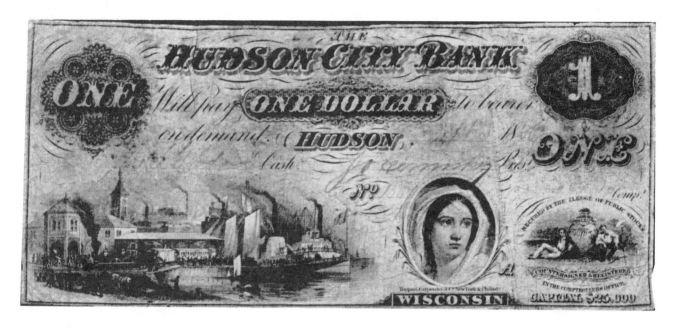

G2 $1   ___18__: 1850s TC.   R-6

G4 $2   ___18__: 1850s TC.

G6 $5   __18__: (1850s) TC.   R-7

C6	$5	__18__: 1846 (!) TC. Photographic cft. of the above.	R-6
R4	$3	__18__: 1850s TC. Raised from $1, G2. The bank issued no $3s.	R-7
R6	$5	__18__: 1850s TC. Raised from $1, G2.	R-7
R8	$10	__18__: 1850s TC. Raised from $1, G2. The bank issued no $10s.	R-7
R10	$10	__18__: 1850s TC. Raised from $2, G4. The bank issued no $10s.	R-7

Uncut Sheet

X1 $1, 1, 2, 5 TC. G2, 2, 4, 6   R-7

WI-272   **ALFRED GROSS, BANKER**

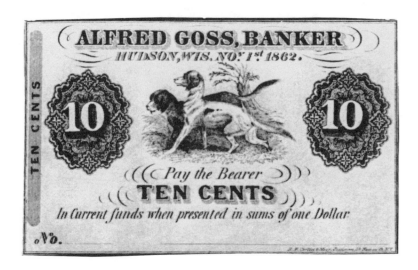

SC 2   10¢   C-F November 1st, 1862.   R-7

WI-274   **SAINT CROIX VALLEY BANK**

SC 1   5¢   September 6, 1862.   7

SC 2   10¢   September 6, 1862.   7

Also see Saint Croix Valley Bank, St. Croix, WI-715.

HUSTISFORD

WI-220   **BANK OF MONEKA**

Established 1858 in Gordon, moved to Viroqua in 1858 and then Hustisford in 1862 and later that year moved to Portage.

G10a	$5	Unknown (ABN). Same as Gordon G2a, except for location & probably date & imprint.	R-7
G12a	$10	Unknown (ABN). Same as Gordon G4a, except for location & probably date & imprint.	R-7

JANESVILLE

WI-275   BADGER STATE BANK, 1853-58

Capital $25,000. Wm. J. Bell, Pres., E L. Dimock, cashier.
Closed $630 specie held for 100% redemption until April 26, 1862.

Genuine Notes, Raised Notes and Counterfeits

| G2 | $1 | ___18__: ____ TCC. Capital: $25,000. No overprint. | R-7 |
| G2b | $1 | ___18__: ____ TCC. Same as above, except for capital ($50,000) and a red 1 1 overprint. | R-7 |

| G4 | $2 | ___18__: ____ TCC. Capital: $25,000. No overprint. | R-7 |
| G4b | $2 | ___18__: ____ TCC. Same as above, except for capital ($50,000) and a red TWO overprint. | R-7 |

| G6 | $3 | ___18__: ____ TCC. Capital: $25,000. No overprint. | R-7 |
| G6b | $3 | ___18__: (1850s) TCC. Same as above, except for capital ($50,000) and a red 3 3 overprint. | R-7 |

G8	$5	___18__: ____ TCC. Capital: $25,000. No overprint.	R-7
G8b	$5	___18__: (1850s) TCC. Same as above, except for capital ($50,000) and a red FIVE overprint.	R-7
R5	$20	___18__: (1850s) TCC. Raised from $1, G2 series.	R-7

Uncut Sheet

| X1 | $1, 2, 3, 5 TCC. G2, 4, 6, 8 | R-7 |
| X2 | $1, 2, 3, 5 TCC. G2b, 4b, 6b, 8b | R-7 |

WI-280   CENTRAL BANK OF WISCONSIN, 1855-63

Organized 1852, opened 1855. Capital $25,000. J. B. Doe & Co., Proprietors, Wm. Norton, Pres., W. A. Lawrence, cashier (1855). In 1863, capital increased to $125,000. E. R. Doe became president & J. B. Doe asst. cashier.

Became the First National Bank of Janesville. Charter #83, in September 1863. In 1882 was rechartered as #2748.

Genuine Notes, Raised Notes and Counterfeits

G2	$1	___18__: ____ TCC. Capital: $100,000. No overprint.	R-6
G2b	$1	___18__: 1850s TCC. As above, except for capital ($25,000) and red ornate overprint.	R-6
G2c	$1	___18__: 1858-60 TCC, ABNCo. mono. Same as G2b, except for imprint, capital ($100,000) and overprint style (block letters).	R-6
G2d	$1	July 1, 18__: 1860s ABN. Same as G2c, except for imprint & capital ($125,000).	R-7

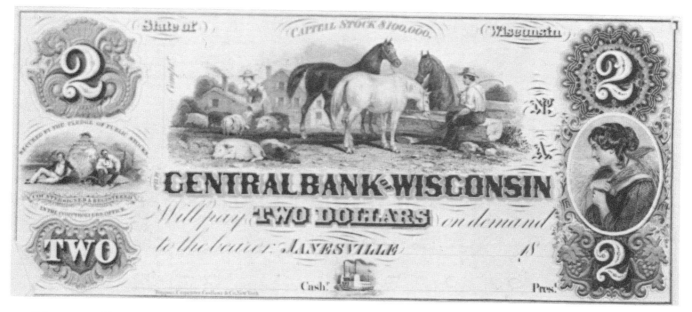

| G4 | $2 | ___18__: ____ TCC. Capital: $100,000. No overprint. | R-7 |
| G4b | $2 | ___18__: 1850s TCC. As above, except for capital ($25,000) and red ornate TWO overprint. | R-7 |

| G4c | $2 | ___18__: 1858-60 TCC, ABNCo. mono. Same as G4b, except for imprint, capital ($100,000) and overprint style (block letters). | R-7 |
| G4d | $2 | July 1, 18__: 1860s ABN. Same as G4c, except for imprint & capital ($125,000). | R-7 |

G6	$3	___18__: ___ TCC. R: Washington, Capital: $100,000. No overprint.	R-7
G6b	$3	___18__: 1850s TCC. As above, except for capital ($25,000) and red ornate overprint.	R-7
G6c	$3	___18__: 1858-60 TCC, ABNCo. mono. Same as G6b, except for imprint, capital ($100,000) and overprint style (block letters).	R-7
G6d	$3	July 1, 18__: 1860s ABN. Same as G6c, except for imprint & capital ($125,000).	R-6
R5	$3	___18__: 1850s (TCC). Raised from $1, G2 series.	R-7
R6	$10	___18__: 1850s (TCC). Raised from $1, G2 series. The bank issued no $10s.	R-7

Uncut Sheet

| X1 | | $1, 1, 2, 3 TCC. G2, 2, 4, 6 | R-7 |

WI-285   JANESVILLE CITY BANK, 1855-58

Capital $25,000. Henry H. Dunster, Pres., Samuel Lightbody, cashier.
Closed forfeiting to redeem its notes. Trust funds deposited with the state were sold to redeem notes at 100% until 1861.

Genuine Notes, Raised Notes and Counterfeits

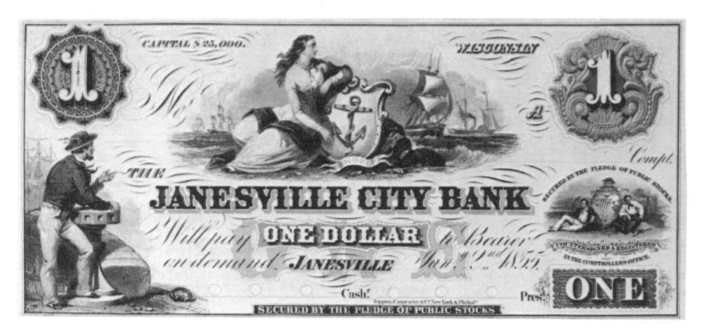

G2 $1   January 2, 1855 TC.   R-7

G4 $2   January 2, 1855 TC.   R-7

| G6 | $5 | January 2, 1865 TC. | R-6 |
| R5 | $10 | January 2, 1855 TC. Raised from $1, G2. The bank issued no $10s. | R-7 |

Uncut Sheet

| X1 | | $1, 2, 5, 5 TC. G2, 4, 6, 6 | R-7 |

WI-290   **PRODUCERS BANK, 1857-58**

Capital $100,000. William A. Barstow, Pres.
Closed 1859. Notes redeemed until 1862.

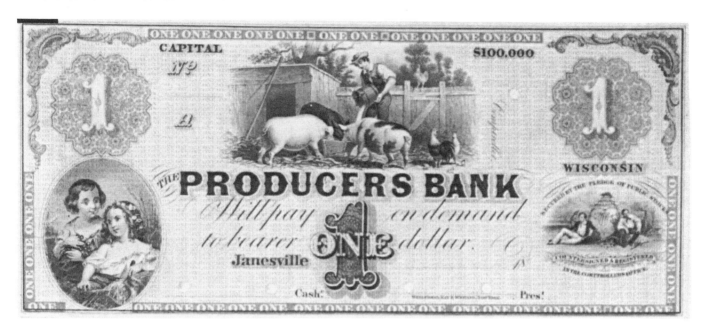

G2a $1   ___18__ (1857-58) WH&W. Tint: Orange lathework over-
            all & counters.   R-7

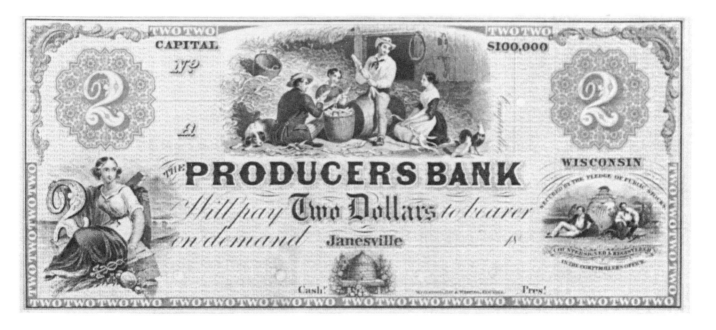

G4a $2   ___18__: 1857-58 WH&W. Tint: Orange lathework overall
            & counters.   R-6

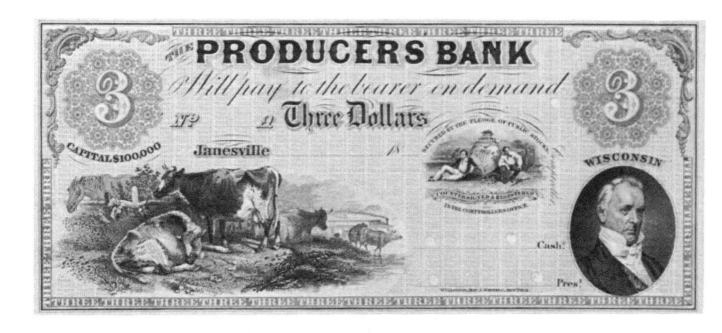

G6a $3   ___18__: (1857-58) WH&W. R: Buchanan. Tint: Orange   R-7
                     lathework overall & counters.

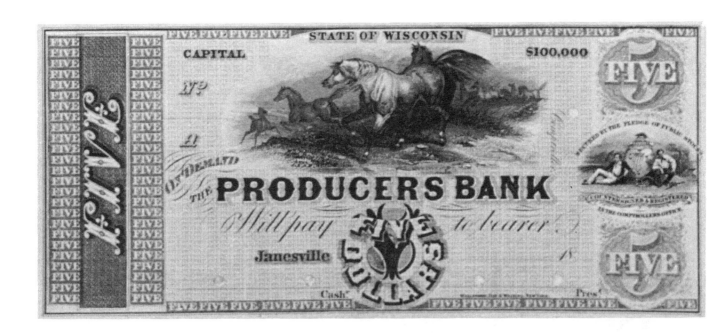

G8a $5   ___18__: 1857-58 WH&W. Tint: Orange lathework overall   R-7
                     & counter.

Uncut Sheet

1X $1, 2, 3, 5 WH&W. G2a, 4a, 6a, 8a   R-7

WI-295   ROCK COUNTY BANK, 1856-65

Capital $50,000. Timothy Jickman, Pres., James B. Crosby, cashier (1863).
Notes redeemed at par to become the Rock County National Bank, Charter #749 in 1865.

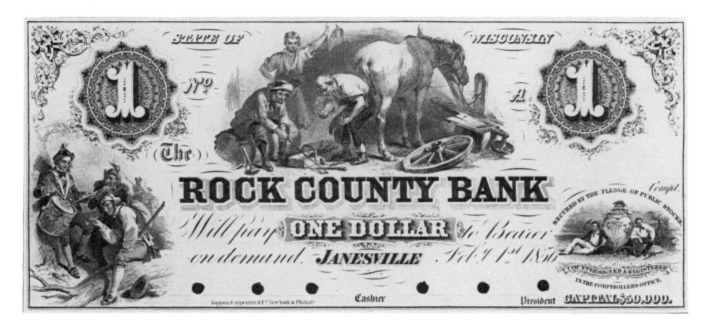

G2	$1	February 1, 1856 TC. No overprint.	R-7
G2a	$1	February 1, 1856 TC. As above except for overprint (probably red ONE.)	R-7

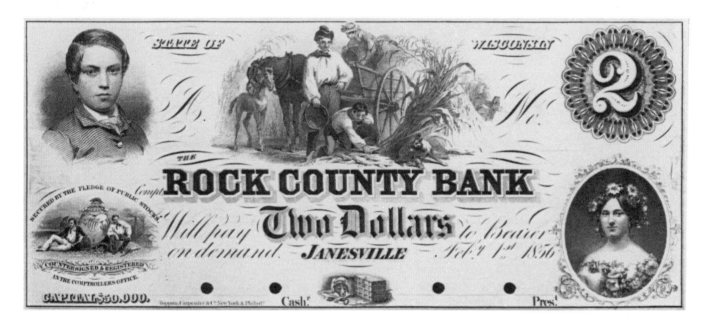

G4	$2	February 1, 1856 TC. No overprint.	R-7
G4a	$2	February 1, 1856 TC. As above, except for red TWO.	R-6

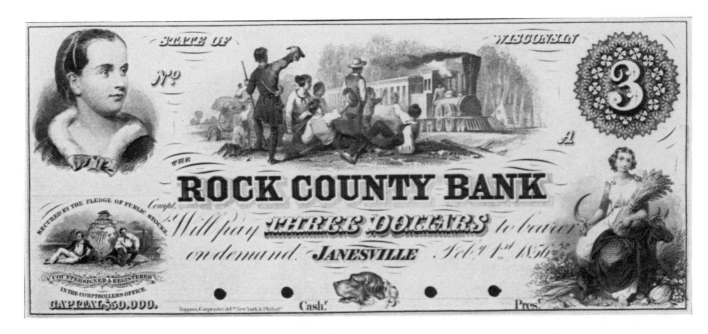

| G6 | $3 | February 1, 1856 TC. No overprint. | R-7 |
| G6a | $3 | February 1, 1856 TC. As above, except for overprint (probably red THREE). | R-7 |

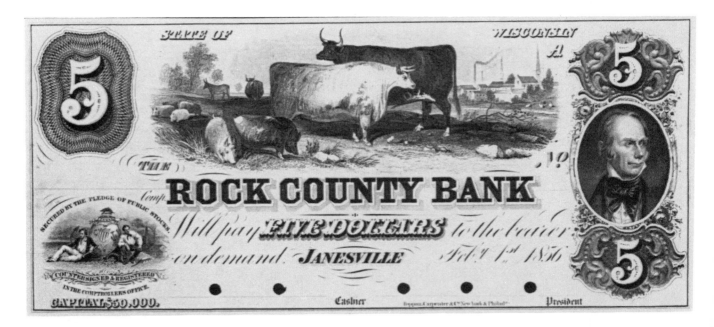

| G8 | $5 | February 1, 1856 TC. R: Clay. No overprint. | R-7 |
| G8a | $5 | February 1, 1856 TC. As above, except for overprint (probably red FIVE.) | R-7 |

Uncut Sheets

| X1 | | $1, 2, 3, 5 TC. G2, 4, 6, 8 | R-7 |

WI-297   F. M. CROSBY AT ROCK COUNTY BANK

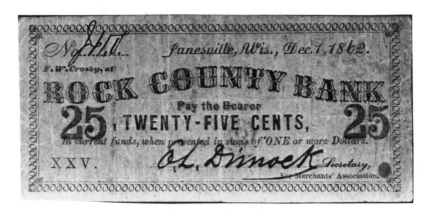

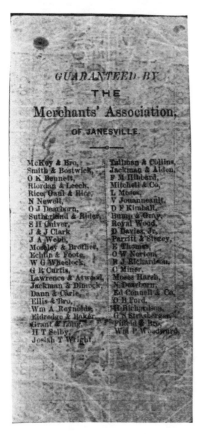

SC 5   25¢   December 7, 1862 for Merchants Association. Green/Red.   R-7

JEFFERSON

WI-300   **BANK OF JEFFERSON, 1855-65**

Capital $50,000. William M. Dennis, Pres., E. McMahon, cashier (1860).
Became the National Bank of Jefferson. Charter #1076, April 28, 1865. Dissolved in August, 1875 to become a state bank, the Jefferson County Bank.

Genuine Notes, Raised Notes and Counterfeits

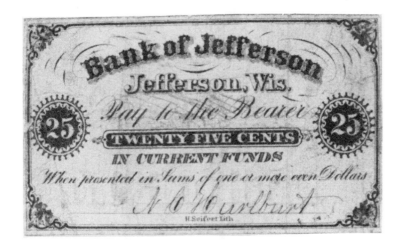

SC 5   25¢   R-7

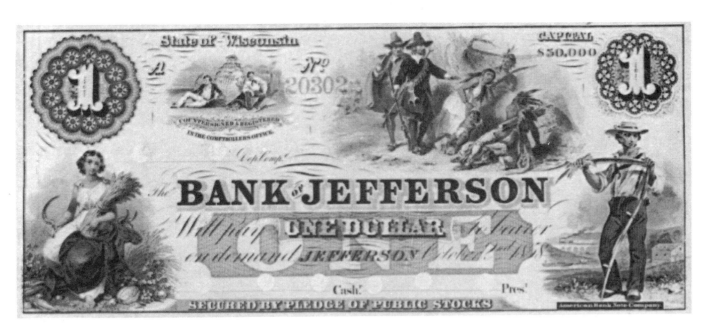

G2a	$1	October 2, 1858 TCC, ABN. Overprint: Red panel outlining a white ONE. Capital: $25,000.		R-6
G2b	$1	October 2, 1858 ABN. As above, except for imprint & capital ($50,000).	Remainder	R-6

G4a	$2	October 2, 1858 TCC, ABN. RC: Jefferson. L: Landing of Roger Williams. Same as G4b, except for imprint and capital ($25,000). Overprint: Red panel outlining a white TWO.		R-7
G4b	$2	October 2, 1858 ABN. As above, except for imprint & capital ($50,000).	Remainder	R-6
R2	$3	October 2, 1855 TCC, ABN. Raised from $1, G2a or 2b. The bank issued no $3s.		R-7
R4	$5	October 2, 1855 TCC, ABN. Raised from $1 G2a or 2b. The bank issued no $5s.		R-7
R6	$10	October 2, 1858 TCC, ABN. Raised from $1, G2a or 2b. The bank issued no $10s.		R-7

Uncut Sheet

| X1 | | $1, 2 ABN. G2b, 4b | | R-7 |

JORDAN

Jordon was located between Stevens Point and Rosholt where the Plover River crosses Highway 66. It was a platted village complete with a dam. A county park marks its location today.

WI-305   PORTAGE COUNTY BANK, 1859-61

Capital $50,000. J. W. Storey, Pres., S. C. Fisher, cashier (1859).
Failed, redeemed notes at 70-3/4¢ per dollar. Outstanding circulation 1863 was $729.

| G2 | $2 | May 20, 1859 ABN. C: Dr. Kane's Arctic Expedition.
No overprint. | R-7 |
| G2a | $2 | May 20, 1859 ABN. As above, except for overprint of a
red panel outlining a white TWO. | R-6 |

| G4 | $3 | May 20, 1859 ABN. No overprint. | R-7 |
| G4a | $3 | May 20, 1859 ABN. As above, except for overprint of a red panel outlining a white THREE. | R-7 |

Uncut Sheet

| X1 | | $2, 3 ABN. G2, 4 | R-7 |

Altered, Spurious and Unattributed Non-Genuine Notes

| N5 | $5 | (1850s) Unknown. C: man at mill carrying bag on shoulder, horse & colt. Possibly altered & raised from $1, Bank of Portage, WI-655-G2 series. | R-7 |

JUNEAU

WI-307   **GOOD TO THE BEARER, JULY ___186__**

SC 1   5¢   Good To Bearer. Black/Green MB.   R-6

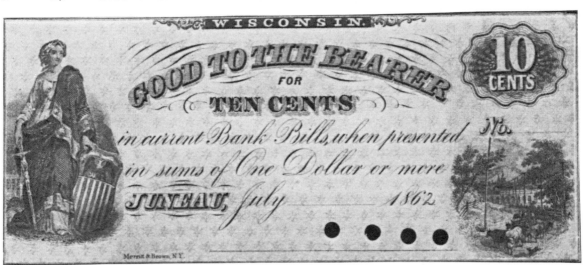

SC 2   10¢   Good To Bearer. Black/Green MB.   R-6

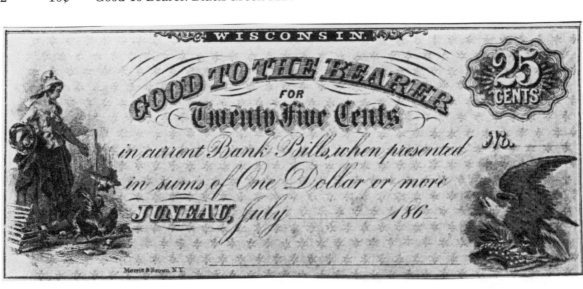

SC 5   25¢   Good To Bearer. Black/Green MB.   R-6

WI-310   CITY BANK OF KANOSHA, (1853)

Apparently the proofs listed below were intended to be for the City Bank of Kenosha, Kenosha, WI-311, and had the city and bank names misspelled in error.

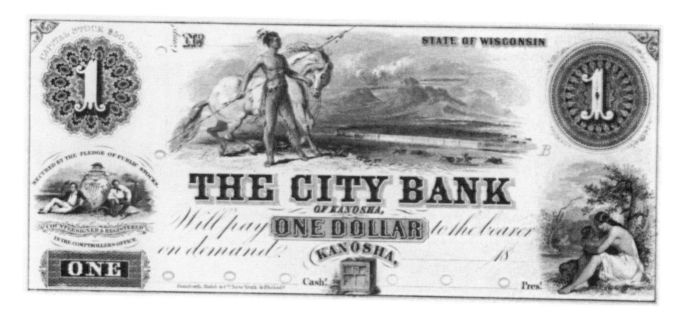

G2 $1   ___18__: ___ DB.

R-7

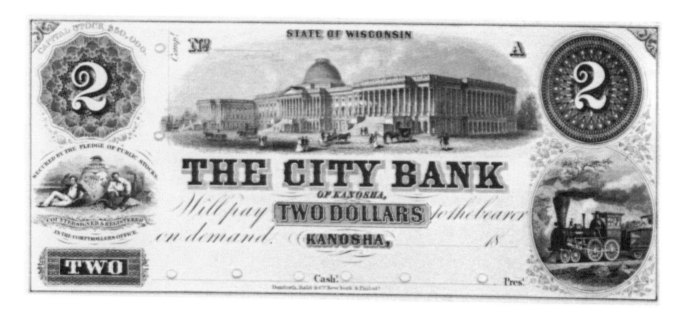

G4 $2   ___18__: ___ DB. C: U.S. Capitol.

R-7

G6 $3   ___18__: ____ DB.   R-7

Uncut Sheet

X1 $1, 1, 2, 3 DB. G2, 2, 4, 6   R-7

WI-311   CITY BANK OF KENOSHA, 1853-64

Capital $30,000.
Became the First National Bank of Kenosha. Charter #212 in 1864. Also see City Bank of Kanosha, Kanosha, WI-310.

Genuine Notes, Raised Notes and Counterfeits

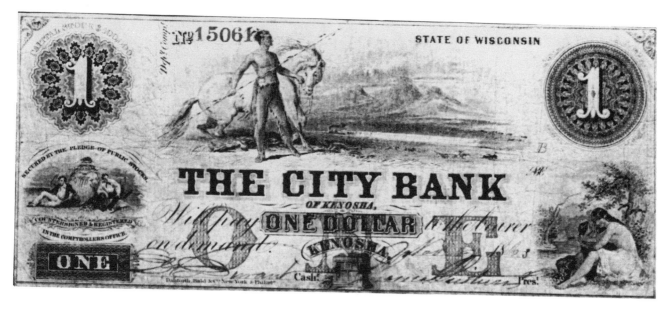

G2	$1	___18__: 1850s DB.	R-7
G2a	$1	___18__: 1850s DB. As above, except for capital (10,000). No overprint.	R-7
G2b	$1	___18__: late: 1850s-60s DB, ABNCo. mono. Same as G2a, except for the imprint, green ONE overprint and a printed serial number.	R-6

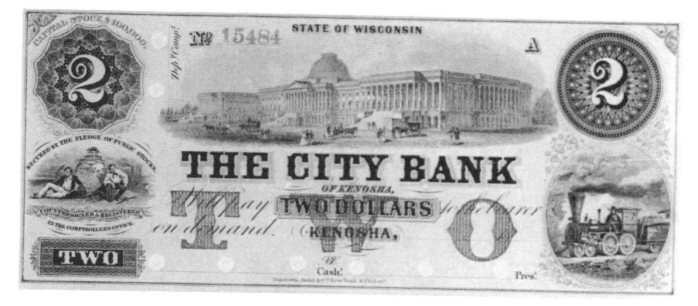

G4	$2	___18__: 1850s DB.	R-7
G4a	$2	___18__: 1850s DB. As above, except for capital ($100,000). No overprint.	R-7

G4b	$2	___18__: (late 1850s-60s) DB, ABNCo. mono. Same as G4a, except for imprint, green ONE overprint and a printed serial number.	Remainder (PC)	R-6
G4a				
R2	$2	___18__: 1850s DB. Raised from $1, G2.		R-7

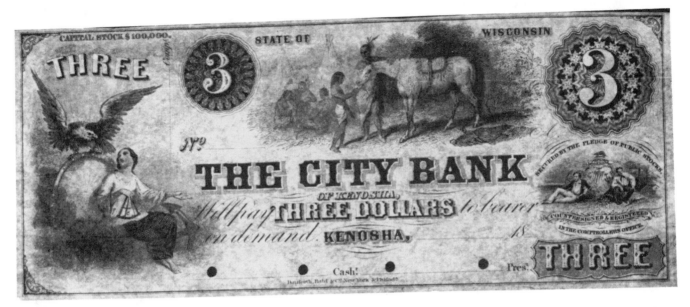

G6	$3	___18__: 1850s DB. Same as G6a, except for capital ($50,000).		R-7
G6a	$3	___18__: (1850s) DB. As above, except for capital ($100,000). Handwritten serial number, no overprint.	Remainder	R-6
G6b	$3	___18__: (late 1850s-60s) DB, ABNCo. mono. Same as G6a, except for the imprint, green THREE overprint and a printed serial number.	Remainder (PC)	R-6

R3	$3	___18__: 1850s-60s DB. Raised from $1, G2 series.	R-6
R4	$5	___18__: 1850s DB. Raised from $1, G2 series. The bank issued no $5s.	R-7
R5	$5	___18__: 1850s DB. Raised from $2, G4 series. The bank issued no $5s.	R-7

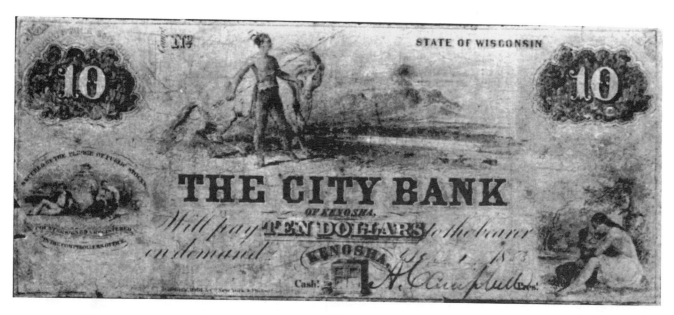

R7	$10	___18__: 1850s-60s DB. Raised from $1, G2 series. The bank issued no $5s.	R-6
R9	$10	___18__: 1850s DB. Raised from $2, G4 series. The bank issued no $10s.	R-7
R12	$20	___18__: 1850s DB. Raised from $1 or $2, G2 series or G4 series. The bank issued no $20s.	R-7

Uncut Sheets

| X1 | | $1, 1, 2, 3 DB, ABNCo. mono. G2b, 2b, 4b, 6b | R-7 |

WI-315 **KENOSHA COUNTY BANK, 1855-62**

Capital $25,000. J. C. Colman, Pres., J. H. Kimball, cashier (1855); E. G. Rucles, Pres. H. W. Habbard, cashier (1863).
Closed 1862.

Genuine Notes, Raised Notes and Counterfeits

G2a	$1	March 1, 1855 WHH&W. Capital: $25,000. Overprint: Red script ONE.	R-7
G2b	$1	March 1, 1855 WHH&W. As above, except for capital ($35,000).	R-7
G2c	$1	March 1, 1855 WHH&W & ABNCo. mono. As above, except imprint and capital ($50,000).	R-6

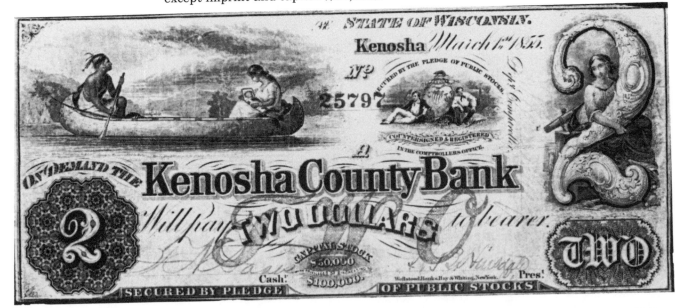

G4a	$2	March 1, 1855 WHH&W. Capital: $25,000. Overprint: Red script TWO.	R-7
G4b	$2	March 1, 1855 WHH&W. As above, except for capital ($35,000).	R-7
G4c	$2	March 1, 1855 WHH&W & ABNCo. mono. As above, except for imprint and capital ($50,000).	R-6

Uncut Sheet

X1	$1, 2 WHH&W. G2a, 4a	R-7

WI-317   SAVINGS AND EXCHANGE BANK

A private branch bank of R. Wells, Grand Rapids, Michigan, issued spurious notes in form of scrip. He disappeared with all the funds and was never heard from again.

G2	$1		R-5
G2a		Same as above, but with red ONE.	R-5

G4	$2	October 1st, 1858.	R-7
G4a		As above, but with red TWO.	R-7

| G6 | $3 | October 1st, 1858. | R-5 |
| G6a | $3 | As above but with red THREE. | R-5 |

KNAPP

WI-318   **HALL, DANN & CO.**

| 1 | 5¢ | Due Bearer, January 10, 1881 | R-7 |

Knapp is a village located 8 miles west of Menomonie, the home of Knapp, Stout & Co., the early loggers in the area.

LA CROSSE

WI-TN5   **AGRICULTURAL BANK (Tenn)**

G10 $5   ___185_: 1850's WH H&W. Surcharged La Crosse. See   R-5
Racine for similar notes.

WI-320   BATAVIAN BANK, 1862-ca. 65

Capital $40,000. Gysbert Van Stienwyck, Pres., J. P. D. Vaswinkel, cashier (1862). L. R. Mitchell became cashier in 1868.
Became the Batavian National Bank. Charter #7347 in July 1904.

| G2 | $1 | November 20, 1861 ABN. No overprint. | | R-7 |
| G2a | $1 | November 20, 1861 ABN. As above, except for overprint of a green panel outlining a white ONE. | Remainder | R-6 |

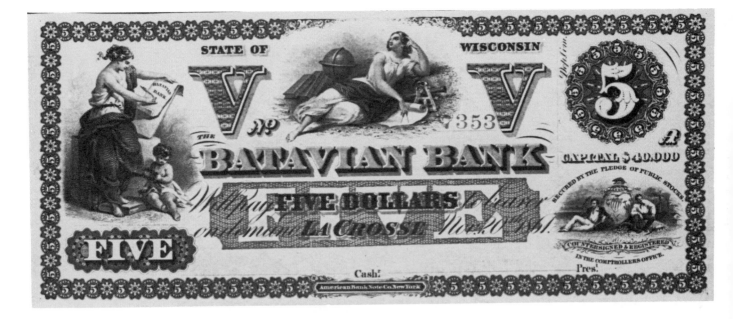

| G4 | $5 | November 20, 1861 ABN. No overprint. | | R-7 |
| G4a | $5 | November 20, 1861 ABN. As above, except for overprint of a green panel outlining a white FIVE. | Remainder | R-6 |

Uncut Sheet

| X1 | | $1, 5 ABN G2, 4 | | R-7 |

WI-325   **BANK OF THE CITY OF LA CROSSE, 1857-58**

Capital $25,000. John M. Levy, Pres., E. D. Campbell, cashier (1857). $367 held in specie for redemption of notes prior to May 6, 1862.
Closed 1858.

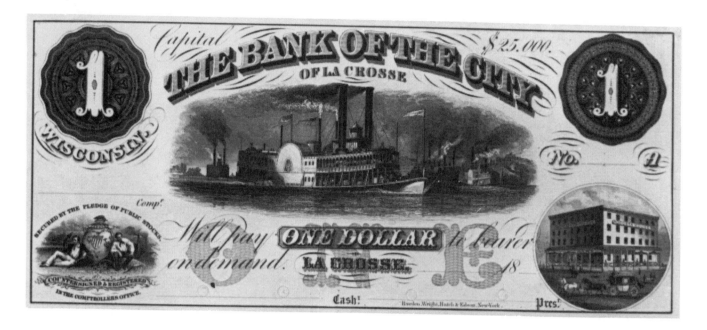

G2a $1   ___18__: (1850s) RWH&E. Overprint: Ornate red ONE.   R-7

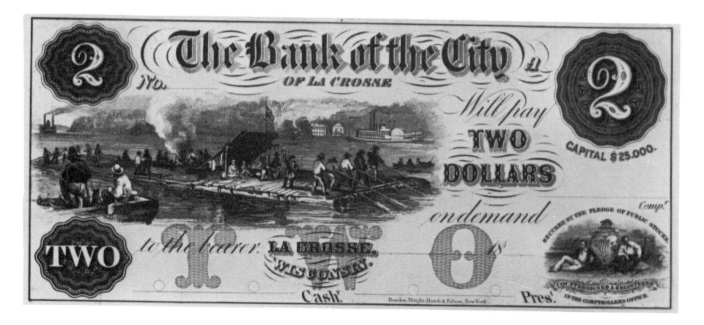

G4a $2   ___18__: (1850s) RWH&E. Overprint: Ornate red TWO.   R-7

| G6a | $3 | ___18__: (1850s) RWH&E. Overprint: Ornate red THREE. | R-7 |

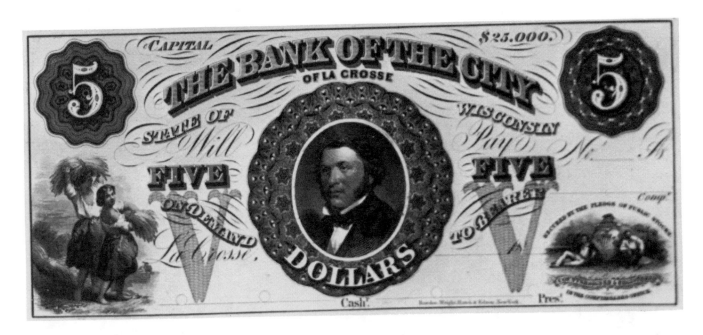

| G8a | $5 | ___18__: (1850s) RWH&E. Overprint: Red V V. | R-7 |

Uncut Sheet

| X1 | | $1, 2, 3, 5 RWH&E. G2a, 4a, 6a, 8a | R-7 |

WI-420   GREEN BAY BANK, 1860

Capital $35,000. Daniel Wells, Jr., Pres., N. Ludington, cashier (1862). Wm. H. Rogers became cashier in 1863.
Bank issued notes while in Maranett (e) 1856-58. Then moved to Oconto in 1858 and in 1860 moved to La Crosse.

NOTES ISSUED AT LA CROSSE

G8a $1   ___18__: 1860s ABN. Overpint: Red ONE.   R-6

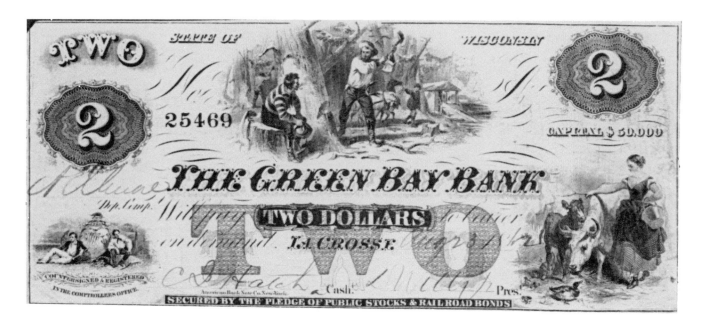

G10a $2   ___18__: 1860s ABN. Overpint: Red TWO.   R-6

G16a $20   October 15, 1862 NBN. Tint: Green ends & counters.   Remainder   R-6
                       Capital: $50,000.

WI-330   **KATANYAN BANK, 1856-61**

Capital $25,000. Wilson Colwell, Pres., George A. Beck (1856), cashier.
Failed 1861. Notes redeemed at 79¢ per dollar, $2,356 outstanding in 1863.

Genuine Notes, Raised Notes and Counterfeits

G2	$1	July 1, 185_: ___ TC. Capital: $25,000. No overprint.	R-7
G2a	$1	July 1, 185_: ___ TC. As above, except for red ornate 1 overprint.	
G2b	$1	July 1, 185_: 1857-58 TC. Same as G2, except for capital ($50,000).	R-7
G2c	$1	___18__: 1859 ABN. Same as G2a, except for capital ($50,000). Imprint & red 1 overprint is slightly larger.	R-6

G4	$2	July 1, 18__: ___ TC. Capital: $25,000. No overprint.	R-7
G4a	$2	July 1, 185_: 1856 TC. As above, except for red overprint.	R-7
G4b	$2	July 1, 185_: 1857-58 TC. Same as G4, except for capital ($50,000). No overprint.	R-7
G4c	$2	___18__: 1859 ABN. Same as G4a, except for capital ($50,000). Imprint and probably modified overprint.	R-7

G6	$5	___18__: ___ TC. Capital: $50,000. No overprint.	R-7
G6a	$5	___18__: 1857-58 TC. As above, except for red FIVE overprint.	R-6
G6b	$5	___18__: 1859 ABN. As above, except for imprint and possibly modified overprint.	R-7
R5	$10	July 1, 185_: (1856) TC. Raised from $1, G2 or another variety. The bank issued no $10s.	R-7

Uncut Sheets

X1	$1, 2, TC. G2, 4	R-7
X2	$1, 2, 5, 5 TC. G2, 4, 6, 6	R-7
X3	$1, 2, 5, 5 TC. G2b, 4b, 6b, 6b	R-7

Altered, Spurious and Unattributed Non-Genuine Notes

| N5 | $2 | (1850s) Unknown. C: farm scene. L: milkmaid. R: state die. | R-7 |

Banking gains respectability
By Carol Darrow

MONEY and credit were scarce commodities in the territories of the Upper Midwest as Minnesota, Iowa and Wisconsin were being organized. Up until the Civil War, there was no national currency. People exchanged gold and silver or specie (coins). Notes were issued by banks and traded with other banks.

Notes were supposed to be backed by gold and silver on deposit and in some cases by the notes of other banks. Holders of notes were supposed to be able to redeem them for 'hard' money whenever they wished.

But without government regulation, it was common for people to carry on speculative banking — the practice of issuing notes in excess of any ability to redeem them in specie.

Speculators frequently traded bank notes in order to finance risky land, mining and transportation schemes. But since many notes lacked financial backing, anyone who accepted a bank note in payment for livestock or real estate risked accepting a piece of paper that might well be worthless.

The situation reached such serious proportions that in 1838 Wisconsin Territorial Gov. Henry Dodge announced banking as a 'system of swindling and robbery.' The Wisconsin legislature in 1838 dissolved existing banks and in 1841 effectively outlawed banking in the Territory.

While some companies, notably the Wisconsin Marine and Fire Insurance Company of Milwaukee, got around the provisions of the anti-banking law by issuing certificates of deposit, the ban on banking lasted until 1852.

Into this chaotic world of finance came Gysbert van Steenwyk, a native of Utrecht in the Netherlands. He arrived in New York in 1849 and moved rapidly to Albany, Buffalo and then by lake steamer to Chicago. Van Steenwyk was offended by the ugliness of Chicago and chose to move on to Milwaukee.

There van Steenwyk became close friends with Samuel Marshall and James K. Illsley, founders of the Marshall and Illsley Bank; John P. MacGregor, who founded the Northwestern National Fire Insurance Co. and Alexander Mitchell, who operated the Wisconsin Marine and Fire, which later became the Marine Bank.

In Milwaukee, van Steenwyk became associated with a law firm and found that his services were in demand among Hollanders and other immigrants who wanted assistance in their business affairs and correspondence with the old country.

Van Steenwyk, who was fluent in several languages, built a thriving business and was soon commissioned by The Hague as the consul of the Netherlands to the state of Wisconsin. He soon added commissions to Michigan and Minnesota.

Van Steenwyk was named Commisioner of Immigration for Wisconsin in 1852 and moved back to New York. His job was to secure for Wisconsin "a thrifty, industrious and temperate class of settlers among the foreigners then flocking to America."

Van Steenwyk returned to Wisconsin and moved to the new town of Newport in central Wisconsin which expected to be on the route of the La Crosse and Milwaukee railroad. The railroad was moved two miles north to Kilbourn City, later to become Wisconsin Dells and most of the people moved from Newport to Kilbourn City.

Van Steenwyk lived there for the next eight years. He served as a member of the legislature from Sauk County for one term and in 1860 was elected bank controller for the state.

After the repeal of the anti-banking law in 1852, banks opened — and closed— rapidly. La Crosse pioneer John Levy opened the Bank of the City of La Crosse in 1856 with capital of $25,000 and circulating notes on $22,000. In the same year, Wilson Colwell opened the Kantanyan Bank with capital of $25,000 and circulation of $24,999.

The Panic of 1857 hurt both banks. The Bank of the City closed in 1858 while the Kantanyan Bank called upon its debtors to pay up. It closed in April of 1861.

Banks were allowed to issue currency to the par value of bonds of any one of the states of the U.S. deposited with the state bank controller. When the Civil War broke out, many of these state bonds, especially of newly seceded southern states, had little value. Therefore, the currency secured by their deposit was also worth little unless additional securities of adequate value were deposited with the bank comptroller. It was his duty to see that such deposit was made or that the notes were redeemed in gold. Otherwise, it was the bank controller's job to close the bank. In 1860, the first year of his two-year term as state bank controller, van Steenwyk closed 40 banks in Wisconsin.

This process left the field of banking wide open throughout the state and by the time his term ended in 1862, van Steenwyk had moved to La Crosse where he incorporated the Batavian Bank. The name came from the Teutonic tribe that in Ceasar's time dwelt near the mouth of the Rhine and from whom the Hollanders believed themselves descended. The bank opened for business in La Crosse on January 16, 1862, in a building on the south side of Main St. between Front and Second Sts. and was the only banking operation in the city at that time.

Van Steenwyk's son, Gysbert van Steenwyk, Jr., who later served as president of the Batavian Bank, writes that the Batavian Bank was always remarkably free from financial difficulties, the only real one occurring in the Panic of 1873.

"One day in that year, a run started on the bank, not having enough currency to meet it, closed for the balance of the day. However, my father made it amply clear to the leading businessmen of La Crosse how sound the bank's condition actually was, and obtained from them a guaranty of the bank's deposits which was posted on the bank's door, and when the bank opened again either that day or the next morning, the run was over and business proceeded as usual."

Van Steenwyk went on to serve a one-year term as La Crosse mayor in 1873 and was also a member of the State Senate. He was involved in the formation of a new incandescent electric light company in La Crosse which later purchased the gas company that was already in existence.

Van Steenwyk was also associated with the Victor Flouring Mill, the La Crosse Linseed Oil Mill, the La Crosse Street Railway Co., the La Crosse Tannery and the East Fork Improvement Co., a lumber company.

Gysbert van Steenwyk, Jr., ends his essay on his father by describing the elder van Steenwyk as a man who was "extremely scrupulous in all matters of personal conduct, notably so in his business dealings, refusing to take advantage of financial opportunities that most men would have considered legitimate, if he thought that he might, in any way, be using a position of trust for his own special benefit."

These qualities were obviously those which stood van Steenwyk and Batavian Bank in solid regard in a community that was taking its first steps in economic development.

WI-335 **BANK OF LA CROSSE, 1862-64**

Capital $25,000. W. D. Banister, Pres., E. D. Campbell, cashier (1863).
Closed.

Genuine Notes, Raised Notes and Counterfeits

| G2 | $1 | November 20, 1861 ABN. | R-7 |

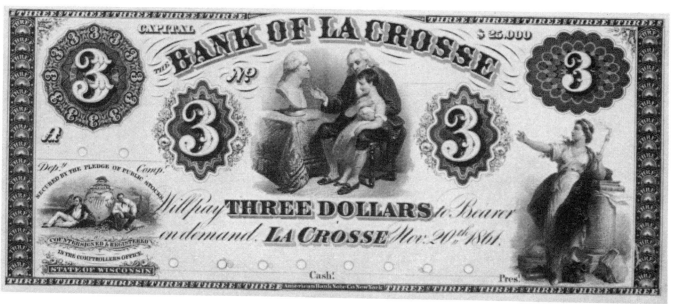

| G4 | $3 | November 20, 1861 ABN. | R-7 |

Uncut Sheet

| X1 | | 1, 3 ABN. G2, 4 | R-7 |

As only proof note is known, the bank probably never opened.

Scrip

| 1 | 5¢ | Pay to Bearer H. Siefert, Milwaukee. | R-5 |
| 2 | 10¢ | Pay to Bearer H. Siefert, Milwaukee. | R-6 |

WI-317   BANK OF LA CROSSE

SC 1   5¢   Pay to Bearer H. Siefert, Milwaukee.   R-5

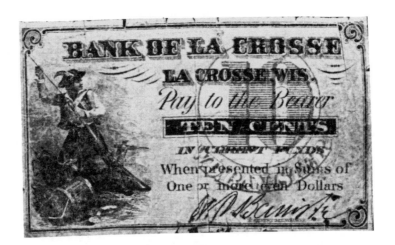

SC 2   10¢   Pay to Bearer H. Siefert, Milwaukee.   R-6

WII-240   **LA CROSSE COUNTY BANK, 1858-61**

Capital $25,000. W. H. Lathop, Pres., W. W. Webb, cashier (1858).
Closed 1861.

Genuine Notes, Raised Notes and Counterfeits

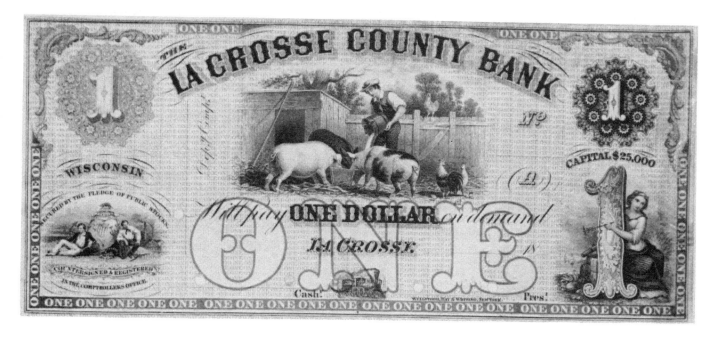

G2a	$1	___18__: (1858-60) WH&W. Tint: Orange microlettering overall and an outlined white ONE.	R-7
G2b	$1	___18__: 1861 ABN. As above, except for imprint.	R-7

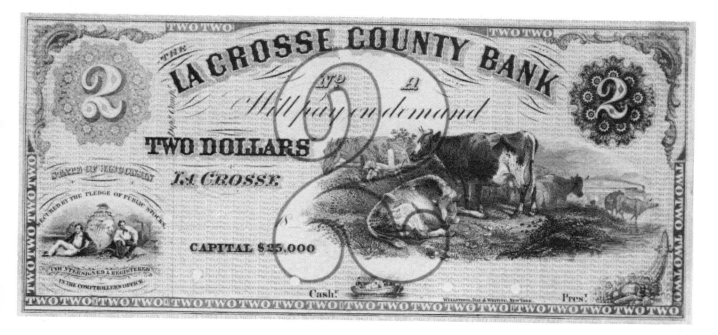

G4a	$2	___18__: (1858-60) WH&W. Tint: Orange microlettering overall and an outlined large white 2.	R-7
G4b	$2	___18__: 1861 ABN. As above, except for imprint.	R-7

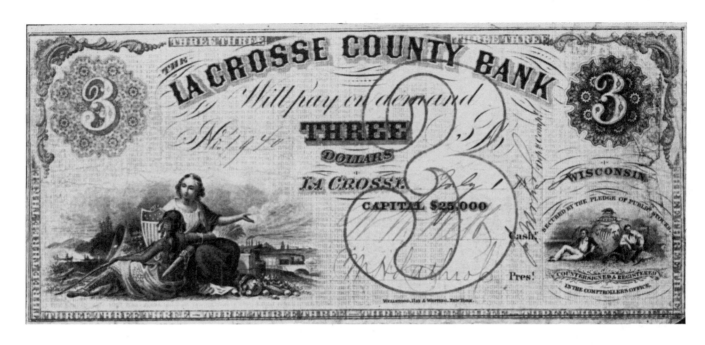

| G6a | $3 | ___18__: 1858-60 WH&W. Tint: Orange microlettering overall and an outlined large white 3. | R-6 |
| G6b | $3 | ___18__: 1861 ABN. As above, except for imprint. | R-7 |

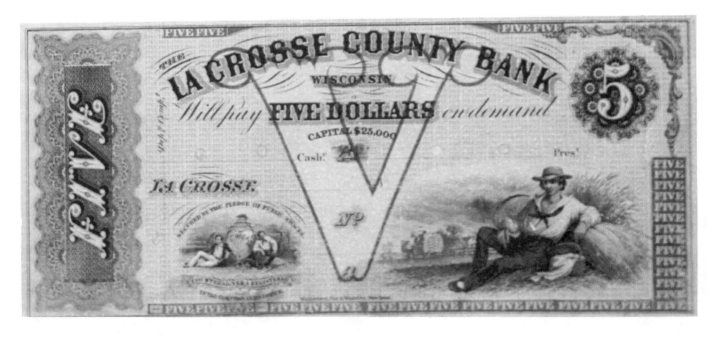

G8a	$5	___18__: (1858-60) WH&W. Tint: Orange microlettering overall and an outlined large V.	R-7
G8b	$5	___18__: 1861 ABN. As above, except for imprint.	R-7
R5	$5	___18__: 1858-60 WH&W. Raised from $1, G2a.	R-7

Uncut Sheet

| X1 | | $1, 2, 5, 5 TC. G2, 4, 6, 6 | R-7 |

LA POINTE

WI-345   FRONTIER BANK, 1858-62

Capital $35,000. L. F. McGowen, cashier; only purpose was to issue notes for circulation.
Later location: Stevens Point (moved ca. 1862).

Notes probably dated only at La Pointe.
Closed.

G2a	$5	January 1, 1858 BC, ABNCo. mono. Capital: $25,000. Overprint: Red FIVE.	R-7
G2b	$5	January 1, 1858 BC, ABNCo. mono. As above, except for capital ($80,000).	R-7
G2c	$5	January 1, 1858 BC, ABNCo. mono. As above, except for capital ($200,000).	R-7

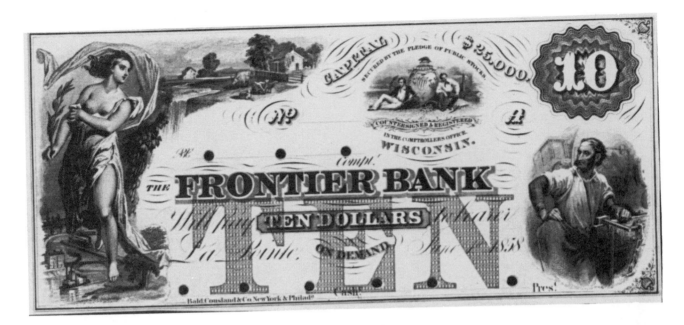

G4a	$10	January 1, 1858 BC, ABNCo. mono. L-LC: large figure of semi-nude woman holding grain, small view of city below, waterfall and farm scene at upper rt. RC: state die. R: 10-3/4-length figure of mechanic. Overprint: Red TEN.	R-7
G4b	$10	January 1, 1858 (BC, ABNCo. mono.) As above, except for capital ($80,000).	R-7
G4c	$10	January 1, 1858 (BC, ABNCo. mono.) As above, except for capital ($200,000).	R-7

Uncut Sheet

| X1 | | $5, 10 BC, ABNCo. mono. G2a, 4 | R-7 |

APOSTLE ISLANDS

Madeline Island, on which is located the village of La Pointe, contains the oldest settlement in northern Wisconsin; and, if we include the primitive races, goes back to the remotest ages. The Jesuits, including Father Marquette, located on this island in the latter part of the seventeenth century. After living here several years, they finally abandoned the place. In 1800, M. Cadotte, an old French trader, settled on the island, and erected fortified dwellings, the location now being known as the "Old Fort." Here he lived the remainder of his life, and died July 8, 1837. At the commencement of the present century, the American Fur Company established its head-quarters here, on the south side of the island; but the harbor being a poor one, they removed across the island to the present village of La Pointe, in 1835. Warehouses and docks were built. Here poured in the trade of the surrounding country, and La Pointe saw its palmiest days. The company's buildings were afterwards burned and the place abandoned. Indistinct traces of these ruins can yet be found near the Catholic cemetery. In 1830 the Rev. Sherman Hall established a mission here. It was afterward removed to Bad River. On July 28, 1835, the Rt. Rev. Frederick Baraga arrived on the island. He says: "I found some Canadians and Catholics who were in the service of the American Fur Company; also some half-breeds, who were civilized and had been baptized." Bishop Baraga partially completed a church by August 29. He then celebrated his first mass in the imperfect church. In order to secure funds for the completion of the edifice, he left for Europe September 29, 1836, and returned October 8, 1837, having received by contributions enough to finish the church, which was effected in August, 1838, and called St. Joseph's. It was dedicated September 27 of the same year. This building was demolished, and a new church built and dedicated, August 1, 1841. August 14, 1844, Bishop Henni arrived, and confirmed 122 Indians. Bishop Baraga continued here many years, going finally to Marquette, where he died. He was succeeded by Father Chebul, who remained for several years. Since his departure, services have been held mostly by missionaries.

Built into the wall of the present Catholic Church is an old structure supposed to have been erected 200 years ago. This supposition is erroneous, as the church dates but half a century back. In the present church is a painting, which is known to be 200 years old, but if one should judge by the canvas and nails, it might date back several hundred years.

On March 28, 1843, the first treaty on this island was made at La Pointe by Robert Stuart, United States Commissioner, with the Chippewa Indians, whereby they ceded all their lands in Michigan and Wisconsin to the Government, the Indians stipulating the right to hunt on these lands. By this treaty $75,000 were allowed them by the Government for the satisfaction of debts to the white men. One of the largest items was some $27,000 to the Astors, then connected with the American Fur Company. In 1854, another treaty was made by Commissioners Gilbert and Harriman, when the Indian reservations were defined. At this time La Pointe Indian Agency was established. La Pointe, in its early days, was mostly governed by the American Fur Company. John W. Bell came here in 1835. The population at that time was about 2,000, composed of Indians, *voyageurs,* traders and half-breeds. The only persons known to be living now, who were there at that time are: John W. Bell, Theophilus Remilliard, Ignace Roberdoux and Matilda Perinier. A dock was built in an early day, but is now in ruins. The village has a good school-house; but where once was a prosperous busy little city, now only few fishermen remain. The area of the island is 14,804 acres. La Pointe for a long time was the county seat of Ashland County, and the head center of the town of La Pointe, Ashland County. This town was vacated on June 17, 1879, and the territory added to the towns of Ashland and Butternut.

Basswood Island has an area of 1,980 acres, and is noted for its brown stone quarries, from which the stone was taken for the Milwaukee Court-house. Michigan Island, with an area of 1,556 acres, has a few farmers; a Government light-house stands on this island. Presque Isle, area 10,054 acres, has good stone quarries; Outer Island, area 7,999 acres, has a Government light-house; Hemlock Island, area 1,340 acres; Oak Island, area 5,077 acres; Raspberry Island, area 224 acres, has a Government light-house; Willey's Island, area 350 acres, the fishermen have made some improvements; Rice Island, area 1,100 acres; Bear Island, area 1,824 acres; York Island, area 104 acres: Sand Island, area 2,868 acres; Steam-boat Island, area 24 acres. The other islands are named Little Steam-boat, Ironwood, Devil's, Wilson's, Gull, and Long Island, upon which is a light-house. These islands, twenty-two in number, contain good soil for all kinds of vegetables. Grain and fruits grow well. The islands are heavily wooded with almost every kind of timber natural to this latitude. Being surrounded by water, the soil is protected from early frost. The Winters are somewhat warmer than on the mainland. The majority contain five undeveloped stone quarries. The greatest length of the islands is thirty-five miles, and the greatest breadth twenty miles.

From *History of Northern Wisconsin*, 1881.

WI-350   BANK OF LA POINTE, 1858-60

Closed with $9,070 in specie to satisfy notes totaling that amount, redemption expired April 19, 1863.

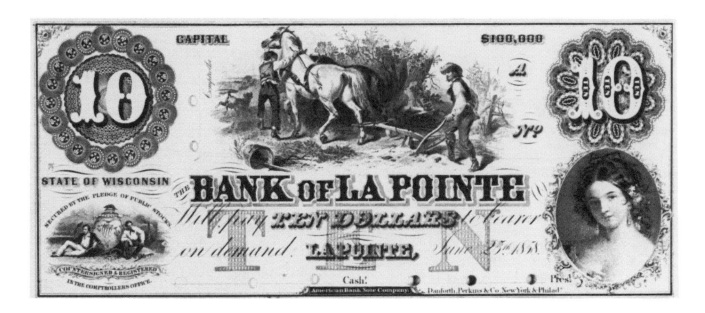

G2 $10   ?: (1858-60) (ABN). C: man plowing with two horses, boy   R-7
leading the horses. L: 10/state die. R: 10/oval female
portrait.

G4 $20   ?: (1858-60) (ABN). C: 3/4-length figures of farmer, sailor   R-7
and mechanic. L: 20/state die/TWENTY. R: 20/por-
trait of young woman holding dove.

La Pointe is located on the southeast end of Madeline Island in Lake Superior, the oldest settlement in the state. The 1850 population was 489: 5 farms and 74 dwellings. It was originally settled by the North-west Fur Trading Co.

LANCASTER

WI-343   LANCASTER

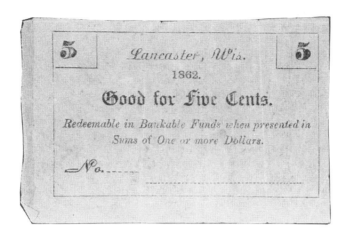

| SC 1 | 5¢ | 1862 Lancaster in script type. | R-7 |

| SC 1a | 5¢ | 1862 no overprint. | R-7 |
| SC 1b | 5¢ | 1862 Blue/dull orange overprint. | R-7 |

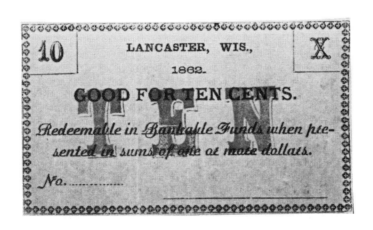

| SC 2a | 10¢ | 1862 no overprint. | R-7 |
| SC 2b | 10¢ | Blue/dull orange overprint. | R-7 |

WI-344   **BANK OF GRANT COUNTY**

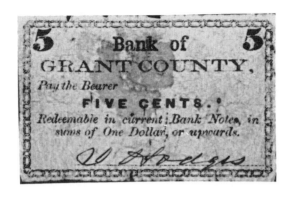

SC 1   5¢   Pay to Bearer. Blue   R-7

The exact location of the Bank of Grant County is unknown. Lancaster is the County Seat of Grant County.

LAPORTE

WIII-355   OCONTO COUNTY BANK, 1858-61

Capital $100,000. John Wright, Pres., G. A. Miller, cashier (1858). M. L. Wright, cashier (1859).
Moved to Oconto in 1859. Had no place of business or banking house.
Failed 1861. Notes redeemed at Milwaukee and Madison at 75¢ per dollar in 1862. In 1863 there was
$825 outstanding.

Genuine Notes, Raised Notes and Counterfeits

G2a $5   August 1, 1857 RWH&E. Overpint: Red 5 5.   R-7

G4a $10   August 1, 1857 RWH&E. Overprint: Red TEN.   R-7

Uncut Sheet

X1 $5, 10 RWH&E. G2a, 4a   R-7

WI-43   **JAMES McCLOUD**

SC 6   50¢   November 25th 1862. Will pay to Bearer. Actual size   R-7
                   38mm.

WI-45   **MERCANTILE BANK**

Moved to Lodi in 1859 from Beaver Dam.

II - NOTES DATED AT LODI

G8a	$1	?: (1860s) ABN. Same as Beaver Dam G2a, except for location, imprint, date (probably) and overprint color changed to blue or green.	R-7
G10a	$2	?: (1860s) ABN Same as Beaver Dam G4a, except for location, imprint, date (probably) and overprint color changed to blue or green.	R-7
G12a	$5	?: (1860s) ABN. Same as Beaver Dam G6a, except for location, imprint, date (probably) and overprint color changed to blue or green.	R-7

MADISON

WI-360   BANK OF THE CAPITOL, 1856-60

Capital $50,000. John T. Martin, Pres., Edward T. Martin, cashier (1856). $3,789 held for like amount of redemption.
Failed.

Genuine Notes, Raised Notes and Counterfeits

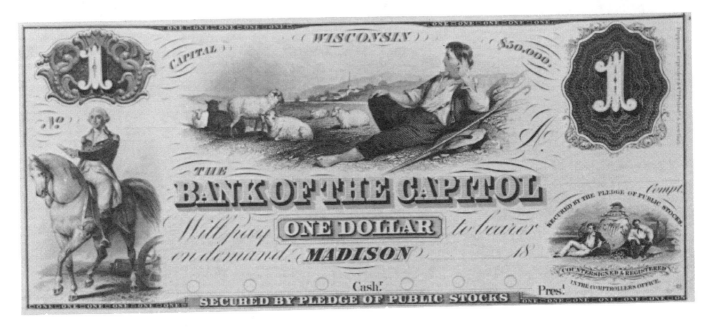

| G2 | $1 | ___18__: ____ TC. L: Washington. No overprint. | R-7 |
| G2a | $1 | ___18__: 1850s TC. As above except for red overprint. | |

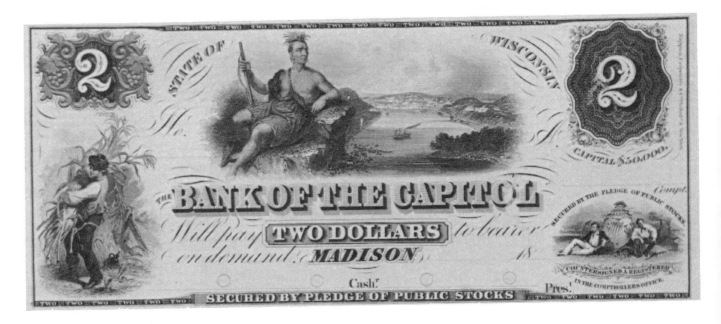

| G4 | $2 | ___18__: ____ TC. No overprint. | R-7 |
| G4a | $2 | ___18__: 1850s TC. As above, except for red overprint. | R-7 |

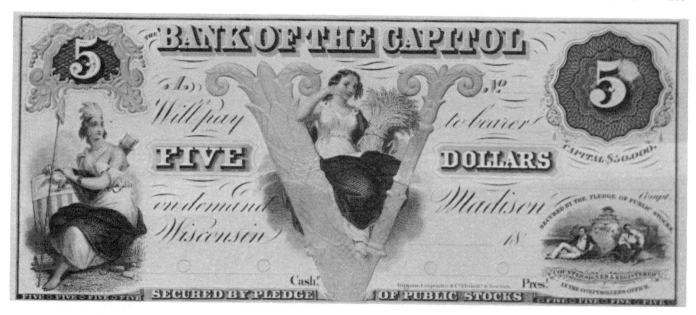

G6	$5	___18__: ____ TC. No overprint.		R-7
G6a	$5	___18__: (1850s) TC. As above, except for red 5 5 overprint.	Remainder	R-6
C6a	$5	___18__: 1850s TC. Photographic cft. of the above.		R-7
R4	$5	___18__: 1850s TC. Raised from $1, G2 or 2a.		R-7
R6	$10	___18__: 1850s TC. Raised from $1, G2 or 2a. The bank issued no $10s.		R-7
R8	$20	___18__: 1850s TC. Raised from $1, G2 or 2a. The bank issued no $20s.		R-7

Uncut Sheet

X1		$1, 2, 5, 5 TC. G2, 4, 6, 6		R-7

Altered, Spurious and Unattributed Non-Genuine Notes

A5 $2   August 1, 1854 BA. R: Pierce. Tint: Blue panel in bank   R-6
                title. Overprint: Red 2. Altered from $2 Bank of Ana-
                castia, Anacastia, DC-35-4a.

A10 $2   December 1, 1852 DB. Overprint: Blue panel over bank   R-6
                title. Altered from $2 Peoples Bank, Georgetown, DC-
                135-G4.

S5 $5   ___18__: 1850s None. Overprint: Blue panel bearing white FIVE.   R-6

WI-365   DANE COUNTY BANK, 1854-63

Capital $50,000. George A. Mason, Pres., Timothy Brown, cashier (1863).
Became the First National Bank of Madison in 1863.

Genuine Notes, Raised Notes and Counterfeits

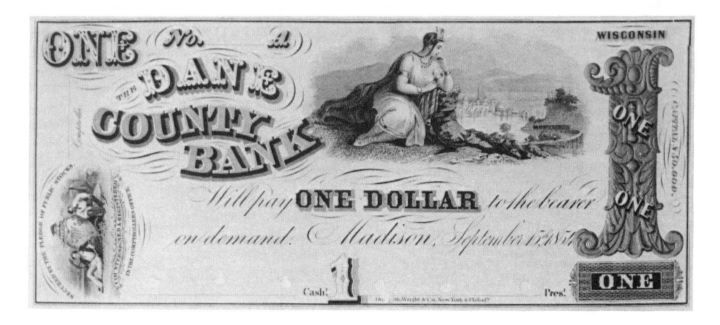

G2 $1   September 15, 1854 DW. Capital: $50,000.   R-6

G4 $2   September 15, 1854 DW. Capital: $50,000.   R-7

| G6 | $3 | September 15, 1854 DW. Capital: $50,000. | R-7 |

G8	$5	September 15, 1854 DW. Capital: $50,000.	R-7
R5	$5	September 15, 1854 DW. Raised from $2, G4.	R-7
R10	$10	September 15, 1854 DW. Raised from $2, G4.	R-7

| G12 | $20 | January 1, 1855 DW. Capital: $100,000. | R-7 |

Uncut Sheets

| X1 | $1, 2, 3, 5 DW. G2, 4, 6, 8 | R-7 |
| X2 | $10, 20 DW. G10, 12 | R-7 |

WI-370   **BANK OF MADISON, 1860-ca. 67**

Capital $50,000. Simeon Mills, Pres., James Hill, cashier.
Closed.

Genuine Notes, Raised Notes and Counterfeits

G2	$1	___18__: ____ ABN. No overprint.	R-7
G2a	$1	___18__: (1860s) ABN. As above, except for red ornate 1 1 overprint.	R-7
G2b	$1	October 1, 1860 ABN. Same as G2a, except for date, removal of "ONE DOLLAR ONE DOLLAR" at bottom and overprint color (green.)	R-7
G2c	$1	?: (1862) ABN. Same as G2b, except for date & green tint instead of overprint.	R-7

G4	$2	___18__: ____ ABN. No overprint.	R-7
G4a	$2	___18__: (1860s) ABN. As above, except for overprint of a red panel outlining a white TWO.	R-7
G4b	$2	October 1, 1860 ABN. As above, except for date & overprint color (green.)	R-6
G4c	$2	?: (1862) ABN. As above, except for probable date change & green tint instead of overprint.	R-7

Uncut Sheets

X1		$1, 2 ABN. G2,4	R-7
X2		$1, 2 ABN. G2a, 4a	R-7

Altered, Spurious and Unattributed Non-Genuine Notes

S5	$3	September 10, 18_: 1860s ABN. Overprint: Red 3, lazy 3 & 3.	R-6

Reverse of all denominations showing list of members of Merchant Association.

WI-375   **MADISON BANK, 1863**

Capital $50,000. Simeon Mills, Pres., James L. Hill, cashier (1863).
Probably never opened.

G2 $1   October 2, 1854 TCC.   R-7

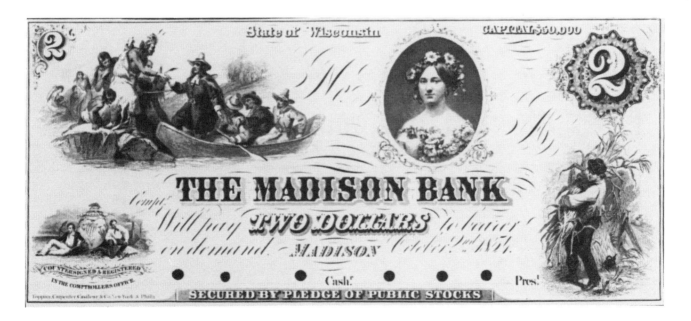

G4 $2   October 2, 1854 TCC. L: Landing of Roger Williams.   R-7

Uncut Sheet

X1 $1, 2 TCC. G2, 4   R-7

WI-370   MERCHANTS ASSOCIATION

SC 1   5¢   November 10, 1862   R-6

SC 2   10¢   R-6
SC 3   25¢   R-7

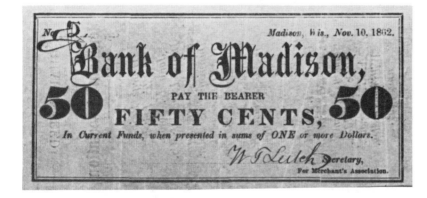

SC 5   50¢   R-7

Common Reverse.

WI-380   **MERCHANTS BANK, 1856-58**

Capital $50,000. A. A. Bliss, Pres., C. T. Flowers, cashier. $1,388 held in 1860 for redemption of that amount of notes. Redemption date February 19, 1862. Closed.

Genuine Note, Raised Notes and Counterfeits

| G2 | $1 | ___18__: ____ DW. No overprint. | R-7 |
| G2a | $1 | ___18__: 1856-58 DW. As above, except for red overprint. | R-7 |

| G4 | $3 | ___18__: ____ DW. No overprint. | R-7 |
| G4a | $3 | ___18__: 1856-58 DW. As above, except for red overprint. | |

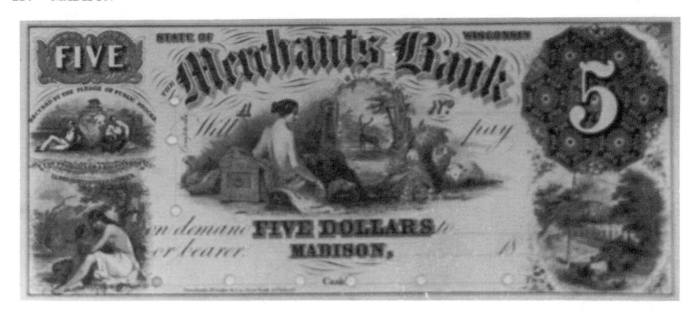

G6	$5	___18__: ____ DW. No overprint.	R-7
G6a	$5	___18__: 1856-58 DW. As above, except for red FIVE overprint.	R-6
R4	$5	___18__: 1856-58 DW. Raised from $1, G2 or 2a.	R-7
R6	$5	___18__: 1856-58 DW. Raised from $3, G4 or 4a.	R-7
R8	$5	___18__: 1856-58 DW. Raised from $1, G2 or 2a. The bank issued no $10s.	R-7
R10	$10	___18__: 1856-58 DW. Raised from $3, G4 or 4a. The bank issued no $10s.	R-7
R12	$20	___18__: 1856-58 DW. Raised from $1, G2 or 2a. The bank issued no $20s.	R-7
R14	$20	___18__: 1856-58 DW. Raised from $3, G4 or 4a. The bank issued no $20s.	R-7

Uncut Sheet

| X1 | | $1, 1, 3, 5 DW. G2, 2, 4, 6 | R-7 |

Altered, Spurious and Unattributed Non-Genuine Notes

A5 $1   October 20, 1854 None. Altered from $1 Merchants Bank, Stillwater, MN-180-G2.   R-6

A10 $2   September 1, 185_: mid-1850s D&B. C: small eagle: Ceres std., hardware at left and upright sheaf at rt., train on bridge and canoe locks in bkgd. L: 2/nude Indian brave on prancing horse. R: 2/deer on hill. BS: Indian in canoe. Altered from $2 Merchants Bank, Mankato City, MN-75-G4.   R-7

A15 $5   September 1, 185_: 1850s None (D&B). C: small eagle; Indian man stdg. on cliff, right hand on bow and left arm raised, watching train at rt. L: Indian woman stdg. with left elbow and left foot propped on rocks, holding bow/FIVE. R: 5/man std. on anchor, ship in left bkgd. BS: Indian in canoe. Altered from $5 Merchants Bank, Mankato City, MN-75-G6.   R-7

A20a	$5	October 20, 1854 None. Overprint: Red FIVE. Altered from $5 Merchants Bank, Stillwater, MN-180-G6.	R-6
N5	$2	(1850s) Unknown. C: large ship. L: portrait. R: ship.	R-7
N10	$3	(1850s) Unknown. C: woman with sheaves, cows, train on bridge & canal lock in bkgd.	R-7
N15	$5	(1850s) Unknown. C: two persons std., griffin on chest.	R-7
N-20	$10	(1850s) Unknown. C; two persons std., griffin on chest.	R-7
N25	$20	(1850s) Unknown. C: two persons std., griffin on chest.	R-7
N30	$50	(1850s) Unknown. C: two persons std., griffin on chest.	R-7

WI-385   **RAIL ROAD BANK, ca. 1858**

Capital $100,000.
Possibly never opened.

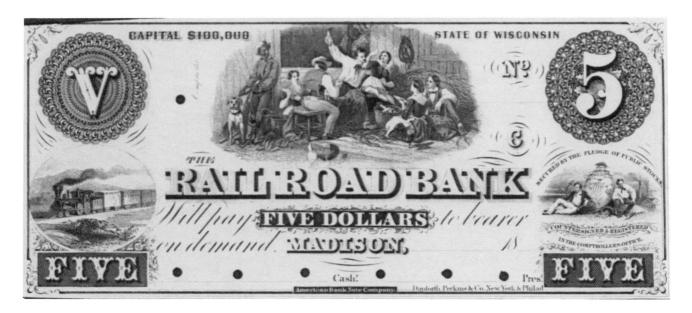

| G2 | $5 | ___18__: ____ DnP, ABN. No overprint. | R-7 |
| G2a | $5 | ___18__: ____ DnP, ABN. As above, except for red FIVE overprint. | R-7 |

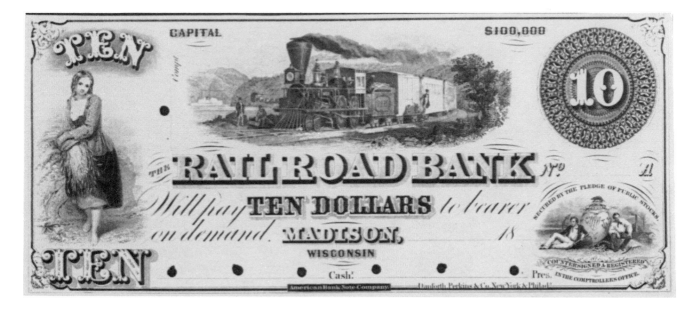

| G4 | $10 | ___18__: ____ DnP, ABN. No overprint. | R-7 |
| G4a | $10 | ___18__: ____ Dnp, ABN. As above, except for red TEN overprint. | R-7 |

Uncut Sheet

| X1 | | $5, 5, 5, 10 DnP, ABN. G2a, 2a, 3a, 4a | R-7 |

WI-390   STATE BANK, 1853-65

Capital $50,000.

First bank in Wisconsin to organize under the new banking laws of November 1851. Organized 1853 by Samuel Marshall, President, and Charles E. Ilsley. Located at 7 Pinckney St. They also opened a bank in Milwaukee but did not issue notes. The bank at Madison later closed, moving to Milwaukee to become known as Marshall and Ilsley Bank (M&I) and most recently merged with the Valley Bank to become Wisconsin's largest banking institution.

Liquidated, all outstanding notes redeemed at par.

Genuine Notes, Raised Notes and Counterfeits

G2	$1	January 1, 1853 DB. No overprint; plain back.	R-7
G2a	$1	January 1, 1853 DB. As above, except for a brown-orange back.	R-6
G2b	$1	January 1, 1853 DB, ABNCo. mono. Same as G2a, except for imprint, lack of a printed back and has an overprint of a green panel outlining a white ONE.	R-6
G2c	$1	January 1, 1853 DB, ABNCo. mono. Same as G2b, except has a printed serial number, lacks an overprint and has a brown-orange back.	R-6

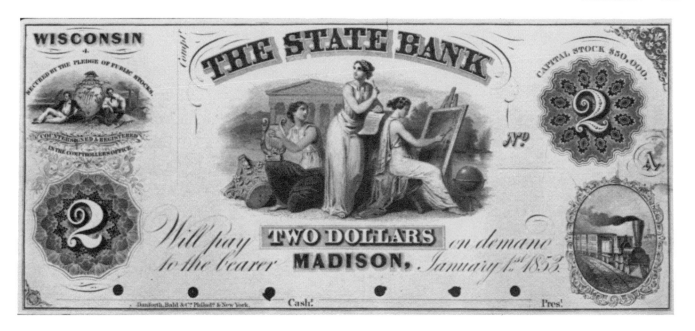

G4	$2	January 1, 1853 DB. No overprint; plain back.	R-7
G4a	$2	January 1, 1853 DB. As above, except for a brown-orange back.	R-7
G4b	$2	January 1, 1853 DB, ABNCo. mono. Same as G4a, except for imprint, lack of a printed back and has an overprint of a green panel outlining a white TWO.	R-7
G4c	$2	January 1, 1853 DB, ABNCo. mono. Same as G4b, except has a printed serial number, lacks an overprint and has a brown-orange back.	R-7

G6	$5	January 1, 1853 DB. No overprint; plain back.		R-7
G6a	$5	January 1, 1853 DB. As above, except for a brown-orange back.	Remainder	R-6
G6b	$5	January 1, 1853 DB, ABNCo. mono. Same as G6a, except for imprint, lack of a printed back and has an overprint of a green panel outlining a white FIVE.		R-6
G6c	$5	January 1, 1853 DB, ABNCo. mono. Same as G6b, except has a printed serial number, lacks an overprint and has a brown-orange back.		R-7
R5	$5	January 1, 1853 DB. Raised from $1, G2 series.		R-7
R6	$10	January 1, 1853 DB. Raised from $1, G2 series. The bank issued no $10s.		R-7

Uncut sheet

X1		Obverse $1, 1, 2, 5 DB. G2, 2, 4, 6		R-7
		Reverse $1, 1, 2, 5 G2, 2, 4, 6		R-7

WI-395   BANK OF THE WEST, 1854-55

Capital $100,000. S. A. Lowe, Pres., W. L. Hinsdale, cashier.
Closed.

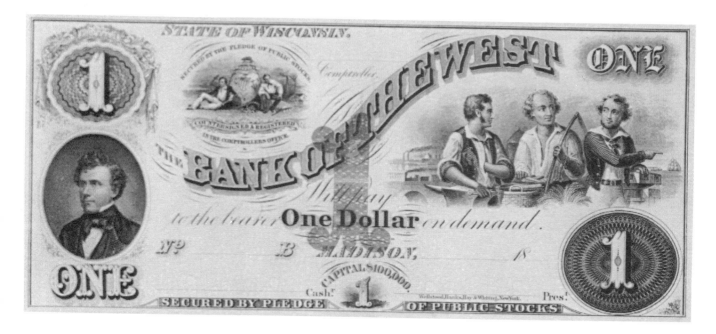

G2	$1	___18__: ___ WHH&W. Same as G2a, except lacks an overprint.	R-7
G2a	$1	___18__: (1854-55) WHH&W. As above, except for a red 1 overprint.	R-6

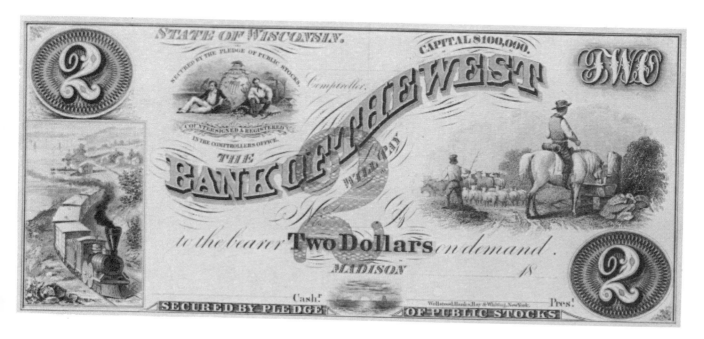

G4	$2	___18__: ___ WHH&W. Same as G4a, except lacks an overprint.	R-7
G4a	$2	___18__: (1854-55) WHH&W. As above, except for a red 2 overprint.	R-6

G6 $3   ___18__: ____ WHH&W. Same as G6a, except lacks an   R-7
      overprint.

G6a $3   ___18__: (1854-55) WHH&W. As above, except for a red   Remainder   R-6
      THREE overprint.

Uncut Sheet

X1 $1, 1, 2, 3 WHH&W. G2a, 2a, 4a, 6a   R-7

WI-400   BANK OF WISCONSIN, 1858-65

Capital $50,000. Wm. M. Dennis, Pres., Peter V. Brown, cashier (1858).
Notes were dated at Madison, but the bank was apparently located in Watertown. Was a redemption center for Wisconsin Bank of Mineral Point. Became the Wisconsin National Bank of Watertown #1010 on February 27, 1865, closed 1934.

Genuine Notes, Raised Notes and Counterfeits

G2a $1   ___18__: (1850s-60s) TC. L: Juneau. Tint: Orange bank   R-7
                title and ONE ONE.

G4a $2   ___18__: (1950s-60s) TC. Tint: Orange bank title and   R-7
                TWO.

| G6a | $5 | ___18__: (1850s-60s) TC. Lower L: Dr. Kane's Arctic Expedition. Tint: Orange bank title and large 5. | R-7 |

| R5 | $5 | ___18__: (1850s-60s) TC. Raised from $1, G2a. | R-7 |

| R10 | $10 | ___18__: (1850s-60s) TC. Raised from $2, G4a. The bank issued no $10s. | R-7 |

Uncut Sheet

| X1 | | $1, 1, 2, 5 TC. G2a, 2a, 4a, 6a | R-7 |

WI-405   WISCONSIN BANK OF MADISON, 1857-60s

Capital: $100,000. M. D. Miller, Pres., Noah Lee, cashier (1857); C. B. Miller, cashier (1863). 1863 capital was $25,000. See Wisconsin Bank, Mineral Point.
Genuine Notes, Raised Notes and Counterfeits

Fate unknown.

G2a $1   ___18__: 1850-60s WH&W. Tint: Orange microlettering   R-6
overall, frame and counter.

G4a $2   ___18__: (1850s-60s) WH&W. Tint: Orange microletter-   R-6
ing overall, frame and counter.

| G6a | $5 | ___18__: (1850s-60s) WH&W. Tint: Orange counters & panel of microlettering with outlined white FIVE. | R-6 |
| R6 | $5 | ___18__: 1850s-60s WH&W. Raised from $1, G2. | R-7 |

G8a	$10	___18__: 1950s-60s) WH&W. Tint: Orange microlettering overall, counters & outlined large white X.	R-7
R8	$10	___18__: 1850s-60s WH&W. Raised from $1, G2.	R-7
R10	$20	___18__: 1850s-60s WH&W. Raised from $1, G2. The bank issued no $20s.	R-7

Uncut Sheets

| X1 | $1, 1, 1, 2 WH&W. G2a, 2a, 2a, 4a | R-7 |
| X2 | $5, 5, 5, 10 WH&W. G6a, 6a, 6a, 8a | R-7 |

MALCOLM

Malcolm was located in Langlade County.

WI-407   HENRY SHERRY

SC 1   5¢   Black with overall green tint, reverse brown. M&L.   R-7

SC 2   10¢   ML&E.   R-7

25¢ and 50¢ per probably issued.

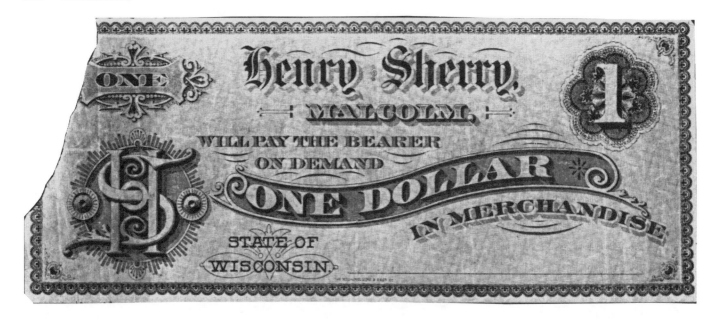

SC 7 $1   ML&E.   R-7

8        $2   ML&E.   R-7

10        $5   ML&E.   R-7

(Note the reverses of the $1, 2, and 5 are identical to the Knapp Stout & Co., notes issued at Menomonie. The fractional notes are of a different design.)

MANITOWOC

WI-410   LAKE SHORE BANK, 1858-61

Capital $25,000. Martin Adams, Pres. G. W. Adams, cashier.
Failed 1861. Redeemed at 77¢ per dollar. $739 outstanding in 1863.

| G2 | $1 | December 1, 1858 ABN. Same as G2a, except lacks an overprint. | R-7 |
| G2a | $1 | December 1, 1858 ABN. As above, except for red ONE overprint. | R-6 |

| G4 | $3 | December 1, 1858 ABN. No overprint. | R-7 |
| G4a | $3 | December 1, 1858 ABN. As above, except for red THREE overprint. | R-7 |

| G6 | $5 | December 1, 1858 ABN. No overprint. | R-7 |
| G6a | $5 | December 1, 1858 ABN. As above, except for red FIVE overprint. | R-6 |

Uncut Sheet

| X1 | | $1, 1, 3, 5 ABN. G2, 2, 4, 6 | R-7 |
| X2 | | $1, 1, 3, 5 ABN. G2a, 2a, 4a, 6a | R-7 |

WI-415   BANK OF MANITOWOC, 1858-65

Capital $100,000 (1858); $25,000 (1863). C. C. Barnes, Pres., J. C. Barnes, cashier (1860). C. Inleng, cashier (1863).

Became the First National Bank of Manitowoc in March 1865. Liquidated 1891. Followed by the State Bank of Manitowoc in 1891.

Genuine Notes, Raised Notes and Counterfeits

G2a	$1	___18__: (1857) None (TC). Upper L: Franklin. Upper RC: Washington. Tint: Orange lathework overall outlining white ONE ONE. Capital: $50,000.	R-7
G2b	$1	___18__: 1858 (ABN). As above, except for capital ($100,000) and probably imprint.	R-7
G2c	$1	___18__: 1858-60s (ABN) . Same as G2b, except for capital ($125,000).	R-7

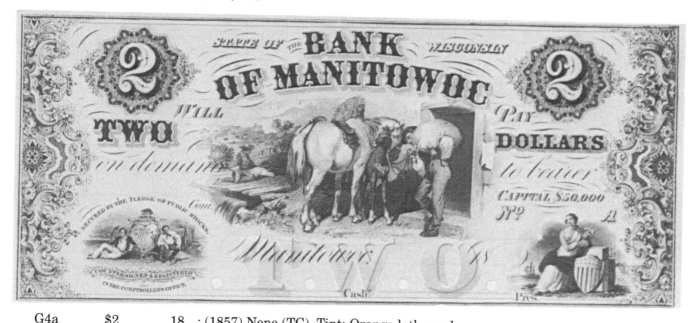

G4a	$2	___18__: (1857) None (TC). Tint: Orange lathework overall outlining white TWO. Capital: $50,000.	R-7
G4b	$2	___18__: 1858 (ABN). As above except for capital ($100,000) and probably imprint.	R-7
4Gc	$2	___18__: 1858-60s (ABN). Same as 4Gb, except for capital ($125,000).	R-7

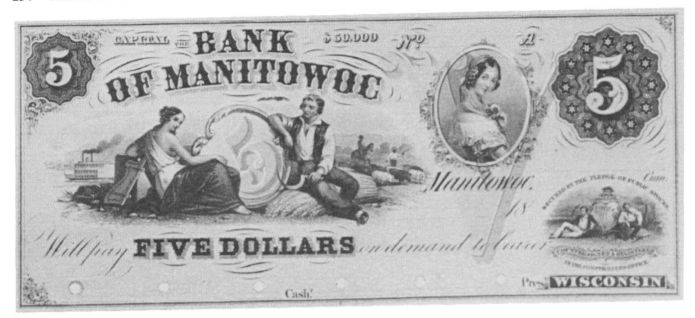

G6a	$5	___18__: 1857 TC. Tint: Orange lathework overall & large ornate V. Capital: $50,000.	R-6
G6b	$5	___18__: 1858 (ABN). As above, except for capital ($100,000) and probably imprint.	R-7
G6c	$5	___18__: 1858-60s (ABN). Same as G6b, except for capital ($125,000).	R-7
R4	$5	___18__: 1850s TC. Raised from $1, G2a series.	R-7
R6	$5	___18__: 1850s (TC). Raised from $2, G4a series.	R-7
R8	$5	___18__: 1850s (TC). Raised from $1, G2a series. The bank issued no $10s.	R-7
R10	$10	___18__: 1850s (TC). Raised from $2, G4a series. The bank issued no $10s.	R-7
R12	$20	___18__: 1850s (TC). Raised from $1, G4a series. The bank issued no $20s.	R-7
R14	$20	___18__: 1850s (TC). Raised from $2, G4a series. The bank issued no $20s.	R-7

Uncut Sheet

| X1 | | $1, 1, 2, 5 (TC). G2a, 2a, 4a, 6a | R-7 |

WI-417   MERCHANTS SCRIP

SC 6 $3   ___185_; 1850s GWH & Co.

R-7

This is a generic piece of scrip with the city and merchant's name changeable.

SC 8 $5   ___185_; GWH&Co.

R-7

MARANETT

WI-420   GREEN BAY BANK, 1856-64

Capital $35,000. Daniel Wills, Pres., N. Ludington, cashier (1857).
Later locations: Oconto, La Crosse (moved in 1858 & 60).
Fate: closed

Genuine Notes, Raised Notes and Counterfeits

G2	$1	___18__: ____ TC. Capital: $25,000. No overprint.	R-7
G2a	$1	___18__: 1850s TC. As above, except for red ONE over-print.	R-7
G2c	$1	___18__: 1850s TC, ABNCo. mono. Same as G2a, except for imprint and capital ($35,000).	R-6

G4	$2	___18__: (1850s) TC. Capital: $25,000. No overprint.	R-7
G4a	$2	___18__: 1850s TC. As above, except for red TWO over-print.	R-6
G4c	$2	___18__: 1850s TC, ABNCo. mono. Same as G4a, except for imprint and capital ($35,000).	R-6

R2 $5   ___18__: 1850s TC. Raised from $1, G2 series. The bank
                issued no $5s.   R-7

R4 $10   ___18__; 1850s TC. Raised from $1, G2 series. The bank
                issued no $10s.   R-6

R6 $10   ___18__; 1850s TC. Raised from $2, G4 series. The bank
                issued no $10s.   R-7

R8 $20   ___18__; 1850s TC. Raised from $1, G2 series. The bank
                issued no $20s.   R-7

R10 $20   ___18__; 1850s TC. Raised from $2, G4 series. The bank
                issued no $20s.   R-7

Uncut Sheets

X1 $1, 2 TC, G2, 4

X2 $1, 1, 2, 5 (TC), G2a, 2a, 4a, 6a   R-7
                                                                         F-7

MARATHON CITY

WI-425   MARATHON CITY, ca. 1858

Probably never opened.

G2a	$3	July 1, 1858 ABN. Tint: Red-orange bank title & ornate 3 3.	R-7
G4a	$5	July 1, 1858 ABN. LC: mechanic stdg. with one hand on large V. factories in bkgd. RC: child with rabbits, in oval. L: young woman holding hen & chicks, in oval/ small 5. R: 5/state die. Tint: Red-orange.	R-7

MARKESAN

WI-160   MARKESAN

Laborer's Bank.

Markesan was formerly named Eliside and issued notes under that name. Notes with the name Markesan probably were never produced.

MARQUETTE

WI-430   NORTH WESTERN BANK, 1856-61

Capital $60,000. Alonzo Wood, Pres., W. W. Wood, cashier (1856).
Later location: Stevens Point (moved ca. 1859).
Closed/failed.

I: NOTED DATED AT MARQUETTE

Genuine Notes, Raised Notes and Counterfeits

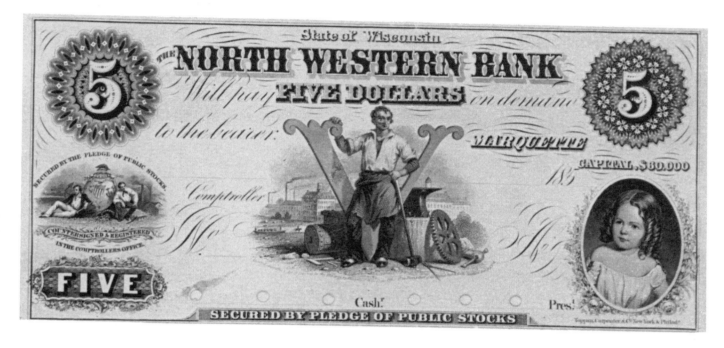

| G6 | $5 | ___18__; 185_s ___TC. Capital: $60,000. No overprint. | R-7 |
| G6b | $5 | ___18__; 185_s TC. (AMBCo. mono.) As above, except for capital ($100,000) and probably imprint. | R-7 |

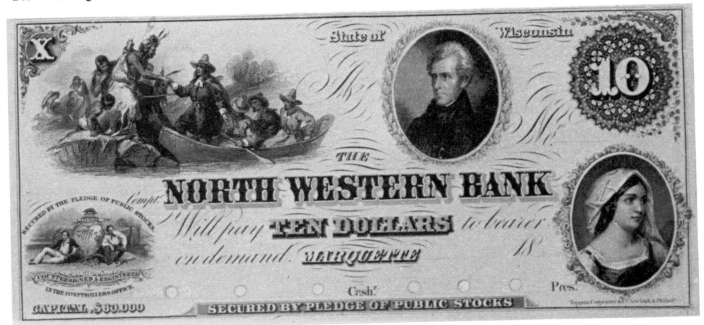

| G8 | $10 | ___18__; 185_s ___TC. L-LC: Landing of Roger Williams. RC: Jackson. Capital: $60,000. No overprint. | R-7 |
| G8b | $10 | ___185_: 1858-61 TC, (ABNCo. mono). As above, except for capital ($100,000) and probably imprint. | R-7 |

Uncut Sheet

| X1 | | $5, 10 TC. G6, 8 | R-7 |

MARSHFIELD

WI-436   C.M. UPHAM & BRO.

| 5 | 25¢ | February 1, 1879. Black. | R-7 |

WI-437   UPHAM MANUFACTURING CO.

| 1 | 5¢ | January 1, 1886. Black. Green and red rev. | R-7 |

JOHN H. RUSSELL, engineer, Marshfield, was born in Canada, February 1, 1833. In 1834, his father moved to Clarence Hollow, Erie Co., N. Y., where they lived until 1845, when they removed to Westfield, Chautauqua Co., N.Y. Then to Milton, Rock Co., Wis., in 1848. Lived there three years; then moved to Dakota, Waushara Co. At the age of twenty-three, he learned engineering. Has followed this business at Madison and Milwaukee. In 1877, he went to farming, in Clark County, which he followed four years, and in the Fall of 1880 came to Marshfield as engineer for Upham & Bro. He was married April 2, 1858, to Miss Mary Ann Reifsnider. They have seven children - Fred, Mary, John, Hilda, Jessie, Vincie and Neva.

WILLIAM H. UPHAM, lumberman, Marshfield, was born in Westminster, Mass., May 3, 1842. After the death of his father, Alvin Upham, the family moved, in 1851, to Racine, Wis. His mother died in 1878. He received his common and high school education at Racine. In April, 1861, he enlisted in Co. F, of the 2d Wis. I.; was badly wounded (shot through the left lung) at the first battle of Bull Run, July 21, 1861; was taken prisoner and confined in the old tobacco-factory prison at Richmond, until March, 1862, the week of the "Monitor fight." He was appointed by Pres. Lincoln, in June, a cadet to West Point. He was graduated in the class of 1866. Was officer of the guard over Jeff. Davis, while prisoner at Fortress Monroe, and received the appointment of first lieutenant of artillery. He resigned his position in the army, in November, 1869, and soon after went to Kewaunee, Wis., where he remained about a year; then, in partnership with his brother, C. M. Upham, engaged in the manufacture of lumber at Angelica, Shawano Co., Wis. There this firm continued in business until in 1878, when they bought lands and built mills and a store, and transferred their business to Marshfield. Mr. W. H. Upham was married December 19, 1867, to Miss Mary C. Kelly, daughter of James H. Kelly, Esq., of Racine. They have two children, Elsie and Carrie. Mr. Upham is one of the corporators and the business manager of the proposed Neillsville & Marshfield Railroad. He has furnished a room and started a public library and reading room. This library has been largely increased by a donation of books from Mr. J. J. Marsh of Haverhill, Mass., for whom the town was named.

From the *History of Northern Wisconsin*, 1881.

MENASHA

WI-438   **CHANGE TICKET**

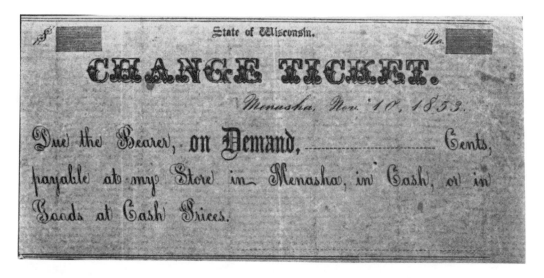

SC 0   – cents November 10, 1853. Black.   R-7

MENOMONEE

WI-435   MENOMONEE BANK, 1858-62

Closed.

| G2 | $1 | ___18__: ____ TC. No overprint. | | R-7 |
| G2a | $1 | ___18__: (1850s) TC. As above, except for ornate red 1 overprint. | Remainder | R-6 |

| G4 | $2 | ___18__: ____ TC. No overprint. | R-7 |
| G4a | $2 | ___18__: 1850s TC. As above, except for red overprint. | R-7 |

| G6 | $3 | ___18__: ____ TC. C: Dr. Kane's Arctic Expedition. No overprint. | R-7 |
| G6a | $3 | ___18__: 1850s TC. As above, except for red overprint. | R-7 |

| G8 | $5 | ___18__: 1850s TC. No overprint. | R-7 |
| G8a | $5 | ___18__: 1850s TC. As above, except for red overprint. | R-7 |

Uncut Sheet

1X $1, 2, 3, 5 TC. G2, 4, 6, 7

MENOMONIE

WI-337   KNAPP, STOUT & COMPANY

SC 1   5¢   Undated. ML&E. Black with overall green underprint   R-7
                    (very faint on circulated specimens. Brown reverse.

SC 1a   5¢   As above but surcharged in orange "Payable only at the
                    place of business in Dunn and Barron Counties, Wis."

SC 2   10¢   Undated. ML&E. Black with overall green underprint   R-7
                    (very faint on circulated specimens. Brown reverse.

SC 2a   10¢   As above but surcharged in orange "Payable only at the
                    place of business in Dunn and Barron Counties, Wis."

SC 5	25¢	Undated. ML&E. Black with overall green underprint very faint on circulated specimens. Brown reverse.	R-7
SC 5a	25¢	As above but surcharged in orange "Payable only at the place of business in Dunn and Barron Counties, Wis."	R-7
SC 5g	25¢	As SC 5 but with printed signature of company and payable in cull lumber, Plain Rev.	

SC 6	50¢	Undated. ML&E. Black with overall green underprint very faint on circulated specimens. Brown reverse.	
SC 6a	50¢	As above but surcharged in orange "Payable only at the place of business in Dunn and Barron Counties, Wis."	
SC 6g	50¢	As SC 6 but surcharged with printed signature of the company. Plain rev.	R-7
SC 7	$1	Undated. ML&E. Black with overall green underprint very faint on circulated specimens. Brown reverse.	R-7
SC 7a	$1	Undated. B/W ML&E.	R-7

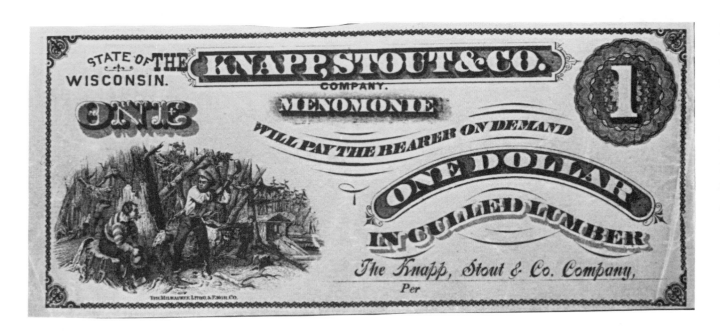

SC 7b	$1	As above, but with printed signature of company and payable in cull lumber, Plain Rev.	R-7
SC 8	$2	Undated. ML&E. Black with overall green underprint very faint on circulated specimens. Brown reverse.	R-7
SC 8a	$2		R-7

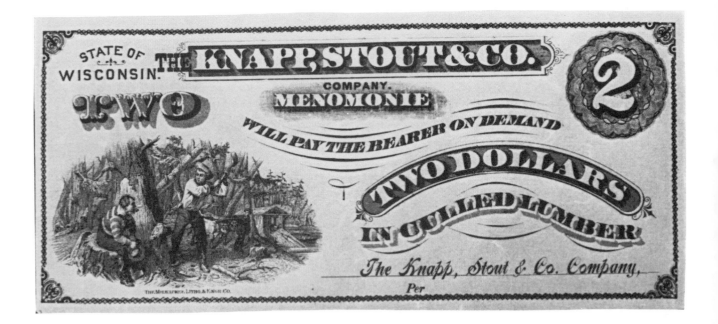

| SC 8b | $2 | As above, but with printed signature of company and payable in cull lumber, Plain Rev. | R-7 |
| SC 9 | $3 | Undated. ML&E. Black with overall green underprint very faint on circulated specimens. Brown reverse. | R-7 |

SC 9a $3   As above, but with printed signature of company.

SC 10 $5   R-7

SC 10a $5   As above, but with printed signature of company and   R-7
                  payable in Cull Lumber. See appendix for history of
                  Knapp Stout & Co Company. Also see Prairie Farm &
                  Rice Lake.

Cull Lumber notes were printed in sheets of three vertical notes of 1, 1, 1 and 2, 2 & 5. A sheet of 25¢
notes of three vertical notes has also been observed, as has a sheet of two 50¢ & two 25¢ horizontal.

Uncut Sheet

                                                                                 F-7

A sheet of two 50¢ and two 25¢.

A sheet of three 25¢ vertical is known to exist.

A sheet of three $1.00 vertical is known to exist.

A sheet of three $2.00, $2.00 and $5.00 is known to exist.

All are payable in Cull Lumber.

A sheet of three 7B $1.00 vertical is known to exist.

A sheet of three 2/8B & 10B vertical is known to exist.

MILLVILLE

WI-440   **WISCONSIN VALLEY BANK, 1858-61**

Capital $100,000. A. W. Balch, Pres., Henry D. Patcher, cashier (1858); A. L. Bostedo, cashier (1859).
Later location: Weyauwega (moved in 1859).
Failed 1861. Redeemed notes at 77¢ per dollar in 1862. Outstanding circulation 1863 $935.

Located in Grant County on the south side of the Wisconsin River midway between Mount Hope and the river, from whence it took its title.

G2a $5   July 1, 1857 WH&W. Tint: Red microlettering overall, counters & outlining white V V.   R-7

| G4a | $10 | July 1, 1857 WH&W. Tint: Red microlettering overall, counters & outlined white X. | R-7 |

Uncut Sheet

| X1 | | $5, 10 WH&W. G2a, 4a | R-7 |

WI-441   **BOOTH & MAYNARD**

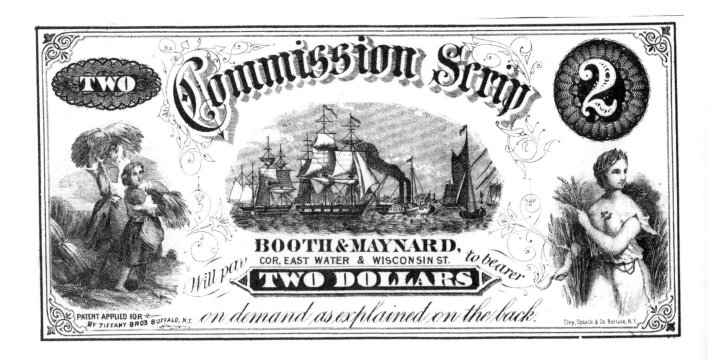

| SC 8 | $2 | Commission Scrip. | R-7 |

MILWAUKEE

WI-445   BANK OF COMMERCE, 1854-ca.58

Capital $100,000. G. W. Peckham, Pres., Joseph S. Colt, cashier.
Closed prior to 1862.
Also see Mechanics Bank, Superior, WI-780.

Closed.

G2	$1	___18__: (1850s) RWH&E. No overprint.	R-7
G2a	$1	___18__: 1850s RWH&E. As above, except for red ONE overprint.	R-7

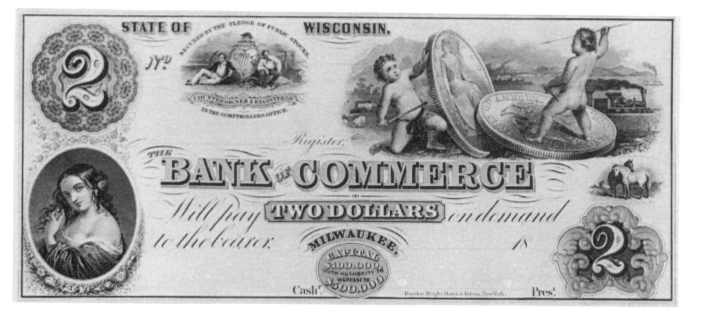

G4	$2	___18__: (1850s) RWH&E. No overprint.1850s	R-7
G4a	$2	___18__: 1850s RWH&E. As above, except for red TWO overprint.	R-7

| G6 | $5 | ___18__: (1850s) RWH&E. No overprint. | R-7 |
| G6a | $5 | ___18__: 1850s RWH&E. As above, except for red FIVE overprint. | R-6 |

Uncut Sheet

| X1 | | $1, 1, 2, 5 RWH&E. G2, 2, 4, 6 | R-7 |

WI-450   **EXCHANGE BANK OF WM. J. BELL & CO., 1854-ca.55**

Capital $50,000. W. J. Bell, Pres.; J. B. Kellog, cashier.
Fate: closed.

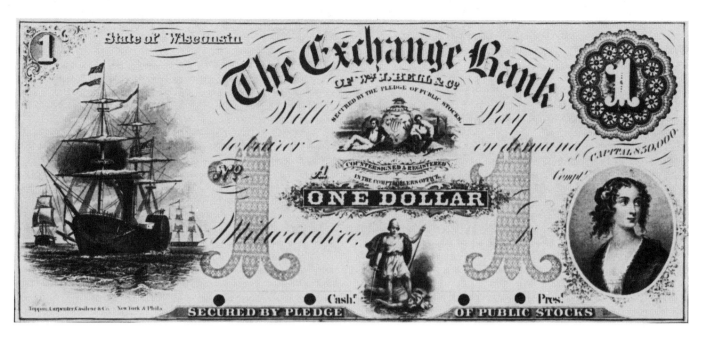

G2a $1   ___18__:____ TCC. Overprint: Red 1 1.   R-7

G4a $2   ___18__:____ TC. Overprint: Red TWO.   R-7

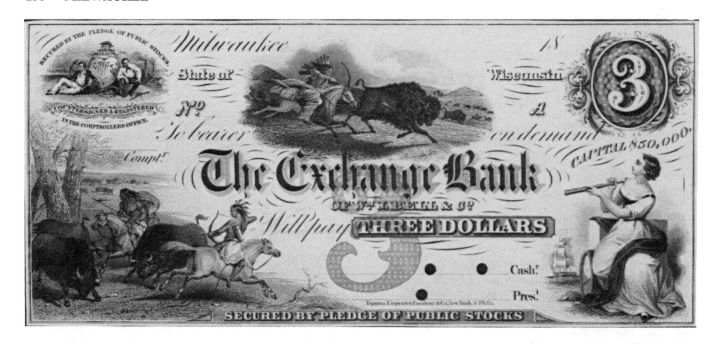

G6a $3   ___18__:___ TC. Overprint: Red 3.   R-7

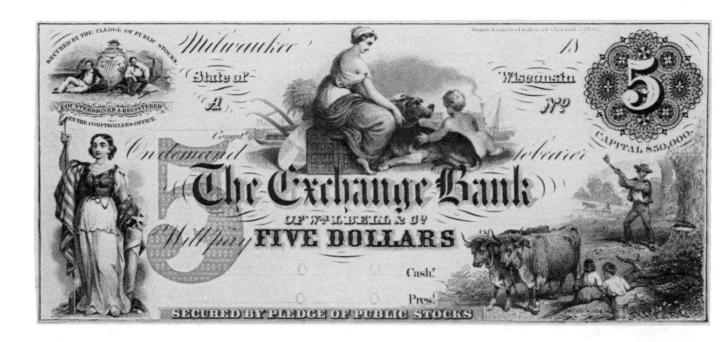

G8a $5   ___18__:___ TC. Overprint: Red 5.   R-7

Uncut Sheet

X1 $1, 2, 3, 5 TC. G2a, 4a, 6a, 8a   R-7

WI-455   FARMERS & MILLERS BANK, 1853-62

From July 1853 — *Bankers* magazine.

This new bank has at length received its strong box, and is ready to go on with business.

N. C. Cleveland, President. J. A. Hoover, V. Pres., C. D. Nash, cashier.

Its owners are the following gentlemen from abroad: Messrs. G. W. Peckham and S. H. Alden, late of Albany, N.Y. N. C. Cleveland of New York and C. D. Nash of Middlebury, Vermont, together with Mssrs. J. A. Hoover, J. W. Medbury and M. B. Medbury of this city. All of them persons of well established business reputation.

Capital 1853 $50,000; 1863 $250,000. Edward H. Brodhead, Pres., Hoel H. Camp, cashier (1863).

Organized 1853, Second Bank to organize under laws passed in November 1851. Became the Farmers & Millers Bank of Milwaukee, WI-460. Began with 10, 25 and 50¢ notes.

Genuine Notes, Raised Notes and Counterfeits

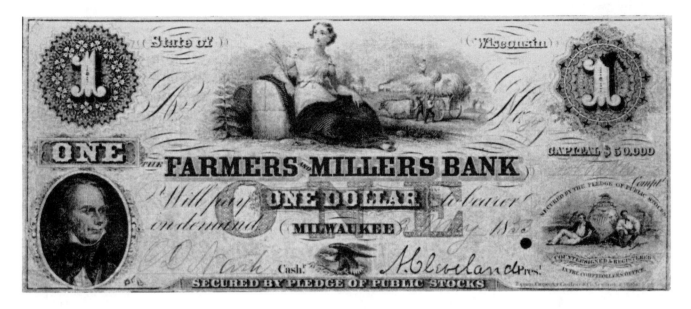

G2	$1	___18__:___ TCC. L: Clay. Capital: $50,000. No overprint.	R-7
G2a	$1	___18__: 1850s TCC. As above, except for red ONE overprint.	R-6
G2b	$1	___18__: 1850s TCC. Same as G2a, except for capital ($100,000).	R-7

G4	$2	___18__:____ TCC. Capital: $50,000. No overprint.	R-7
G4a	$2	___18__: 1850s TCC. As above, except for red TWO overprint.	R-7
G4b	$2	___18__: 1850s TCC. Same as G4a, except for capital ($100,000).	R-7

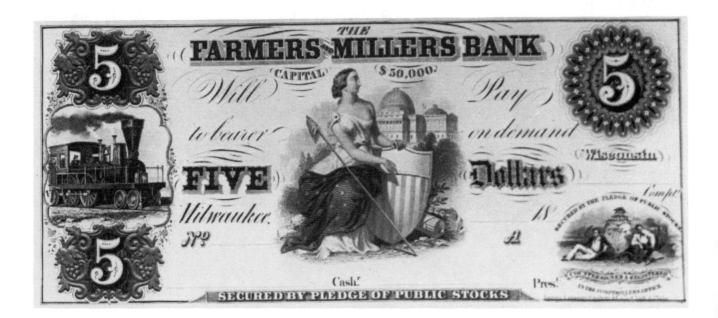

| G6 | $5 | ___18__:____ TCC. Capital: $50,000. No overprint. | R-7 |

| G6b | $5 | ___18__: 1850s TCC. As above, except for red 5 5 over-print. | R-6 |
| G6c | $5 | ___18__: 1850s TCC. Same as G6b, except for capital ($100,000). | R-6 |

| R3 | $5 | ___18__: 1850s TCC. Raised from $1, G2a. | R-6 |
| R5 | $10 | ___18__: (1850s) TCC. Raised from $1, G2. The bank issued no $10s. | R-7 |

Uncut Sheet

X1 $1, 1, 2, 5 TCC   R-7

Altered, Spurious and Unattributed Non-Genuine Notes

A5 $3   ___18__; 1840s DS&H. SH&D. Altered from $3 Farmers   R-6
                   and Millers Bank of Hagerstown, MD-235-G12.

WI-460   **FARMERS AND MILLERS BANK OF MILWAUKEE, 1862-63**

Formerly Farmers and Millers Bank, Milwaukee, WI-455.

Became the First National Bank of Milwaukee #64 — recharter #2715 then reclaimed #64. Predecessor today — 1st Wisconsin Bank, just renamed First Star.

SC 2   10¢   Pay to Bearer, blue & light brown underprint with JN & Co dropped out. (John Mazr & Co) LL.

SC 5   25¢   Pay to the Bearer. Green. October 22, 1862. LL.   R-7

SC   50¢   Pay to the Bearer. Black with light LL. Brown underprint with the initials J. N. & Co. dropped out (John Mazn Co).   R-7

G2a $1   ___18__: 1862 TCC, ABNCo. mono. Overprint: Red ONE.   R-6

G6c $5   November 1, 1862 ABN. No overprint.   R-7

G6d $5   November 1, 1862 ABN. As above, except for red over-   R-7
                 print.

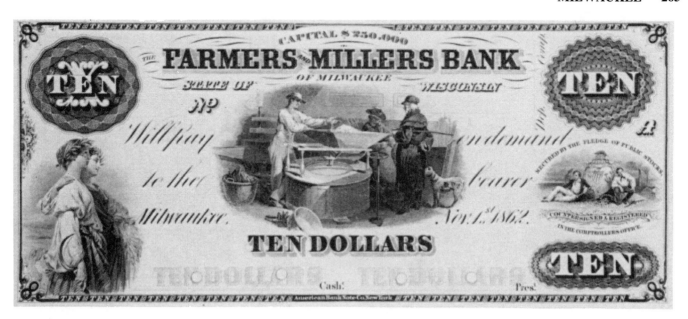

| G8 | $10 | November 1, 1862 ABN. No overprint. | R-7 |

| G8a | $10 | November 1, 1862 ABN. As above, except for red overprint. | R-7 |

Uncut Sheet

| X1 | | $5, 10 ABN. G6c, 8 | R-7 |

WI-465   GERMANIA BANK OF G. PAPENDICK & CO., 1854-55

Capital $50,000. Geo. Papendick, Pres., Ch. H. Papendick, cashier (1854). Suspended business in 1854 and resumed the same year.
Liquidated in 1859. Held $25 in specie for redemption of notes.

G2 $1   ___18__: (1850s) TCC. L: Washington.   R-7

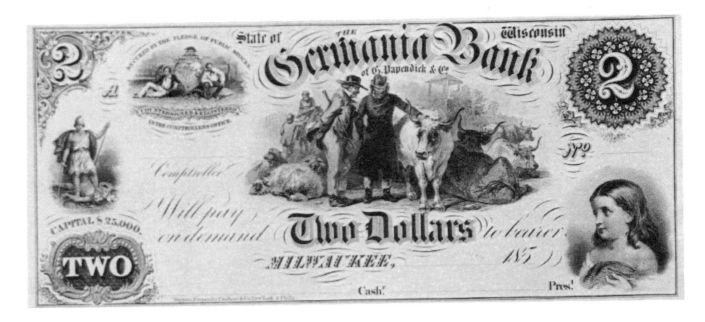

G4 $2   ___18__: (1850s) TCC.   R-7

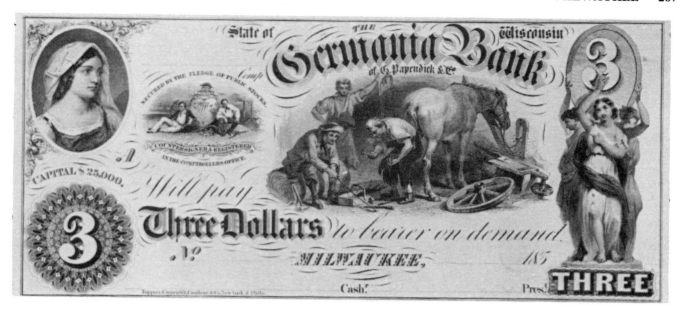

G6 $3 ___18__: (1850s) TCC. R-7

G8 $5 ___18__: (1850s) TCC. R-7

Uncut Sheet

X1 $1, 2, 3, 5 TCC. G2, 4, 6, 8 R-7

WI-470   GLOBE BANK, 1857-58

Cash capital $125,000. Asabel Finch Jr. Pres., William R. Freeman, cashier.
Relinquished business in 1858. Notes redeemed until October 22, 1860. $100 in specie held in 1860 further redemption.

G2a $1   ___18__: (1857-58) TC. L: Atlas kneeling holding globe on   R-7
                        shoulders. Tint: Red lathework overall and panel of
                        microlettering with outlined white ONE.

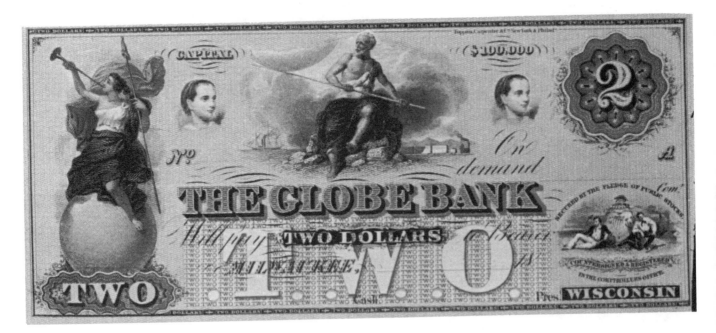

G4a $2   ___18__: (1857-58) TC. C: Archimedes raising globe with   R-7
                        lever. Tint: Red lathework overall and panel of micro-
                        lettering with outline white TWO.

Uncut Sheet

X1 $1, 2 TC. G2a, 4a   R-7

***WI-475*   HEMENWAY'S BANK OF DEPOSITE & EXCHANGE, ca. 1849**

Fate probably failed.

Only certificates of deposit, dated 1849, are known from this bank.

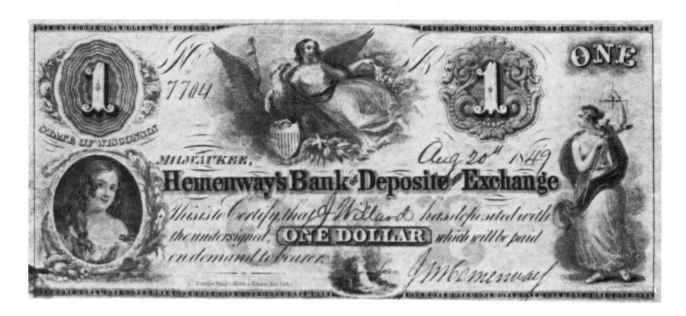

G2 $1   ___18__: 1849 RWH&E.   R-4

G4 $2   ___18__: 1849 RWH&E.   R-4

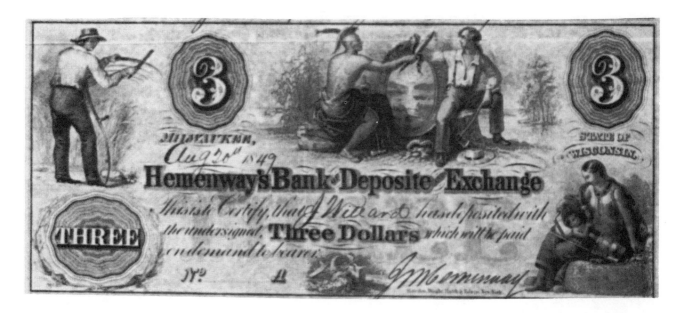

G-6 $3   ___18__: 1849 RWH&E.   R-4

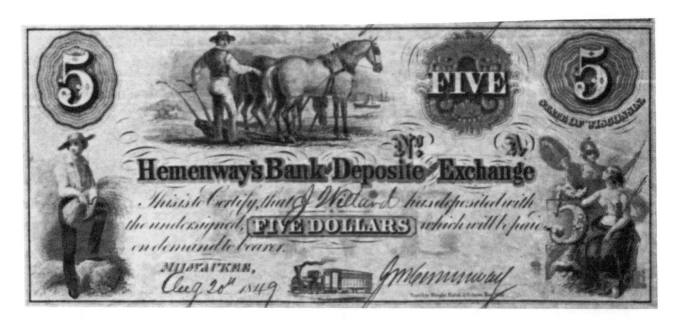

G-8 $5   ___18__: 1849 RWH&E.   R-4

Uncut Sheets

X1   G2, 3, 5, 8 $1, 2, 3, 5 RWH&E   Remainder   R-7

WI-480   JUNEAU BANK, 1857-65

Commenced business – August 24th, 1857. Capital $25,000, one-half of which is owned by Eastern Capitalists and Bankers; the other half is owned in Milwaukee. James B. Cross, Pres., Samuel B. Scott, cashier.

1863 capital $200,000. Anthony Green, Pres., James A. Pirie (1865). Elected Pres. and cashier of National City Bank of Milwaukee. Succeeded by National City Bank (#1483) org., in July, commenced business August 1st, 1865. Date of vol. liquidation February 24th, 1875.

G2	$1	___18__: late 1850s TC. C: Juneau. Tint: Red-orange lathework overall with an outlining white ONE.	R-6
G2a	$1	___18__: 1860s ABN. As above, except for imprint.	R-7

G4	$5	___18__: (late 1850s) TC. LC: Juneau. Tint: Red-orange lathework overall with an outlined large white 5.	R-7
G4a	$5	___18__: (1860s) ABN. As above, except for imprint. Remainder	R-6

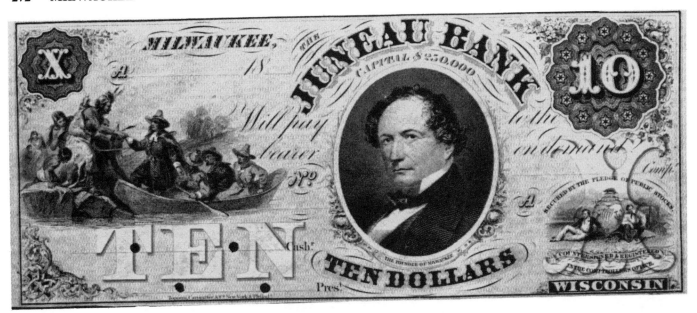

| G6 | $10 | ___18__: (late 1850s) TC. L: Landing of Roger Williams. RC: Juneau. Tint: Red-orange lathework overall with outlined white TEN and X. | | R-7 |
| G6a | $10 | ___18__: (1860s) ABN. As above, except for imprint. | Remainder | R-6 |

Uncut Sheets

| X1 | $1, 1 TC. G2, 2 | R-7 |
| X2 | $5, 10 TC. G4, 6 | R-7 |

SOLOMON JUNEAU — Was born August 9, 1793, in the parish of L'Assumption, Canada. In 1818, as clerk for his father-in-law, Jacques Vieux (or Vieau), a French fur trader, who at that date had a trading-post in an Indian village at the site of the present city of Milwaukee, he entered the mouth of the Milwaukee river in a Mackinaw boat for the first time, and here he continued to reside, although not the first white resident, until after 1846. At that date — 1818 — there were no white persons outside this immediate locality, residing in what is now the state of Wisconsin, nearer than at the head of Green bay, in the present Brown county. A few years after his arrival, Juneau left the employment of his father-in-law, and commenced business for himself. After the death of his neighbor, John Baptiste Soloman. Juneau remained the only white resident of the place as late as the year 1833, when Americans began to arrive and take up their abode there. He continued to reside in Milwaukee, rearing a family of fourteen children, thirteen being born there. He was at one time a large proprietor of the site of the city. When, in 1835, a post-office was established there, he was appointed postmaster, holding the office for nine years. In 1846, when Milwaukee became a city, he was chosen the first mayor. Shortly afterward he removed to Dodge county. He died November 14, 1856.

From *Historical Atlas of Wisconsin*, 1878.

WI-447   CHAS. BIGELOW

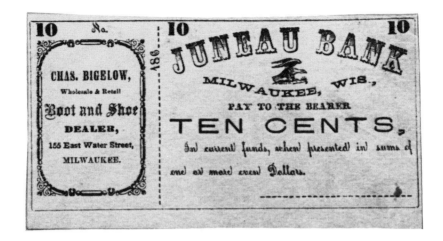

SC 2   10¢ $ undated.   R-7

WI-493   D. P. KENT

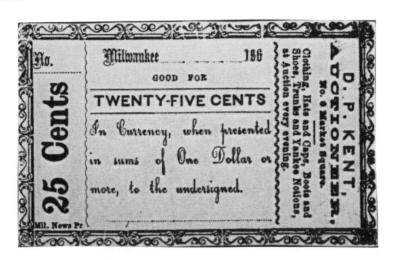

SC 5   25¢   ___18__: ____ MNP Black.

SC 6   50¢   ___18__: ____ MNP Black.   R-7

WI-485   MARINE BANK, 1856-59

Capital $50,000. J. A. Hoover, Pres., J. H. Skidmore, cashier.
Closed prior to 1860. $2,844 specie held in 1860 for redemption of notes amounting to a like figure, expired April 18, 1863.

Genuine Notes, Raised Notes and Counterfeits

| G2 | $1 | ___18__: (1850s) TC. No overprint. | R-7 |
| G2a | $1 | ___18__: (1850s) TC. As above, except for red ONE overprint. | R-6 |

| G4 | $2 | ___18__: (1850s) TC. No overprint. | R-7 |
| G4a | $2 | ___18__: (1850s) TC. As above, except for red 2 2 overprint. | R-6 |

G6	$5	___18__: (1850s) TC. No overprint.	R-7
G6a	$5	___18__: (1850s) TC. As above, except for red 5 5 overprint.	R-6
S10	$5	(1850s) Unknown. C: steamer. Lacks state die.	R-7
S15	$5	(1850s) Unknown. C: woman with sheaf.	R-7
S20	$10	(1850s) Unknown. C: woman with sheaf.	R-7
S25	$10	(1850s) Unknown. C: steamer. Lacks state die.	R-7
S30	$20	(1850s) Unknown. C: woman with sheaf.	R-7

Uncut Sheet

| X1 | | $1, 1, 2, 5 TC. G2, 2, 4, 6 | R-6 |

Altered, Spurious and Unattributed Non-Genuine Notes

| S5 | $3 | (1850s) Unknown. C: steamer. Lacks state die. | R-7 |

WI-487   **MARINERS BANK**

SC 5   50¢   Promise to pay. Black/with red surcharge, Milwaukee   R-7
                     November 9. '62.

MARINE AND FIRE INSURANCE CO.

See Mississippi Marine and Fire Insurance Co., Sinipee, WI-740.

WI-780   **MECHANICS BANK**

Moved to Milwaukee from Superior.

NOTE DATED AT MILWAUKEE

G6 $5   ABN. Same as Superior G2, except for city & possibly   R-7
                     date.

WI-490   **MERCHANTS BANK, 1862-65**

Capital $50,000. E. H. Goodrich, Pres., S. P. Scott, cashier.
Became the Merchants National Bank in July 1865 #1438 and liquidated June 1870.

| G2a | $5 | July 1, 1862 NBN. Tint: Green. Back: Green. | R-7 |
| G4a | $5 | July 1, 1862 NBN. Tint: Green. Back: Green. Note similarity to G2a. Capital: $50,000. | R-7 |

| G6a | $10 | April 1, 1863 NBN. Tint: Green. Back: Green. Capital: $100,000. | R-6 |

Uncut Sheets

X1		$5, 5 NBN. G2a, 2a	R-7
X2		$5, 5 NBN. G4a, 4a	R-7
X3		$10, 10 NBN. G6a, 6a	R-7

WI-495   BANK OF MILWAUKEE (1st), 1836-39

Territorial bank.
Never opened because of opposite views by two Board of Directors, which accounts for two distinct type of notes.

DEMAND NOTES

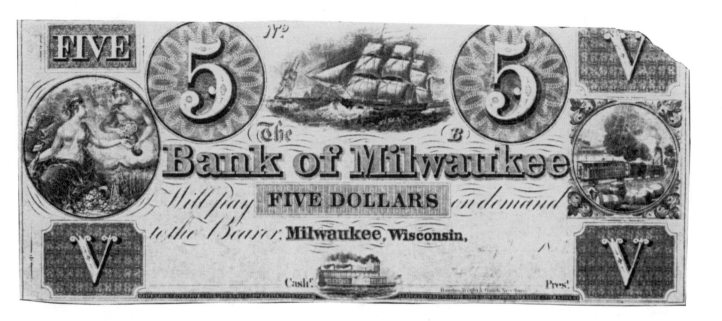

G2 $5   ___18__: (1830s) RW&H.   Remainder   R-3

G4 $5   ___18__: (late 1830s) Durand.   R-7

G6 $5   ___18__: SH&D, DS&H.   Remainder   R-6

G8 $5   ___18__: (1830s).   R-6

G12 $10 ___18__: (1830s).   R-7

G13 $10 ___18__: (1830s) RW&H.   R-7

G14 $10   ___18__: (1830s) Durand.   RW&H   R-7 Ill

G16 $20   ___18__: (1830s) RW&H.   NDA   R-7

G18 $20   ___18__: (1830s) TP. C: plowing scene, in oval; white   R-7
                  woman std. with left hand on shoulder of stdg. Indian
                  male; beehive, in oval. L: XX/men and rowboat/XX. R:
                  20/two men reaping/20. BS: anchor, etc.

G20 $50   ___18__: (1830s TP. C: L; Hebe std. pouring drink for   R-7
                  eagle at left. L: L: 50/woman stdg. bowl of fruit above
                  shield bearing anchor at rt./50. R: 50/farmer stdg.
                  holding grain/50. BS: anchor and implements.

G24 $100   ___18__: (1830s) TP. L: Samson slaying lion. R: Washing-   R-7
                         ton at Dorchester Heights, 1775.

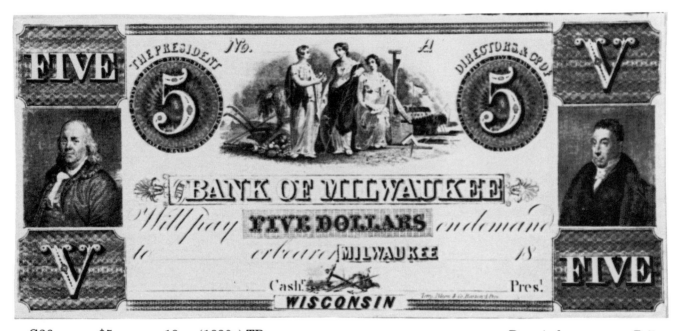

G26 $5   ___18__: (1830s) TP.   Remainder   R-5

| G28 | $10 | ___18__: (1830s) RW&H. C: 10; Moneta std. receiving bag of coin from Mercury in clouds at rt. griffin on chest at left; 10. L: X/train, in circle/10. R: X/canal scene (?), in circle/10. BS: sailing ship. | Remainder | R-5 |

WI-500   **BANK OF MILWAUKEE (2nd), 1855-65**

Capital $100,000. Charles D. Mosh, Pres., Wm. G. Fetch, cashier (1863). T. R. B. Eldridge had been cashier in 1857.

Organized 1854 was 3rd bank to be granted charter after banking was legalized in November 1851. Became the National Exchange Bank of Milwaukee in April 1865. Merged with the Marine National Bank in 1930 & became the Marine National Exchange Bank.

Genuine Notes, Raised Notes and Counterfeits

G2	$1	January 2, 1855 TC. Capital: $50,000. No overprint.		R-7
G2a	$1	January 2, 1855 TC. As above, except for red ONE overprint.		R-7
G2b	$1	January 2, 1855 TC. As above, except for capital ($100,000).		R-7
G2c	$1	January 2, 1855 TC. As above, except for capital ($200,000).		R-7
G2d	$1	January 2, 1855 TC, ABNCo. mono. As above, except for capital ($300,000) and imprint	Remainder	R-6

| G4 | $2 | January 2, 1855 TC. Capital: $50,000. No overprint. | Signed Note | R-6 |

| R4 | $3 | January 2, 1855 TC. Raised from $1, G2 or another variety. | | R-7 |

G6	$5	January 2, 1855 TC. L: Santa Claus visiting sleeping children. Capital: $50,000. No overprint.		R-7
G6a	$5	January 2, 1855 TC. As above, except for red FIVE overprint.		R-7
G6b	$5	January 2, 1855 TC. As above, except for capital ($100,000).		R-7
G6c	$5	January 2, 1855 TC. As above, except for capital ($200,000).		R-7
G6d	$5	January 2, 1855 TC, ABNCo. mono. As above, except for capital ($300,000) and imprint.	Remainder Signed Note	R-6 R-6
R6	$5	January 2, 1855 TC. Raised from $1, G2 or another variety.		R-7

G8	$10	___18__: (1860s) NBN. Tint: Green border, large TEN, etc. Capital $150,000.	Remainder	R-6
R8	$10	January 2, 1855 TC. Raised from $1, G2 or another variety.		R-7

G10	$20	___18__: (1860s) NBN. Tint: Green border ctr. panel. etc. Capital: $150,000.	Remainder	R-6
R10	$20	January 2, 1855 TC. Raised from $1, G2 or another variety.		R-7

Uncut Sheet

X1		$1, 1, 2, 5 TC. G2, 2, 4, 6		R-7
2		10¢ Seifert		R-7

SC 2   10¢   Pennsylvania Oil Company. Blue. HS.   R-7

SC 3   15¢   Pennsylvania Oil Company. Blue. HS.   R-7

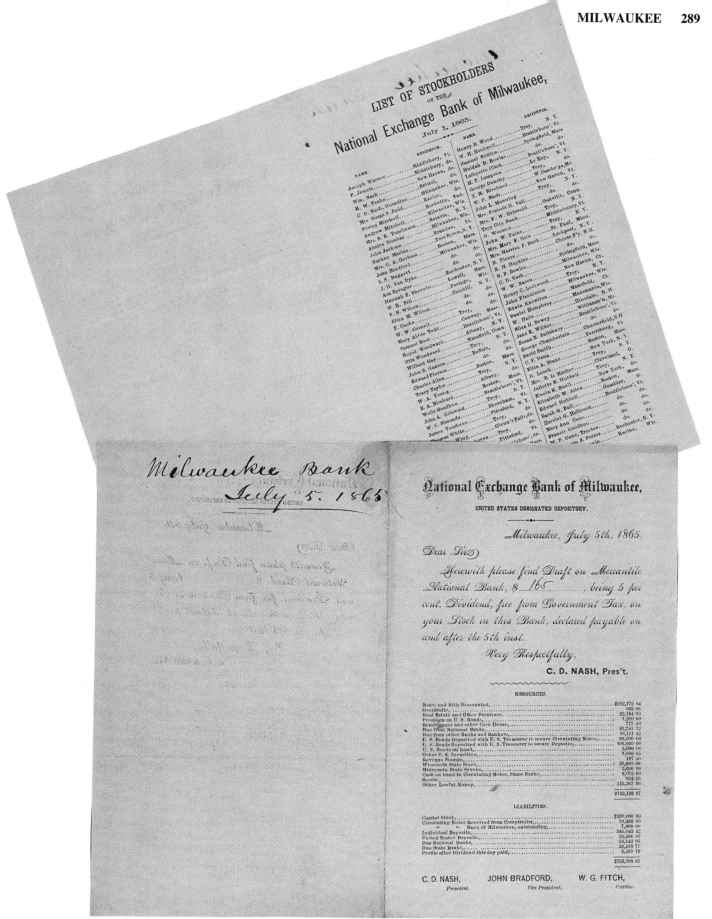

Bank of Milwaukee statement and list of stockholders as of July 1, 1865, after having become a National Bank in April 1865. Only John Bradford, S.S. Daggett, H.H. Van Dyhe, W.G. Fitch, C.D. Nash, John Plankington hailed from Milwaukee. The latter three were all very prominent in Milwaukee Banking circles.

WI-505   **MILWAUKEE BANK, 1858**

Might not have opened.

Genuine Notes, Raised Notes and Counterfeits

G2 $1   ___18__: (1855) RWH&E.   R-7

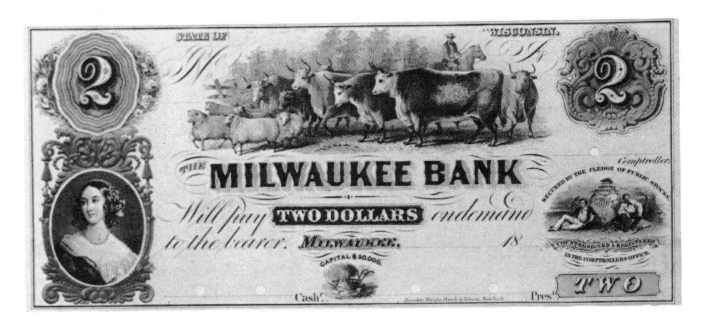

G4 $2   ___18__: (1855) RWH&E.   R-7

G6 $3   ___18__: (1855) RWH&E.   Remainder   R-6

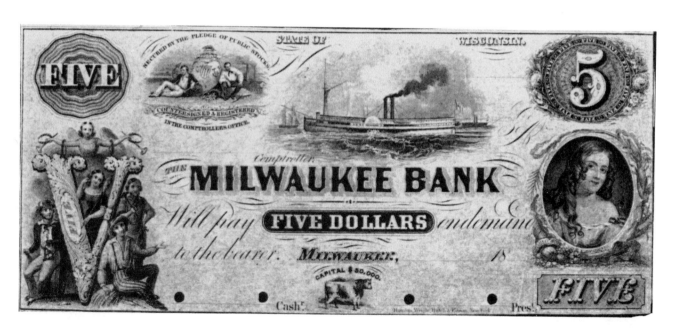

G8 $5   ___18__: (1855) RWH&E.   Remainder   R-6

Uncut Sheet

X1 $1, 2, 3, 5 RWH&E. G2, 4, 6, 8   R-7

WI-506   **MILWAUKEE BUSINESS UNIVERSITY, Milwaukee, Wis.**

15        $500   College Currency.   R-7

WI-510   MILWAUKEE CITY BANK, ca.1856

Probably never opened.

The plate was officially altered to the Forest City Bank, Waukesha, WI-830.

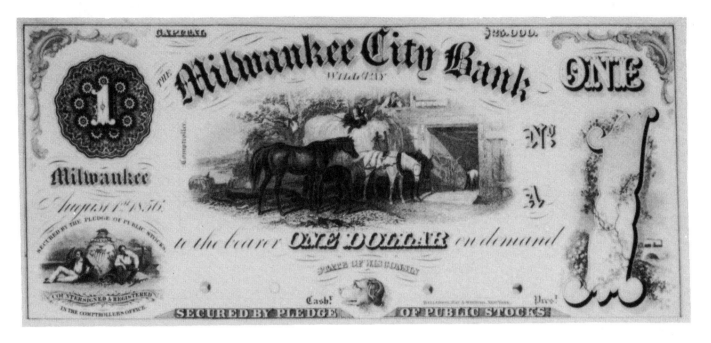

G2 $1   August 1, 1856 WH&W.   R-7

G4 $2   August 1, 1856 WH&W.   R-7

| G6 | $3 | August 1, 1856 WH&W. | R-7 |

Uncut Sheet

| X1 | | $1, 1, 2, 3 WH&W.G2, 2, 4, 6 | R-7 |

WI-515   **MILWAUKEE COUNTY BANK, 1862-ca.65**

Capital $50,000. John Armstrong, Pres., J. L. Spink, cashier (1862). Louis Scheffer, cashier (1865). Formerly Banking House of Armstrong, Spink & Co.
Closed.

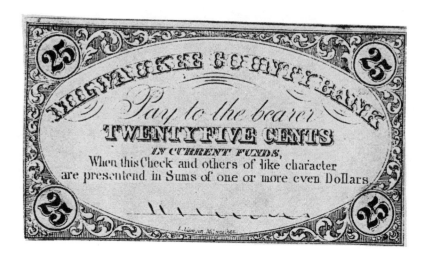

SC 5   25¢   Payable to the Bearer Black. LL.   R-7

G2 $5   September 1, 1862 ABN. Tint: Green end & ctr. panels,   Remainder   R-6
                  ornate V V etc.

| G4 | $10 | September 1, 1862 ABN. C: View of Niagara Falls. Tint: Green border, panel at left & large ctr. die. | Remainder | R-6 |

Uncut Sheet

| X1 | | $5, 10 ABN. G2, 4 | | R-7 |

WI-516   MILWAUKEE LOAN & EXCHANGE OFFICE

SC 1   5¢   John Taylor or Bearer. November 1, 1862.   R-7

WI-517   MILWAUKEE TELEPHONE EXCHANGE

SC 2   10¢   Good for one conversation, cardboard.   R-7

WI-518   NATIONAL EXCHANGE BANK, 1854

Issued no State Bank notes but merged with the Marine Bank in 1865 and became the National
Exchange Bank of Milwaukee in April 1865.

WI-525   PEOPLE'S BANK OF HAERTEL, GREENLEAF & COMPANY, 1854-58

Capital $25,000. H. Haertel, Pres., E. B. Greenleaf, cashier.
Liquidated 1859. $805 specie held for redemption of a like amount of notes until March 12, 1862.

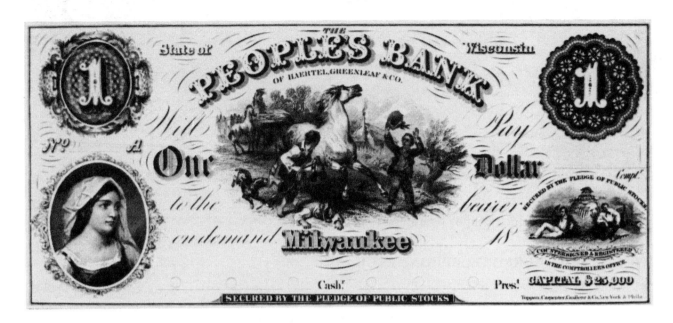

| G2 | $1 | ___18__: ____ TCC. No overprint. | R-7 |
| G2a | $1 | ___18__: mid 1850s TCC. As above, except for red over-print. | R-7 |

G4	$2	___18__: ____ TCC. No overprint.	R-7
G4a	$2	___18__: mid-1850s TCC. As above, except for red over-print.	R-7
G6	$2	___18__: ____ TCC. No overprint.	R-7

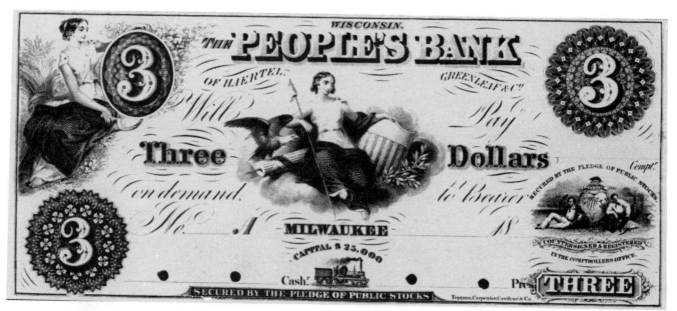

G6a $3   ___18__: (mid-1850s) TCC. As above, except for red 3 3   Remainder   R-6
               overprint.

Uncut Sheet

X1 $1, 1, 2, 3 TCC. G2, 2, 4, 6   R-7

WI-530   SECOND WARD BANK, 1956-64

Capital $25,000. A. C. Williams, Pres., W. H. Jacobs, cashier.
Failed 1862. Notes redeemed in gold at comptroller's office. In 1928 was Wisconsin's 2nd largest state bank. Taken over by First Wisconsin National Bank.

Genuine Notes, Raised Notes and Counterfeits

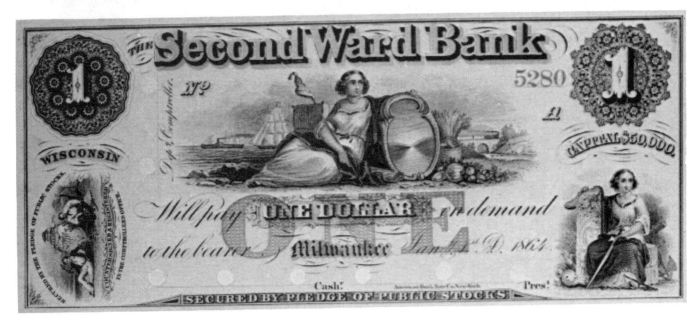

G2a	$1	___18__: (1850s) WH&W. Capital: $25,000. Overprint: Red ONE.		R-7
G2b	$1	January 1, 1864 ABN. As above, except for date, imprint, capital ($50,000), addition of "Dept. of" before "Comptroller" and style of overprint (thicker letters).	Remainder	R-6

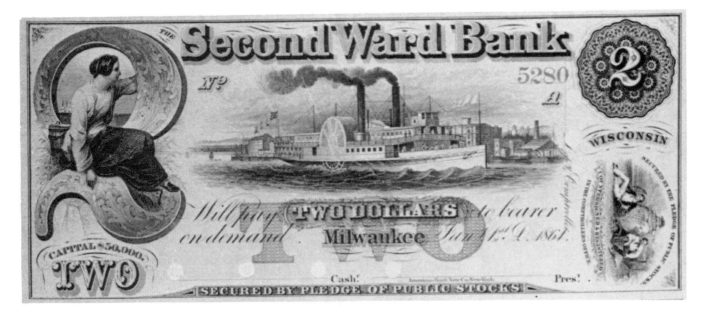

G4a	$2	___18__: (1850s) WH&W. Capital: $25,000; Overprint: Red TWO.		R-7
G4b	$2	January 1, 1864 ABN. As above, except for date, imprint, capital ($50,000), addition of "Dept. of" before "Comptroller" and style of overprint (thicker letters).	Remainder	R-6

G6a	$5	___18__: (1850s) WH&W. Capital: $25,000. Overprint: Red 5.		R-7
G6b	$5	January 1, 1864 ABN. As above, except for date, imprint, capital ($50,000), & addition of "Dept. of" before "Comptroller".	Remainder	R-6
R5	$5	___18__: 1850s WH&W. Raised from $1, G2.		R-7
R6	$10	___18__: 1850s WH&W. Raised from $1, G2. The bank issued no $10s.		R-7
R7	$20	___18__: 1850s WH&W. Raised from $1, G2. The bank issued no $20s.		R-7

Uncut Sheets

X1	$1, 1, 2, 5 WH&W. G2a, 2a, 4a, 6a	R-7
X2	$1, 1, 2, 5 ABN. G2b, 2b, 4b, 6b	R-7

SC 2	10¢	Pay to the Bearer. Green HS	R-7

SC 5	25¢	Pay to the Bearer black with solid pink underprint with Valentine Blatz dropped out. HS.	R-7

WI-335   **R. SUHM & CO.**

SC 5   25¢

R-7

WI-535   STATE BANK OF WISCONSIN, 1853-65

Capital 1853 $50,000. Eliphdlet Cramer, Pres., M. S. Scott, cashier (1853). Capital 1863 $250,000.
E. Cramer, Pres., T. L. Baker, cashier (1863).
Became the Milwaukee National Bank in April 1865. Liquidation 1912, and merged with the First Wisconsin National Bank.

Genuine Notes, Raised Notes and Counterfeits

| G2 | $1 | ___18__: ____ TCC.L: Webster. Capital: $150,000. No overprint. | R-7 |
| G2a | $1 | ___18__: 1850s TCC. As above, except for red overprint. | R-7 |

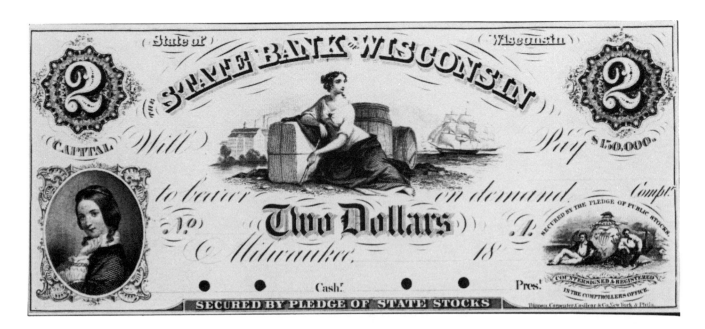

| G4 | $2 | ___18__: ____ TCC. Capital: $150,000. No overprint. | R-7 |
| G4a | $2 | ___18__: 1850s TCC. As above, except for red overprint. | R-6 |

G6	$5	___18__: ____ TCC. RC: Clay. Capital: $150,000. No overprint.	R-7
G6a	$5	___18__: 1850s TCC. As above, except for red overprint.	R-7
G6b	$5	___18__: (1850s) TCC. Same as G6a, except for capital ($100,000).	R-7
G6c	$5	September 17, 1862 (ABN). Same as G6b, except for date, probably imprint & capital ($250,000).	R-7

G8	$10	___18__: ___ TCC. Same as G8b, except for capital ($150,000) and lack of an overprint.	R-7
G8a	$10	___18__: 1850s TCC. As above, except has a red over-print.	R-7
G8b	$10	___18__: 1850s TCC. Same as G8a, except for capital ($100,000).	R-7
G8c	$10	September 17, 1862 (ABN). Same as G8b, except for date, probably imprint & capital ($250,000).	R-7
R5	$10	___18__: 1850s TCC. Raised from $1, G2.	R-7

Uncut Sheets

X1	$1, 2, 5, 10 TCC. G2, 4, 8	R-7
X2	$5, 10 TCC. G6a, 8a	R-7

WI-540   **UNION BANK, 1858-59**

Capital $50,000. W. F. Hubert, cashier.
Closed prior to 1860. In 1860 $566 of specie was held to redeem a like amount of notes.

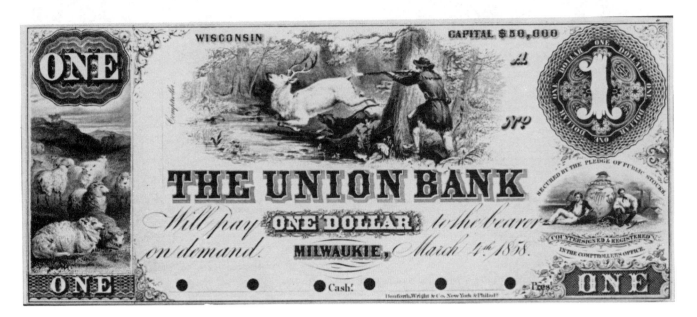

| G2 | $1 | March 4, 1858 DW. No overprint. | R-7 |
| G2a | $1 | March 4, 1858 DW. As above, except for red ONE overprint. | R-7 |

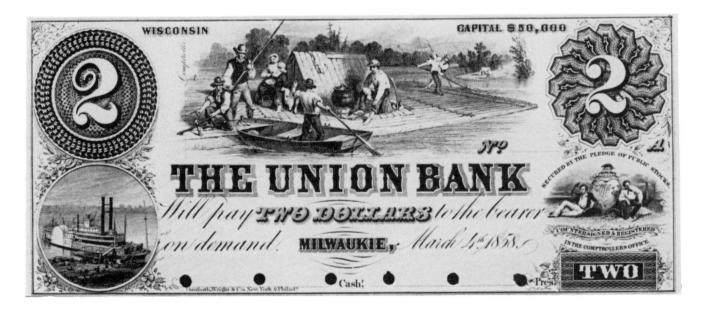

| G4 | $2 | March 4, 1858 DW. No overprint. | R-7 |
| G4a | $2 | March 4, 1858 DW. As above, except for red TWO overprint. | R-7 |

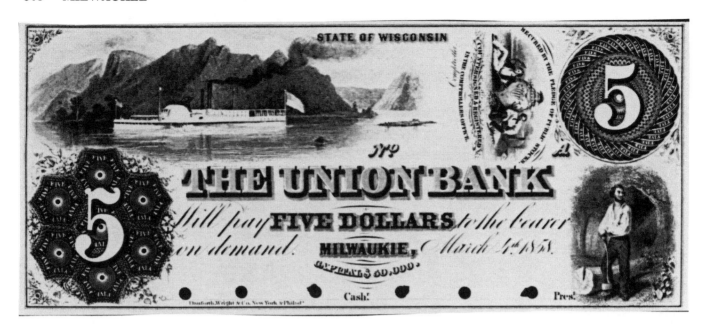

G6	$5	March 4, 1858 DW. No overprint.	R-7
G6a	$5	March 4, 1858 DW. As above, except for red 5 overprint.	R-7

Uncut Sheets

X1	$1, 1, 2, 5 DW. G2a, 2a, 4a, 6a	R-7
X2	$1, 1, 2, 5 DW. G2a, 2a, 4a, 6a	R-7

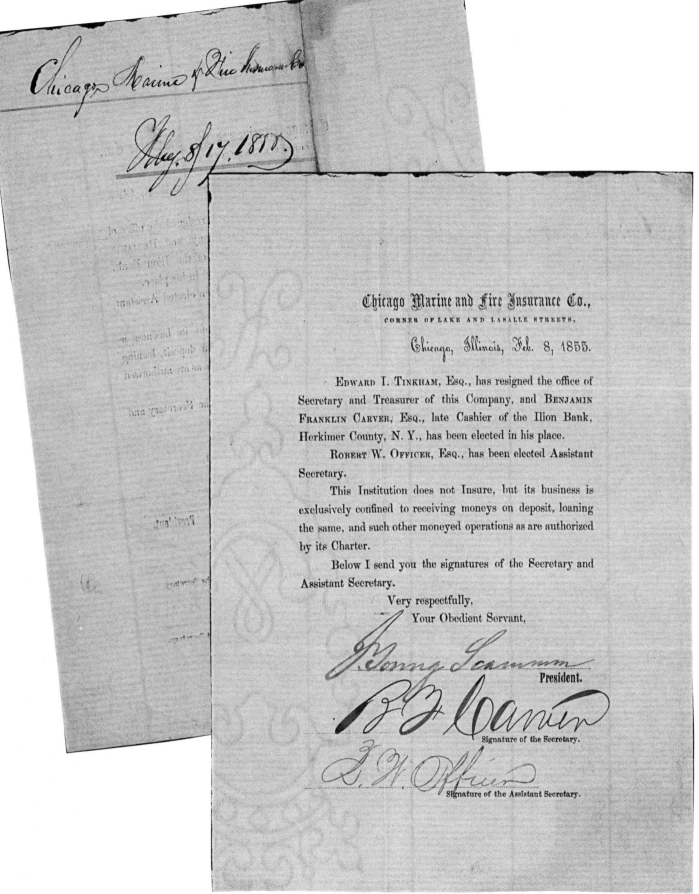

Note paragraph three which states that the bank is not in the insurance business, rather to receive and loan monies. The Chicago Marine & Insurance Co. were the owners of the Milwaukee Marine & Fire Insurance Co. namely Geo. Smith, Alex (Alexander) Mitchell, grandfather of Billy Mitchell of WWII Air Force fame and after which the Milwaukee airport is named.

WI-940 WISCONSIN MARINE & FIRE INS. CO., 1839-52

Issued only $147,000 worth of certificates of deposit, signed by Geo. Smith, Pres., A. A. Mitchell, cashier (1839). All redeemed at par. The rarest of all Wisconsin obsolete notes.

CERTIFICATES OF DEPOSIT

G2	$1	___18__: 1840s Unknown.	R-7

G4	$1	___18__: late 1840-early 50s RWH&E.	R-7
G6	$2	___18__: 1840s Unknown.	R-7
G8	$2	___18__: late 1840s-early 50s RWH&E.	R-7
C8	$2	___18__: late 1840s-early 50s RWH&E.	R-7

Courtesy Chicago Historical Society.

G9	$3	___18__; 1830s RWH&E.	R-7

C10 $5   ___18__: 1840s Unknown.   R-7

G16 $10   ___18__: late 1840s-early 50s RWH&E. C: std. with   R-7
                     stalks of grain in rt. hand, sheaf, plow & produce at
                     left, train in rt. bkgd. L: 10/farmer stdg. sharpening
                     scythe. R: TEN/Minerva stdg. looking to left, resting
                     shield on short column at rt. BS: steamship.

C16 $10   ___18__: late 1840s-early 50s RWH&E. Cft. of the above.   R-7

DEMAND NOTES

ALTERED, SPURIOUS AND OTHER NON-GENUINE NOTES

N5 $10   (1840s) Unknown. C: woman & cattle. L: Indian. R: R-7
                     woman with scales, bust of Washington & sword.

ALEXANDER MITCHELL — May correctly be called the representative of commercial interests in the West, having been long identified with its development, and intimately related to its prosperity. By strict fidelity to the laws of business, he has accumulated a wealth and a commercial status that has not an equal in the west, and but few in the United States. He was born in the Parish of Ellon, Scotland, October 18, 1817. His father was a prosperous farmer, and was regarded by his neighbors as a wise advisor and a just artibtrator, being frequently called upon for that purpose. Alexander received his common-school education. After this he began the study of law, at the same time giving some attention to Latin. Having continued this study about two years, he abandoned the idea of being a lawyer, and became a clerk in the bank at Peterhead. Here he was first initiated into the business in which he has in later days become so prominent. He came to America about 1839, as secretary of a Scottish joint-stock company, known as the Wisconsin Marine and Fire Insurance Company. He located in Milwaukee, which, at that time, had a population of about twelve hundred. He soon succeeded to the presidency of the company. His banking career in this country took shape in May, 1839, when he occupied a very indifferent building on Broadway, and did a fair little business. This, however, increased, and compelled him time and again to seek larger and more commodious quarters, until 1846, when he erected suitable buildings on the corner of East Water and Michigan streets. This was destroyed by fire in 1853, but was immediately rebuilt, and served his purpose until 1876, when it was torn down to give place to the present magnificent structure, a piece of architecture that has not its equal in the west. It is 120 by 80 feet, and seven stories high, including basement, being constructed in a most substantial and elaborate manner. Not only as a banker has Mr. Mitchell become distinguished, but he likewise holds a prominent place as a railroad man. His principal interest has always centered in the Chicago, Milwaukee & St. Paul road, at the head of which he has stood for years. He is at present president of this line and its branches, embracing in all about fifteen hundred miles which ramify throughout the entire northwest, and bring to the doors of Milwaukee the product of this extensive region. He is also president of the Western Union road; director of the reorganized Northern Pacific; president of the Northwestern Fire Insurance Company; director of the Milwaukee Gas Company, as well as the life of many smaller concerns. In 1870, he was elected to congress, and returned in 1872. A third nomination was proffered him, but he declined. Mr. Mitchell is a genuine Scotchman, having great love for the home of his childhood. His name has been accorded a high place by a Scottish writer on "Prominent Scotchmen in America." He was the first president of St. Andrew's Society, whose picnics and games have annually delighted the people of the queen city of the lakes since 1859. Mr. Mitchell's residence, on Grand Avenue, for beauty of situation and completeness of detail, has not an equal west of New York City. He was married in October, 1841, to Miss Martha Reed, daughter of Seth Reed, an early settler of Milwaukee. She is a woman of excellent qualities, prominent in national, local and individual charities.

From *Historical Atlas of Wisconsin*, 1878.

WI-545   WISCONSIN MARINE & FIRE INSURANCE COMPANY, 1853-1900

Capital 1863 was $100,000. Alexander Mitchell, Pres., David Ferguson, cashier (1863).
Succeeded a corporation of the same name (founded in 1839), which probably issued only certificates of deposit.
Became the Marine National Bank, now Bank One.

Genuine Notes, Raised Notes and Counterfeits

SC 5   25¢   HS. Kahn Bros. Black & green.   R-7

G2 $2   ___18__: (1850-60s) TCC.   R-7

G4 $3   ___18__: (1850s-1860s) TCC.   Remainder   R-6

G6	$5	___18__: (1850s-60s) TCC.	R-7
R2	$5	___18__: 1850s TCC. Raised from $2, G2.	R-7
R4	$10	___18__: 1850s TCC. Raised from $2, G2. The bank issued no $10s.	R-7
R6	$20	___18__: 1850s TCC. Raised from $2, G2. The bank issued no $20s.	R-7
R8	$50	___18__: 1850s TCC. Raised from $2, G2. The bank issued no $50s.	R-7

Uncut Sheet

| X1 | $2, 3, 5, 5 TCC. G2, 4, 6, 6 | R-7 |

MINERAL POINT

WI-549   THE CORPORATION OF MINERAL POINT

$1	21st of December 1839 ___ 1837 HT, L&Co.	R-7

WI-550   IOWA COUNTY BANK, 1860-61

Joel C. Squires, Pres., L. H. Whittlesey, cashier. (Squires was Wis. Comptroller of the Currency). Closed 1861. Redeemed notes at par.

G2	$1	?: 1860-61 (ABN). C: female portrait. L: state die/1. R: ONE DOLLAR/sailor stdg. by capstan & anchor, farmer std., boy, dog & grain/1.	R-7
G4	$3	?: 1860-61 (ABN). C: THREE across 3; woman stdg. with sword. L: 3/state die. R: 3/dog & game.	R-7

Uncut Sheet

X1	$1, 3 (ABN). G2, 4	R-7

WI-555   BANK OF MINERAL POINT, 1836-41

Territorial bank chartered November 30, 1836, repealed February 1842. Closed 1841. Largest and most speculative of all chartered territorial banks. Its officers hailed from Green Bay. Speculated in lead futures and issued illegal postdated notes. First redeemed at 50¢, later 20¢.

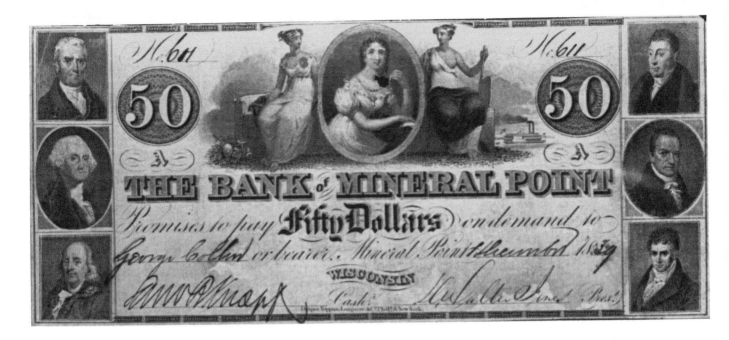

G10 $50   ___18__: late 1830s-40s DTL. L: Marshall/Washington/   R-7
                      Franklin. R: Lafayette/DeWitt Clinton/Robert Ful-
                      ton.

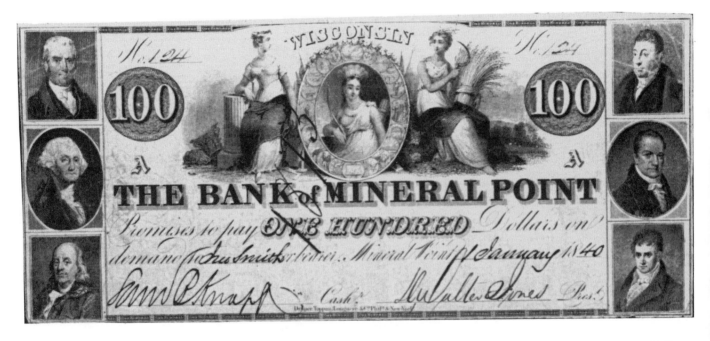

G12 $100   ___18__: late 1830s-40s DTL. L: Marshall/Washington/   R-7
                      Franklin. R: Lafayette/DeWitt Clinton/Robert Ful-
                      ton.

WI-560   **MINERAL POINT BANK, ca. 1836-41**

Territorial bank. Fate: failed.

DEMAND NOTES

| G2 | $5 | ___18__: late 1830s-40 RW&H. Back: Brown. | R-1 |
| G2a | $5 | ___18__: late 1830s-40 RW&H. Same as above, except for plain back. | R-2 |

| G4 | $10 | ___18__: late 1830s-40 RWH&. Back: Brown. | R-1 |
| G4a | $10 | ___18__: late 1830s-40 RW&H. Same as above. | R-2 |

| G6 | $20 | ___18__: late 1830s-40 RWH&. Back: Brown. | R-1 |
| G6a | $20 | ___18__: late 1830s-40 RW&H. Same as above, except for plain back. | R-2 |

G8	$50	___18__: late 1830s-40 RW&H. Back: Brown.	R-6
G8a	$50	___18__: late 1830s-40 RW&H. Same as above, except for plain back.	R-6
G10	$100	___18__: late 1830s-40 RW&H. Back: Brown.	R-7
G10a	$100	___18__: late 1830s-40 RW&H. Plain back.	R-7

POST NOTES

The notes have "Payable (on some date in 1849 or 1841)" written across one end and often, "on demand" crossed out.

| G14 | $5 | ___18__: late 1830s-40 RW&H. Same as G2, brown back, except for handwritten "Payable" statement. | R-1 |
| G14a | $5 | ___18__: late 1830s-40 RW&H. Same as G2a, except for handwritten "Payable" statement. | R-2 |

| G16 | $10 | ___18__: late 1830s-40 RW&H. Same as G4, brown back, except for handwritten "Payable" statement. | R-1 |
| G16a | $10 | ___18__: late 1830s-40 RW&H. Same as G4a, except for handwritten "Payable" statement. | R-7 |

| G18 | $20 | ___18__: late 1830s-40 RW&H. Same as G6, brown back, except for handwritten "Payable" statement. | R-1 |
| G18a | $20 | ___18__: late 1830s-40 RW&H. Same as G6a, except for handwritten "Payable" statement. | R-2 |

WI-565   **WISCONSIN BANK, 1853-56**

Capital $50,000. Notes redeemed at par until December 24, 1859.
Closed. Capital: $25,000. Became a station to pay out and redeem notes of the Bank of Hallowell, Maine. Both Banks were founded by Cadwallader Washburn, whose brother was cashier of the Hallowell Bank. By July 2, 1853 the Wisconsin Bank had $20,863 in circulation. Circulated notes have never been reported. The State Bank of Madison located in Watertown also paid out its Hallowell notes as did the Bank of Galena, (Ill.)

Genuine Notes, Raised Notes and Counterfeits

G2 $1   ___18__: (1850s) TCC. L: Franklin.   R-7

G4 $2   ___18__: (1850s) TCC.   R-7

| G6 | $3 | ___18__: (1850s) TCC. | R-7 |

| G8 | $5 | ___18__: (1850s) TCC. | R-7 |
| R5 | $10 | ___18__: 1850s TCC. Raised from $1, G2. The bank issued no $10s. | R-7 |

Uncut Sheet

| X1 | | $1, 2, 3, 5 TCC. G2, 4, 6, 8 | R-7 |

CADWALLADER C. WASHBURN — Was born in the town of Livermore, Maine, on the twenty-second day of April, 1818. He received a common-school education. He afterward read law and practiced his profession. He removed to Wisconsin in the year 1842, and settled at Mineral Point. He was elected to congress from the second district in 1854, and again in 1856 and 1858. In 1860, he declined a re-election. While a member of the thirty-fourth and thirty-fifth congresses, he served on the committees on private land claims and expenditures on the public buildings. When a member of the thirty-sixth congress, he served as chairman of the committee on private land claims. He was also a member of the special committee of thirty-three, and a delegate of the "Peace Congress" of 1861. The same year he entered the union service as colonel of the Second Wisconsin cavalry regiment. In June, 1862, he was appointed brigadier-general, and in November, a major-general. He resigned June 1, 1865. He was a delegate to the "Soldiers' Convention," held at Pittsburgh, in 1866, and was the same year elected to congress from the La Crosse district, and re-elected 1868. As a member of the fortieth and forty-first congresses, he was placed on the committees on foreign affairs, expenditures on the public buildings, and appropriations. In November, 1871, Washburn was elected governor of Wisconsin, holding the office for the years 1872 and 1873. In November of the latter year, was defeated for the same office by W. R .Taylor. Since that time he has taken no active part in public affairs, his extensive business interests receiving his whole attention.

From the *Historical Atlas of Wisconsin*, 1878.

MONROE

WI-570   **BANK OF MONROE, 1856-64**

Capital $25,000. John A. Bangham, Pres., Julius B. Galusha, cashier (1856). Asa Richardson, Pres. (1863).
Became the First National Bank of Monroe #230 in 1864.

Genuine Notes, Raised Notes and Counterfeits

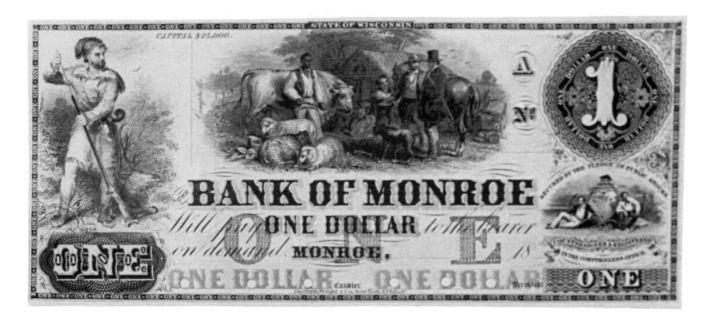

G2a $1   ___18__: (1850s-60s) DW. Overprint: Red ONE.   Remainder   R-6

G4a $2   ___18__: (1850s-60s) DW. Overprint: Red TWO.   Remainder   R-6

G6a $3   ___18__: (1850s-60s) DW. Overprint: Red THREE.   R-7

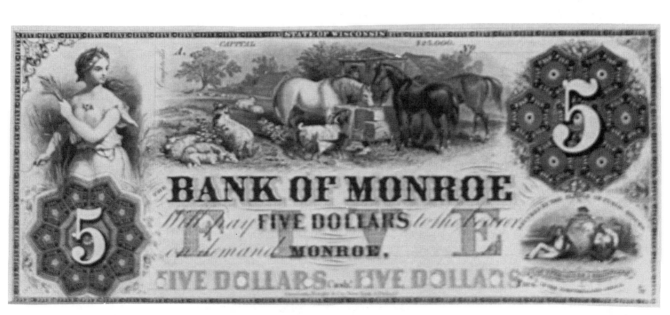

G8a $5   ___18__: (1850s-60s) DW. Overprint: Red FIVE.   R-7

R4 $5   ___18__: 1850s DW. Raised from $2, G4a.   R-7

R6 $10   ___18__: 1850s DW. Raised from $2, G4a. The bank   R-7
                   issued no $10s.

R8 $20   ___18__: 1850s DW. Raised from $2, G4a. The bank   R-7
                   issued no $20s.

Uncut Sheet

X1 $1, 2, 3, 5 DW. G2a, 4a, 6a, 8a   R-7

MONTELLO

WI-575   BANK OF MONTELLO, 1858-60

Capital $25,000. E. B. Kelsey, Pres., C. S. Kelsey, cashier (1858). Had no office or banking house.
Later location: Princeton. Became the First National Bank of America #230.
Closed 1860, notes protected. $8,122 specie held in 1860 for redemption of notes.

| G2a | $1 | ___18__: (late 1850s) WH&W. L: Buchanan. Capital: $25,000. Overprint: Red ONE. | R-7 |
| G2b | $1 | ___18__: late 1850s WH&W. As above, except for capital ($50,000). | R-7 |

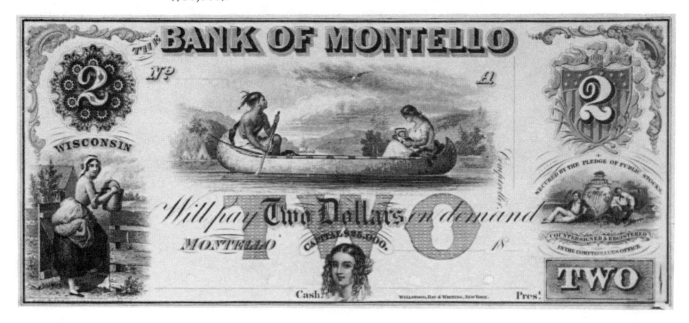

| G4a | $2 | ___18__: (late 1850s) WH&W. Capital: $25,000. Overprint: Red TWO. | R-7 |
| G4b | $2 | ___18__: late 1850s WH&W. As above, except for capital ($50,000). | R-7 |

Uncut Sheet

| X1 | | $1, 2 WH&W. G2a, 4a | R-7 |

NECEDAH

WI-877 **GOOD TO THE BEARER FOR MERCHANDISE**

SC 6   50¢   Good to the Bearer for Merchandise.

R-7

SC 7 $1   ___185_: Good to the Bearer for Merchandise. Imprint lower left corner. "Entered according to Act of Congress in the year 1858 by Hatch & Co. in the clerks office of the District Court of the United States for the Southern District of New York." H&Co.

R-7

WI-879   **T. WESTON & CO.**

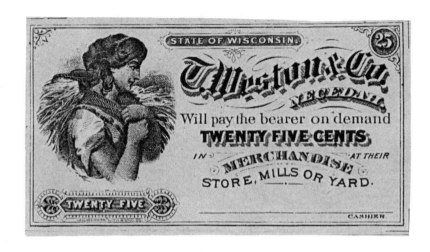

SC 6   50¢   Will pay to the bearer on demand. ML&E.   R-7

NEENAH

WI-878   **S.G. BURDICK**

SC 1   5¢   Will Pay to Bearer. Black/green TP.   R-7

SC 2   10¢   Will Pay to Bearer. Black and green. TP.   R-7

SC 3   15¢   Will Pay to Bearer Black/green TP.   R-7

SC 4   20¢   Will Pay to Bearer TP.   R-7

Tribune Print, Chicago.

WI-580 WINNEBAGO COUNTY BANK, 1854-61

Capital $25,000. C. C. Townsend, Pres., A. H. Cronkhite, cashier.
Closed 1861, notes paid at 57¢ per dollar in 1862. In 1863 there was $1,754 of outstanding circulation.

Genuine Notes, Raised Notes and Counterfeits

| G2 | $1 | September 18, 1855 WHH&W. | R-7 |

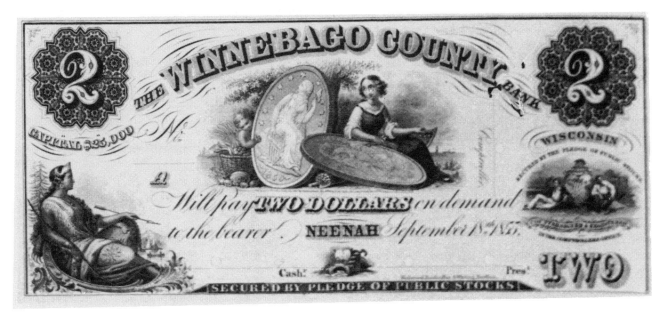

G4	$2	September 18, 1855 WHH&W.	R-7
R5	$5	September 18, 1855 WHH&W. Raised from $1, G2. The bank issued no $5s.	R-7
R6	$10	September 18. 1855 WHH&W. Raised from $1, G2. The bank issued no $10s.	R-7

Uncut Sheet

| X1 | | $1, 2 WHH&W. G2, 4 | R-7 |

NEW LONDON

WI-585   **BANK OF NEW LONDON, 1858-62**

Closed.

G2a $1   ___18__: (1858-60s) TC, ABNCo. mono. Tint: Orange   R-7
                   counter, bank title and ONE ONE.

G4a $5   ___18__: (1858-60s) TC, ABNCo. mono. Tint: Orange   R-7
                   counter, bank title and FIVE FIVE.

Uncut Sheet

X1 $1, 5 TC, ABNCo. mono. G2a, 4a   R-7

WI-590   OSBORN BANK OF NEW LONDON, 1859-61

Capital $50,000. H. K. Lawrence, Pres., George Sea, cashier.
Formerly Osborn Bank of Gemekon, WI-210.
Failed. 1861 redeemed notes at 65¢ per dollar in 1862. Outstanding circulation 1863 $835.00.

G2	$5	Unknown (TC, ABNCo. mono.) Same as $5 Osborn Bank of Gemekon, Gemekon, WI-210-G2, except for city and probably date.	R-7
G4	$10	Unknown (TC, ABNCo. mono.) Same as $10 Osborn Bank of Gemekon, Gemekon, WI-210-G4, except for city and probably date.	R-7

NEWBURG

WI-581   JOS. REICHL & SON

SC 5	25¢	Jos. Reichl & Son, black on white paper.	R-7
SC 5	25¢	Jos. Reichl & Son, purple (grey) paper.	R-7
SC 5	25¢	Jos. Reichl & Son, red/orange paper.	R-7

NORTH PEPIN

WI-595   OAKWOOD BANK, 1855-62

Capital $50,000. O. B. Connor, Pres., A. C. Alan, cashier.
Closed 1862.

| G2a | $5 | September 3, 1855 DW. Tint: Large brown-orange die bearing 5, FIVE, and FIVE DOLLARS. Same as G2b, except for capital ($50,000). | R-7 |

Uncut Sheet

| X1 | | $5, 5 DW. G2a, 2a | R-7 |

NORTHHOUSEN

WI-600   BUFFALO COUNTY BANK, 1858-62

Bank never opened; proofs only printed.

G2a $1   ___185_: ___ TC. Tint: Red-orange bank title and   R-7
                                    counter at upper rt.

G4a $5   ___185_: ___ TC. Tint: Red-orange bank title and   R-7
                                    counters.

G6a $10   ___185_: ____   TC. Tint: Red-orange bank title and   R-7
                       counter.

Uncut Sheet

X1 $1, 1, 5, 10 TC. G2a, 2a, 4a, 6a   R-7

OCONOMOWOC

***WI-605*   SUMMIT BANK, 1859-63**

Capital $25,000. H. K. Edgerton, cashier. First oldest established bank.
Became H. K. Edgerton, Banker, then Bank of Oconomowoc.

| G2 | $2 | October 1, 1859 ABN. No overprint. | | R-7 |
| G2a | $2 | October 1, 1859 ABN. As above, except for overprint of a red panel outlining a white TWO. | Remainder | R-1 |

G4	$3	October 1, 1859 ABN. No overprint.		R-7
G4a	$3	October 1, 1859 ABN. As above, except for overprint of a red panel outlining a white THREE.	Remainder	R-1
			Signed	R-5
			Note	

Uncut Sheet

| X1 | | $2, 3 ABN. G2, 4 | | R-1 |

WI-634   SUMMIT BANK/JOHN S. ROCKWELL

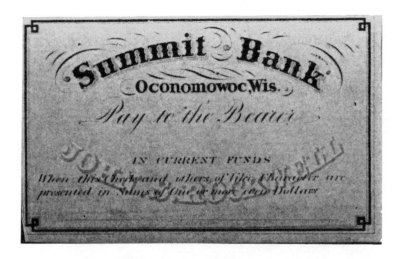

SC 0   Pay to the Bearer in current funds, non denominated.   R-7
                    Green with light brown underprint.

OCONTO

WI-610   BANK OF OCONTO, 1859-61

Capital $100,00. E. Hart, Pres., J. F. Woodruff (1858).
Failed 1861.

G2a	$1	___18__: (1850s) RWH&E. Tint: Green lathework overall, with an outlined white 1 1/ONE. Capital: $50,000.	R-7
G2b	$1	___18__: 1859-61 RWH&E, (ABNCo. mono.) As above, except for capital ($100,000) and probably imprint.	R-7

G4a	$3	___18__: (1850s) RWH&E. Tint: Green lathework overall, with an outlined large white 3. Capital: $50,000.	R-7
G4b	$3	___18__: 1859-61 RWH&E, (ABNCo. mono. As above, except for capital ($100,000) and probably imprint.	

| G6a | $5 | ___18__: 1850s RWH&E. R: Buchanan. Tint: Green lathework overall, with an outlined white FIVE. Capital: $50,000. | R-7 |
| G6b | $5 | ___18__: 1859-61 RWH&E (ABNCo. mono.) As above, except for capital ($100,000) and probably imprint. | R-7 |

| G8a | $10 | ___18__: (1850s) RWH&E. Tint: Green lathework overall, with an outlined white X and TEN. Capital: $50,000. | R-7 |
| G8b | $10 | ___18__: 1859-61 RWH&E, (ABNCo. mono.) As above, except for capital ($100,000) and probably imprint. | R-7 |

Uncut Sheet

| X1 | | $1, 3, 5, 10 RWH&E. G2a,4a, 6a, 8a | R-7 |

WI-355   OCONTO COUNTY BANK, 1858

Moved from La Porte in 1859 to Oconto; never issued notes from La Porte.

O'NEILSVILLE

WI-615 **CLARK COUNTY BANK, 1858-61**

Capital $250,000. W. J. Lyons, cashier.

Later location: Chippewa Falls (moved ca.1859).
Closed/failed.

G2a	$5	___18__: late 1850s DW. Capital: $25,000. Overprint: Red FIVE.	Proof 7	R-6
G2b	$5	___18__: ca.1859 DW & probably ABNCo. mono. As above, except for capital ($50,000) and imprint.		R-7
G2c	$5	___18__: ca.1859-61 DW & probably ABNCo. mono. As above, except for capital ($100,000).		R-7
G2d	$5	___18__: ca.1859-61 DW & probably ABNCo. mono. As above, except for capital ($250,000).		R-7

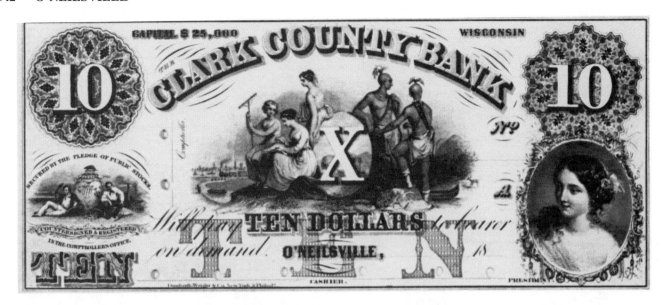

G4a	$10	___18__: (1858) DW. Capital: $25,000. Overprint: Red TEN.	R-7
G4b	$10	___18__: ca.1859 DW & probably ABNCo. mono. As above, except for capital ($50,000) and imprint.	R-7
G4c	$10	___18__: ca.1859 DW & probably ABNCo. mono. As above, except for capital ($100,000).	R-7
G4d	$10	___18__: ca.1859 DW & probably ABNCo. mono. As above, except for capital ($250,000).	R-7

Uncut Sheet

| X1 | $5, 10 DW. G2a, 4a | R-7 |

OSHKOSH

WI-620 BANK OF OSHKOSH, 1852-64

Capital $30,000. Oldest bank in Central Wisconsin.
Became the First National Bank of Oshkosh in 1904. Liquidated in 1883 and was succeeded by the National Bank of Oshkosh. Liquidated in 1903 and became the Old National Bank of Oshkosh. In 1919 changed its name to The Old Commercial National Bank of Oshkosh. In 1925 the name changed to the First National Bank of Oshkosh.

Genuine Notes, Raised Notes and Counterfeits

G2 $3   ___18__: (1850s-60s) TC.   R-7

G4	$5	___18__: (1850s-60s) TC.	R-7
C4	$5	___18__: 1850s-60s TC. Cft. of the above.	R-7
R10	$20	___18__: 1850s-60s TC. Raised from $3, G2. The bank issued no $20s.	R-7

Uncut Sheet

| X1 | $3, 5 TC. G2, 4 | R-7 |

WI-625   OSHKOSH CITY BANK, ca.1854-59

Capital $50,000. J. Knutland, Pres., B. S. Henning, cashier.
Failed in the mid 50s but as securities had been deposited with the state depositors were paid in full.
An additional $99 held in specie held after 1860.

Genuine Notes, Raised Notes and Counterfeits

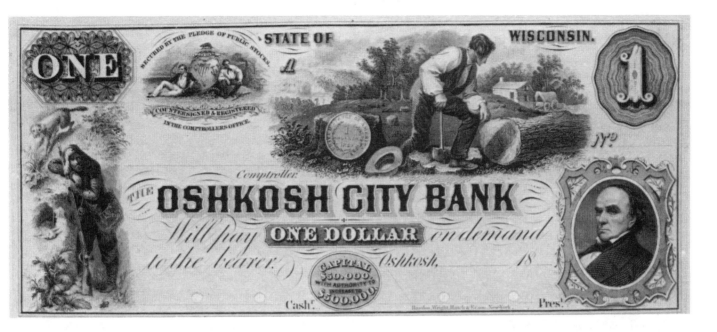

G2 $1   ___18__: (1850s) RWH&E. R: Webster.   Remainder   R-7

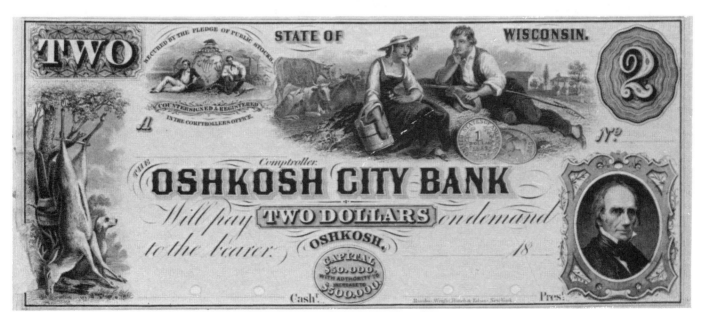

G4 $2   ___18__: (1850s) RWH&E. Clay.   R-7

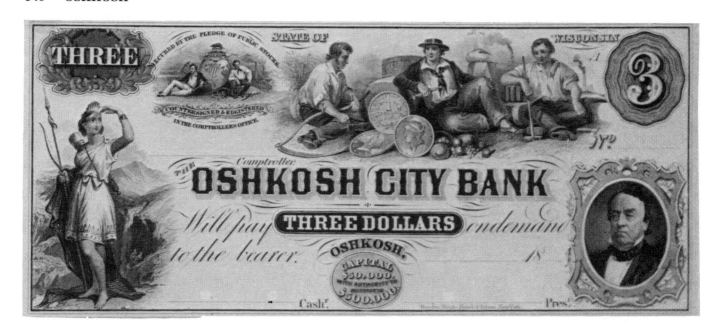

G6 $3   ___18__: (1850s) RWH&E.   R-7

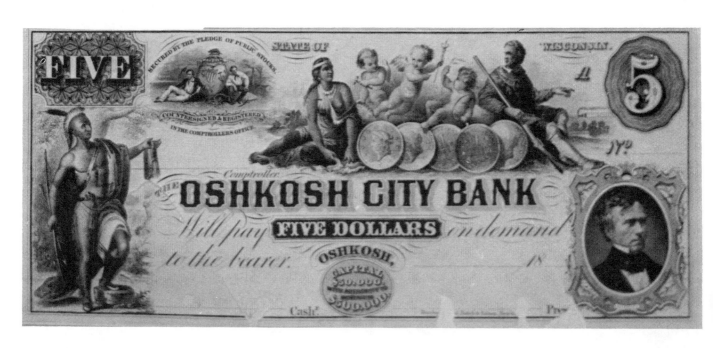

G8 $5   ___18__: (1850s) RWH&E.   R-7

Uncut Sheet

X1 $1, 2, 3, 5 RWH&E. G2, 4, 6, 8   R-7

WI-75   CITIZENS BANK, 1859-62

Capital $50,000. W. D. Martin, Pres., Sue Bolkin, cashier.
Moved from Black River Falls in 1859. Closed 1862. Only business was to circulate notes. Redeemed at
72¢ per dollar. $679 outstanding in 1863.

NOTES DATED AT OSHKOSH

G6a	$1	?: early 1860s(ABN). Same as G2a, except for city and probably imprint.	R-7
G8a	$2	?: early 1860s(ABN). Same as G4a, except for city and probably imprint.	R-7

Uncut Sheet

X1	$1, 2 WH&W. G2a, 4a	R-7

WI-630   OSHKOSH COMMERCIAL BANK, 1856-ca.65

Capital $50,000 (1856); $30,000 (1863). Henry Strong, Pres.
Became the Commercial National Bank #1568 September 1865. Thomas T. Reeve Pres., Gilbert Roe, cashier. Liquidated 1871. Then became the Commercial Bank.

Genuine Notes, Raised Notes and Counterfeits

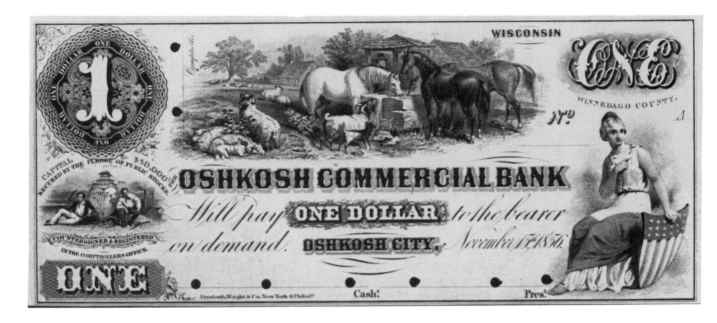

| G2 | $1 | November 15, 1856 DW. | R-7 |
| C2 | $1 | November 15, 1856 DW. Photographic cft. of the above. | R-7 |

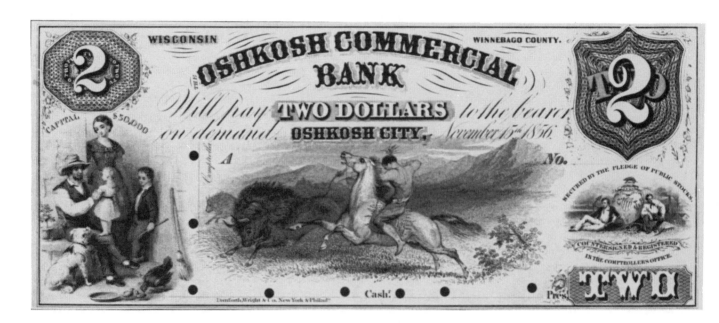

| G4 | $2 | November 15, 1856 DW. | R-7 |

| G6 | $3 | November 15, 1856 DW. | | R-7 |

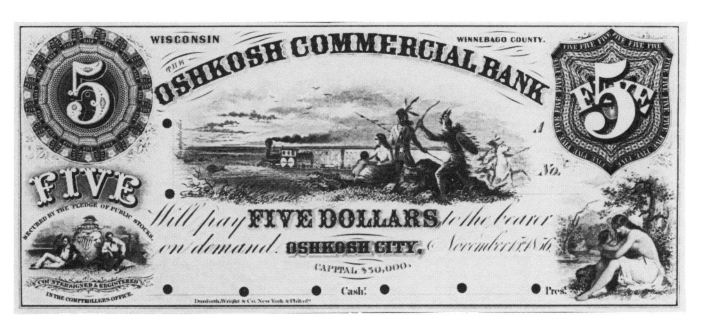

G8	$5	November 15, 1856 DW.		R-7
R5	$5	November 15, 1856 DW. Raised from $2, G4.		R-7
R10	$10	November 15, 1856 DW. Raised from $1, G2. The bank issued no $10s.		R-7
R15	$10	November 15, 1856 DW. Raised from $2, G4. The bank issued no $10s.		R-7

R20 $20   November 15, 1856 DW. Raised from $2, G4. The bank   R-6
                    issued no $20s.

Uncut Sheet

X1 $1, 2, 3, 5 DW. G2, 4, 6, 8   R-7

Altered, Spurious and Unattributed Non-Genuine Notes

A5 $2   July 10, 1856 DW. C: Steamship, sailing ship at left. L: R-7
                    2/Indian woman std. by stream, holding spear in rt.
                    hand, in circle. Altered from $2 Commercial Bank of
                    New Jersey, Perth Amboy, NJ-445-G42 series.

WI-632   OSHKOSH

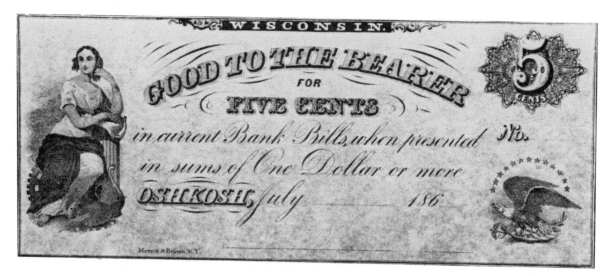

SC 1   5¢   Good to the Bearer. Black M & B.   R-7

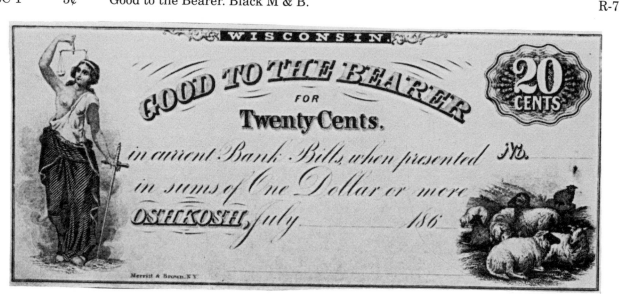

SC 4   20¢   Good to the Bearer. Black M & B.   R-7

SC 6   50¢   Good to the Bearer. Black M & B.   R-7

In all probability other denominations of these notes were also printed.

WI-633   OSHKOSH (Due Bearer)

SC 2a   10¢   On demand we will pay. Red. K&B.   R-7

SC 5a   25¢   On demand we will pay. Blue. K&B.   R-7

SC 6a   50¢   On demand we will pay. Black. K&B   R-7

PEKWECOWA

WI-635   **WISCONSIN MINERS BANK, ca 1859**

Non-existent bank; represented only by fraudulent notes. Non-existent city.

S5 $3   May 2, 1859 None.   R-7

PEPIN

WI-640   CHIPPEWA BANK, 1856-61

Capital $50,000. E. Lathrop, Pres., J. C. Mann, cashier (1857).
Closed. Redeemed notes at 77.5¢ per dollar. $1,695 outstanding 1863. Maintained no banking house.

Genuine Notes, Raised Notes and Counterfeits

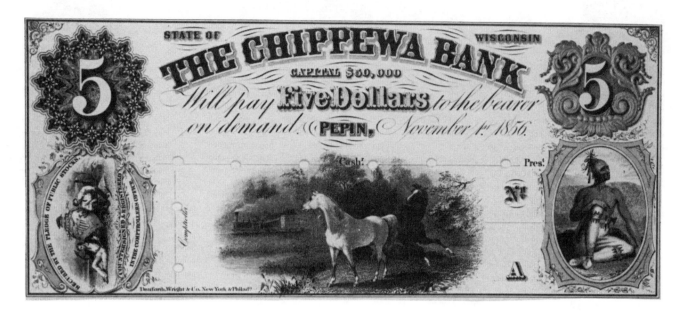

G4	$5	November 1, 1856 DW. Letters A or B.	R-3
G4a	$5	Unknown. DW, ABNCo. mono. Same as G4, except for imprint and possibly date.	R-7
C4	$5	November 1, 1856DW. Cft. of the above. Letter A only.	R-3

Uncut Sheet

Genuine   Counterfeit
Note non-conforming type used on counterfeited note.

| X1 | $5, 5 DW. G4,4 | R-7 |

Altered, Spurious and Unattributed Non-Genuine Notes

S5a $10   November 1, 185__: 1856 DW. Similar to cft. of $5, C4.   R-6
               Overprint: Red lazy X.

PESHTIGO

WI-641   **THE PESHTICO COMPANY**

2   10¢   ___186_.   R-7

(Note: Spelling error in the word Peshtigo; is spelled Peshtico.) The city of Peshtigo was destroyed by a forest fire in 1871 the same date as the great Chicago fire. It caused many more deaths than the Chicago fire but because of it remoteness in northeastern Wisconsin little was known about the fire and its devastation until years later. This note is probably one of the few surviving pieces of memorabilia from the pre-fire era.

PESHTIGO

Peshtigo is a place of 1,200 inhabitants, situated on the river by that name, six miles south of Marinette. Although settlements were made in its vicinity at quite an early day, there are no "ancient landmarks" standing to keep alive an interest in its youthful times - all swept away, with hundreds of human lives, in that awful baptism by fire in 1871. The history of Peshtigo, as it is, dates from October 8, 1871.

The village is located on the Peshtigo River, about seven miles from its mouth, and six miles directly south of Marinette.

BUSINESS INTERESTS

The Peshtigo Company, a business power in Northern Wisconsin, was organized in October, 1856, as the Peshtigo Lumber & Manufacturing Company. The name was afterward changed to that by which it is at present known. When the company was organized, a mill on each side of the river had been operated for years. The one on the west side was torn down and a very large mill erected on its site in 1857. This was burned in 1867. The old building on the east side was enlarged, containing finally a circular, lath, planing and grist mill, sash and door factory and machine shop, all in one. It was burned in the fire of 1871, and has not been rebuilt, but a saw-mill, with two large circulars, was erected on the west side in 1872, and is now in operation. Its capacity is 100,000 feet of lumber, and 33,000 lath per day. It is run by water power and employs fifty men. To facilitate the transportation and marketing of this large manufacture, the Peshtigo Company has constructed a railroad line from Peshtigo to Peshtigo Harbor, eight miles, where it connects with its line of barges, and thus a continuous route is opened to Chicago. At Peshtigo Harbor the company owns and operates a steam saw-mill, the largest and most productive in this section of the State. It was built in 1867-68, going into operation during the Spring of the latter year. Its capacity (eleven hours per day) is 200,000 feet of lumber, 33,000 lath and 40,000 shingles. The number of men employed in the mill is 125. The barge line, mentioned above, consists of a magnificent $50,000 tug, "The Boscobel," which was built this season, and six fine barges. The company has also in operation at Peshtigo a flourishing general store, and a first-class boarding house. Its lands comprise 160,000 acres, located on both sides of the Pestigo River. This season's estimated manufacture is 50,000,000 feet. Present officers of the company: President, Wm. E. Strong; Vice-president, Isaac Stephenson; Secretary, Wm. A. Ellis; Assistant Secretary and Treasurer, George C. Hempstead.

Machine Shops and Planing Mill of S. G. Lister, is the only manufacturing establishment in Peshtigo, outside the mill and shops owned by the Peshtigo Company. The shops were first erected in 1870, by David Lister & Son, but were burned in the great fire. They were rebuilt the next year, the senior proprietor selling out to his sons, David Lister, and S. G. Lister, who operated them until 1876, as Lister Brothers. The former disposed of his interest to F. J. Bartels, who remained in partnership with the latter for a year, since which time S. G. Lister has been sole proprietor.

About a dozen hands are employed in the foundry, machine shop and planing mill.

Peshtigo has, of course, a number of general stores, which do a good business, and has after ten years grown up to be the only settlement of importance in the county, outside of Marinette.

THE GREAT FIRE OF OCTOBER 8, 1871

For months previous to that shocking human sacrifice on October 8, 1871, earth and air seemed to have entered into a conspiracy to lay the foundation of the altar broad and raise its structure high. The previous Winter had been scant of snow, the Spring had withheld its cooling showers, and July, only, finally vouchsafed a refreshing drought to the parched land, which quickly and greedily drank it. The atmosphere panted, and everything on the earth right in sight of Lake Michigan's grand old arm - Green Bay - was parched and cracked. The swamps of tamarack and the marshes of cedar which stretched along both of its shores were black, dry and cheerless. In September the clouds opened and sifted down a scanty shower, which served rather to tantalize than to satisfy. The panting of air and earth went on. One might almost imagine that some fiery atmosphere of judgement from above was yoking itself to the infernal breath of the pit and preparing to ride, flaming and rough-shod, over the villages and forest of the land. The swamps and marshes were peat, prepared for burning, the forests of pine were tinder, ready and anxious for a suicide by fire. All nature was so dry and so miserable that it cried out for death. The human victims for the coming holocaust were not yet prepared for death, if they ever were. Little adder tongues of flame first shot in and out, darting down among the roots of trees, stealthily following their prey underground, then springing up to the air and licking a bush or a small tree. Soon a whole body came into sight, the spirit of destruction grew bolder, a forest pine was wrapped in its folds and came tumbling to earth, its enemy hissing and darting around it. Then, as if by magic, a whole forest of pines were surrounded and invaded, and eaten by a grand mass of fire, and all the world was in the flames. To be more historical, the local fires commenced to be really noticeable and create wide-spread alarm up both shores of Green Bay in the early part of September. A dark pall of smoke already hung over the pine forests, or was wafted and wandered slowly over the country. Red and lurid flames were dancing among the tree-tops on both sides of the bay. People in the farming sections were commencing to look with alarm in each other's faces, and, with the enemy in the rear, to take their families and their household goods to the settlements, or the villages, where, they thought, a more effective stand could be maintained. The large settlements, such as those located in the "Upper, Middle and Lower Sugar Bushes," a few miles southwest of Peshtigo, breathed easily in comparison with isolated farmers scattered over a broad expanse of country. Especially was the feeling gloomy on the eastern shore of the bay, where the farming settlements were few and small. By the middle of the month the forest fires were raging up and down the shores of Green Bay, encompassing and apparently dooming to destruction

Sturgeon Bay, Little Suamico, Pensaukee, Oconto, the Sugar Bushes, Peshtigo, and all other settlements and villages where such crowds were fleeing for safety. The whole population of the bay counties turned out to fight the flames, and for the time they were driven back. With the exception of the thousands of acres of valuable timber destroyed, and the burning of railroad ties, bridges and camps belonging to the Chicago & Northwestern Company, whose line was then being built from Fort Howard to Menominee, Mich., up to the middle of September the loss of property was light and the loss of life nothing. After that date the fire drew closer and closer around the settlements. It had fed upon the forest, even eating the upper soil of the land, leaving in its place nothing but ashes. Like a hungry lion which, after he has cleared the forests of lower game, is driven by gnawing and fierce hunger to rush for his prey even into cities and the haunts of men, what were to be the great fires of October, 1871, raged around the villages of Northwestern Wisconsin, preparing in their famished state to sweep into them and bear away their victims. Twice did doomed Peshtigo escape only by the brave resistance of its people. On the twenty-first, Little Suamico fought nobly. Oconto, Pensaukee, all the villages on the west shore were being glared at by hungry eyes. To add to the horror of the situation, by the latter part of September not only were earth and heaven in flames, but telegraph communication with Green Bay, and thus with the remainder of the State, was completely severed. Anyone who has observed the intimate association between these towns and settlements on the western shore, which were so sorely pressed, can realize to some extent the horror of uncertainty, in addition to the horror of reality, which was born of this fact. Green Bay and Fort Howard also were entered by the foe, and narrowly escaped being swallowed. While the cities and villages were trembling in doubtful fear, isolated saw-mills and farm-houses were being destroyed throughout Oconto, Shawano, Marinette, Brown, Kewaunee and Door counties. A terrible battle had been waged and won, on the twenty-fourth, by the people of Peshtigo. The fire finally gave up the battle and swept around the town, burning large quantities of hay in the marshes between it and Marinette. The latter village itself was threatened, and only saved by being soaked with water and covered with wet blankets. By the end of September there was no sleep for the people of five counties, who rested upon their arms and waited in dread the approach of a fearful enemy, and one with whom they so seldom had to deal. Thus had the drought of six months, which made the earth tinder and the air gaseous and explosive vapor; the destruction of all the unpopulated districts of the State around those which were thickly settled, and the exhaustive conflict with the insatiable flames which raged for weeks, led up to that fatal Sunday - that fatal union and onset of tornado and fire - which makes the 8th of October, 1871, a sadder day to the people of Northern Wisconsin than to the business men of Northern Illinois. How, in that immense ocean of fire which rolled over Chicago and bore away so much of its pride and wealth, so few souls were carried, too, is the mystery. But the blank made on this earth by the loss of a thousand souls is not to be filled in a day.

It is uncertain when or where the tornado first formed, which was to put the finish upon this already desolate region. It is uncertain whether one tornado formed near the lower waters of the bay and there split, one-half rushing up it eastern shore and the other along its western banks, or whether each was formed alone and pursued its own destructive course. But certain it is, that the whirlwinds drove the flames together into one mass on both the shores and then swept the newly formed body swiftly along. As it passed over the peaty swamps and marshes, gases were there generated which it rolled together and threw before it in great balls. These exploded and set fire to whatever material had escaped the local conflagrations, and so the phalanx moved on, pushed from behind by an irresistible tornado, and fed and sustained, and strengthened by its prey before. It lashed itself and roared, like a wild beast. Nothing in its way could withstand it. Oconto escaped its fury. Then it swept upon the settlements of the Sugar Bushes, and here the scene was sickening. The forward movement of the wind was not rapid, but its rotary motion was so fearful that great trees were uprooted and twisted like twigs. It tore up the earth; it threw fire-balls in all directions; it hurled torrents of fire after flying families. Houses and barns were swept away like toys. Amid the war of the tempest and fire and the falling of trees, sounded agonizing shouts and screams for help. Some fell to the earth, and with their mouth upon its hot bosom, managed to sustain the breath of life until the fury passed over them. Others fled to the highest points they could find and were swept away, not to be distinguished from charred limbs and trunks of trees. Some who escaped fire were smothered by gases. Others were drowned in the streams to which they had fled, and lay there with dead fish, who rose to the surface in thousands. Fathers became crazed, and taking their children in their arms ran wildly before the flames and were swallowed up. One father seeing that escape was hopeless, cut his own throat, and killed his three children in the same way. Many suicides occurred in crouching moments of the horror which every one feels toward death by fire. Poor women, in that scene of confusion of death, gave birth to life. The fire passed over death and ruin, on to Pestigo. In the three Sugar Bush settlements, consisting of three hundred families, but eight houses remained, those of A. Phillips, A. Place, John Hutchins, and Jacob Empy, in the upper; Mr. Fetterly, in the lower; Daniel Sage and Joseph Vallier, in the middle, and Charles Schwartz in the village. In the Lower Bush settlement but four persons escaped death, and they by setting down in a shallow pool of water. It is impossible to tell the exact number of persons who perished in this region, but the number can not be less than three hundred.

It was now about 9 o'clock on that Sunday night. As is usual with the atmosphere in advance of a tornado, the air was oppressive and heavy around Peshtigo. Fires in the woods had raged around for weeks, and this particular Sunday night was no exception. The smoke from burning and smoldering forests just formed a faint illumination, which was beginning to spread up from the southwestern horizon. The churches were dismissed; a breeze which had been briskly blowing in the afternoon, had died away into a pretentious calm; faint hearts beat fast, and strong ones were oppressed, and some restlessly walked the streets, to be taken, if need be, at their best. By 10 o'clock, many had "retired to rest;" little they knew how long a one. There had come a great change. A hot wind was blowing strongly from the southwest, the whole sky in that direction was ablaze; a distant roar swept toward the village, the flames could now be plainly seen galloping and surging over the tree-tops, then the air was afire, and the earth and Peshtigo was doomed. Men, women, children, cattle, horses, every thing, every body, were borne along toward the river and plunged in. Crowds rushed for the bridge, but found it in flames. Many rushed upon it, notwithstanding, to escape the flames pursuing them, and when it fell, were drowned. Debris from the burning town was cast upon the mass of strugglers in the water, and some even who were not drowned or burned, were killed by shooting timber and bricks. Burning logs hissed as they floated flaming down the river. Roofs of buildings were lifted almost entire and cast along like sheets of paper. Some seventy persons, who considered themselves fortunate at the time, rushed for the Peshtigo Company's boarding-house, and there sheltered themselves from the fury of the fiery storm. In a few minutes the hurricane had reached them there, passed on and left their charred bodies there. In less than one hour Peshtigo and 800 people were annihilated. The only building which escaped in a measure was one unfinished dwelling house on the east side of the river. When Monday morning came, this stood alone, as if in mockery, while the victims of the fire, and the ruins of the fire, were heaped together, oftentimes in inseparable confusion. It is unnecessary to picture the shriveled and blackened bodies of the dead, in detail, or draw the scenes of suffering in distinct lines. Every one is content to forget all this, and will be satisfied with obtaining a general view, which is much more difficult of successful and correct execution. In addition to the loss of 800 lives, the loss of property in the village was large. At the same time of her own calamity, Peshtigo contained a population of 1,500, and was one of the most brisk places of business on the bay. Among the principal losers were the Peshtigo Company, whose immense factory of wooden ware (the largest in the United States), lumber mill, machine shop, sash, door and blind factory, grist mill, boarding house, and a large number of tenant houses, were destroyed. Judge F. J. Bartels, Harter & Horvath, Charles Johnson, McDonald & Murray, P. J. Marshall, Williams Brothers, who mostly carried on general stores; Nicholas Cavoit, a small saw-mill; David Lister, foundry and machine shop; Edward Kittner, wagon and blacksmith shop; and the Congregational and Roman Catholic societies, which lost fine churches. It has been estimated that a quarter of a million of dollars were lost in Peshtigo and vicinity, of which the Company suffered to the extent of one-half. Peshtigo, and half her people, many of them strangers who had fled to her for protection, was as completely destroyed as if by an earthquake, and in taking a sad leave of her and following

the path of the destroyer, it would be inexcusable not to pay tribute to the useless yet heroic endeavors of such men as William A. Ellis, general manager of the Peshtigo Company, and Judge F. J. Bartels, with many mill hands and private citizens, less well known, and who afterward, when the worst had been accomplished, labored so earnestly in the noble work of relief.

The fire, after leaving Peshtigo, swerved a little in its course to the eastward, and sweeping along toward Marinette and Menominee, half a dozen miles distant was broken up in its course by the "sand hills," mounds formed of that material which lie midway between the Peshtigo and Menominee rivers. This was all that saved Marinette. The main tornado of wind, fire, gas, sand, and burning debris, passed along to the west of the village, taking with it the planing mill of Messrs. Bagley & Curry, and saw-mill of McCartney & Co., and the Catholic church. The branch caused by the divide enveloped and destroyed the village of Menekaune, and then made a grand leap of nearly a quarter of a mile at the business life of Menominee across the river. From the large saw-mill of Spaulding, Houghteling & Johnson, now the Menominee River Lumber Company, leaped the river and soon leveled to the ground the "Gilmore mill," owned by R. Stephenson & Co. The fire then swept out over Green Bay, but as the shipping there narrowly escaped, its destruction was checked at this point. The body of the divided fire, which scorched Marinette, passed on to the west of the village and following the Menominee River for fourteen miles, swept away thousands of acres of valuable timber, making a dreary and barren waste of the entire tract.

The total loss in property which had been caused along the west shore of Green Bay by that fierce sweep of fire, of only a few hours of duration, has been placed at $5,000,000. The heaviest loss at Menekaune was sustained by Spalding, Houghteling & Johnson — $116,000. Besides their fine saw-mill, a large boarding-house and ten tenement houses were consumed. Two saw-mills, thirty-five dwellings, three stores, one planing-mill, sash, door and blind factory, two hotels, a number of scows, nearly, 1,000,000 feet of lumber, the bridge to Philbrook's Island, warehouse and dock at the steamboat landing, Philbrook's shipyard and shops and the Catholic Church were destroyed. So far as known, no lives were lost directly by the fire, though several deaths undoubtedly occurred from fright and exhaustion. Had it not been, however, for the excellent management of some of the prominent citizens of Marinette, Menominee and Menekaune, it is doubtful if either of the first two places could have escaped the fate of the latter. When Menekaunee was given up as lost, Messrs. Isaac Stephenson, A. C. Brown, A. C. Merryman, D. C. Prescott, Fred. Carney and other mill owners marshaled their men, put them to work hauling water, digging trenches, wetting down buildings and putting blankets upon them for protection from the falling cinders and flying debris, etc. They and their co-laborers did all that human strength could accomplish, and carried the day. Both Marinette and Menominee were saved. The men worked with greater coolness and effect from the fact that they knew their wives and children were safe, as they had seen the dear ones on board the steamer "Union," and pass between the fires of Menekaune and Menominee to a place of refuge below. What a contrast between the fates of Menekaune and Peshtigo!

But the flames were not yet satisfied. Birch Creek, to the northeast of Marinette, about a dozen of miles, received the visitation before midnight of that October Sunday. It was a farming settlement, of 100 people. Its property was swept away, and nineteen persons perished. Here the tornado seems to have exhausted itself and rested, after thus desecrating the Sabbath with its wicked work. In four hours, the fire had cut a path forty miles in length by ten in width, destroying millions of dollars worth of property, and twelve hundred human lives.

Having followed the course of the fire up the western shore of Green Bay, its track and destruction should be traced along its eastern shore. The settlements here were fewer and less populous, and for that very reason, those whose property was destroyed, and who escaped only with their lives, suffered more than those who were burned out in the western counties. Relief was longer in coming to them. The destruction at New Franken and Robinsonville, in Brown County, northeast of Green Bay, have been described in the history of that county, with the progress of the flames through that region. The fire continued, with about the same rapidity, up the eastern shore as it did along the western shore, the tornado moving it northeast. Passing out of Brown County, it swept over fully half of Kewaunee County, the loss being particularly heavy in the towns of Casco, Red River, Lincoln and Ahnapee. The villages escaped. One hundred houses were burned, the loss of property being estimated at $250,000. School-houses were burned — every thing perishable in the path of the tempestuous fire disappeared. Hundreds of families were made homeless, and many deaths occurred through fright, as well as by actual burning. The fire sped up the peninsula into Door County, and clearing the timbered land and scattering houses and barns, and human and brute beings, before it, approached Williamsonville. This was a small settlement of about eighty persons, six miles south of Little Sturgeon, which had been built up by the Williamsons, father and sons, who were operating a flourishing shingle mill. Connected with it was a store, boarding-house and a number of dwelling houses. The other buildings were such as would go to make up a growing and hopeful little village. The family of eleven, and the mill hands, had, for two weeks previous to the great fire, been fighting the flames in the woods, all around the settlement, and had apparently subdued them. A clearing of ten acres had been made, and around this the fire continued to burn in spots, but with no appearance of concerted action. On Sunday afternoon, it entered what was called the potato-patch, but was extinguished without trouble. Water was hauled to the mill, as a measure of precaution, but the general opinion was that the worst of the danger had been met. Late at night, after the same hush which preceded the death-blow at Peshtigo, heavy puffs of wind commenced to surge up from the southwest. Next the fire balls appeared in advance of the tornado - and to this phenomena nearly every survivor bears witness; then the rumbling and the roar was heard, and the huge body of the fire came rolling through the woods and over the trees. The woods fell and crackled, and the Williamsons, and the whole village of men, women and children, were either busy changing their clothing for woolen goods, wetting down the buildings and covering them with blankets, or huddling together in the clearing. The women and children had at first all gathered in the boarding-house, but were led to the potato-patch clearing, when it became evident that the fire was advancing rapidly toward the settlement. It reached the village, and the scenes of Peshtigo were repeated, only on a smaller scale. Men and women fell on their faces, and attempted to get a breath of air not charged with blinding fire and smoke and stifling vapors; others rushed wildly on, and when they saw the race was useless, attempted to dash out their brains against stumps or tress; some perished in their houses; groans and screams of agony pieced even the roar of the tempest; horses galloped and snorted, in speechless terror, through the whirling flames; oxen bellowed. But the fury of the tornado passed quickly on, and out of four score, only seventeen escaped. Of the Williamson family, only Mrs. Williamson and her son, Thomas, remained. They save themselves by wrapping wet blankets around their bodies. Thirty-five of the dead lay together in one heap, in the center of the clearing. A few feet off sat Mrs. Williamson, badly burned, but alive, with the charred head of a dead woman resting upon her blanket. Of seven persons who jumped into a well, five came out alive. These fortunate cases were exceptions. Williamsonville was nothing but a name. The town of Nasewaupee suffered severely. Gardner, Union, Brussels, Forestville and Clay Banks were swept, and hundreds of narrow escapes are recorded. Green Bay and the drenching rain of Monday night, October 9, stayed the further progress to the north of this awful devastation.

PHILLIPS

WI-642   **JOHN R. DAVIS LUMBER CO.**

SC 1   5¢   Due Bearer, Black/Brown.   R-7

COUNTY OF PIERCE

WI-643   **PIERCE COUNTY**

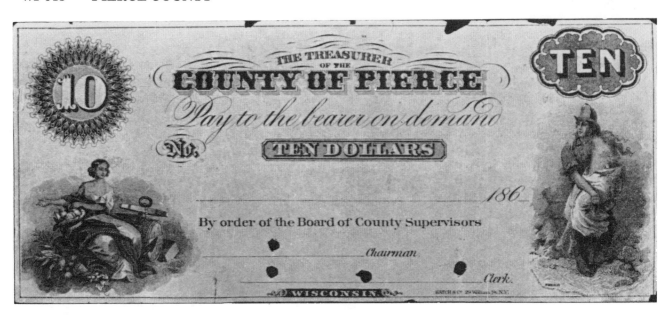

SC 2 $10   ___186-: Pay to the Bearer. Black. H & Co.   R-7

PLATTEVILLE

WI-645   **E.R. HINKLEY & COMPANY'S BANK OF GRANT COUNTY, 1857-65**

Capital $50,000. E. R. Hinckley, Pres., L. McCarn, cashier (1858). John H. Roundbee, Pres. (1863). Closed.

| G2a | $1 | February 21, 1857 DW. Tint: Orange lathework overall, panel at left and large ornate 1. Capital: $50,000. | R-7 |
| G2b | $1 | February 27, 1858 DW, ABNCo. mono. Same as G2a, except for date, imprint and capital ($75,000). | R-7 |

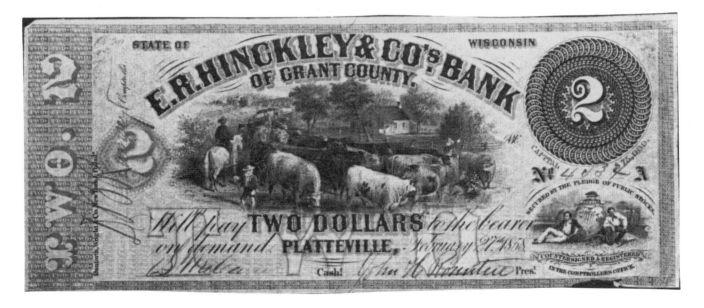

| G4a | $2 | February 21, 1857 DW. Tint: Orange lathework overall, panel at left and outlined in white TWO. Capital: $50,000. | R-6 |
| G4b | $2 | February 27, 1858 DW, ABNCo. mono. Same as G4a, except for date, imprint and capital ($75,000). | R-6 |

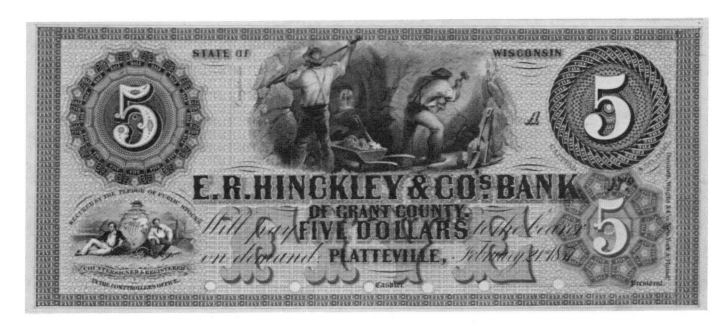

| G6a | $5 | February 21, 1857 DW. Tint: Orange lathework overall, counters and ornate FIVE. Capital: $50,000. | R-6 |
| G6b | $5 | February 27, 1858 DW, ABNCo. mono. Same as G6a, except for date, imprint and capital ($75,000). | R-7 |

| G8a | $10 | February 21, 1857 DW. Tint: Orange lathework overall, counter and ornate TEN. Capital: $50,000. | R-7 |

Uncut Sheet

| X1 | | $1, 2, 5, 10 DW. G2a, 4a, 6a, 8a | R-7 |

PORTAGE CITY

WI-648   COLUMBIA CO. BANK, (1850s)

Non-existent bank, represented only by altered notes, apparently intended to pass for those of the Columbia County Bank, Portage, WI-650.

A5	$3	___18__: 1850s DB. L: Franklin. Altered from $3 Columbia Bank, Washington, DC-195-G4.3.	R-6
A10	$5	___18__: 1850s DB.C: three allegorical women reclining with sheaf, pole and cap, globe and quadrant/FIVE. L: FIVE/Minerva stdg. with spear, helmet and shield/FIVE. R: oval portrait of Washington. Altered from $5 Columbia Bank, Washington, DC-195-G6.	R-7

WI-650 COLUMBIA COUNTY BANK, 1854-74

Capital $25,000. S. Marshall, Pres., H. S. Haskell, cashier (1854). John P. McGregor, Pres., H. E. Wells, cashier (1868).
Failed 1874.

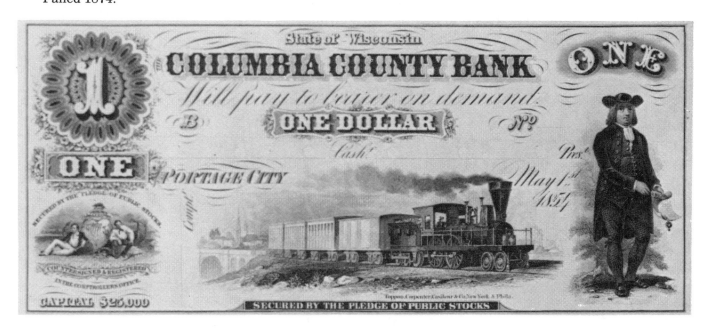

G2	$1	May 1, 1854 TCC. R: Penn. Capital: $25,000. No overprint.		R-7
G2b	$1	May 1, 1854 TCC. As above, except for capital ($50,000) and red ONE overprint.	Remainder Signed Note	R-5 R-6
G2c	$1	May 1, 1854 TCC, ABNCo. mono. As above, except for imprint.		R-6
G2d	$1	Unknown ABN. As above, except for imprint, addition of "Dept. of" before "Comptroller" and probably date.		R-7

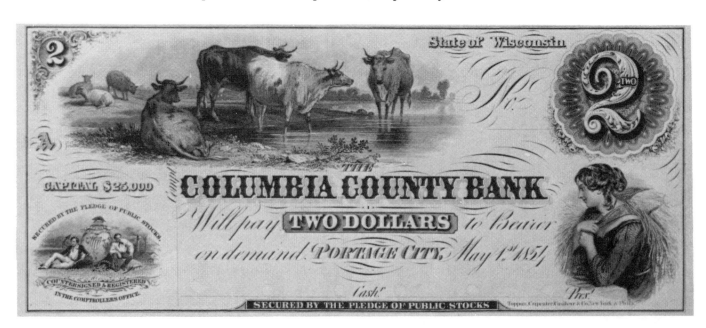

G4	$2	May 1, 1854 TCC. Capital: $25,000.	R-7
G4b	$2	May 1, 1854 TCC. As above, except for capital ($50,000) and red TWO overprint.	R-7

| G4c | $2 | May 1, 1854 TCC, ABNCo. mono. As above, except for imprint. | R-7 |
| G4d | $2 | Unknown ABN. As above, except for imprint, addition of "Dept. of" before "Comptroller" and probably date. | R-7 |

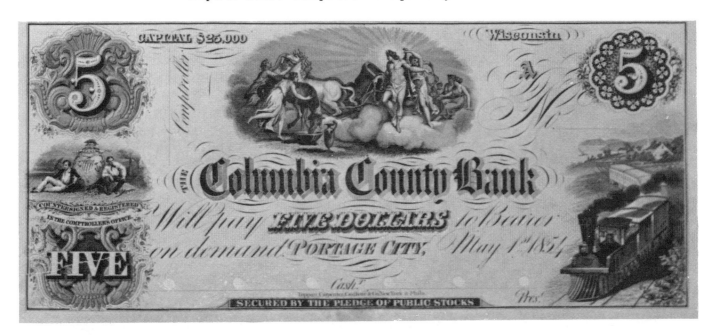

G6	$5	May 1, 1854 TCC. Capital: $25,000. No overprint.	R-7
G6b	$5	May 1, 1854 TCC. As above, except for capital ($50,000) and red FIVE overprint.	R-7
G6c	$5	May 1, 1854 TCC, ABNCo. mono. As above, except for imprint.	R-7
G6d	$5	Unknown ABN. As above, except for imprint, addition of "Dept. of" before "Comptr." and probably date.	R-7
R5	$10	May 1, 1854 TCC. Raised from $1, G2 or 2b. The bank issued no $10s.	R-7

Uncut Sheet

| X1 | | $1, 1, 2, 5 TCC. G2, 2, 4,6 | R-7 |

PORTAGE

WI-220   **BANK OF MONEKA, 1862**

Capital $50,000. J. H. Cole, Pres., J. Cole, cashier.
Was begun in Gordon in 1858 but moved that year to Viroqua. In 1862, it moved to Hustisford before settling in Portage. No notes were ever issued at Viroqua, Hustisford or Portage. In fact, only proof notes are known, thus it is possible none circulated.

WI-655   BANK OF PORTAGE, 1858-61

Capital $50,000. D. Verdercook, Pres., H. L. Norton, cashier.
Failed. 1862 notes redeemed at 78.6¢ per dollar in 1862.

Genuine Notes, Raised Notes and Counterfeits

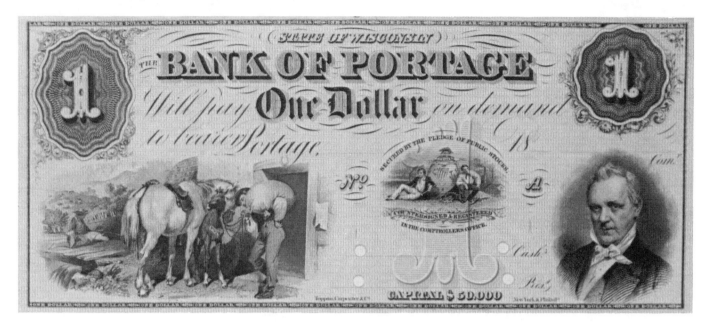

| G2a | $1 | ___18__: 1858 TC. Lower R: Buchanan. Tint: Red-orange ornate 1 and lathework overall. | R-6 |
| G4a | $1 | ___18__: (1859-61) TC, ABNCo. mono. Lower R. Clay. Overprint: Ornate red 1. | R-7 |

| G6a | $2 | ___18__: (1858) TC. Tint: Red-orange ornate 2 and lathework overall. | R-7 |
| G6b | $2 | ___18__: (1859-61) TC, ABNCo. mono. As above, except for imprint and replacement of tint by red ornate 2 overprint. | R-7 |

| G8a | $3 | ___18__: (1858) TC. Tint: Red orange ornate 3 and lathework overall. | R-7 |
| G8b | $3 | ___18__: (1859-61) TC, ABNCo. mono. As above, except for imprint and replacement of tint by red ornate 3 overprint. | R-7 |

G10a	$5	___18__: 1858 TC. Tint: Red-orange lathework overall and panel of microlettering with an outlined white FIVE.	R-6
G10b	$5	___18__: 1859-61 TC, ABNCo. mono. As above, except for imprint and replacement of tint by a red FIVE overprint.	R-7
R5	$5	___18__: late 1850s TC. Raised from $1, G2a or G4a.	R-7
R6	$10	___18__: late 1850s TC. Raised from $1, G2a or G4a. The bank issued no $10s.	R-7

Uncut Sheets

| X1 | $1, 2, 3, 5 TC. G2a, 6a, 8a, 10a | R-7 |
| X2 | $1, 2, 3, 5 TC, ABNCo. mono. G4a, 6b, 8b, 10b | R-7 |

POUND

WI-657   **JACOB BROOKS**

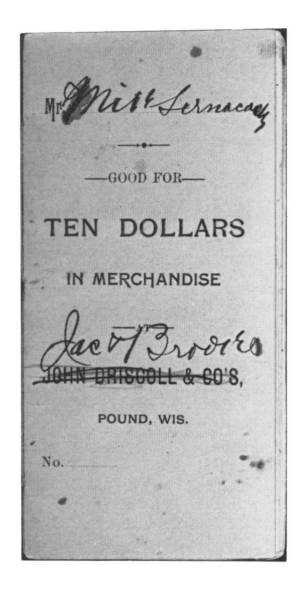

SC 10 $10   In Merchandise. An account book to record merchandise   R-7
                    (produce) received.

PRAIRIE DU CHIEN

WI-660   BANK OF PRAIRIE DU CHIEN, 1857-67

Capital $50,000. This bank began operations in 1856 and then suspended them until 1862 and again suspended operations in 1867. From 1862 to 1867 Anson Eldred served as President and Charles Ray as cashier. RWH&E printed notes for the first period, ABN for the second.
Closed.

Genuine Notes, Raised Notes and Counterfeits

SC 1   5¢   Pay to the Bearer. Blue. CP.   R-7

SC 2   10¢   Pay to the Bearer. Blue. CP.   R-7

G2	$1	___18__: ____ RWH&E. No overprint.	R-7
G2a	$1	___18__: (1850s) RWH&E. As above, except for red ONE overprint.	R-7
G2c	$1	___18__: 1860s ABN. As above, except for imprint, addition of "Dept. of" before "Comptroller" and overprint color (green).	R-7

G4	$2	___18__: ____ RWH&E. No overprint.	R-7
G4a	$2	___18__: (1850s) RWH&E. As above, except for red TWO overprint.	R-7
G4c	$2	___18__: 1860s ABN. As above, except for imprint, addition of "Dept. of" before "Comptroller" and overprint color (green).	R-7

| G6 | $3 | ___18__: ____ RWH&E. No overprint. | R-7 |

G6a $3 ___18__: (1850s) RWH&E. As above, except for red lazy 3 overprint. R-7

G6c $3 ___18__: 1860s ABN. As above, except for imprint, addition of "Dept. of" before "Comptroller" and overprint color (green). R-7

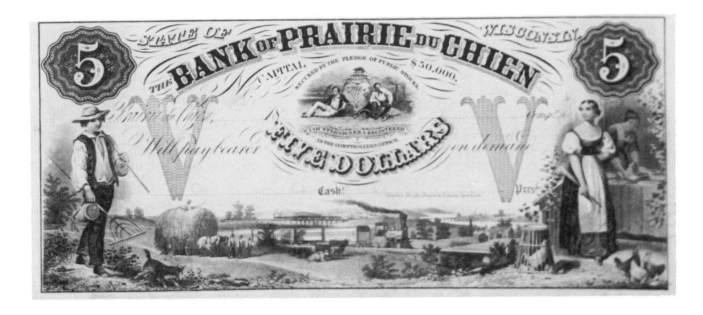

G8 $5 ___18__: ____ RWH&E. Same as G8a, except for lack of an overprint. R-7

G8a	$5	___18__: (1850s) RWH&E. As above, except for red ornate V V overprint.	R-7
G8c	$5	___18__: 1860s ABN. As above, except for imprint, addition of "Dept. of" before "Comptroller" and overprint color (green).	R-7
R5	$5	___18__: 1850s RWH&E. Raised from $1, G2a.	R-7
R6	$10	___18__: 1850s RWH&E. Raised from $1, G2a. The bank issued no $10s.	R-7
R7	$20	___18__: 1850s RWH&E. Raised from $1, G2a. The bank issued no $20s.	R-7

Uncut Sheet

| X1 | | $1, 2, 3, 5 RWH&E. G2a, 4a, 6a, 8a | R-7 |

WI-656   PRAIRIE DU CHIEN FERRY COMPY. (Wisconsin Territory)

| SC 8a | $3 | January 10, 1838. | R-6 |

PRAIRIE FARM

WI-662   **KNAPP, STOUT & CO.**

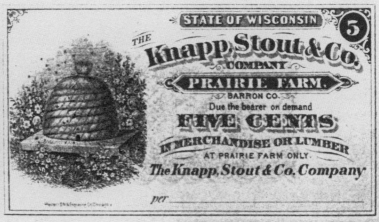

SC 1   5¢   Due Bearer in Merchandise or Lumber, blue front, brown   R-7
               back WBN&E.

SC 2   10¢   Due Bearer in Merchandise or Lumber, blue front, brown   R-7
               back WBN&E.

SC 5   25¢   Due Bearer in Merchandise or Lumber, blue front, brown   R-7
                    back WBN&E.

SC 6   50¢   Due Bearer in Merchandise or Lumber, blue front, brown   R-7
                    back WBN&E.

SC 7 $1   Due Bearer in Merchandise or Lumber, blue front, brown   R-7
                    back WBN.

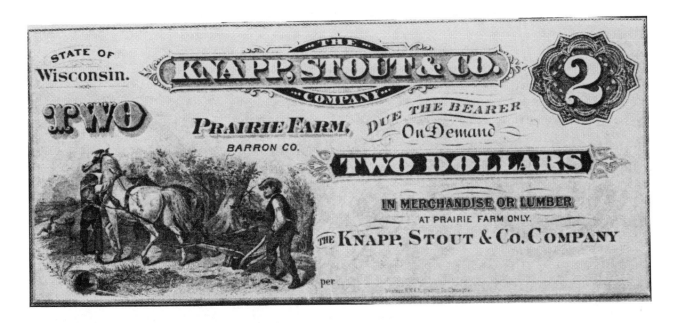

SC 8 $2   Due Bearer in Merchandise or Lumber, blue front, brown   R-7
                      back WBN&E.

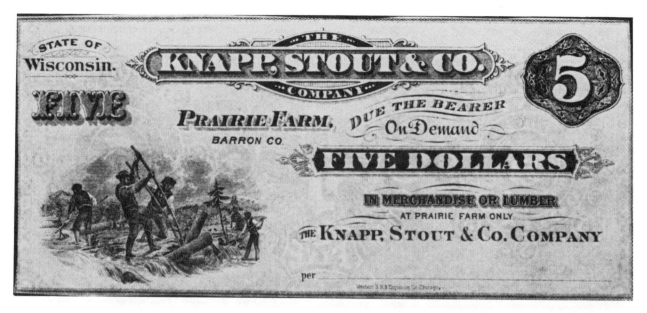

SC 10 $5   Due Bearer in Merchandise or Lumber, blue front, brown   R-7
                back WBN&E.

Uncut Sheet

1   Front uncut sheet of 12 notes. Back uncut sheet of 12   R-7
                notes

Litho by Western B.N. & Engraving Co., Chicago 9.

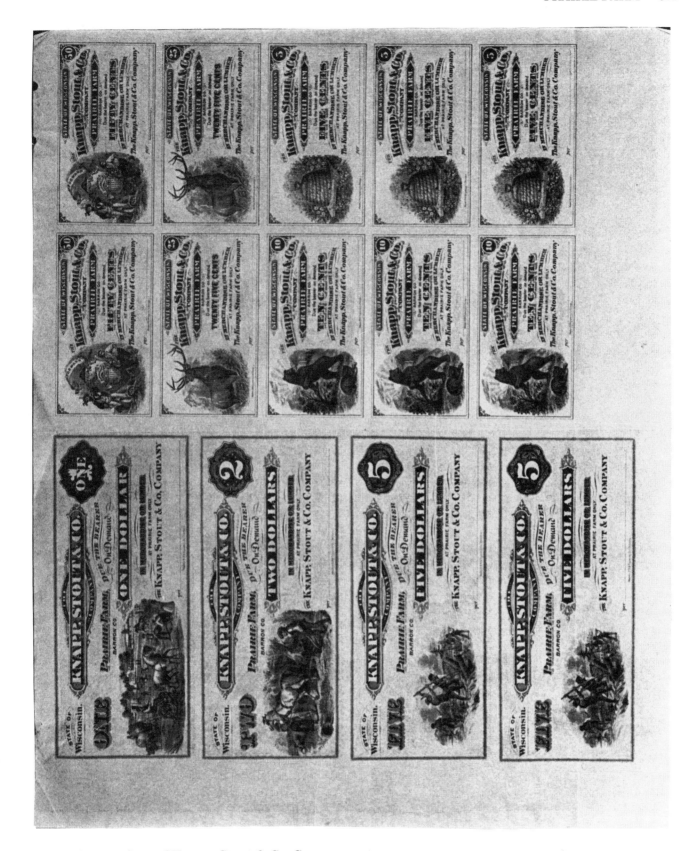

Front of uncut sheet of Knapp, Stout & Co. Company notes.

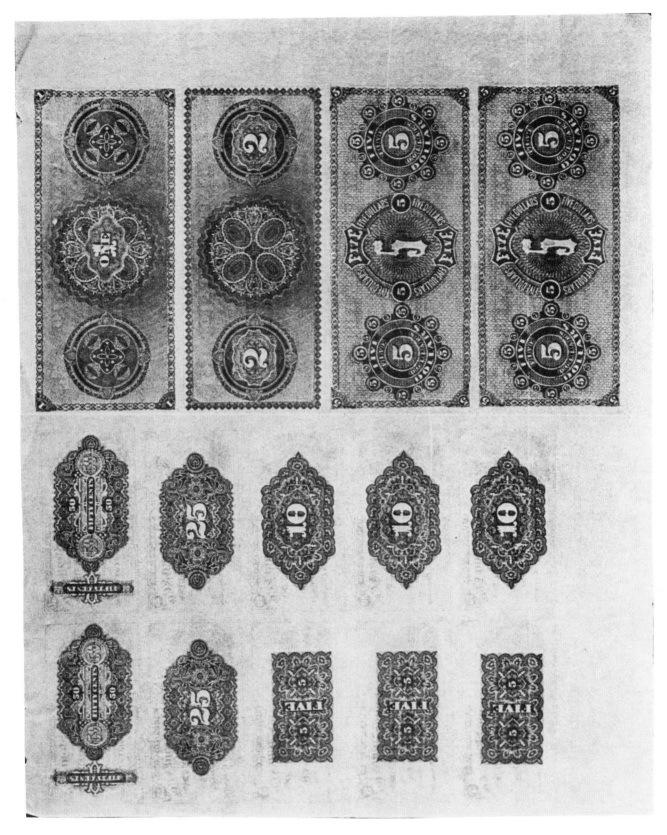

Reverse of Knapp, Stout & Co. Company notes.

PRESCOTT

WI-665   CITY BANK OF PRESCOTT, 1858-65

Capital $50,000. Charles Miller, Pres., W. P. Westfall, cashier.
Closed.

G2a	$1	___18__: (1857) TC. Tint: Red-orange lathework overall and panel of microlettering bearing large ONE. Capital: $25,000.	Remainder	R-6
G2b	$1	___18__: late 1850s TC, ABNCo. mono. As above, except for imprint and capital ($50,000).		R-7
G2c	$1	___18__: 1860s TC, ABNCo. mono. Same as G2b, except for capital ($75,000).		R-7

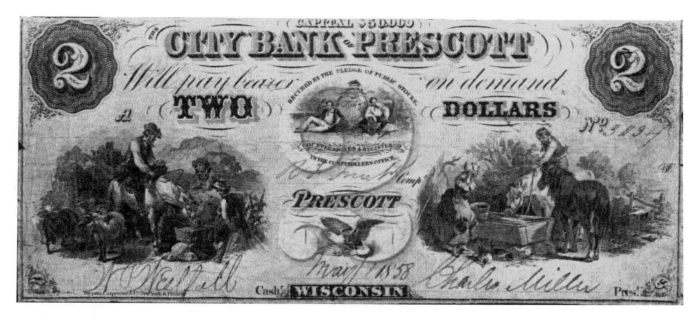

G4a	$2	___18__: (1857) TC. Tint: Red-orange lathework overall outlining large ornate 2. Capital: $25,000.	R-7
G4b	$2	___18__: late 1850s TC, ABNCo. mono. As above, except for imprint and capital ($50,000).	R-6
G4c	$2	___18__: 1860s TC, ABNCo. mono. Same as G4b, except for capital ($75,000).	R-7

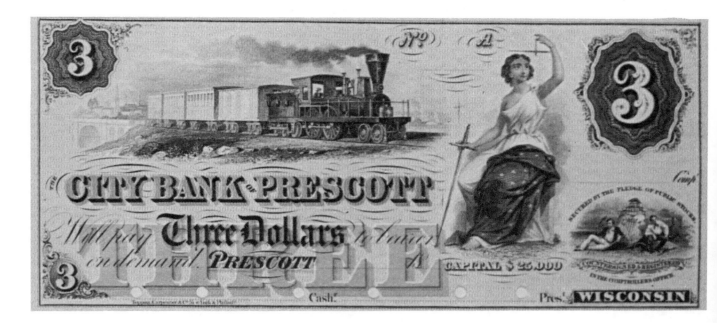

G6a	$3	___18__: (1857) TC. Tint: Red-orange lathework overall and large THREE. Capital: $25,000.	R-7
G6b	$3	___18__: late 1850s TC, ABNCo. mono. As above, except for imprint and capital ($50,000).	R-6
G6c	$3	___18__: 1860s TC, ABNCo. mono. Same as G6b, except for capital ($75,000).	R-7

G8a	$5	___18__: (1857) TC Tint: Red-orange lathework overall and panel of microlettering with outlined white FIVE. Capital: $25,000.	R-7
G8b	$5	___18__: late 1850s TC, ABNCo. mono. Same as G8a, except for imprint and capital ($50,000).	R-7
G8c	$5	___18__: 1860s TC, ABNCo. mono. Same as G8b, except for capital ($75,000).	R-7

Uncut Sheet

| X1 | | $1, 2, 3, 5 TC. G2a, 4a, 6a, 8a | R-7 |

WI-666   **PRESCOTT CITY BANK**

SC 3   15¢   Pay the Bearer, October 12, 1862.   R-7

PRINCETON

WI-575   **BANK OF MONTELLO**

Moved from Montello in 1850s; did not issue notes from Princeton.

RACINE

TN5   **AGRICULTURAL BANK, BROWNSVILLE, TENN.**

G1 $1   ___185__; 1850s WHH&W.   R-5

Surcharged. Racine — See LaCrosse for similar surcharge of these notes.

G2 $2   ___185__; 1850s Black WHH&W.   R-5

WI-670   CITY BANK OF RACINE, 1854-59

Capital $50,000. Gilbert Knapp, Pres., A. LeClerg, cashier.
Closed in 1860. $3,496 held for redemption of notes until December 31, 1862.

G2	$1	___185__: ___TCC. Same as G2a, except for lack of an overprint.		R-7
G2a	$1	___185__: 1850s TCC. As above, except for a red lazy overprint.	Remainder	R-6

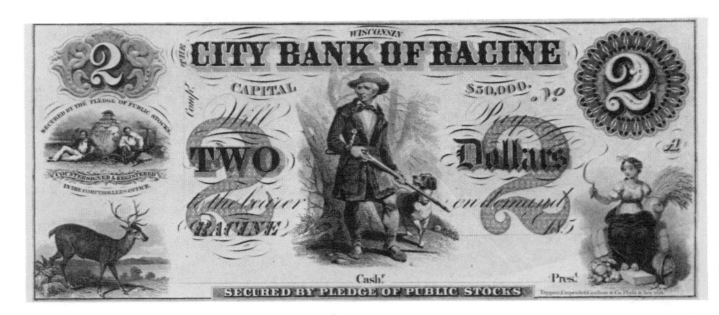

G4	$2	___185__: ___TCC. C: Daniel Boone. No overprint.		R-7
G4a	$2	___185__: (1850s) TCC. As above, except for a red ornate 2 2 overprint.	Remainder	R-6

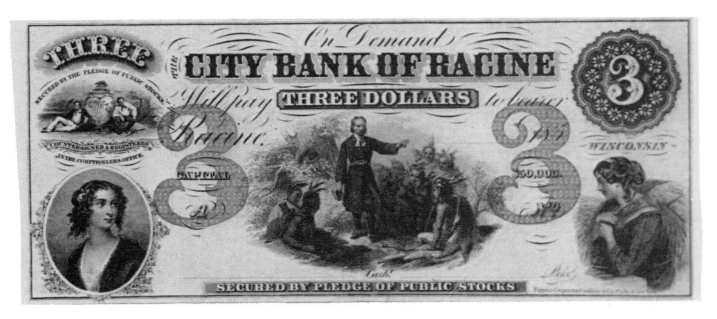

G6 $3   ___185__: ___TCC. C: Eliot preaching to the Indians.   —
                       Same as G6a, except for lack of an overprint.

G6a $3   ___185__: (1850s) TCC. As above, except for a red ornate   Remainder   R-6
                       33 overprint.

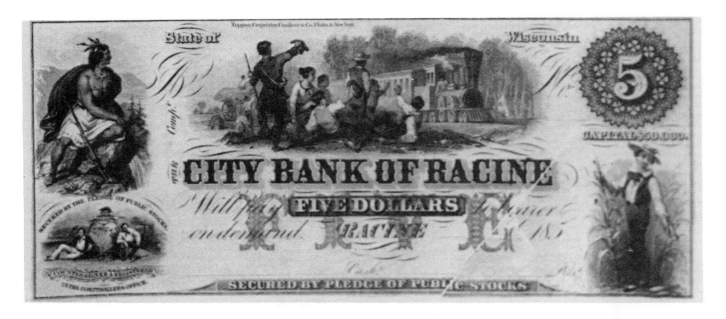

G8 $5   ___185__: ___TCC. Same as G8a, except for lack of an   —
                       overprint.

G8a $5   ___185__: (1850s) TCC. As above, except for a red ornate   Remainder   R-6
                       FIVE overprint.

Uncut Sheet

X1 $1, 2, 3, 5 TCC. G2, 4, 6, 8   R-7

X2 $1, 2, 3, 5 TCC. G2a, 4a, 6a, 8a   R-7

WI-675   COMMERCIAL BANK OF RACINE, ca.1856-63

Capital $100,000 (1858); $25,000 (1863). H. S. Durand, Pres., Jacob W. Moore, cashier.
Closed 1862.

Genuine Notes, Raised Notes and Counterfeits

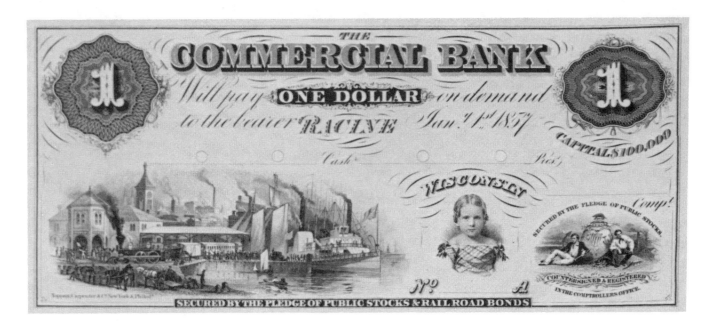

| G2 | $1 | January 1, 1857 TC. No overprint. | Remainder | R-6 |
| G2a | $1 | (January 1, 1857) (TC). As above, except for a red over-print. | | R-7 |

| G4 | $1 | January 1, 1857 TC. No overprint. | | R-7 |
| G4a | $1 | (January 1, 1857) (TC). As above, except for a red over-print. | | R-7 |

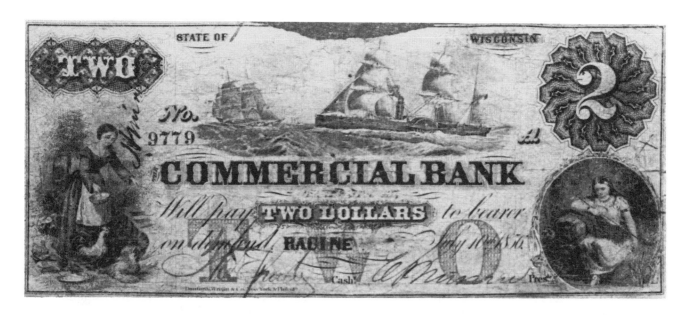

| G6 | $2 | January 1, 1857 TC. No overprint. | R-7 |
| G6a | $2 | (January 1, 1857) (TC). As above, except for a red over-print. | R-7 |

G8	$3	January 1, 1857 TC. No overprint.	R-7
G8a	$3	(January 1, 1857) (TC). As above, except for a red over-print.	R-7
R5	$10	January 1, 1857 TC. Raised from $1, G4. The bank issued no $10s.	R-7

Uncut Sheet

| X1 | | $1, 1, 2, 3 TC. G2, 4, 6, 8 | R-7 |

Altered, Spurious and Unattributed Non-Genuine Notes

A5 $1   July 10, 1856DW. C: three horses drinking from well, sheep at left. L: ONE/male reaper std. under tree. R: 1/sailor std. on board ship, telescope in left hand. Altered from $1 Commercial Bank of New Jersey, Perth Amboy, NJ-445-G40.   R-7

A10 $2   July 10, 1856 DW. Altered from $2 Commercial Bank of New Jersey, Perth Amboy, NJ-445-G42 series.   R-6

A15 $5   July 10, 1856 DW.C: whaling scene, men in boat in fore-ground, ship in rt. bkdg. L: 5/sailing ship, in circle. R: 5-1/2-length figure of sailor at ship's wheel, in circle. Altered from $5 Commercial Bank of New Jersey, Perth Amboy, NJ-445-G44 series.   R-7

WI-686   RACINE & MISSISSIPPI RAILROAD CO.

Formed March 29, 1856, by consolidation of: (a) Racine and Mississippi Rail Road Company, a consolidation of The Rockton and Freeport Railroad Company (52), and (b) Savanna Branch Railroad Company.
Wisconsin division deeded to The Western Union Rail Road Company June 5, 1867.
Illinois division deeded to The Western Union Rail Road Company August 25, 1868.
After a series of subsequent mergers and name changes it became the Chicago, Milwaukee, St. Paul and Pacific Railroad Company in 1927.

SC 7 $1.00   Will Pay to Phillips & Lighthard, Contractors $125,000 for road between Beloit and Freeport (Ill.)___185_.   R-7

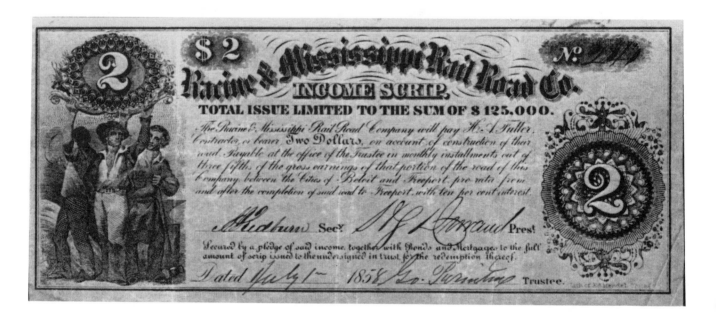

SC 8 $2.00   ___185_.   R-7

SC 7 $1.00   ___188_ Black. Will Pay to H.R. Fuller, Contractors   R-7
                        $200,000 for road between Freeport and Savanna
                        (Ill.).

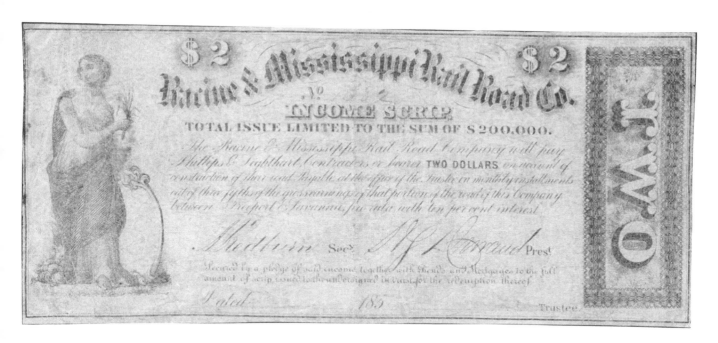

SC 8 $2.00   ___185_.   R-7

WI-680   BANK OF RACINE, 1853-72

Capital $50,000 (1852); $25,000 (1863). McCrea, Bell & Neman, Proprietors, Augustus McCrea, Pres., Henry J. Ulman, cashier 1853. Daniel Neman became cashier in 1863.
Closed 1872.

Genuine Notes, Raised Notes and Counterfeits

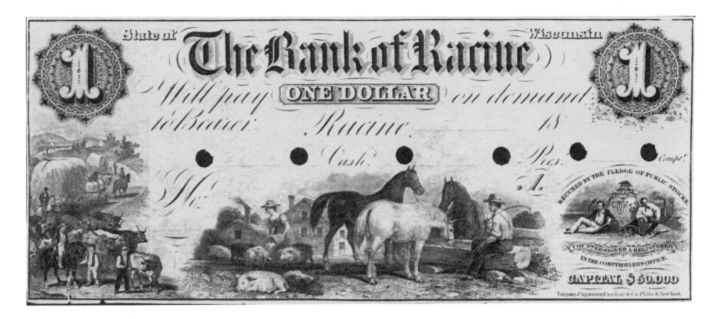

G2 $1   __18__: (1850s) TCC.   Remainder   R-6

G4 $2   __18__: (1850s) TCC.   R-7

G6 $3   ___18__: (1850s) TCC.   R-7

G8 $5   ___18__: (1850s) TCC.L: Washington. R: Webster.   Remainder   R-6

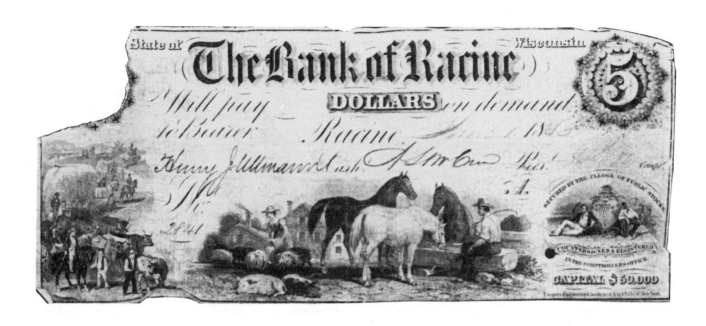

R5	$5	___18__: 1850s TCC.Raised from $1, G2.	R-6
R6	$10	___18__: 1850s TCC.Raised from $1, G2. The bank issued no $10s.	R-7
R7	$20	___18__: 1850s TCC.Raised from $1, G2. The bank issued no $20s.	R-7
R8	$50	___18__: 1850s TCC.Raised from $1, G2. The bank issued no $50s.	R-7

Uncut Sheets

| X1 | $1, 2, 3, 5 TCC. G2, 4, 6, 8 | R-7 |

WI-685   RACINE COUNTY BANK, 1854-64

Capital $100,000. Reubin M. Norton, Pres., George C. Northrop, cashier (1854). N. D. Fratt, Pres., Darwin Andrews, cashier (1863).
Became the First National Bank of Racine #457 in May 1864.

Genuine Notes, Raised Notes and Counterfeits

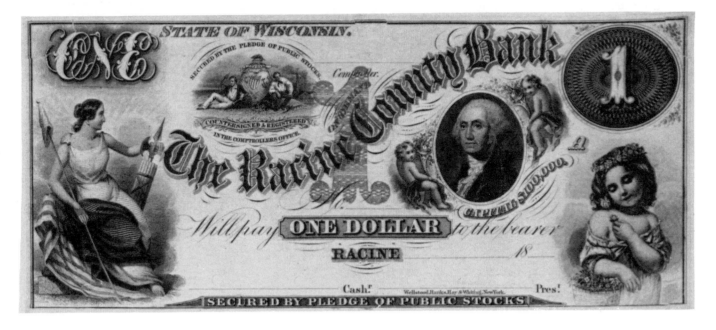

G2	$1	___18__: ____ WHH&W. RC: Washington. No overprint.	R-7
G2a	$1	___18__: (1850s-60s) WHH&W. As above, except for a red 1 overprint.	R-7

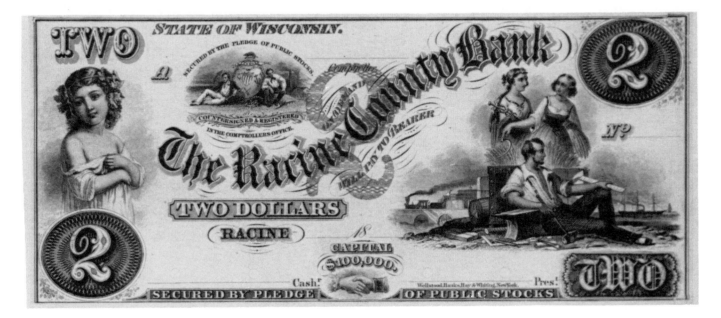

G4	$2	___18__: ____ WHH&W. No overprint.	R-7
G4a	$2	___18__: (1850s-60s) WHH&W. As above, except for a red 2 overprint.	R-7
R2	$2	___18__: 1850s WHH&W. Raised from $1, G2 or 2a.	R-7

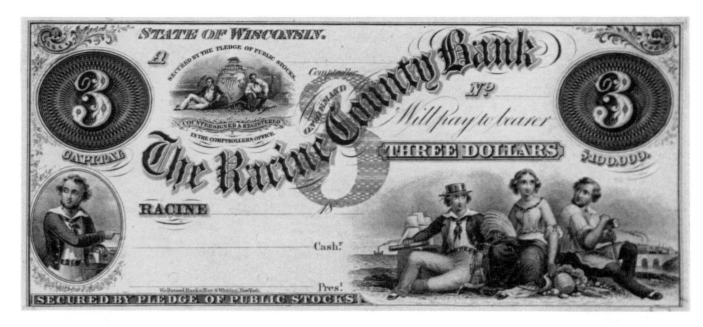

G6	$3	___18__: ____ WHH&W. No overprint.	R-7
G6a	$3	___18__: (1850s-60s) WHH&W. As above, except for a red 3 overprint.	R-7
R4	$3	___18__: 1850s WHH&W. Raised from $1, G2 or 2a.	R-7

G8	$5	___18__: ____ WHH&W. No overprint.	R-7
G8a	$5	___18__: 1850s WHH&W. As above, except for a red ornate FIVE overprint.	R-6
G8b	$5	___18__: 1860s WHH&W. Same as G8a, except for overprint style (block letters).	R-6

R6	$5	___18__: 1850s WHH&W. Raised from $1, G2 or 2a.	R-7
R8	$10	___18__: 1850s WHH&W. Raised from $1, G2 or 2a. The bank issued no $10s.	R-7
R10	$20	___18__: 1850s WHH&W. Raised from $1, G2 or 2a. The bank issued no $20s.	R-7

Uncut Sheets

| X1 | $1, 2, 3, 5 WHH&W. G2, 4, 6, 8 | R-7 |
| X2 | $1, 2, 3, 5 WHH&W. G2a, 4a, 6a, 8a | R-7 |

WI-690   RICHMOND'S EXCHANGE BANK, ca.1852-60s

A private bank.
Unknown.

Genuine Notes, Raised Notes and Counterfeits

G2 $1   ___185__: 1850s RWH&E.   R-4

G4 $2   ___185__: 1850s RWH&E.   R-4

G6 $3   ___185__: 1850s. RWH&E. Black.   R-4

R5 $5   ___185__: 1850s RWH&E. Raised from $1, G2.   R-6

REEDSBURGH

WI-695   REEDSBURGH BANK, 1859-61

Capital $50,000. George Ege, Pres., H. M. Haskell, cashier.
Failed 1861. Notes redeemed in 1862 at 75-1/2¢ per dollar. $682 outstanding in 1863.

Genuine Notes, Raised Notes and Counterfeits

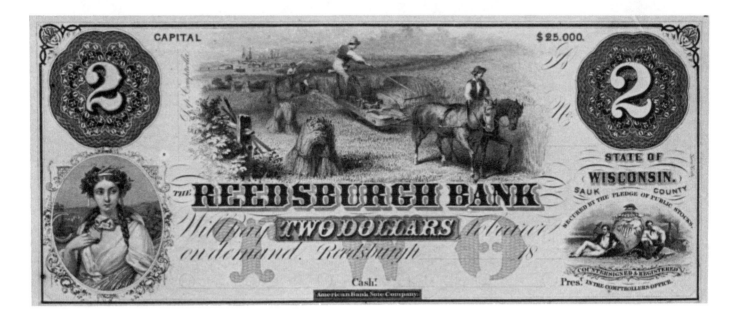

G2a	$2	___18__: ca.1859 ABN. Capital: $25,000. Overprint: Red TWO.	R-6
G2b	$2	___18__: ca.1860-61 ABN. As above, except for capital ($50,000).	R-7

| G4a | $3 | ___18__: (ca.1859) ABN. Overprint: Red THREE. Same as G4b, except for capital ($25,000). | R-7 |
| G4b | $3 | ___18__: ca.1860-61 ABN. As above, except for capital ($50,000). | R-6 |

Uncut Sheet

| X1 | | $2, 3 ABN. G2a, 4a | R-7 |

Altered, Spurious and Unattributed Non-Genuine Notes

| N5 | $10 | Unknown. C: Man feeding hogs. The bank issued no $10s. | R-7 |

RICE LAKE

WI-714   **KNAPP, STOUT & CO. COMPANY**

SC 1   5¢   Due Bearer on Demand in Merchandise or Lumber WBN.   R-3

SC 2   10¢   Due Bearer on Demand in Merchandise or Lumber WBN.   R-3
                        Face, black.

SC 5   25¢   Due Bearer on Demand in Merchandise or Lumber WBN.   R-3
                        Black, green.

SC 6   50¢   Due Bearer on Demand in Merchandise or Lumber WBN.   R-3

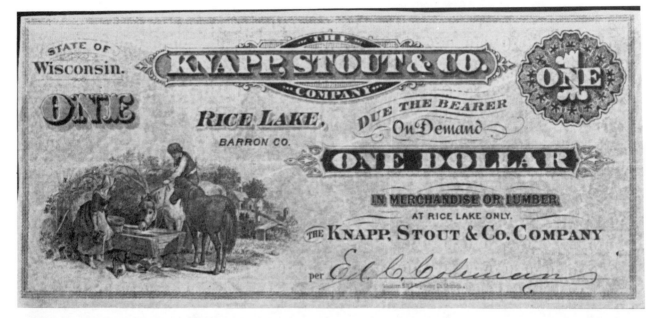

SC 7 $1   Due Bearer On Demand in Merchandise or Lumber   R-6
                         WBN.

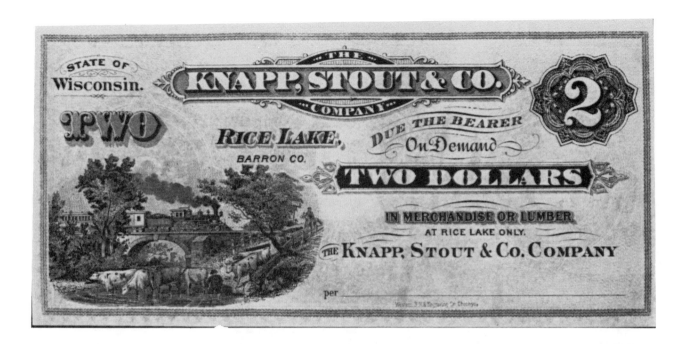

SC 8 $2   Due Bearer On Demand in Merchandise or Lumber WBN.   R-5

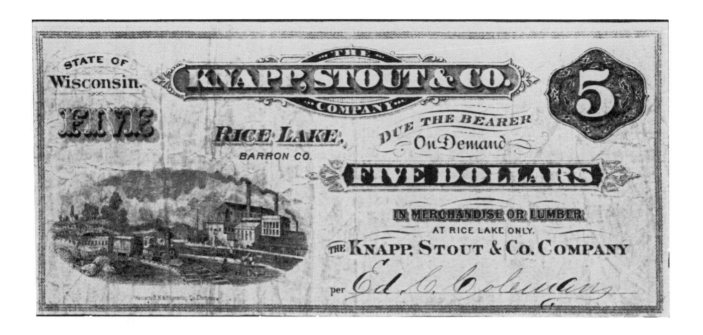

SC 10 $5   Due Bearer on Demand in Merchandise or Lumber WBN.   R-5

*Sheet — none known. Unique.
Litho by Western B N & Engraving Co., Chicago.
*See Prairie Farm for sheet configuration.
See Appendix A for a history of the Knapp, South & Co. Company.

RICHLAND CENTER

WI-700   **RICHLAND COUNTY BANK, ca. 1858**

Probably never opened.

G2a $1   August 1, 1858 BC, ABN. Overprint: Red ONE.   R-7

G4a $2   August 1, 1858 BC, ABN. Overprint: Red TWO.   R-7

RIPON

WI-705   **PRAIRIE CITY BANK, ca.1860-63**

Capital $25,000.
Fate: closed.

| G2 | $2 | ___18__: ____ ABN. No overprint. | R-7 |
| G2a | $2 | ___18__: 1860s ABN. As above, except for overprint (probably red 2 2). | R-7 |

| G4 | $3 | ___18__: ____ ABN. No overprint. | R-7 |
| G4a | $3 | ___18__: 1860s. ABN. As above, except for red 3 3 overprint. | R-6 |

Uncut Sheet

| X1 | | $2, 3 ABN. G2, 4 | R-7 |

WI-710   **BANK OF RIPON, 1856-64**

Capital $25,000. Richard Catlin, Pres., E. P. Brockway, cashier (1857). Geo. L. Field, cashier, (1863). Became the First National Bank of Ripon #425 in 1864. Merged with American National Bank and became the First National Bank in 1930.

G2 $1   ___18__: (1850s-60s) TC.   R-1

G4 $2   ___18__: ___ TC.   R-7

G6 $5   ___18__: (1850s-60s) TC.   R-7

Uncut Sheet

X1 $1, 1, 2, 5 TC. G2, 2, 4, 6   R-7

WI-712   PECK & CO.

SC 3   15¢   Pay the Bearer WLSH.   R-7

WI-713   DODGE & SAUB

SC 1   5¢   June 5, 1862 HS. Payable in Currency.   R-7

ST. CROIX FALLS

WI-715   **ST. CROIX VALLEY BANK, 1857-62**

Capital $50,000 (1858); $100,000 (1859); $25,000 (1863). John R. Wheeler, Pres., D. W. Armstrong, cashier
(1863); Silas Staples, Pres., 1865. No place of business or banking house.
Closed before May, 1862.

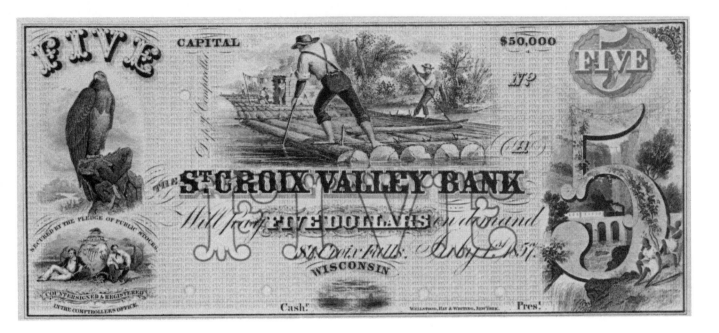

| G2 | $5 | July 1, 1857 WH&W. Tint: Red counter and microletter-ing overall with an outlined white FIVE. Capital: $50,000. | R-7 |
| G2a | $5 | (July 1, 1857) (WH&W). As above, except for capital ($100,000). | R-7 |

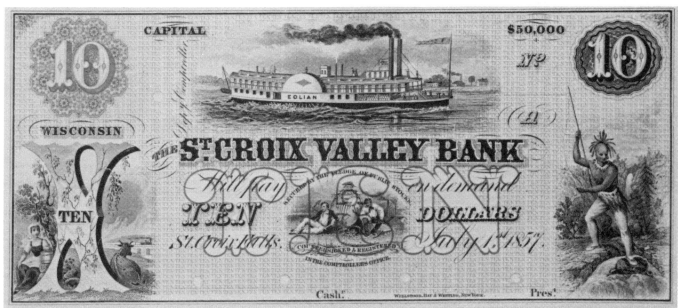

G4	$10	July 1, 1857 WH&W. Tint: Red counter and microlettering overall with an outlined white TEN. Capital: $50,000.	R-7
G4a	$10	(July 1, 1857 (WH&W). As above, except for capital ($100,000).	R-7

Uncut Sheet

X1		$5, 10 WH&W. G2, 4	R-7

SAUK CITY

WI-720   **SAUK CITY BANK, 1858-65**

Capital $50,000. D. K. Tenny, Pres., George B. Burrows, cashier (1863).
Fate: closed.

Genuine Notes, Raised Notes and Counterfeits

G2	$1	November 1, 1858 WH&W, ABN. No overprint.	R-5
C2	$1	November 1, 1858 WH&W, ABN. Photographic cft. of the above.	R-7
G2a	$1	November 1, 1858 WH&W, ABN. As above, except for red ONE overprint. Written serial number.	R-5

G2b	$1	November 1, 1858 WH&W, ABN. Same as G2a, except for printed serial number.	R-5

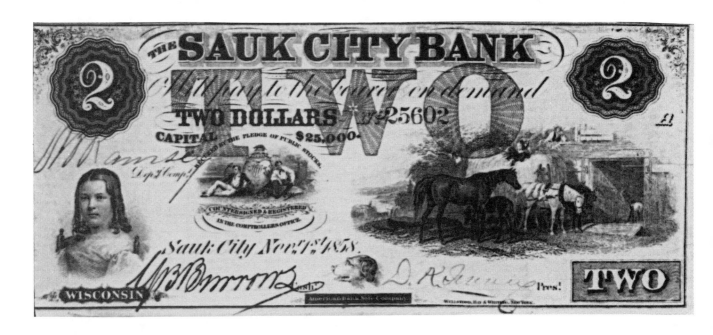

G4	$2	November 1, 1858 WH&W, ABN. No overprint.	R-7
C4	$2	November 1, 1858 WH&W, ABN. Photographic cft. of the above.	R-7
G4a	$1	November 1, 1858 WH&W, ABN. Same as G4, except for red TWO overprint. Written serial number.	R-7
G4b	$2	November 1, 1858 WH&W, ABN. Same as G4a, except for printed serial number.	R-5
R5	$5	November 1, 1858 WH&W, ABN. Raised from $1, G2 or 2a. The bank issued no $5s.	R-7
R6	$5	November 1, 1858 WH&W, ABN. Raised from $2, G2 or 2a. The bank issued no $5s.	R-7
R7	$10	November 1, 1858 WH&W, ABN. Raised from $1, G2 or 2a. The bank issued no $10s.	R-7
R8	$20	November 1, 1858 WH&W, ABN. Raised from $1, G2 or 2a. The bank issued no $20s.	R-7

Uncut Sheets

| X1 | | $1, 2 WH&W, ABN. G2, 4 | R-7 |
| X2 | | $1, 2 WH&W, ABN. G2a, 4a | R-7 |

Altered, Spurious and Unattributed Non-Genuine Notes

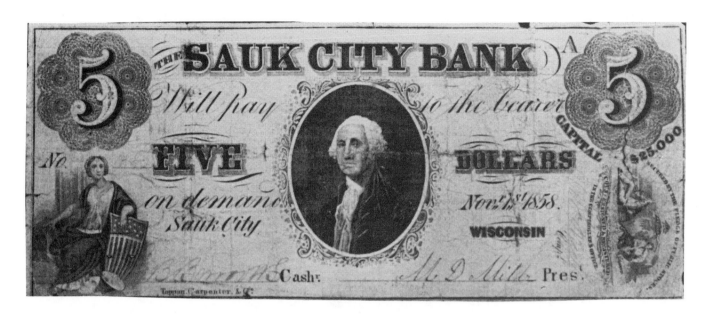

S5 $5   November 1, 1858 TC. C: Washington. The bank issued   R-5
                  no $5s.

SCANDINAVIA

WI-721   **SCANDINAVIA ACADEMY**

(College currency)

For use in the Business Department.

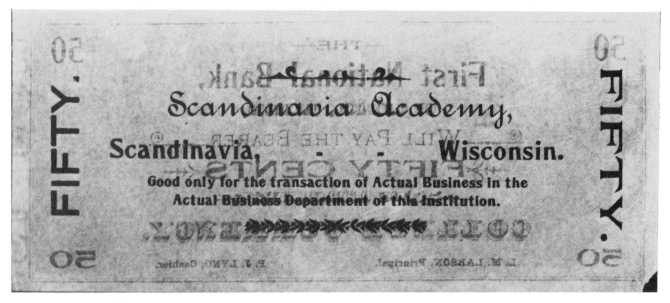

SC 6   50¢   Black/Light Brown tint.   R-7

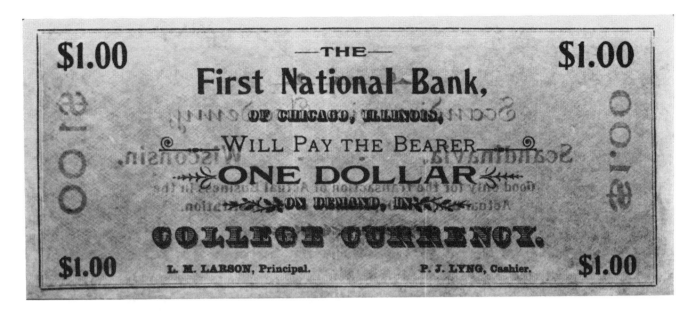

SC 7 $1   Black/Light Brown tint.   R-7

SC 10 $5   Black/Green tint.   R-7

These notes were printed on very thin paper and printing on both sides was highly readable.

SEYMOUR

WI-724   **P. HAMMEL & CO.**

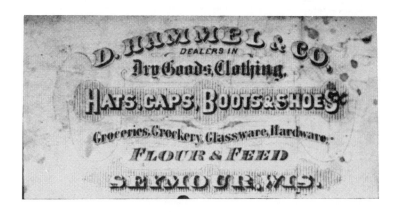

SC 6   50¢   ___18__. Will Pay to Bearer. Front: Blue/Green. Back: R-7
         Green.

SHAWANAW

WI-725   SHAWANAW BANK, 1857-1865

Capital $100,000. S. A. Bean, Pres. 1860; J. O. Thayer, 1863. E. P. Niles, cashier 1858; H. Madgeburg 1860 and M. Grasser 1863. Capital 1863 was $35,000.
This bank moved to Chilton in 1858 and to Sheboygan in 1863. While only $5 and $10 are known to exist, the author suggests that $1 and $2 also were issued without an overprint. The $1 and $2 of Chilton carry green overprints, as do the $5 and $10 of Sheboygan.
Fate: closed.

NOTES DATED AT SHAWANAW

Genuine Notes, Raised Notes and Counterfeits

G2	$5	June 1, 1857 DW. Capital: $50,000.	Remainder	R-6
C2	$5	June 1, 1857 DW. Photographic cft. of the above.		R-7

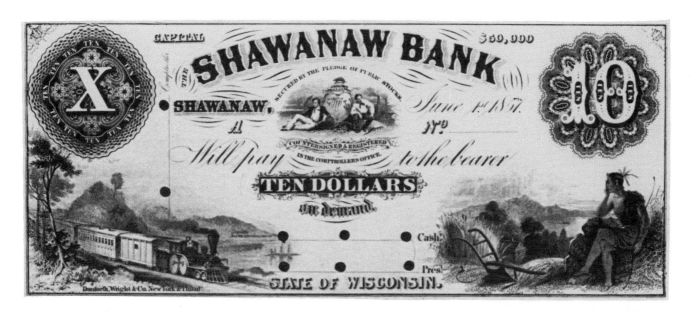

G4	$10	June 1, 1857 DW. Capital: $50,000.	Remainder	R-6

Uncut Sheet

X1		$5, 10 DW. G2, 4		R-7

Early Banking In Shawano County

In 1852, Wisconsin legislature in act of the law, "An act to authorize the business of banking." Under this act a bank was organized by William A. Loordayet, of Chicago, in 1857, and filed its incorporation papers in the office of the register of deeds in Shawanaw on May 16, 1857.

The bank started business on June 1, 1857, but stayed only about two years and moved its charter to Chilton, Wisconsin and later to Sheboygan, Wisconsin. The bank was known as the Shawanaw Bank. Apparently Shawano had no banking facilities until 1881 when F. W. Humphrey organized the Shawano County Bank under a charter and operated the same until about 1900 when the bank was reorganized and rechartered as a national bank under the laws of the United States. Prominent in the banking business for many years in Shawano, were F. W. Humphrey, V. H. George, W. C. Zachow, M. J. Wallrich, D. E. Wescott, A. C. Weber, King Weeman, and Yuma Mittlestadt. The original bank building was erected in about 1887. About 1902, a new bank was organized by a group of citizens headed by Antone Kuckuk, Z. R. Stier, Ira Wheat, Frank K. Martin, and others. This bank was organized as the German-American Bank, but later changed its name to The Wisconsin National Bank. In 1910, a new state bank was organized by a group of local citizens; The Citizens State Bank with Fred G. Brener as cashier. Other associates of the new bank were Judge F. A. Jaeckel, Paul J. Winter, Chow Tiehl, Charles Raisler, August Kleeman, W. J. B. Gordon, and others.

Taken from the *Shawano County Centurawno,* 1953.

SHAWANO

WI-726   **UPHAM & RUSSEL**

SC 1   5¢   November 4, 1886. Due to the Bearer. Black front, blue
                        back.

SC 2   10¢   May 1, 1878. Due the Bearer. Black front, blue back.   R-7

William Upham was governor of the state of Wisconsin from 1895 - 1897. His home was in Marshfield where his company name was Upham Manufacturing Co. The reverses of notes from Marshfield are similar and bear the inscription One Price Only. His home has been preserved as a museum. See Marshfield for biographies for both Upham & Russel.

WI-730   **GERMAN BANK, 1856-ca.67**

Authorized capital $50,000. John Ewing, Pres. J. H. Mead, cashier. Succeeded by Security National Bank #11150.

Genuine Notes, Raised Notes and Counterfeits

| G2a | $1 | ___18__: (1850s) RWH&E. Overprint: Red ONE and "CAPITAL $25,000". | R-7 |
| G2c | $1 | ___18__: (1860s) ABN. As above, except for imprint and "CAPITAL $50,000" is engraved. | R-7 |

| G4a | $2 | ___18__: (1850s) RWH&E. Overprint: Red TWO and "CAPITAL $50,000" is engraved. | R-6 |

G6a	$3	____18__: (1850s) RWH&E Overprint: Red lazy 3 and "CAPITAL $25,000".		R-7
G6c	$3	____18__: (1860s) ABN. As above, except for imprint and "CAPITAL $50,000" is engraved.	Remainder	R-6

G8a	$5	____18__: (1850s) RWH&E. Overprint: Red 5 and "CAPITAL $25,000".	R-7
G8c	$5	____18__: 1860s ABN. As above, except for imprint and "CAPITAL $50,000" is engraved.	R-7
R5	$10	____18__: 1850s-60s RWH&E or ABN. Raised from $1, G2a or 2c. The bank issued no $10s.	R-7

Uncut Sheet

X1		$1, 2, 3, 5 RWH&E. G2a, 4a, 6a, 8a	R-7

SHEBOYGAN

WI-736   **W.A. PFISTER**

SC 5   25¢   Good Until 15 Day of January, 1890. ML&E.   R-7

WI-725   **SHAWANAW BANK, 1858-1865**

Capital $35,000. J. O. Thayor, Pres., M. Grasser, cashier.
This bank was founded at Shawanaw (Shawano) 100 miles to the northwest. It also was located at Chilton about 40 miles northwest before moving to Sheboygan is 1863.

NOTES DATED AT SHEBOYGAN

G10a	$1	(July 1), 1863 ABN. Same as Shawanaw G6a, except for date, city and capital ($35,000).	R-7
G12a	$2	(July 1), 1863 ABN. Same as G8a, except for date, city and capital ($35,000).	R-7

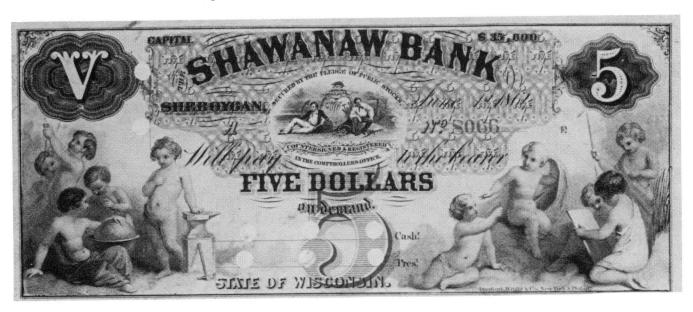

G14a	$5	June 1, 1864 DW. Tint: Green lathework, etc. panel and large 5.	Remainder	R-6

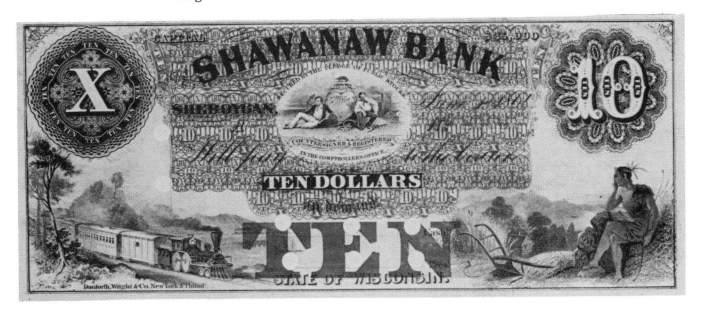

G16a	$10	June 1, 1864 DW. Tint: Green lathework, etc. panel and large TEN.	Remainder	R-6

Uncut Sheet

X1	$5, 10 DW. G14a, 16a	R-1

WI-735   BANK OF SHEBOYGAN, 1856-73

Capital $25,000 (1859). W. W. King, Pres., F. R. Townsend, cashier (1859-63).
Became the First National Bank of Sheboygan #2123 in 1873. Liquidated in 1879. Continued as the Bank
of Sheboygan.

G2a	$1	___18__: (1850s) DW. Tint: Red lathework overall and large ornate 1 1.		R-7
G2b	$1	___18__: (1860s) DW, ABNCo. mono. As above, except for imprint.	Remainder	R-5

G4a	$2	___18__: (1850s) DW. Tint: Red lathework overall and TWO.		R-7
G4b	$2	___18__: 1860s DW, ABNCo. mono. As above, except for imprint.	Remainder	R-5

G6a	$3	___18__: (1850s) DW. Tint: Red lathework overall and panel of microlettering bearing THREE.		R-7
G6b	$3	___18__: (1860s) DW, ABNCo. mono. As above, except for imprint.	Remainder	R-5

G8a	$5	___18__: (1850s) DW. Tint: Red lathework overall and panel of microlettering bearing FIVE.		R-7
G8b	$5	___18__: (1860s) DW, ABNCo. mono. As above, except for imprint.	Remainder	R-5

Uncut Sheets

X1	$1, 2, 3, 5 DW. G2a, 4a, 6a, 8a	R-7
X2	$1, 2, 3, 5 DW, ABNCo. mono. G2b, 4b, 6b, 8b	—

BANK OF SHEBOYGAN

S.S. Miller Printer.

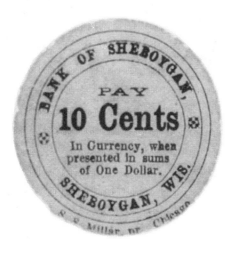

SC 2   10¢   38mm green actual size.   R-7

SC 3   25¢   38mm pale yellow actual size.   R-7

SHEBOYGAN FALLS

WI-737   **SHEBOYGAN FALLS**

SC 3   3¢   At sight. Black S, S&Co.   R-7

SHERRY

Sherry is located about 20 miles west of Stevens Point.

WI-737   SHERRY LUMBER CO.

SC 1   5¢   January 1, 1888. Front: Black/Red. Back: Green. PL.   R-7

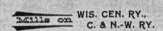

Letter sent by Henry Sherry January 20, 1897.

SINIPEE

WI-740   **MISSISSIPPI MARINE & FIRE INSURANCE COMPANY, ca.1844**

A non-existent institution, represented only by fraudulent notes.

Similar to $5 The Bank of Milwaukee

I - NOTES PAYABLE IN MILWAUKEE

The city name is engraved.

A2 $1   ___18__: 1844 SH&D, DS&H. Altered from $1 Missis-   R-6
                    sippi Marine & Fire Insurance Co., Sinipee, WI-740-
                    G2.

G2 $1?   ___18__: 1844 SH&D, DS&H. As Design 1A, except for   R-6
                    the engraved city name.

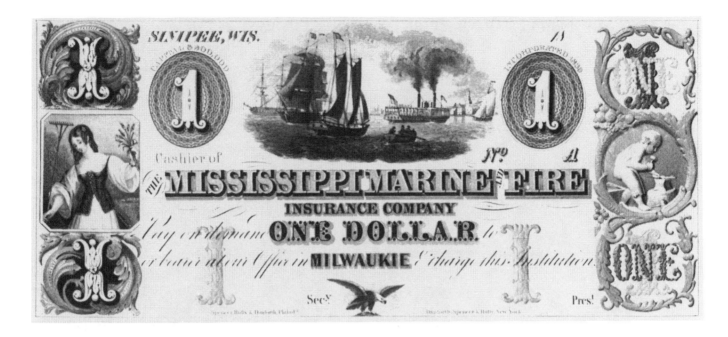

G2a   Similar to 2G, but Grant County is deleted and Insurance
                       Co. added.

G4 $2   ___18__: 1844 SH&D, DS&H.   Remainder   R-6

G4a   Similar to G4, but Grant County deleted and Insurance
                         Co. added.

Uncut Sheet

X1 $1, 2   2 Ga, G4a   R-7

II - NOTES PAYABLE IN THE COMPANY'S OFFICE IN CHICAGO

The city name is written in.

G8 $1   ___18__: 1844 SH&D, DS&H. Design 1A.   R-2

G10 $2   ___18__: 1844 SH&D, DS&H. Design 2A.   R-2

G12 $5   ___18__: 1844 SH&D, DS&H. Design 5A.   R-6

Design similar to $5 Bank of Milwaukee.

III - NOTES PAYABLE AT THE CLEVELAND INSURANCE CO.

"Cleveland Insurance Co." is written above the engraved "MARINE FIRE INSURANCE CO." and "Cleveland, O." is written in the space below.

G14 $1   ___18__: 1844 SH&D, DS&H Design 1A.   R-6

G16 $2   ___18__: 1844 SH&D, DS&H. Design 2A.   R-6

IV - NOTES ON WHICH THE PLACE PAYABLE IS NOT FILLED IN

G20 $1   ___18__: ____ SH&D, DS&H. Design 1A   R-7

G22 $2   ___18__: ____ SH&D, DS&H. Design 2A.   R-7

G24 $5   ___18__ : ____DS&B   R-7
                     Sheet of 2 notes plates A&B.   R-7

V - NOTES ON WHICH GRANT COUNTY HAS BEEN DELETED, REPLACED BY INSURANCE COMPANY.

SINIPEE

In the early 1830's, before present day Wisconsin was even a territory, most of the 3,000 white inhabitants living in this wild area were clustered in what are now Grant and Lafayette Counties. They were there to mine lead.

These men with their crude mining operations were ever dependent on Galena, a river community fifty miles to the south in Illinois. It was from the Galena merchants they bought their supplies. It was to the Galena river docks they brought lead for shipment down the Mississippi.

The local tradesmen charged the miners whatever the traffic would bear. Because Galena had no competition, charges were high. In fact so high that in 1836 several of the more imaginative miners met with the idea of developing their own Mississippi River port.

They chose for their site the mouth of a small steep valley, which terminated at the Mississippi. A creek ran through this valley called the Sinipee.

The owner of this land was an enterprising young native of North Carolina, Payton Vaughn, who had, with his wife, migrated to the area several years earlier.

Vaughn and the entrepreneuring miners formed the Sinipee Company. The valley floor was soon platted. Vaughn received what at that time was an immense sum of $12,000 for the land he sold to the company.

It was mutually agreed that he would use half of the money to build a grand hotel. The same year present day Wisconsin became a territory, 1836, construction started on the building.

It was an all stone structure with walls two feet thick, fireplaces in every room, and a ballroom which occupied most of the second floor. The village sprang up both with size and speed. Choice lots sold for $2,000.

Sinipee, in addition to Stone House, which the hotel was appropriately named, soon included several stores, a bank, church, blacksmith shop, mill, post office and a score of homes. The hostelry became the focal point for the social activity of the area.

At this time a garrison of Territorial troops was stationed forty miles up river at Fort Crawford near the village of Prairie du Chien. Zachary Taylor, who subsequently became President of the United States, was commandant of the garrison and Jefferson Davis, later President of the Confederacy, was stationed there as a young lieutenant. It is on record that both of these men on more than one occasion enjoyed the hospitality of Stone House.

For a year or two Sinipee looked like it might eventually rival Galena and Dubuque, perhaps even St. Louis. But suddenly all ended. In the spring of 1839 early thaws and heavy rains flooded the valley, doing damage to many buildings in the village. No one was overly concerned because repair could be made.

As the water receded stagnant pools remained in the village. And with hot weather Sinipee's doom was spawned in these very pools. In a matter of days, an epidemic of Malaria spread over the town. Those who did not die during the first devastating weeks, and there were few who survived, abandoned the village.

Sinipee became a ghost town. Nothing can be more poignant than a letter written shortly afterward by an early Mineral Point settler, Theodore Rodolph, who wanted to buy one of the abandoned village stores and move it to Mineral Point, Rodolph wrote:

"When we finally rode down the ravine to the Mississippi River, and the bankrupted city burst upon our view, a singular sensation took hold of me. The buildings were all new, showing no sign of decay or deterioration by usage or the weather, having stood there but a little over a year. I expected momentarily to see the occupants come out to bid us welcome. There was, however, not a living soul to be seen or heard, neither a dog, nor a cat, nor a fox, nor a rat - I think not even a bird gave life to the desolation. The quiet of a churchyard reigned. The houses, all painted white, seemed to loom up as monuments of departed greatness."

What remains of Sinipee today?

First the traveler must find the William Fenley farm whose neat white buildings are nestled under a massive sandstone bluff some three miles north of the bridge crossing the Mississippi to Dubuque. Mr. Fenley, the great grandson of Sinipee's founder, should prove to be a willing guide.

For a quarter of a mile from his house a barely discernible road winds through heavy woods. A portion of this road was the village's main street over a century and a quarter ago.

The Stone House stood on the east side of the road hard against a large bluff. A spring, which still cascades out of the sandstone wall, supplied the hostelry with water. The vague outline of the foundation is all that remains.

If your legs are strong and your clothes expendable, climb up to a precipitous ravine to Sinipee Heights. On the top of the bluff, four hundred feet above the ghost town, is located what must be the state's most secluded and dramatic cemetery.

Under the sixty or seventy weather-beaten headstones lie the remains of Sinipee's pioneers. To the north and south the broad Mississippi stretches like a giant silver ribbon.

It takes little imagination, looking down from the precipitous Heights of Sinipee, to picture the bustling river port of one hundred and forty years ago.

A thirty mile drive from Sinipee over some of Wisconsin's most picturesque roads will bring the traveler to another ghost town.

Courtesy *Wisconsin Tales & Trails.*

SPARTA

WI-745   MONROE COUNTY BANK, 1860-ca.65

Capital $50,000. E. H. Goodrich, Pres., James Meyers, cashier.
Fate: closed.

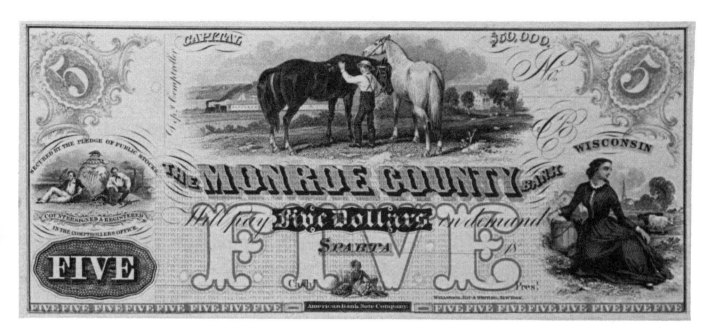

| G2a | $5 | ___18__: (1858-60s) WH&W, ABN. Tint: Red counters and microlettering panel with an outlined white FIVE. | F-7 |

Uncut Sheets

| X1 | $5, 5 | WH&W, ARN. G2a, 2a | R-7 |

WI-750   BANK OF SPARTA, 1858-65

Capital $25,000. J. T. Hemphill, Pres., S. McCord, cashier, 1858 and Thomas W. Wilson in 1863.

Mr. Hemphill came from the M&I Bank of Milwaukee & Mr. McCord from their Associated Bank in Madison. They came to Sparta on the first train that rolled in to Sparta; the Chicago, Milwaukee & St. Paul & Pacific Railroad.

Became the First National Bank of Sparta #1115 in 1865. Liquidated in 1878 and became the Bank of Sparta.

G2	$1	August 2, 1858 ABN. No overprint.	R-7
G2a	$1	August 2, 1858 ABN. Same as G2, except for a red ONE overprint.	R-6
G2b	$1	August 2, 1858 ABN. Same as G2a, except for overprint of a red panel outlining a white ONE.	R-7

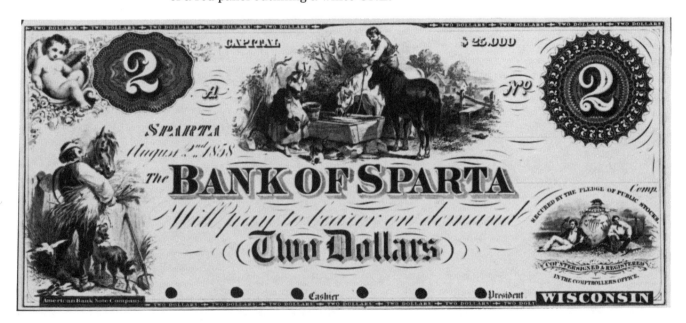

G4	$2	August 2, 1858 ABN. No overprint.	R-7
G4a	$2	August 2, 1858 ABN. Same as G4, except for a red TWO overprint.	R-7
G4b	$2	August 2, 1858 ABN. Same as G4a, except for overprint of a red panel outlining a white TWO.	R-7

G6	$3	August 2, 1858 ABN. No overprint.	R-7
G6a	$3	August 2, 1858 ABN. Same as G6, except for a red THREE overprint.	R-7
G6b	$3	August 2, 1858 ABN. Same as G6a, except for overprint of a red panel outlining a white THREE.	R-7

G8	$5	August 2, 1858 ABN. No overprint.	R-7
G8a	$5	August 2, 1858 ABN. Same as G8, except for a red FIVE overprint.	R-7
G8b	$5	August 2, 1858 ABN. Same as G8a, except for overprint of a red panel outlining a white FIVE.	R-7

Uncut Sheet

| X1 | $1, 2, 3, 5 ABN. G2, 4, 6, 8 | R-7 |
| X2 | $1, 2, 3, 5 ABN. G2b, 4b, 6b, 8b | R-7 |

STEVENS POINT

WI-345   FRONTIER BANK

Capital $30,000. W. W. Wood, Pres., L. F. McGowan, cashier. No business except to issue notes for circulation.
Moved from La Pointe in Barron County in 1862; probably never issued notes from Stevens Point.

Also see Frontier Bank, La Pointe, WI-345.

WI-755   **BANK OF STEVENS POINT, 1863-65**

Capital $50,000. John Armstrong, Pres., George Gall, cashier (1863). Private bankers.
Fate: closed.

G2a $5   December 1, 1862 NBN. C: Clay. Tint: Green frame, 5 5   R-7
                        and panel.

G4a $10   December 1, 1862 NBN. Tint: Green frame, counter and   R-7
                        x.

Uncut Sheets

X1 $5, 10 NBN. G2a, 4a   R-7

WI-430   NORTHWESTERN BANK 1856-61

Moved from Marquette 1859. Closed 1861 with $948 outstanding redeemed at 66.5¢.
NOTES DATED AT STEVENS POINT

| G12 | $1 | ___18__:___ ABN. RC-R: Dr. Kane's Arctic Expedition. Capital: $50,000. No overprint. | R-7 |
| G12a | $1 | ___18__: 1859-61 ABN. As above, except for large red ornate 1 overprint. | R-7 |

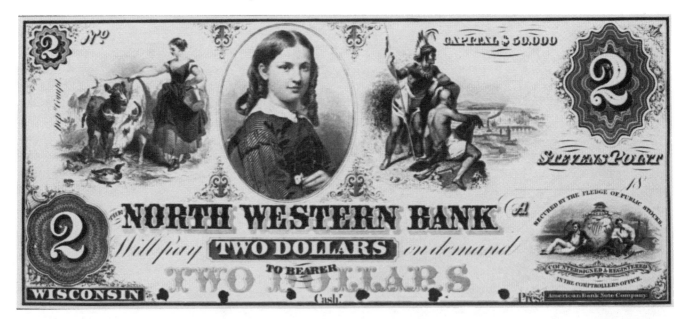

| G14 | $2 | ___18__:___ ABN. Capital: $50,000. No overprint. | R-7 |
| C14a | $2 | ___18__: 1859-61 ABN. As above, except for red overprint. | R-7 |

Uncut Sheet

| X2 | $1, 2 | ABN. G12, 14 | R-7 |

Altered, Spurious and Unattributed Non-Genuine Notes

| N5 | $5 | (1850s) Unknown. C: view of suspension bridge. | R-7 |

WI-760   **WISCONSIN PINERY BANK, 1858-62**

Capital $50,000. Herman Huyson, Pres., L. Scheffer, cashier.
Closed 1862. Had $46,361 in circulation in 1861. Located in inacessable point. Bank of circulation only.

Genuine Notes, Raised Notes and Counterfeits

G2	$1	July 1, 1858 DnP, ABN. No overprint.	R-7
G2a	$1	July 1, 1858 DnP, ABN. As above, except for a red ONE overprint.	R-7

G4	$2	July 1, 1858 DnP, ABN. No overprint.	R-7
G4a	$2	July 1, 1858 DnP, ABN. As above, except for a red TWO overprint.	R-7

| G6 | $3 | July 1, 1858 DnP, ABN. No overprint. | R-7 |
| G6a | $3 | July 1, 1858 DnP, ABN. As above, except for a red 3 3 overprint. | R-6 |

G8	$5	July 1, 1858 DnP, ABN. No overprint.	R-7
G8a	$5	July 1, 1858 DnP, ABN. As above, except for a red FIVE overprint.	R-7
R5	$5	July 1, 1858 DnP, ABN. Raised from $1, G2 series.	R-7
R6	$10	July 1, 1858 DnP, ABN. Raised from $1, G2 series. The bank issued no $10s.	R-7

Uncut Sheets

| X1 | | $1, 2, 3, 5 DnP, ABN. G2, 4, 6, 8 | R-7 |
| X2 | | $1, 2, 3, 5 DnP, ABN. G2a, 4a, 6a, 8a | R-7 |

Altered, Spurious and Unattributed Non-Genuine Notes

| N5 | $10 | Unknown. Unknown. C: woman, corn and basket. The bank issued no $10s. | R-7 |

WI-761 **EXCHANGE BANK OF GEO. W. GREEN**

SC 5   30¢   November 15, 1862. Blue. Lipman.   R-7

STILES

WI-765   HOWARD BANK, ca. 1858-59

Later location: Chippewa Falls.
Probably never opened although proofs are known dated at both locations.

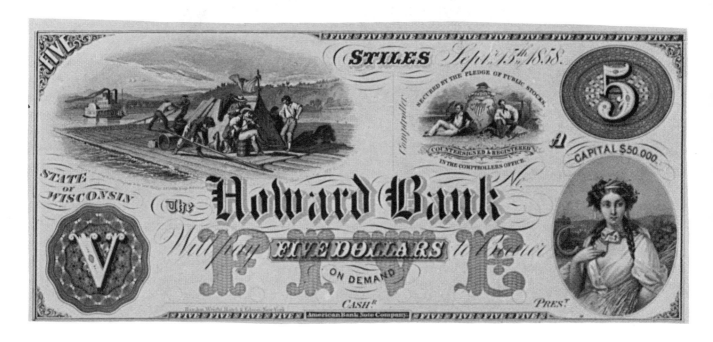

G2a $5   September 15, 1858. ABN. Overprint: Red FIVE.   R-7

G4a $10   September 15, 1858. ABN. Overprint: Red TEN.   R-7

Uncut Sheet

X1 $5, 10   ABN G2a, 4a   R-7

STRATFORD

WI-766   R. CONNER CO.

SC 3   15¢   Redeemable in Premiums, black. White cardboard.   R-7

SUN PRAIRIE

WI-770   **SUN PRAIRIE BANK, 1860-63**

Capital $30,000.
Closed.

G2	$1	October 1, 1860 ABN. No overprint.	R-7
G2a	$1	October 1, 1860 ABN. As above, except for overprint of a green panel outlining a white ONE.	R-7

G4	$5	October 1, 1860 ABN. Lower R: Clay. No overprint.	R-7
G4a	$5	October 1, 1860 ABN. As above, except for overprint of a green panel outlining a white FIVE.	R-7

Uncut Sheet

X1	$1, 5 ABN. G2, 4	R-7
X2	$1, 5 ABN. G2a, 4a	R-7

WI-775   **WHEAT GROWERS BANK, ca.1862-65**

Capital $25,000. M. Helmer, Pres., J. S. Helmer, cashier. May have originally been located in Whitewater. Closed.
Wheat at that time was the principal crop in Wisconsin. It was the primary reason railroads were built north and west of Milwaukee. While it is hard to believe, Wisconsin was the largest wheat growing state in the U.S. in 1858.

G2a $5   ___18__: (1860s) NBN. Tint: Green frame, counters and   R-7
                     panel.

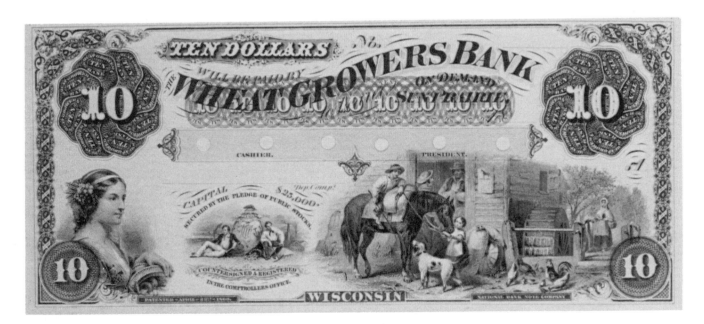

G4a $10   ___18__: (1860s) NBN. Tint: Green frame, counters and   R-7
                     panel.

Uncut Sheet

X1 $5, 10 NBN. G2a, 4a   R-7

SUPERIOR (and SUPERIOR CITY)

WI-780   **MECHANICS BANK, ca.1858-61**

Closed 1861. Agreed to have their circulation redeemed at Milwaukee or Madison.

G2 $5   July 1, 1858 ABN. Overprint: Ornate red FIVE.   R-7

Uncut Sheet

X1 $5, 5 ABN. G2, 2   R-7

WI-785   BANK OF NORTH AMERICA, 1859-61

Capital $100,000. T. M. Turley, Pres., H. M. Hunter, cashier. Both lived in Cook County, Illinois. Closed 1861. Notes redeemed at 95.5¢.
Later location: Grand Rapids.
Apparently issued notes only from Superior City.

Closed.

Genuine Notes, Raised Notes and Counterfeits

G2a $5   ___18__: *1858-60s) ABN. Tint: Red bank title and 5   R-7
                FIVE 5.

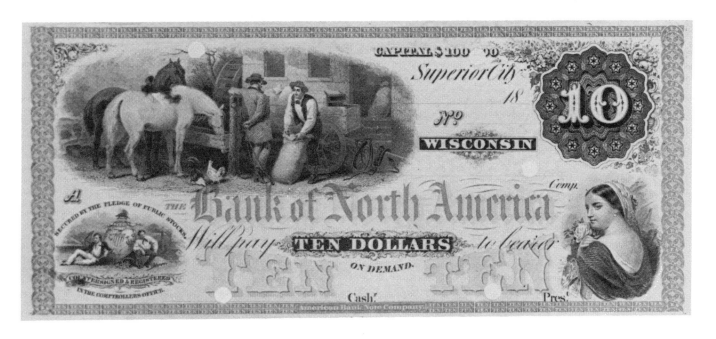

G4a $10   ___18__: (1858-0s) ABN. Tint: Red bank title and TEN   R-7
                TEN.

| G6a | $20 | ___18__: (1858-60s) ABN. Tint: Red bank title, counters and TWENTY. | R-7 |

Uncut Sheet

| X1 | | $5, 5, 10, 20 ABN. G2a, 2a, a, 6a | R-7 |

Altered, Spurious and Unattributed Non-Genuine Notes

| S5 | $5 | ___18__: 1860: DW. Overprint: Red FIVE. | R-6 |
| N5 | $5 | Unknown. Unknown. C: Train. | R-7 |

WI-790   ST. LOUIS BANK, 1858-62

Fate: closed.

G2 $5   October 1, 1857 RWH&E. Tint: 5; red panel bearing   R-7
                      white FIVE; 5.

G4 $10   October 1, 1857 RWH&E. Tint: Red XX/panel bearing   R-7
                      white TEN.

G6 $20   October 1, 1857 RWH&E. Tint: Red panel bearing white   R-7
                       TWENTY.

Uncut Sheets

X1 $5, 5, 10, 20 RWH&E. G2, 2, 4, 6   R-7

WI-795   **BANK OF SUPERIOR, ca.1858-61**

Closed.

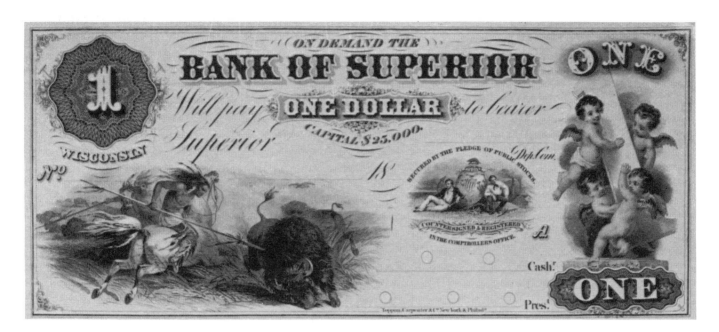

G2	$1	___18__: ____ TC. No overprint.		R-7
G2a	$1	___18__: (1858-61) TC. As above, except for a red ONE overprint.	Remainder	R-6

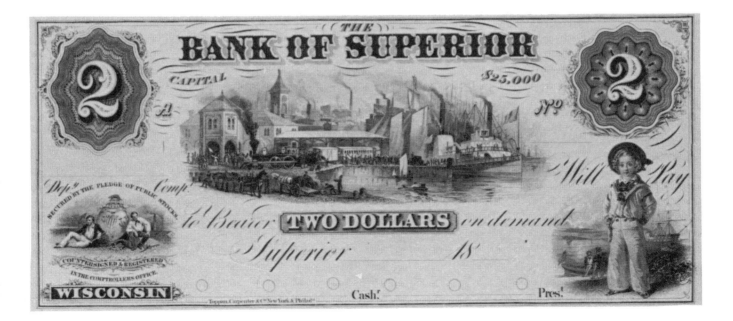

G4	$2	___18__: ____ TC. No overprint.	R-7
G4a	$2	___18__: 1858-61 TC. As above, except for a red overprint.	R-7

G6 $3   ___18__: ____ TC. No overprint.   R-7

G6a $3   ___18__: 1858-61 TC. As above, except for a red over-   R-7
                print.

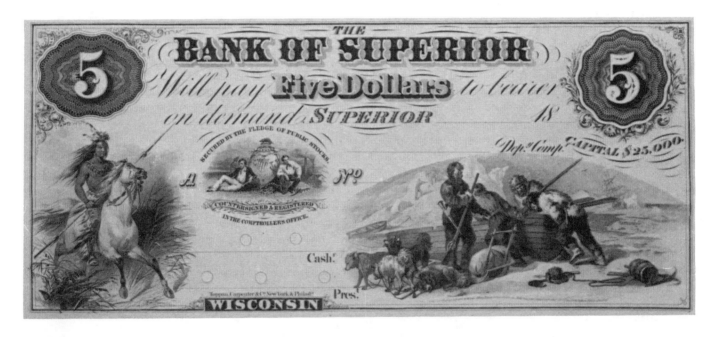

G8 $5   ___18__: ____ TC. Lower R: Dr. Kane's Arctic Expedition.   R-7

G8a $5   ___18__: 1858-61 TC. As above, except for a red over-   R-7
                print.

Uncut Sheet

X1 $1, 2, 3, 5 TC. G2, 4, 6, 8   R-7

TWO RIVERS

WI-800   FARMERS BANK OF TWO RIVERS, 1859-61

Capital $50,000. J. W. Medbury, Pres., J. H. Perkins, cashier. No place of business or banking house.
The $10 plate used for this bank was officially altered from the Farmers Bank of Chippewa, WI-105.
Closed 1861.

Genuine Notes, Raised Notes and Counterfeits

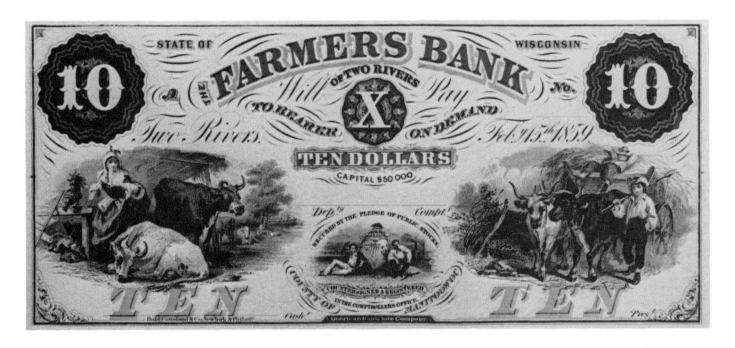

G8a	$10	February 15, 1859 ABN. Tint: Red bank title and denomination panel.	R-7

Altered, Spurious and Unattributed Non-Genuine Notes

N5	$10	Unknown C: woman; state arms. L: 10/farmer feeding hay to horse. R: 10. Tint: Red.	R-6

WI-801   **MERCHANDISE**

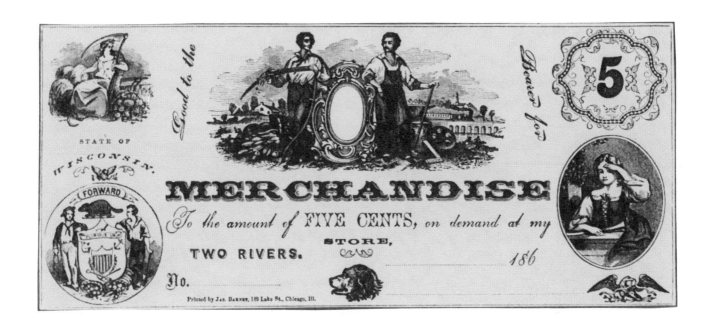

| SC 1 | 5¢ | Good to the Bearer for ___186_ JB. | R-7 |
| SC 2 | 10¢ | Good to the Bearer for ___186_JB. | R-7 |

| SC 5 | 25¢ | Good to the Bearer for ___186_. | R-7 |

It seems logical that these notes also would have been issued in 50¢ notes.

WI-805   **MANITOUWOC COUNTY BANK, 1857-61**

Capital $50,000. Charles Kuehn, Pres., L. Kemper, cashier (1858).
Closed 1861. Redeemed at 93¢. Outstanding circulation $1,162.

Genuine Notes, Raised Notes and Counterfeits

G2a $1   ___18__: (late 1850s) Tint: Orange bank title, ONE. ONE,   R-7
                    etc.

G4a $2   ___18__: (late 1850s) Tint: Orange bank title, TWO.   R-7
                    TWO, etc.

| G6a | $5 | ___18__: (late 1850s) TC. Tint: Orange bank title, 5 FIVE 5, etc. | R-7 |

| R5 | $10 | ___18__: 1850s TC. Raised from $1, G2a. The bank issued no $10s. | R-7 |
| R10 | $10 | ___18__: 1850s TC. Raised form $2, G4a. The bank issued no $10s. | R-6 |

Uncut Sheet

| X1 | $1, 1, 2, 5 | TC. G2a, 2a, 4a,6a | R-7 |

VIROQUA

WI-220   BANK OF MONEKA, 1859

Capital $75,000. J. H. Cole, Pres., J. Cole, cashier.
Began in Gordon, moved to Viroqua in 1858. In 1862 moved first to Hustisford, later to Portage. No notes are reported as being issued from Viroqua. As only proof notes are known on Gordon, none probably ever circulated.

WI-810   LUMBERMAN'S BANK, 1859

Capital $150,000. Andrew Proudfit, Pres., Jas. K. Proudfit, cashier.
Later locations: Conterelle, Beloit (moved in 1858, 62).

Became the Second National Bank of Beloit in 1882.

Notes dated at Viroqua

G2	$5	___18__: 1857 WH&W. Same as G6, except for city.	R-7
G4	$10	___18__: 1857 WH&W. Same as G8, except for city.	R-7

WARRENSVILLE

WI-815   ORIENTAL BANK, (1858)

Probably never opened. The plate originally prepared for this bank was officially altered to the Beloit Savings Bank, WI-55.

Genuine Notes, Raised Notes and Counterfeits

G2 $5   ___18__: ___BC, ABN.   R-7

G4 $10   ___18__:_ ___BC, ABN.   R-7

Uncut Sheet

X1 $5, 10 BC, ABN. G2, 4   R-7

WATERTOWN

WI-820   **JEFFERSON COUNTY BANK, ca. 1854-64**

Capital $25,000, later $50,000 (1854). Charles G. Harger, Pres., Daniel Jones, cashier (1854), H. B. Gallup, cashier (1863).
Closed.

Genuine Notes, Raised Notes and Counterfeits

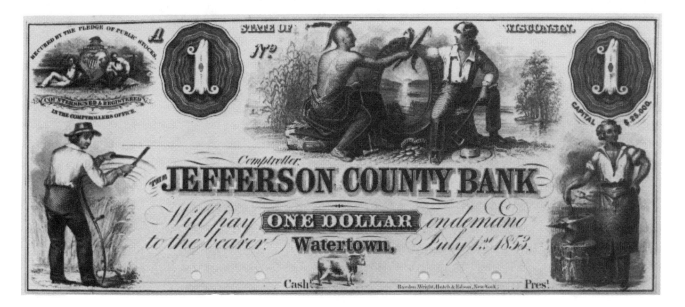

G2	$1	July 1, 1853 RWH&E. Capital: $25,000. No overprint.	R-6
G2a	$1	July 1, 1853 RWH&E. As above, except for a red ONE overprint.	R-7
G2b	$1	July 1, 1853 RWH&E. Same as G2, except for capital ($50,000).	R-6
G2c	$1	July 1, 1853 RWH&E. Same as G2, except for capital ($75,000) and possibly date.	R-7

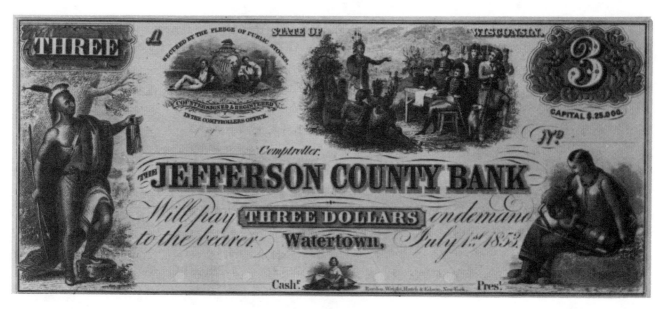

| G4 | $3 | July 1, 1853 RWH&E. Capital: $25,000. No overprint. | R-7 |

| G4a | $3 | July 1, 1853 RWH&E. As above, except for a red THREE overprint. | R-7 |

| G4b | $3 | July 1, 1853 RWH&E. Same as G4, except for capital ($50,000). | R-7 |

| G4c | $3 | July 1, 1853 RWH&E. Same as G4, except for capital ($75,000) and possibly date. | R-7 |

| C4 | $3 | July 1, 1853 RWH&E. Cft. of G4, 4a or 4b. | R-7 |

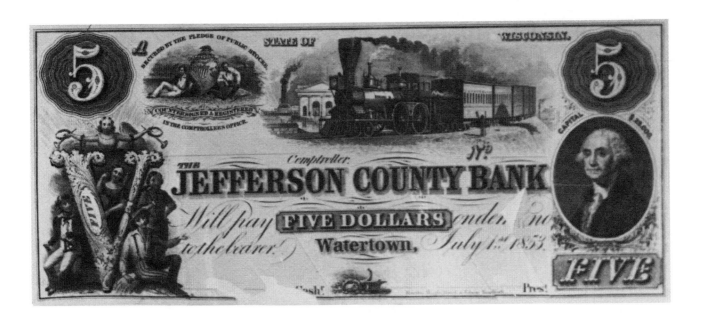

G6	$5	July 1, 1853 RWH&E. Capital: $25,000.	R-7
G6a	$5	July 1, 1853 RWH&E. As above, except for a red FIVE overprint.	R-7
G6b	$5	July 1, 1853 RWH&E. Same as G6, except for capital ($50,000).	R-7
G6d	$5	July 1, 1853 RWH&E. Same as G6, except for capital ($75,000) and possibly date.	R-7
R4	$5	July 1, 1853 RWH&E. Raised from $1, G2 or 2a.	R-7
R6	$10	July 1, 1853 RWH&E. Raised from $1, G2 or 2a. The bank issued no $10s.	R-7
R8	$10	July 1, 1853 RWH&E. Raised from $3, G4 or 4a. The bank issued no $10s.	R-7
R12	$20	July 1, 1853 RWH&E. Raised from $1, G2 or 2a. The bank issued no $20s.	R-7
R16	$100	July 1, 1853 RWH&E. Raised from $3, G4 or 4a. The bank issued no $100s.	R-7

Uncut Sheet

X1		$1, 1, 3, 5 RWH&E. G2, 2, 4, 6	R-7

Altered, Spurious and Unattributed Non-Genuine Notes

N5	$3	(1850s) Unknown. C: man plowing with oxen.	R-7

WI-825   BANK OF WATERTOWN, 1854-60s

Capital $50,000. W. H. Angel, Pres., Louis L. Angel, cashier. (1855). Albert L. Pritchard, Pres., H. Clark, cashier (1863).
Continued as state bank without circulation. Signed notes are scarce.

Genuine Notes, Raised Notes and Counterfeits

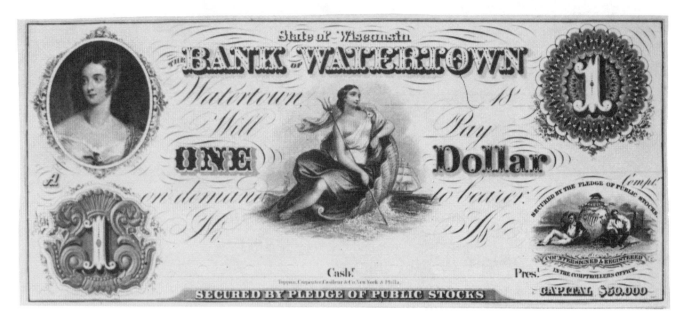

G2	$1	___18__: ____ TCC. Capital: $50,000. No overprint.		R-7
G2a	$1	January 8, 1856 TCC. As above, except for date & red 1 1 overprint. Capital: $100,000. Written serial number.		R-6
G2b	$1	September 1, 1863 TCC, ABNCo. mono. As above except for date, imprint and printed serial number.	Remainder	R-3

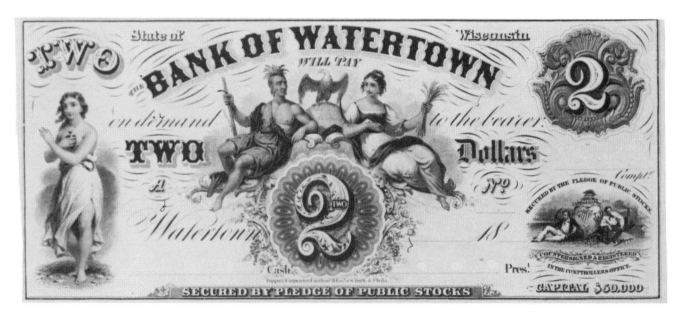

G4	$2	___18__: ____ TCC. Capital: $50,000. No overprint.		R-7
G4a	$2	January 8, 1856 TCC. As above, except for date & red 2 2 overprint. Capital: $100,000. Written serial number.		R-6
G4b	$2	September 1, 1863 TCC, ABNCo. mono. As above, except for date, imprint and written serial number.	Remainder	R-3

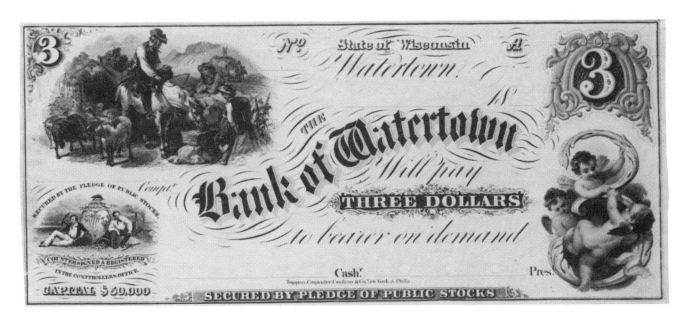

G6	$3	___18__:___ TCC. Capital: $50,000. No overprint.	Remainder	R-7
G6a	$3	January 8, 1856 TCC. As above, except for date & red 3 overprint. Capital: $100,000. Written serial number.	Remainder	R-6
G6b	$3	September 1, 1863 TCC, ABNCo. mono. As above, except for date, imprint and printed serial number.	Remainder	R-3

G8	$5	___18__: (1855) TCC. Capital: $50,000. No overprint.		R-7
G8a	$5	January 8, 1856 TCC. As above, except for date & red lazy 5 overprint. Capital: $100,000. Written serial number.	Remainder	R-6
G8b	$5	September 1, 1863 TCC, ABNCo. mono. As above except for date, imprint and printed serial number.	Remainder	R-3

R6	$5	___18__: 1850s TCC. Raised from $1, G2.	R-7
R8	$10	___18__: 1850s TCC. Raised from $1, G2. The bank issued no $10s.	R-7
R10	$10	___18__: 1850s TCC. Raised from $2, G4. The bank issued no $10s.	R-7
R12	$20	___18__: 1850s TCC. Raised from $1, G2. The bank issued no $20s.	R-7

Uncut Sheets

| X1 | $1, 2, 3, 5 TCC. G2, 4, 6, 8 | R-7 |
| X2 | $1, 2, 3, 5 TCC, ABNCo. mono. G2b, 4b, 6b, 8b | R-3 |

WI-400   BANK OF WISCONSIN

This bank located in Watertown but notes were dated in Madison. See Madison.

WAUKESHA

WI-830 FOREST CITY BANK, 1857-65

Capital 1859 $50,000, 1863 $40,000. Sidney A. Bean, Pres., Orson M. Tyler, asst. cashier, M. G. Townsend, cashier.

Became Farmers National Bank #1159 in 1865 & liquidated in 1866 and became the Forrest City Bank. The plate for this bank was originally prepared for the Milwaukee City Bank, WI-510, then officially altered in 1857.

Genuine Notes, Raised Notes and Counterfeits

G2a	$1	March 1, 1857 WH&W. Overprint: Red ONE.	R-6
G2c	$1	March 1, 1857 ABN. As above, except for imprint and lack of an overprint. Handwritten serial number.	R-6
G2d	$1	March 1, 1857 ABN. Same as G2c, except for red ONE overprint and printed serial number.	R-7

G4a	$2	March 1, 1857 WH&W. Overprint: Red TWO.	R-6
G4c	$2	March 1, 1857 ABN. As above, except for imprint and lack of an overprint. Handwritten serial number.	R-7
G4d	$2	March 1, 1857 ABN. Same as G4c, except for red TWO overprint and printed serial number.	R-7

G6a	$3	March 1, 1857 WH&W. Overprint: Red THREE. Same as G6d , except for imprint.	R-7
G6c	$3	March 1, 1857 ABN. As above, except for imprint and lack of an overprint.	R-7
G6d	$3	March 1, 1857 ABN. Same as G6c, except for red THREE overprint.	R-6
R2	$5	March 1, 1852 WH&W or ABN. Raised from $1, G2a or 2c. The bank issued no $5s.	R-7
R4	$10	March 1, 1857 WH&W or ABN. Raised from $1, G2a or 2c. The bank issued no $10s.	R-7
R6	$20	March 1, 1857 WH&W or ABN. Raised from $1, G2a or 2c. The bank issued no $20s.	R-7

Uncut Sheet

X1		$1, 1, 2, 3 WH&W. G2a, 2a, 4a, 6a	R-7

WI-835   **WAUKESHA COUNTY BANK, 1855-65**

Capital $25,000. A. Minor, Pres., C. C. Barnes, cashier (1855). Absalam Minor, Pres., Charles Minor, cashier, 1863. Capital increased to $50,000.
Became the Waukesha National Bank #1086 in 1865.

In 1862, Andrew Jay Frame became an office boy in Waukesha County Bank. In 1880, was appointed President of the Waukesha National Bank, and was active until October, 1932, as Chairman of the Board. Seventy years a banker. He was the dean of Wisconsin Bankers, and known in financial circles as "America's Greatest Country Banker.
From *Philadelphia Public Ledger* — October 5, 1932

Genuine Notes, Raised Notes and Counterfeits

G2	$1	July 16, 1855 WHH&W. Capital: $25,000. No overprint.		R-7
G2a	$1	July 16, 1855 WHH&W. As above, except for capital ($50,000).		R-7
G2c	$1	July 16, 1855 WHH&W. Same as G2a, except for capital ($100,000) and red 11 overprint.	Remainder	R-6
G2d	$1	January 1, 1859 ABN. Same as G2c, except for date, addition of gray ONE ONE in the signature spaces at bottom and style of overprint (not sides of the 1s).	Remainder	R-6

G4a	$2	January 1, 1859 ABN. Overprint: Red panel outlining white TWO. Capital: $100,000.	Remainder	R-6
C4	$2	January 1, 1859 ABN. Photographic cft. of the above, except lacks the overprint.		R-6
R6	$5	Unknown. Unknown. Raised from $1, G2 series. The bank issued no $5s.		R-7
R8	$10	Unknown. Unknown. Raised from $1, G2 series. The bank issued no $10s.		R-7
R10	$20	Unknown. Unknown. Raised from $1, G2 series. The bank issued no $20s.		R-7

Uncut Sheets

| X1 | | $1, 1, WHH&W. G2, 2 | | R-7 |
| X2 | | $1, 1, 1, 2 ABN. G2b, 2b, 2b, 4 | | R-7 |

WI-836   PEOPLE ACCOMMODATION STORE

| SC 1 | 5¢ | Pay to Bearer ___186_. D&M. Black/Red. | R-7 |

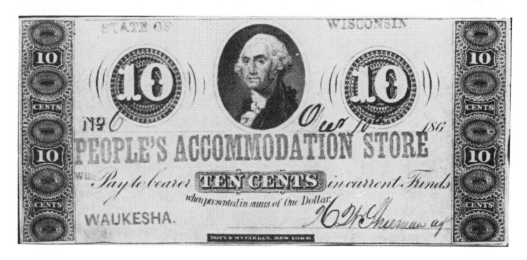

| SC 2 | 10¢ | Pay to Bearer ___186_. D&M. Black/Red. | R-7 |

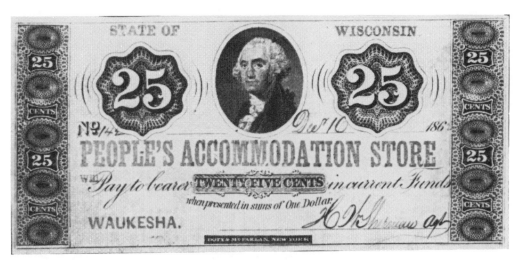

SC 5	25¢	Pay to Bearer ___186_. funds. D&M Black/Red.	R-7
SC 6	50¢	Pay to Bearer ___186_ D&M Black/Red.	R-7
SC 7	$1	Pay to Bearer ___186_ D&M Black/Red.	R-7

Litho by Doty & McFarland, New York.

WI-836.5 PEOPLE'S ACCOMMODATION STORE

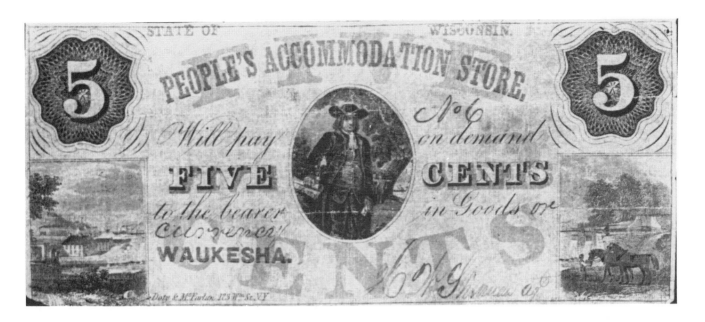

SC 1a   5¢   Will pay on demand to the bearer in goods & currency.   R-7

SC 2a   10¢   Will pay on demand to the bearer in goods & currency.   R-7

SC 5a   25¢   Will pay on demand to the bearer in goods & currency.   R-7

SC 6a   50¢   Will pay on demand to the bearer in goods & currency.   R-7

SC 8aa $3   Will pay on demand to the bearer in goods & currency.   R-7

WAUPACCA

WI-840   CORN PLANTERS BANK, 1859

Capital $50,000. K. A. Darling, Pres., W. D. Wells, cashier.
Closed. No place of business or banking house.

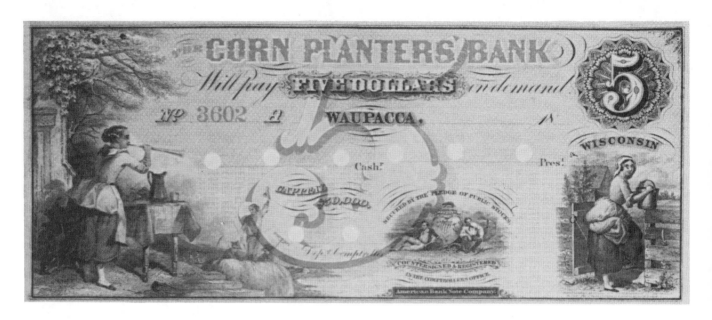

G2a $5   ___18__: (1859-65) ABN. Tint: Orange, outlining large   R-7
                         ornate 5.

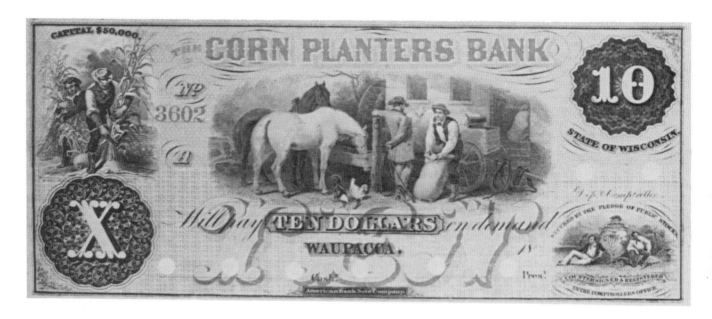

G4a $10   ___18__: (1859-65) ABN. Tint: Orange, outlining ornate   R-7
                         TEN.

Uncut Sheet

X1 $5, 10 ABN. G2a, 4a   R-7

WI-845   WAUPACCA COUNTY BANK, 1858-61

Capital $50,000. N. B. Van Slyke, Pres., E. E. Blunn, cashier (1859).
Failed. Closed 1861. Redeemed notes at 83¢. Outstanding circulation $1225.

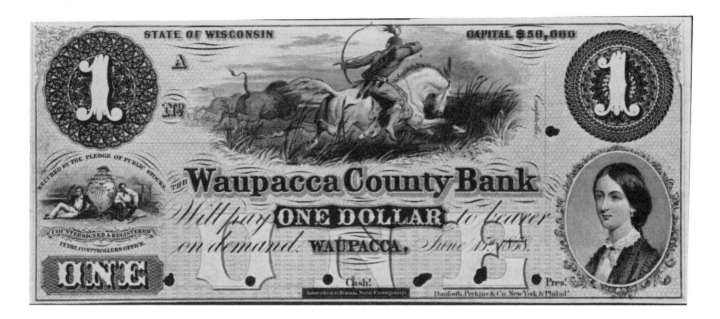

G2a $1   June 15, 1858 DnP, ABN. Tint: Red-brown lathework   R-6
overall & panel of microlettering with an outlined
white ONE.

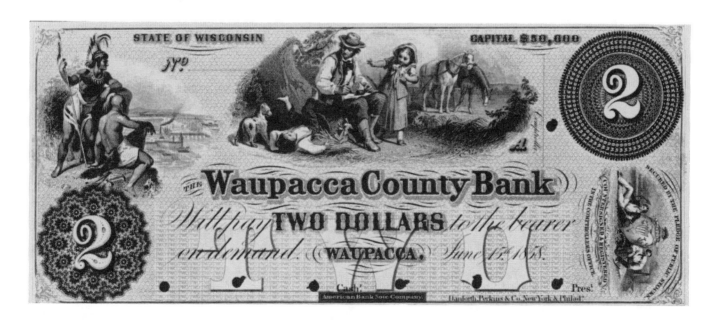

G4a $2   June 15, 1858 DnP, ABN. Tint: Red-brown lathework   R-7
overall & panel of microlettering with an outlining
white TWO.

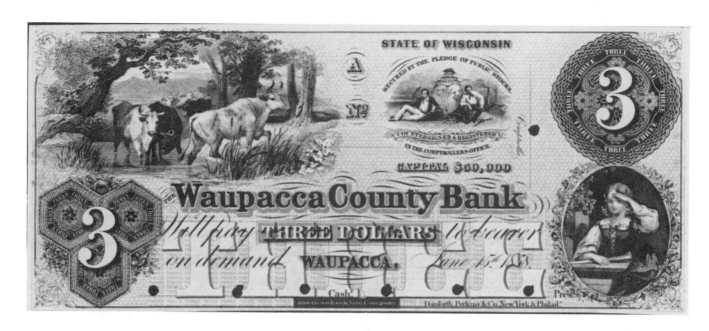

G6a $3   June 15, 1858 DnP, ABN. Tint: Red-brown lathework   R-7
                     overall & panel of microlettering with an outlining
                     white THREE.

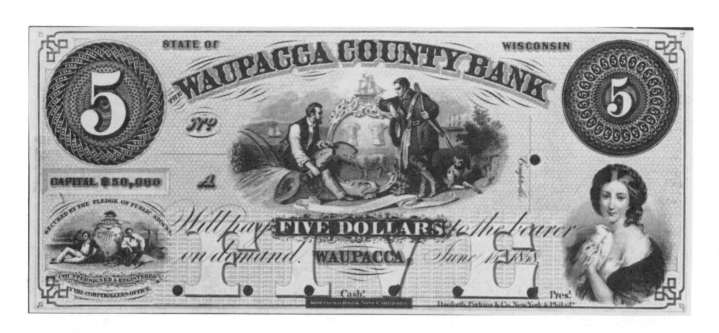

G8a $5   June 15, 1858 DnP, ABN. Tint: Red-brown lathework   R-6
                     overall & panel of microlettering with an outlining
                     white FIVE.

Uncut Sheet

X1 $1, 2, 3, 5 DnP, ABN. G2a, 4a, 6a, 8a   R-7

WAUPUN

WI-850   **CORN EXCHANGE BANK, ca. 1858-63**

Capital $50,000. Andrew Proudfit, Pres., Wm. Habkirk, cashier (1858). David Ferguson, Pres. (1863)
Closed 1863.

G2	$1	___18__:___ RWH&E. Same as G2a, except for lack of an overprint.		R-7
G2a	$1	___18__: (1850s-60s) RWH&E. Same as above, except for a red ONE overprint.	Remainder	R-3

G4	$2	___18__:___ RWH&E. L: Jackson. Same as G4a, except for lack of an overprint.		R-7
G4a	$2	___18__: (1850s-60s) RWH&E. Same as above, except for a red TWO overprint.	Remainder	R-3

G6	$3	___18__:___ RWH&E. R: Webster. No overprint.		R-7
G6a	$3	___18__: (1850s-60s) RWH&E. Same as above, except for a red THREE overprint.	Remainder	R-3

G8	$5	___18__:___ RWH&E. Same as G8a, except lack of an overprint.		R-7
G8a	$5	___18__: (1850s-60s) RWH&E. Same as above, except for red FIVE overprint.	Remainder	R-3

Uncut Sheet

X1		$1, 2, 3, 5 RWH&E. G2a, 4a, 6a, 8a		R-3

WI-855 **WAUPUN BANK, 1856-61**

Capital $25,000. Seth B. Hills, Pres., L. B. Hills, cashier, 1856.
Closed 1862. Redeemed notes at 80¢.

Genuine Notes, Raised Notes and Counterfeits

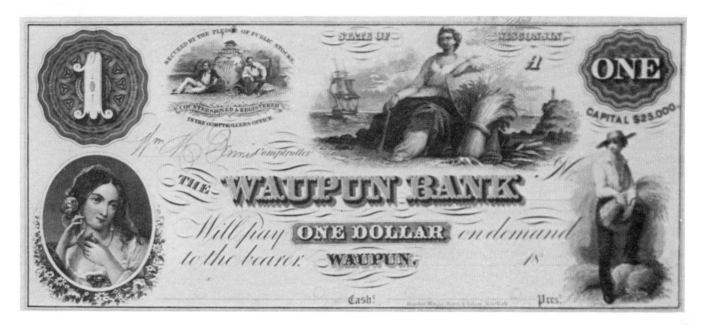

G2 $1   ___18__: (1850s-61) RWH&E.   R-7

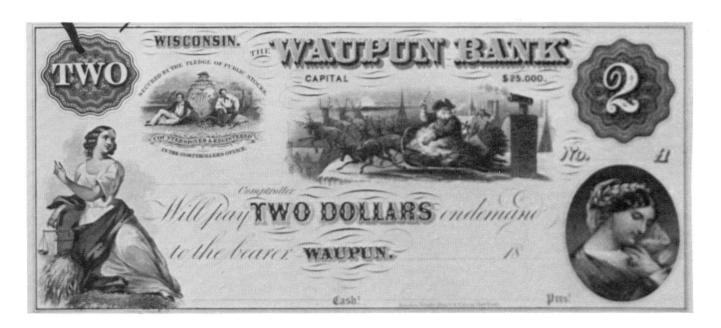

G4 $2   ___18__: (1850s-61) RWH&E. C: Santa Claus on rooftop.   R-7

G6	$3	___18__: (1850s-61) RWH&E. L: Washington.	Remainder	R-6
R5	$5	___18__: 1850s RWH&E. Raised from $1, G2. The bank issued no $5s.		R-7
R6	$5	___18__: 1850s RWH&E. Raised from $2, G4. The bank issued no $5s.		R-7
R8	$10	___18__: 1850s RWH&E. Raised from $1, G2. The bank issued no $10s.		R-7
R9	$10	___18__: 1850s RWH&E. Raised from $2, G4. The bank issued no $10s.		R-7

Uncut Sheet

X1		$1, 1, 2, 3 RWH&E. G2, 2, 4, 6		R-7

WAUSAU

BANK OF THE INTERIOR, 1858-65

Capital $50,000. L. R. Cady Pres., Geo. L. Field, cashier (1858).
Closed.

Genuine Notes, Raised Notes and Counterfeits

G2a $1   ___18__: (1850s-60s) ABN. Tint: Green lathework overall   R-7
            with an outlined white ONE.

G4a $2   ___18__: 1859-60 ABN. Tint: Green lathework overall   R-6
            with an outlined white TWO.

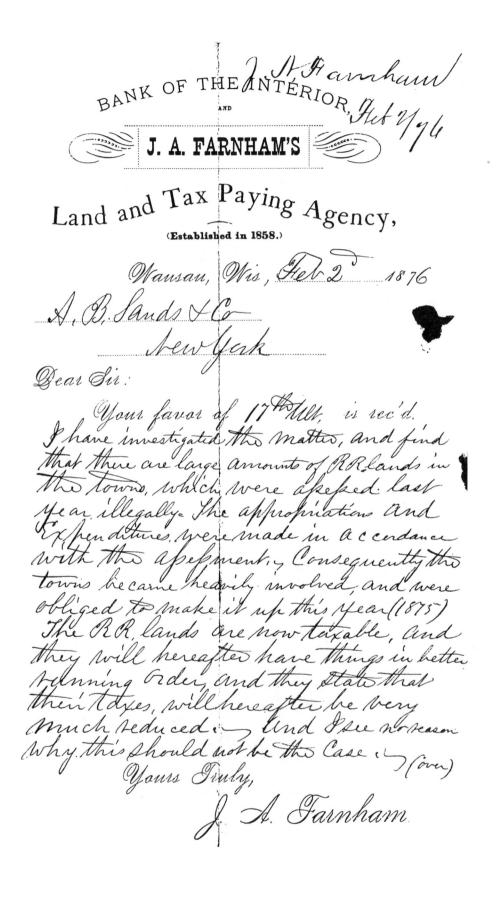

J N Farnham
Feb 2/76

BANK OF THE INTERIOR,

AND

J. A. FARNHAM'S

Land and Tax Paying Agency,

(Established in 1858.)

Wausau, Wis, Feb 2d 1876

A, B, Sands & Co

New York

Dear Sir:

Your favor of 17th Ult, is rec'd.
I have investigated the matter, and find
that there are large amounts of RR lands in
the towns, which were assessed last
year illegally. The appropriations and
Expenditures were made in accordance
with the assessment; Consequently the
towns became heavily involved, and were
obliged to make it up this year (1875)
The RR lands are now taxable, and
they will hereafter have things in better
running order, and they state that
their taxes, will hereafter be very
much reduced. And I see no reason
why this should not be the case. (over)

Yours Truly,

J. A. Farnham.

G6	$5	___18__:___ TC.	R-7
G6a	$5	___18__: 1859-62 TC, ABNCo. mono. As above, except for imprint.	R-7
C6	$5	___18__: 1858-60s TC. Photographic cft. of G6 or 6a.	R-7
G6b	$5	___18__: 1863-65 ABN. Same as G6, except for imprint.	R-7

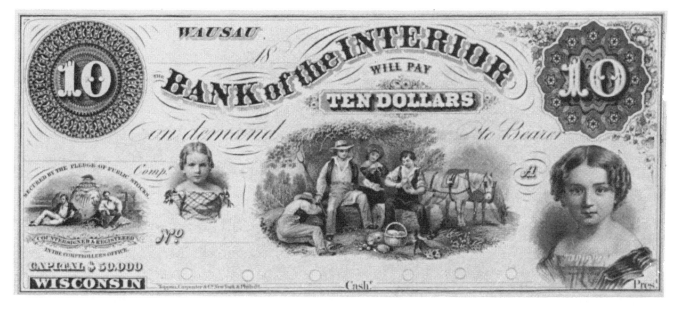

G8	$10	___18__:___ TC.	R-7
G8a	$10	___18__:1859-62 TC, ABNCo. mono. As above, except for imprint.	R-7
G8b	$10	___18__: 1862-65 ABN. As above, except for imprint.	R-7

Uncut Sheets

| X1 | $1, 2 ABN. As above, except for imprint | R-7 |
| X2 | $5. 1- TC. G6, G8 | R-7 |

WAUTOMA

WI-865   **WAUSHARA COUNTY BANK, 1859-61**

Capital 1855 $25,000, 1861 $50,000. H. V. Bogert, Pres., George B. Congdon, cashier 1861.
Failed 1861. Notes redeemed at 73-1/2¢ in 1862, $403 outstanding.

G2	$1	July 1, 1859 ABN. Capital: $25,000.	R-7
G2a	$1	July 1, 1859 ABN. As above, except for capital ($50,000).	R-7

G4	$5	July 1, 1859 ABN. Capital: $25,000.	R-7
G4a	$5	July 1, 1859 ABN. As above, except for capital ($50,000).	R-7

Uncut Sheet

X1	$1, 5 ABN. G2, 4	R-7

WESTPORT

WI-867   **L.M. SMITH**

SC 1   5¢   January 24, 1861. Black.   R-7

WEYAUWEGA

WI-870   BANK OF WEYAUWEGA, 1859-65

Capital 1861 $50,000. 1863 $35,000.
Closed.

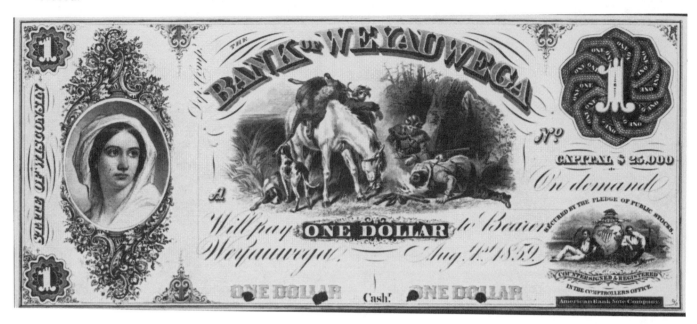

G2	$1	August 1, 1859 ABN. No overprint.	R-7
G2a	$1	August 1, 1859 ABN. As above, except for overprint of a red panel outlining a white ONE.	R-6

G4	$2	August 1, 1859 ABN. No overprint.	R-7
G4a	$2	August 1, 1859 ABN. As above, except for overprint of a red panel outlining a white Two.	R-6

Uncut Sheet

X1	$1, 2 ABN. G2, 4	R-7

WI-440   WISCONSIN VALLEY BANK (See Millville WI-440)

WHITEWATER

WI-250   KOKOMO BANK, 1859-60

Notes dated at Whitewater, 1858.
Failed, $2903 held for redemption of notes.

Genuine Notes, Raised Notes and Counterfeits

G10a	$5	1858 DW, ABNCo. mono. Same as Hillsdale G4a, except for location, date and imprint.	R-7
G12a	$10	1858 DW, ABNCo. mono. Same as Hillsdale G6a, except for location, date and imprint.	R-7

Uncut Sheet

X1		$5, 10 DW. G4a, 6a	R-7

Altered, Spurious and Unattributed Non-Genuine Notes

S5	$1	?: (1850s) Unknown. NDA. The bank issued no $1s.	R-6
S10	$2	?: (1850s) Unknown. C: Liberty std. with pole & cap. The bank issued no $2s.	R-7

S15	$3	___18__: 1859 DrW. The bank issued no $3s.	R-6
S15a	$3	___18__: 1859 None. As above, except for lack of an imprint.	R-6

WI-875   MERCHANTS & MECHANICS BANK, 1857-59

Capital $100,000. D. Graham, cashier.
Originally known as McDonnel Graham & Company's Bank of Whitewater, although no notes were issued under that title. Closed 1859. Specie of $6373 held in 1863 for redemption of notes.

Genuine Notes, Raised Notes and Counterfeits

| G2a | $1 | ___18__: (1857-59) WH&W. Tint: Red microlettering overall, panel at left end and counter. | Remainder | R-6 |

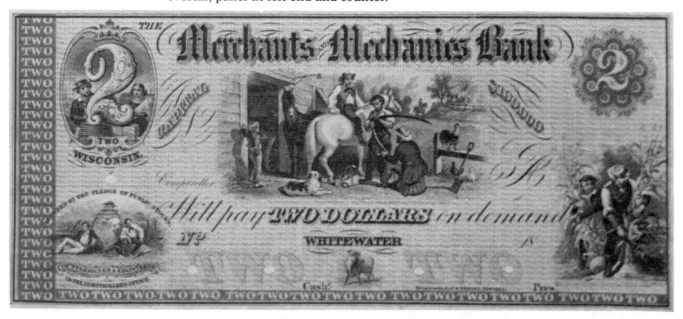

G4a	$2	___18__: (1857-59) WH&W. Tint: Red overall microlettering, panel at left end, counter & TWO TWO.		R-7
R2	$5	___18__: 1857-59 WH&W. Raised from $2, G4a. The bank issued no $5s.		R-7
R4	$10	___18__: 1857-59 WH&W. Raised from $2, G4a. The bank issued no $5s.		R-7
R6	$20	___18__: 1857-59 WH&W. Raised from $2, G4a. The bank issued no $20s.		R-7

Uncut Sheet

| X1 | | $1, 2 WH&W. G2a, 4a | | R-7 |

WI-880   **BANK OF WHITEWATER, ca. 1858-65**

Closed.

G2a	$1	___18__: (1850s) RWH&E. Tint: Green lathework overall and an outlined white ONE. Capital: $25,000.	R-6
G2b	$1	___18__: 1805s Unknown. As above, except for addition of "Depy." before "Compr.", and possible imprint change to ABN.	R-7
G2c	$1	___18__: 1860s Unknown. Same as G2b, except for capital ($50,000).	R-7

G4a	$3	___18__: (1850s) RWH&E. Tint: Green lathework outlining and an outlined white THREE. Capital: $25,000.	R-7
G4b	$3	___18__: 1860s Unknown. As above, except for addition of "Dept." before "Compr." and possible imprint change to ABN.	R-7
G4c	$3	___18__: 1860s Unknown. Same as G4b, except for capital ($50,000).	R-7

Uncut Sheet

| X1 | | $1, 3R WH&E. G2a, 4a | R-7 |

UNIVERSAL NOTES

Type of 1854

25¢   ___1854 No ___   R-6

50¢   Goodrick & Davis   R-7

$1.00   ___1854 No ___   R-7

$2.00   ___1854 No ___   R-7

$3.00   ___ 1854 No ___   R-7

$5.00   ___ 1854 No ___   R-7

*Type of 185_*

25¢	___ 185_ No ____	R-6
50¢	___ 185_ No ____	R-6
$1.00	___ 185_ No ____	R-7
$2.00	___ 185_ No ____	R-7

| $3.00 | ___ 185_ No ____ | R-7 |
| $5.00 | ___ 185_ No ____ | R-7 |

Notes on Wisconsin

APPENDIX I
THE KNAPP, STOUT & CO. COMPANY

The original Knapp, Stout & Company was organized on August 30, 1853. The co-partnership was based on an inventory of an estimate value of $70,000 holdings by the gentlemen who entered into the agreement. The story of the acquiring of the various interests dates from 1846.

William Wilson, a resident of Fort Madison in the then territory of Iowa, who previously had had some experience in lumbering operations in northern Pennsylvania, having been informed that there were vast pineries and excellent inducements and opportunities for investment on the Chippewa River and its tributaries in the territory of Wisconsin, concluded to make personal examination. Accordingly he made the trip to the Chippewa and Red Cedar counties, and his comprehensive business grasp, practical knowledge and keen insight enabled him to see and determine at once that here was a rare opportunity for investment in pine lands and to engage in the manufacture of lumber. He returned to his home full of enthusiasm and confidence, and told his friends of the beautiful rivers, vast forest of pine and rare opportunities for investment and labor and the securing of renumerative reward for each.

He found in John H. Knapp, also of Fort Madison, one who saw like himself his life's best opportunity, and who earnestly and enthusiastically offered to join him in an effort to gain a competency in the almost uninhabitable wilds of the Chippewa Valley. On May 19, 1846 the two men executed a co-partnership agreement for lumbering operations in the Chippewa Valley. They were not, however, the first arrivals or pioneers in this business here, though the enterprise they started in time so far over-shadowed the comparatively insignificant work of their predecessors that the latter has almost been lost sight of. Mr. Freeman's story of the evolution of the Knapp-Stout concern, together with the antecedent facts, referred to at the end of the previous chapter, is as follows.

"He who studies the past growth of this city gets at the same time the history of the city and the story of a great lumber enterprise. Until recent years the history of either well might be taken as the narrative of the other. Among the fruits of that enterprise are two of our city's important benefactions — the Memorial Library and Stout schools. That this lumber business was a great enterprise is a fact attested by tradition, by the pages of contemporarily published lumber magazines and periodicals, by the statements of some now living who were engaged in its later year activities and by the business records of the company that conducted the enterprise.

"A writer for the Wisconsin Historical Society Collections, in a book of the Industries of Wisconsin during and after the Civil War, has stated that Knapp, Stout & Company was said, in the early '70s, to be the greatest lumber corporation in the world; that it in 1873, on the Red Cedar and Chippewa Rivers, owned 115,000 acres of pine lands, and had in its employ 1200 men. The real estate book of this company shows that during its existence it owned in the valley of the Red Cedar River alone some 490,000 acres of pine lands.

"The first occupancy here for the lumber business was in 1822 or 1823. The first permanent settlement, that which has continued to this day, was in 1830. In 1830-31, 100,000 feet of lumber was cut here. At our river mill the last log was sawed in August, 1901. There was a continuous cutting of logs into lumber for 70 years, the once appointed term of a man's life, but more years, by far, than the actual span of life of many a man who in those years worked here.

"It is evident, in the association of past events and in years of settlement, that this is an old city. Its age, measured by years, is best understood by a comparison of its permanent beginning with the time when other cities near had far had their beginnings.

HISTORY OF DUNN COUNTY

"A search of the records of the state shows that Milwaukee was settled but a few years earlier; Madison in 1837, seven years later; Chippewa Falls, 1838, eight years after, and Eau Claire, 1845, fifteen years after. Going outside of the state it is found that Chicago had but two families one year after the site of Menomonie was first occupied; that St. Paul was not settled until 1838, eight years after permanent settlement here.

"In the administrative function of the state it is presumed that every person knows the law. In considering the history of a community, a town or a city it is assumed that every person knows the history of the place where he resides. We all know that as a matter of fact the presumption and the assumption are mere fiction, that there is scant basis of truth for either to stand upon. A decent regard for the feelings of our fellows constrains us to admit that we all do know the history of the place in which we live.

"By way of apology, for considering the history of this city at this time, perhaps it may suffice in connection with the admission that all the permanent residents do know the city history, to suggest that each year ushers in a new generation and each week strangers are welcomed as permanent settlers, and to call attention to the fact that no authoritative publication in book form is available for correct information for the new generation and for the new settlers.

"The books treating of the history of Menomonie are: The History of the Chippewa Valley, published in Chicago; The History of the Lumber Industry of Northern Wisconsin, published in Chicago; A Sketch of Menomonie, by Mrs. Bella French, and An Early History of the Chippewa Valley, written and published by Thomas E. Randall, of Eau Claire, Wisconsin, in 1875; the others are founded upon it so far as the early history of our city is concerned. All of these books are grossly inaccurate in statement as to dates, and as to the personal names of proprietors, and as to the relative times of their ownership, and as to the mutual association of persons in firms or corporations. Even the writer on Civil War industries referred to, whose work was published by the Wisconsin Historical Society, makes the blunder of misnaming the corporation operating here, giving it as "Krapp Stout and Company." It should have been The Knapp Stout & Co. Company. Again, he antedates the operations of this corporation by laying the stress as to his statistics at a time some five years prior to its organization. He refers to 1873 and this corporation was not organized until 1878.

"The matter of a name of a corporation is not a trivial thing. The exact name of a corporation stands to it in the same stead as does the baptismal name of a person. The corporation is an entity, a corporate thing, and at its organization the state stands sponsor for its name. By the name given it, it is known in the law, and by no other name. The corporation operating here was named The Knapp Stout & Co. Company. When a part or parts of this name are eliminated through carelessness its identity is lost. It may not legally contract in a shorter name and it cannot be successfully prosecuted in such shorter name in a civil or a criminal tribunal of the state.

"Of all of the early settlements in this state this settlement has probably the most complete original record evidence of its initial time of commencement and of the precise local place of its beginning. Its first step and all subsequent steps are authenticated, by either the written statement of some one who participated in the events constituting the step, by files or records of the transactions of the step in some court of record of the state, by the extant original instruments attesting transfers or agreements as to transfers of the site or by preserved daily original business entries in business books kept from 1846 continuously to the recent close of the active affairs of the corporation that finally took over and continued the business enterprise here. Any one certain fact in our history may be evidenced by more than one of these testimonies.

"Such being the available material it would seem to be our duty to correct rather than by inaction help to perpetuate the errors that outside narrators have engrafted upon our local history. It were well that some "Truthful James" enter the field and tell in simple language what he knows about the scenes, the persons and the events that make up our aforetime history. As an aid to such a coming result I give to you an abstract of the information that lays open at your door.

"The first location and establishment of a dam and mill in this valley was in 1822-23, on Wilson Creek, at its mouth. These were destroyed by a flood within a few months after commencement of work and before their completion. Both were rebuilt, but not until 1830-31. By March, 1831, 100,000 feet of lumber had been sawed at the Wilson Creek mill, but in June of that year the dam was swept out by a freshnet and the lumber carried away and scattered. This dam at Wilson Creek was probably the exact site of the present dam on that stream.

"There is no definite and well authenticated account of the occupation even temporarily on this river for any purpose before this of 1822-23. Between the occupancy of 1822-23 and that of 1830 it is probable that some private forays were made on the timber growing here, but no mention is found of them. Lawfully, only those having a permit from the United States could then cut timber on this river, and during this period it is believed no such permit was issued.

"In both instances, that of 1822-23 and that of 1830-31, James H. Lockwood and Joseph Rolette, rival fur traders, both of Prairie du Chien, were the backers of the enterprises. In the first venture one Hardin Perkins was interested and a man named Armstrong was a part owner in the second. Perkins lost his services and $1,500 and Lockwood & Rolette divided the remainder of the loss. Armstrong, to get rid of him, was paid $500 for his interest in the business venture of 1830-31, before the dam and mill at Wilson Creek was completed. Then an interest was given to one Isaac Saunders.

"From August 11, 1831, until the fall of 1837 we find no mention of this mill by any one claiming to have been here during that period. John H. Fonda, an early resident of Prairie du Chien, in a published statement, states that he was at the mill on the Menomonie River in the years 1837, 1838 and 1839, in all two years. He calls the mill Lockwood's mill.

"From a statement made by James H. Lockwood, the last known owners before 1841 of the Wilson Creek mill were Lockwood and Rolette, with an interest in Isaac Saunders, given to him to induce him to take charge of the business there. By Fonda's statement it would appear that in 1837, 1838 and 1839, Lockwood owned this mill. There is no evidence of a transfer of the interest of Rolette or of Saunders in and to this mill. Yet it is probable that not only the interests of Rolette, but that of Saunders, was, at some time, conveyed, for by a deed recorded in Crawford County, it appears that a transfer was made of the Wilson Creek mill to James Green by James H. Lockwood and Hiram S. Allen. This deed bears date January 8, 1841. By the same records it appears that Green, by a deed, dated May 18, 1842, conveyed this mill to William Black. The records of the county court of Crawford County show that William Black died in 1844 and that David Black, described in the petition for administration of his estate as the nearest relative living in this vicinity, became administrator of his estate. An inventory was filed which showed only personal property. David Black asked for and got an extention of two years in which to settle the estate, which in fact never was settled so far as the records show. Before the two years for which the extension was given had expired, David Black died. It is conjectured that David Black in some way acquired title to the Wilson Creek property through these administration proceedings, for by a deed recorded in Crawford County, dated June 16, 1846, for a consideration of $2,000, he conveyed to John H. Knapp an undivided one-half interest therein. It was but a few weeks after the giving of this deed that he, David Black, died.

"A partnership was formed between David Black and John H. Knapp at the time of the sale of the one-half interest by which Mr. Knapp was to carry on a lumber business at the mill for the firm styled "Black and Knapp" for a term of five years.

"David Black's estate was administered through the county court of Crawford County and the administrator thereof became authorized to and did give to Mr. Knapp a deed of the one-half interest remaining in David Black. This deed is dated May 4, 1850. For this one-half interest $2,600 was paid. One thousand dollars in cash and two short term notes of eight hundred dollars each. It will be remembered that for the first one-half interest Mr. Knapp paid two thousand dollars. By the record it appears that now John H. Knapp became the sole owner of the Wilson Creek mill, paying therefor the sum of forty-six hundred dollars. As a matter of fact, however, Mr. William Wilson, through whose enterprise this purchase was made, was a joint and equal owner with Mr. Knapp. On the death of David Black it was the legal duty of Mr. Knapp to close up the partnership business, but it is evident that this sacrifice of the property was avoided by a contract entered into with the administrator of Black's estate, by which Mr. Knapp agreed to continue to conduct the business. He did so until 1850 when he bought the remaining one-half interest of the administrator.

"It is not difficult, from this time on, to trace the successive ownership of this property. In 1823, and again in 1830, the right acquired by Lockwood and Rolette rested on a permit from the United States government to cut timber on Indian lands, supplemented by a contract with the Indians by which they were to receive $1,000 per year in goods for their consent to the privilege granted. The first avowed claim to any specific tract of land at Wilson Creek appears in the deed from Lockwood and Allen to Green, wherein the grantors covenant to put the grantee into possession of land on the Menomonie River in Carver Grant, so-called, one-half mile square. By a description of the survey, the mouth of Wilson Creek was placed at the middle of the east boundary line of this square. The deed from Green to William Black conveys the same tract; so also do the deeds of David Black and of the administrator of David Black, to Mr. Knapp. It has been noted that no transfer from William Black to David Black is found, and it is surmised that title came to the latter by administration of William Black's estate.

"The country about here had not been surveyed when the deed of Black to Knapp was given, and it contains this promise: "that whenever the above tracts of land shall be sold by the United States or when the same shall be in the market, that then and in such case the said Black shall either prove up a pre-emption or purchase the same at the land sales and convey the one equal undivided half thereof to said Knapp, he, said Knapp, paying one equal half of the consideration money."

"Black's death occurred before the land was pre-empted or sold and before it came into market.

"In May, 1846, before the purchase by Knapp from Black had been consummated by deed, Mr. Knapp and William Wilson entered into an agreement by the terms of which they were to carry on a lumber business at the Wilson Creek mill for five years. This agreement, although technically not a partnership agreement between Mr. Knapp and Mr. Wilson, was in effect such an agreement to carry out the agreement on the part of Mr. Knapp with David Black. Its effect was to make Knapp, Wilson and Black partners and on the death of David Black, it left Knapp and Wilson the surviving partners, and they conducted the business under the firm name of Black and Knapp until 1850 when the deed was given by the administrator of the estate of David Black to Mr. Knapp.

"The death of David Black made it impossible to secure title to the land described in his deed in the manner therein agreed upon. A United States survey

of the lands was made in 1849, and we find that William Wilson, on April 24, 1851, by pre-emption entered lots 1, 2 and 3, section 26, township 28 north, of range 13 west, which corresponds in area and location closely to the trace conveyed by David Black. Mr. Wilson four days later, April 28, 1851, conveyed these lots to John H. Knapp. On this pre-emption Wilson received a patent dated April 19, 1855. The title granted by this patent, by operation of law, inured to Mr. Knapp and his grantees by virtue of the conveyance to him of April 28, 1851. The remainder of section 26 was pre-empted by other persons in 1855, who were then members of the firm of Knapp, Stout & Company.

"After the conveyance by the administrator of the estate of David Black, and the entry by Wilson, the changes in the associates in business and the title to the property at Wilson Creek mill were rapid. August 19, 1850, Knapp sold a one-third interest to Andrew Tainter, and a new set of books were opened in the firm name of Knapp and Tainter. Knapp and Tainter sold within the next three years interests in the business to B. B. Downs and Henry L. Stout.

"To give a summary of the successive steps in this four-part partnership, — first, Mr. Knapp sold to B. B. Downs a one-twentieth interest; second, Mr. Stout bought the interest of Downs, whereupon Tainter sold to Stout, a one-twelfth of the whole property and Mr. Knapp sold to him seven-sixteenths of the whole business. This gave Mr. Stout a one-fourth interest.

"The new and old owners formed a co-partnership as of August 20, 1853, based on an inventory of an estimated value at $70,000, to be known as Knapp, Stout & Company. The apportionment of interests made on the books shows Knapp, one-half, Tainter, one quarter. Stout one-fifth, and Downs one-twentieth. It will be borne in mind that William Wilson's interest is here included in Mr. Knapp's one-half. In 1854 Knapp sold to Thomas B. Wilson a one-fourth interest in the business with the agreement that the firm name should remain as then fixed, Downs, in the same year, sold his interest to Stout, thus reducing the number of partners to four, each having a one-fourth part of Thomas B. Wilson, he making a declaration of trust showing his father's interest in his share.

"This somewhat circumstantial and detailed account of the organization of the firm of Knapp, Stout & Company is given in the hope that it may correct some of the whimsical and unsatisfactory statements which have appeared in histories of the Chippewa Valley and have been written into the biographies of the deceased members of this firm.

"The private papers and the private records of the last line of owners showing the establishment of their business and the successive firm names of their enterprise have been put in my hands and I have used them, in connection with information found in the public records of Crawford and Dunn counties, in an earnest endeavor to give a correct statement of events, leading from the first settlement here up to the permanent organization of the lumber company as a corporation.

"An investigation will show a certain parallelism of continuous advancement in business and in social development. The temporary logging camp had a force of men, only, independent and self-reliant, unrestrained, save at times of actual work; permanent camp was attended with a self regulated hamlet; a more permanent camp with a politically organized town government and a permanent corporate organized business became seated in a civic organized city.

"After formation of the partnership company Mr. Knapp sold to John H. Douglass an interest and there were then six members of the firm although record title appeared in only five members. These later members were John H. Knapp, William Wilson, Andrew Tainter, Henry L. Stout, Thomas B. Wilson and John H. Douglass, named in order in which their respective interests were taken. These men, at first some of them as a group and later all of them as a group, conducted business under the firm name of Knapp, Stout & Company from August 20, 1853, until March 16, 1878. On June 1, 1878. They formally transferred their firm and individual interests to a corporation organized by them.

"In order to preserve, as nearly as the law would permit, the old firm name under which they had done business there was prefixed to such old name the word 'The,' and affixed thereto the word 'Company', making the name of the corporation 'The Knapp Stout & Co. Company.'

"The capital stock of the corporation was fixed at $2,000,000. John H. Knapp was made president; Andrew Tainter, vice president; Thomas B. Wilson, secretary; and John H. Douglass, treasurer. Of these men, William Wilson, John H. Knapp, Andrew Tainter and Thomas B. Wilson actively identified with the history of Menomonie as residents here. Henry L. Stout was a prominent resident of Dubuque and ended his days there. John H. Douglass moved from Dubuque to St. Louis and ended his days there. John Knapp, son of John H. Knapp, became a stockholder in the corporation, and soon afterward Peter E. Wilson, eldest son of Thomas B. wilson, and William W. Cassidy of Read's Landing, also became stockholders.

"Of the three early mills along the Red Cedar River we have a traditionary account. It has been given by Mr. Thomas F. Randall, now deceased, late of Eau Claire, Wisconsin. Some years ago he wrote a series of sketches on the early history of the Chippewa Valley, printed first as newspaper articles, later published in book form. He did not come to the valley until 1845, and located and lived to the time of his death on the main Chippewa. He and Hiram S. Allen became great friends. An inspection of his book reveals but incidental mention of the Menomonie or Red Cedar River, and for the most part such mention is for the purpose of giving incidents in the life of Mr. Allen. The traditions as given by Randall have been copied in subsequent publications concerning this county as being its early history.

"As given by Randall some of the legendary history runs as follows: 'In the spring of 1828, Street and Lockwood erected at Wilson Creek the first mill built in the Chippewa Valley. This firm constructed a second mill at Gilbert Creek. In 1835 Street and Lockwood sold both mills to H. S. Allen. In 1839 Allen built a sawmill at Irvine Creek, which he rebuilt in 1841. He then owned the three mills called Upper, Middle and Lower Mills. The same year (1841) he sold the Lower mill to Stephen S. McCann; it was burned in 1843; in the fall

of 1841 the Upper mill was sold to one Green, who soon after transferred it to a Mr. Pearson, by whom the first dam across the Menomonie was erected; he soon sold it to an old gentleman by the name of Black, who, in 1844, transferred a half interest to Knapp and Wilson, who, the following year, associated themselves with Mr. Stout under the firm name of Knapp, Stout & Co.; in a later article this event is placed by Randall as of 1846; and that Knapp, Stout & Co. in 1860 sold to Andrew Tainter a one-fourth interest in their business.'

"Generally speaking, it may matter but little to the general reader in giving early local history, whether events be placed within five or even ten years of their real occurrence or whether names of settlers and owners connected with such events be given as Jones or Brown, but, to the local resident it is sometimes exasperating to find the antecedents of his present personal surroundings grossly misstated.

"In this present instance it is well established that the first mill here was built in 1822-23, not in 1828, and that no mill was built here in 1828, but that in 1830 and 1831 this mill was built by Lockwood and Rolette and none at any time by Street and Lockwood; that Mr. Black mentioned by Randall did not in 1844, nor at any other time, transfer the property to Knapp and Wilson, but that another Black did transfer a one-half interest in such property in 1846 to John H. Knapp; that Mr. Stout did not associate himself with Knapp and Wilson in 1844 nor 1846, but not until 1853; that Andrew Tainter acquired an interest in 1850, instead of 1860, and prior to Mr. Stout's purchase.

"The records show that Lockwood and Allen conveyed the Upper Mill to Green, but at the same time it shows that out of a consideration of $5,000 Green gave back a mortgage of $4,671 running to Lockwood. While these transactions might indicate an interest of Allen in the Upper Mill they negative the idea that Allen owned and sold it to Green. There is no direct evidence that Allen ever owned this mill.

"As the records show a deed to Green in January, 1841, and one from Green to William Black in May, 1842, it seems improbable, in the absence of direct evidence, that there was an intermediary named Pearson, as stated by Randall to be the fact, who made some progress in the erection of a dam across the Menomonee River. Regarding the dam across the river, the time when Pearson entered upon its construction, this proviso: that the grantor also transfers an equal undivided interest in and to a contract in relation to the building of a new mill on and a dam across the said Menomonie River. This proviso would seem to indicate a project for the building of a dam and mill rather than the completion of an enterprise already well forwarded. In the accounts of Black and Knapp there is no appearance of this contract having been entered upon or carried out, although the fact is a dam had been constructed across the river before October, 1849. Perhaps the death, soon after this deed was given, of Mr. Black may have put the project in abeyance.

"As to the time when Mr. Stout acquired his interest and as to the time when the co-partnership under the name of Knapp, Stout & Co. was formed, an entry on the firm books of Knapp and Tainter shows it to be as of August 20th, 1853, instead of 1844 as stated by Randall.

"To corroborate Lockwood in his statement that he and Rolette built the mill, we have from the United States Department of the Interior copies of the application of Lockwood for, and of the permit by the War Department to build this mill, which shows that Rolette was associated with Lockwood. Schoolcraft, when in 1831 he was at the Wilson Creek mill, was told by the man in charge that the mill belonged to "Messrs. Rolette and Lockwood." Fonda in 1837 calls this mill Lockwood's. The permit here mentioned required a contract with the Indians through the Government Agent. General Street was at that time such agent at Prairie du Chien. Popular suspicion may have connected him with the enterprise and Randall have merely written the suspicion into his sketch.

"It was long the fashion to write the histories of monarchies by setting forth the facts as to the rise, the reign and fall of monarchs. It may be a suspicion that I have here given you as a history of our city but a list of successive proprietors who have in succession each obtained, held and relinquished the ownership of the Upper Mill, the early name of this site.

"To set out in detail the progressive economic story of the former business period here with its accompanying social advancement would take too much of your time.

"The ground that I have gone over is that whereon chaotic error has heretofore mostly been found, the field wherein wrong statements have been most persistently repeated.

"Up to 1858 the occupied part of the site of Menomonie was that on the north side of the river. The Wisconsin Milling Company office now stands where probably the first cabin was built in 1822-23. It is the spot upon which in 1830-31 stood the trading shanty, upon which, always, ever since, to this time, has stood either a trading shanty, a store or an office. There was not up to that time (1858) any individual ownership of lands or of houses. The lumber company owned everything.

"In 1854 the erection of a grist mill, the first building to be put up on the south side of the river, was begun. In 1857-58 a bridge was built across the river where the present bridge stands. The mill and the bridge were built by the lumber company. In 1858 a village plat on the south side of the river was surveyed. It was plotted and recorded. The next year the sale of lots commenced. From this time on the general histories of this place are for the most part accurate in statement although meager in narrative."

Thus ends Mr. Freeman's narrative as he wrote it. That which follows is derived, as previously stated, from other sources, but is printed with Mr. Freeman's approval.

The single sash sawmill of Black & Green had a capacity for manufacturing from 5,000 to 7,000 feet of "timber" (lumber?) per day. The sawing and rafting of the lumber, running it to market and selling it in those early days devolved mainly upon the proprietors. there was at that time no market for the sale of lumber, or the purchase of food, nor any of the commodities essential to living, even on the frontier, nearer than Prairie du Chien. The only means of communication with the business world was by keel boat down the river or by the Indian trail.

About 1850 a new mill 60 x 100 feet in ground plan, was built by the firm, and two years later a gang saw was placed in the mill. This mill burned December 26, 1856, and the firm then erected a large water saw-mill on the same site, which was enlarged from time to time, and was in operation at the time of the fiftieth anniversary of the company's activities.

They bravely and energetically met every obstacle and disadvantage, each year adding a little to the plant and resources of the firm. The company did not during the first 41 years of existence declare a dividend or divide its profits. The members of the firm clearly perceived that at no far distant day, the value of uncut pine land would of necessity become greatly enhanced, and on this account, as well as the maintenance of their business they used much of their surplus capital in the purchase of large tracts of timber mostly pine lands which in those days were obtainable at low prices.

Among these were the purchases from C. C. Washburn, Cornell University, Russell Sage, Haley & Pitcher, the North Wisconsin and the Omaha railroad companies, the United States government and the state of Wisconsin. The purchase from C. C. Washburn in 1863 was over 10,000 acres of land and the mill at Waubeek. The purchase from the Cornell University in 1879-80 was also over 10,000 acres. The total purchase of pine lands in Wisconsin as shown by its real estate records were about 530,000 acres of which 490,000 acres were in the Red Cedar Valley.

Regarding the extent of the pine forests in this valley, it is a matter of history that they were included in the great pine belt which extended across the states of Wisconsin, Michigan and Minnesota. Some men now living tell of the immense tracts of pine they saw in this valley in an early day. In many instances in solidly covered contiguous sections were found the best quality pine trees that grew in the valley. Many still living can remember seeing in the spring of each year the pond at this place, now Lake Menomin, covered to far above the cemetery with saw logs so thickly massed that scarce a square yard of open water could be seen in the whole area covered, more than 300 acres. This supply was for the current year, the logs to be replaced by the next winter's cut.

The amount of lumber cut by this company was enormous, but there is not sufficient data at hand from which to make even an approximate accurate statement of the total. No estimate based on an average cut per acre of the lands purchased can be of value. In two instances, that of the Washburn and the Haley-Pitcher purchases, a large acreage was of cut-over land. From 1846 to 1851, the pine trees manufactured were cut on government lands under permits from the departments at Washington. Early inventories and sawmill accounts have been destroyed or lost by accident of flood or fire.

The vast area of cut-over land was eventually devoted to agriculture. Some of the finest farms in Barron County, one of the leading dairy communities in the world were developed from lands once covered with dense pine forests and cut-over by Knapp, Stout & Co.

In the 70's Knapp, Stout & Co., was said to be the greatest lumber corporation in the world. It was certainly most excellently situated so far as established facilities for carrying on the lumber business was concerned. It had nearly complete mastery of the Red Cedar Valley; its mill dams and its mills were located at most of the available sites on the main river; its flooding dams were built across every northern tributary and contiguous to each such dam there were located as many logging camps as could be accommodated in their output of logs by the forced artificial flooding capacity of the streams; at the mills were well stocked supply and merchandise stores; on every route from each central mill to its out-lying camps were, at easy stages, stopping places; at these stopping places there was either a farm or a large camp garden; at the mills were local lumber yards and at most of the important towns on the Mississippi River as far down as St. Louis were sales yards, each with its complement of finishing mills.

The efficiency of this system of mills, stores, farms, gardens, stopping places, local and sales yards and the right of exclusive control of the upper streams of the Red Cedar River can best be summed up by citing the remark made by Mr. William Carson, a lumberman of Eau Claire, and one of the founders of Eau Galle this county, made at a time when the price of lumber was, for the producer, ruinously low. He stated that owning to the system of operation here described; the Knapp, Stout & Co. Company could manufacture lumber at the then general market prices and make a profit, while lumbermen on other rivers could not at the same prices get back the cost of production.

In the earlier years in this region men were averse to looking forward to a life of work for wages. It was not uncommon then to see a man buy horses, harness, and a wagon, and haul produce or products under a general contract or at a specific price per load rather than drive an employer's team at daily, weekly or monthly wages. This man cheerfully faced loss rather than take personal service. It was usually in such a case a loss, if the man's income at the end of the year were to be compared with the amount of wages he might have received for the same period of time. Some, or all, of these things, were sure to happen; loss of a horse by disease or accident; lost of time, from lameness of the horse, from laying off for repairs to be made, by the shoeing of horses or in the hauling of hay and feed.

In 1873 the firm owned 115,000 acres of pine lands on the Chippewa and Menomonie Rivers, from which it cut and manufactured during the year, in its various stream and water power mills, 55,000,000 feet of lumber, 20,000,000 shingles and 20,000,000 lath and pickets. It maintained at Menomonie, in addition to its lumber mills, store, and stables, a foundry machine shop and blacksmith shop, a grain warehouse of 40,000 bushels capacity and a grist mill in which its yearly requirement of flour was ground. It owned six large farms in Dunn and Barron counties containing 6,000 to 7,000 acres of improved land; upon which was raised large supplies of wheat and pork. It conducted general merchandise stores, the annual sales of which amounted to $750,000. Its dams and camps were on every available site in the valley. Large lumber yards were maintained at Read's Landing, Dubuque and St. Louis. Twelve hundred men were on its payroll.

As the time approached when the pine timber would be exhausted in Wisconsin, the company looked to other localities for investments. During the five years prior to 1896 it carefully selected, examined and purchased over 400,000 acres of pine lands situated in Missouri, Arkansas and Mississippi. The company also owned extensive and valuable real estate properties in St. Louis, Mo., Dubuque and Fort Madison, Ia. The combined sawing capacity of those mills in the late 90's was over 750,000 feet of lumber a day, allowing 11 hours' work for each day. The mills in Wisconsin were cutting 650,000 feet of lumber per day. This did not include lath and shingles. The principal lumber yards were at St. Louis, Fort Madison, Dubuque and Cedar Falls. The lumber for all the yards located outside of Wisconsin was rafted at the mills and run down the Red Cedar, Chippewa and Mississippi Rivers to the points of destination.

As an indication of the cut per year it may be cited that at a stockholders' meeting in 1887 a proposition was brought before the meeting to limit the board of directors in their operation of the mills in that year to a cut of 87,000,000 feet of lumber with its proportionate cut of shingles and laths.

The annual manufacture of the company for many years was from 80,000,000 to 90,000,000 feet of lumber and 50,000,000 shingles at the several mills at Menomonie, Cedar Falls and Downsville, disposed of at its wholesale yards at various points on the Mississippi River, in addition to an extensive car trade which the company had been enabled to carry on with the western prairie country, through the railroad facilities which had opened direct communications with all parts of the nation. The number of employees on the payroll of the company averaged about 2,000 during the last twenty years of operations. In this number were included the employees at the various business branches in the states where the corporation carried on business.

This concern was one of the oldest lumbering institutions in the country. From the point of view of the business transacted during the last 30 years of its existence, it stood at the head of the list of lumber manufacturers in the United States. There have been associations, or combinations of corporations, that have cut more timber in a given time, to be floated down streams or transported by railway to different points, to be manufactured by different persons, firms and corporations, but no single firm or corporation equaled it in the amount of lumber manufactured.

Perhaps the most significant fact in the whole history of the institution is that while its members may have been prosperous, may have accumulated a competence, yet at the same time hundreds of the employees have been able, through their employment and aid, to purchase and pay for homes and purchase and improve farms, so that there is scarcely a neighborhood in the Red Cedar and the Chippewa valleys where there are not well-to-do and prosperous farmers who received the first dollar that was paid on the purchase price of their homes from Knapp, Stout & Co. Company for services rendered. Nor is this all. It may safely be said that no other lumbering concern in the

Northwest bore so largely and yet uncomplainingly the burdens of taxation nor paid as much into the public treasury. During the last 35 years of the company's operations, it paid, as a firm and corporation over $1,500,000 in Wisconsin alone. This does not include taxes paid by individual members nor taxes paid in other states. During the last 30 years of its activities the company as a firm or corporation paid in taxes in the several states where its business and prosperity has been located, more than $2,000,000.

In the days that saw the beginning of this significant venture, this section was a wilderness covered by splendid pine forests. Civilization followed the woodman's axe. The lumberman literally blazed the way for settlement and progress. The small industry that was taken over in 1846 by Messrs. Wilson and Knapp and which increased and flourished under the wise direction of these men and their associates became the nucleus around which for many years all things in this vicinity centered. From this nucleus was evolved a busy, beautiful and prosperous city. At no time did the interest of these founders in the welfare of the settlement ever flag. Nearly every pioneer now living includes in his biography a period when he was employed in some capacity by Knapp, Stout & Co. Company. the archives of this corporation contain the material from which an almost complete history of Menomonie might be written. Its pay rolls for many years contained the roster of nearly all its bread winners. When gradually the lands were cleared and fertile farms sprang up where the virgin forests had reared their majestic heads, the interest of these sturdy and far-seeing founders did not cease with the passing of the era of lumbering, but continued through that epoch when agriculture was established as the stable and enduring foundation of the communities prosperity.

On August 12, 1896, the members of the corporation, their families and invited guests assembled to celebrate the semi-centennial anniversary of the beginning of this enterprise. The exercises were held during the afternoon and evening of that day at the residence of Senator James H. Stout. The spacious grounds had been appropriately decorated for the occasion, and for two hours were thrown open to the public that all might share in the notable commemoration. A novel feature of this observance was the presence of a band of Chippewa Indians, who had pitched their tepees on the lawn, and as a pleasant reminder of the amicable relations always maintained between the company and the red men in the early days, the leader, Aleck Moose, lit a peace pipe, which was passed among the officers, each of whom puffed heartily at the calumet. At the banquet which was spread out upon the greensward, addresses were delivered and reminiscences recalled by members of the company and pioneers bearing upon the long-continued and honorably conducted activities of the corporation.

Between 1846 and the final cessation of operations in 1901 the company's activities continued practically unabated. The company was never formally dissolved for the reason that its services are still occasionally needed in the clearing of land titles and the like, but while its corporate existence still endures theoretically, the great enterprise like the men who made it what it was, has passed from the field of effort, leaving a permanent monument behind it in the form of other varied and important interests which it made possible.

In 1886 John H. Knapp, on account of failing health, declined serving longer as president of the corporation and Henry L. Stout was elected president. Mr Knapp died in the autumn of 1888, and his widow and children, in the settlement of his estate, became stockholders in the corporation. The next of the founders to depart this life was the oldest of them all, Capt. William Wilson, who died in this city (Menomonie) in 1892 at the age of 85 years. T. B. Wilson, his oldest son, who gave practically his entire life to the company's business having come to Menomonie with his father in 1846, and who enjoyed before his death the distinction of being "the oldest inhabitant" passed away in March, 1898. Capt. Andrew Tainter died October 18, 1899, after an active career here, which began in 1850. Henry L. Stout died at his home in Dubuque on July 17, 1900. It was claimed as a remarkable coincidence that on the day of Mr. Stout's death the rear of the last drive from Rice Lake left that place. At about the same time, James Bracklin of Rice Lake, head woods foreman, and one of the well known characters of the northwest, died, the date of his passing being July 26, 1900.

Singularly enough, the lives of the founders nearly spanned the period of activity of the big lumber company. Though the organization went on, and the mills kept on sawing, in the course of a short time it was necessary to abandon manufacture because of the exhaustion of the supply of material. The Cedar Falls and Downsville mills ceased work in the fall of 1900. The following year the three Menomonie mills - the steam mill, the water mill and the shingle mill - closed business, the last raft being sent down the river on August 12, 1901.

The water power and franchises were sold to the Wisconsin Power Company, which disposed of them to the Chippewa Valley Railway, Light & Power Company, by which they are now owned and operated for the transmission of electric current to various points. The St. Louis property was taken over by the heirs of T. B. Wilson. The Thornton, Ark., interests were acquired by J. H. Stout, who greatly extended them. He died December 10, 1910. F. D. Stout purchased the properties of the company located at Leeper, Mo., Dubuque and Fort Madison, Ia., and in Mississippi. The land holdings in this vicinity went to various parties. The Wisconsin Land Company Purchased a large tract of Barron and Washburn County lands.

Thus closed one of the most interesting chapters in the history of Northern Wisconsin's pioneer industry, the source of its greatest wealth, a chapter without which the annals of settlement and progress in the entire northwest would be incomplete.

APPENDIX II

Urbana Union (Ill)
August 19, 1858
Another Crash

Below we give a list of banks thrown out by Chicago Bankers. It is said that the banks are all amply secured:

Arctic Bank; Bank of Eau Claire; Bank of La Point; Bank of Manitowoc; Bank of Moneka; Bank of North America; Bank of Oconto; Chippewa Bank; Clark County Bank; Laborer's Bank; Lumberman's Bank; Manitowoc County Bank; Marathon County Bank; Mercantile Bank; Northern Wisconsin Bank; Oakwood Bank; Oconto County Bank; Oneida Bank; Shewanaw Bank; State Security Bank; State Stock Bank; St. Croix River Bank; St. Croix Valley Bank; Tradesmen's Bank; Waupacca County Bank; Wisconsin Valley Bank; Wisconsin Pinery Bank.

APPENDIX III

Central Illinois Gazette
April 10, 1861
Forty Two Wisconsin Banks Thrown Out

The bankers of this city this morning determined to throw out the following Wisconsin Banks, the value of whose securities are so far below the value of their circulation, that they are deemed unsafe to hold. The list embraces forty-two, as follows:

Arctic Bank, Eagle Point,
Bank of Albany,
Bank of Beaver Dam,
Bank of Eau Claire, Eau Claire,
Bank of Grant County, Platteville,
Bank of Green Bay, Green Bay,
Bank of Horicon, Horicon,
Bank of Mokena, Gordon,
Bank of Monroe, Monroe,
Bank of Whitewater, Whitewater,
Bank of Wisconsin, Watertown,
Beloit Savings Bank,
Bank of Chippewa, Pepin,
Citizen's Bank, Black River Falls,
Clark County, Chippewa Falls,
Commercial Bank, Racine,
Corn Planters' Bank, Waupacca,
Dodge County Bank, Beaver Dam,
Bank of Elkhorn, Elkhorn,
Farmers' Bank, Two Rivers,
Farmers & Merchants' Bank, Fon du Lac,
Forest City Bank, Waukesha,
Hall & Brothers' Bank, Eau Claire,
Katanyan Bank, La Crosse,
Koshkaonong Bank, Ft. Atkinson,
La Crosse County Bank, La Crosse,
Lake Shore Bank, Manitowoc,
Laborers Bank, Ellisville (Eliside) & Markesan,
Mechanics' Bank, Superior,
Monroe County Bank Sparta,
North Western Bank, Stevens' Point,
Osborne Bank, New London,
Portage County Bank, Jordon,
Bank of Reedsburgh, Reedsburgh,

Rockwell & Co's Bank, Elkhorn,
State Stock Bank, Eau Claire,
Southern Bank, Eau Claire,
St. Croix River Bank, Brinkerhoff,
Sun Prairie Bank, Sun Prairie,
Tradesmen's Bank, Eagle Lake,
Waukesha County Bank, Waukesha,
Wood County Bank, Grand Rapids,

The bills on all these banks will be received at 20 per cent, discount by the brokers of this city, though we advise bill-holders not to dispose of them at a sacrifice unless they are obliged to do so.- *Chicago Journal*

APPENDIX IV

Central Illinois Gazette
June 5, 1861
Wisconsin Currency.

During the past ten days repeated inquiries have been made to us, by parties living in Iowa, Wisconsin and Northern Illinois, whether or not it was safe to sell produce for Wisconsin currency. In answer to these inquiries and also for the general information of our readers, we append a list of the Banks of Wisconsin now received by the bankers at Milwaukee, with the circulation of each, and the value per dollar of the bills, according to the market prices of the securities in the hands of the comptroller of the State on the 20th of May. By reference to this list, it will be seen that the value of the currency generally ranges from 51 to 85 c. on the dollar. There are a few banks ranging 90 c. to 100, but these, it will be seen, are of limited circulation, and we understand their issues rarely if ever see daylight. Few, if any of the Banks redeem their issues in coin or exchange, and in this respect they are no better than the Illinois bank bills — now known as "stumptail," — and hawked about our streets at or about their real value.

Such, therefore, being the case, there is no reason on earth why Wisconsin currency should not share the same fate as that of Illinois. Both are frauds on the community, and were gotten up by heartless speculators, without the remotest intention that they would ever redeem a dollar of the stuff — and our advice to all is, *to take it only at its real value.*

It may be said that if the people have confidence in it, the currency will continue "to go;" but so far as the Northwest is concerned this "confidence game" is "played out." It was tried here by almost every merchant and banker in the State — agreements, contracts, and compromises were tried — but in vain. Water will find its level, as did Illinois currency; and the same inexorable law will work out its results in regard to that of Wisconsin. At the present, in view of the scarcity of good currency, the bankers of Wisconsin are moving heaven and earth to get their circulation into the hands of the people; but it is up-hill work. The people of Illinois repudiate it, and sell only for gold; and their neighbors of Wisconsin, Iowa, and Minnesota are getting hungry for something that is worth one hundred cents on the dollar. Produce brings gold in every market in the world, and there is no reason why the farmers of the Northwest should continue to take paper money worth only from fifty to seventy cents on the dollar.

List of Current Wisconsin Banks

Name of Bank	Circulation	Val per dol.
Bank of Beloit	$18,500	51 cts
Bank of Columbia	63,852	69
Bank of Fox Lake	54,791	85
Bank of Grant Co., Platteville	68,018	59
Bank of Green Bay	44,264	65
Bank of the Interior, Wausau	40,403	73
Bank of Madison	8,897	86
Bank of Jefferson, Gordon	48,700	94
Bank of Moneka	48,265	77
Bank of Monroe	15,278	62
Bank of the Northwest, Stevens Point	83,823	75
Bank of Oshkosh	6,835	101
Bank of Portage	47,233	74
Bank of Prairie du Chien	34,099	94
Bank of Racine	2,327	82
Bank of Ripon	12,212	92
Bank of Sheboygan	23,566	58
Bank of Sparta	18,407	59
Bank of Watertown	43,630	73
Bank of Whitewater	23,300	53
Bank of Weyauwega	42,110	96
Central Bank of Wisconsin, Janesville	56,927	100
City Bank of Kenosha	19,411	59
City Bank of Prescott	49,666	95
Oneida Bank, Berlin	22,154	74
Columbia Bank, Portage	45,940	96
Commercial Bank, Racine	20,560	87
Corn Exchange Bank, Waupun	44,190	96
Corn Planters Bank, Waupacca	37,275	55
Dane County Bank, Madison	14,790	100
Dodge Co. Bank, Beaver Dam	22,257	56
Exch. Bank of Darling & Co., Fond du Lac	27,227	56
Elkhorn Bank	21,649	60
Farmers and Merchants Bank, Burlington	14,460	75
Farmers and Millers Bank, Milwaukee	5,655	68
Forest City Bank, Waukesha	24,006	82
Frontier Bank, La Pointe	28,745	74
German Bank, Sheboygan	38,286	84
Green Bay Bank	22,661	96
Hudson City Bank	21,865	83
Iowa County Bank, Mineral Point	23,451	81
Jefferson County Bank, Watertown	58,700	71
Juneau Bank	7,850	59
Kenosha County Bank	8,300	88
La Crosse County Bank	12,800	52
Lumberman's Bank, Viroqua	55,180	91
Northern Bank, Howard	19,060	52
Oakwood Bank, North Pepin	48,100	96
Oshkosh Com. Bank	23,635	67
Prairie City Bank, Ripon	20,100	74
Racine County Bank	20,510	69
Rock River Bank, Janesville	45,165	69
Rockwell & Co's Bank, Elk Horn	21,286	59
Sauk City Bank	49,992	94
Sauk County Bank, Baraboo	49,026	100
Second Ward Bank, Milwaukee	180	100
Shawanaw Bank, Shawano	59,709	94
State Bank, Madison	10,459	99
State Bank of Wisconsin	21,751	52
St. Croix Valley Bank, Hudson	65,015	76
Summitt Bank, Oconomowoc	17,783	78
Sun Prairie Bank	28,686	70
Walworth County Bank, Delavan	27,455	64
Waukesha County Bank, Wautoma	62,988	59
Waupun Bank	22,065	69
Wis. Bank of Madison	24,625	88
Wis. Marine & Fire Ins. Bk., Milwaukee	35,362	100
Wis Pinery Bank, Stevens Point	45,361	78

Courtesy Jimmy Kaczor

LIST OF STOCKHOLDERS

OF THE

National Exchange Bank of Milwaukee,

July 1, 1865.

NAME.	RESIDENCE.	NAME.	RESIDENCE.
Joseph Warner	Middlebury, Vt.	Henry R. Weed	Troy, N. Y.
P. Jewett	Middlebury, do.	W. H. Rockwell	Brattleboro', Vt.
Wm. Nash	New Haven, do.	Samuel Bowles	Springfield, Mass
R. W. Peake	Bristol, do.	Huldah D. Bowles	do. do.
C D. Nash, Guardian	Milwaukee, Wis.	Lafayette Clark	Brattleboro', Vt.
Mrs Susan S. Judd	Racine, do.	M. P. Lampson	Le Roy, N. Y.
Perley Mitchell	Rockville, Ind.	George Dauchy	W.Cambr'ge,Ma.
Andrew Mitchell	Milwaukee, Wis.	N. M. Birchard	New Haven, Vt.
Mrs. S. E. Tomlinson	Batavia, N. Y.	W. P. Nash	Troy, N. Y.
Almira Dunbar	Milwaukee, Wis.	John L. Manning	do. do.
John Jackson	Brandon, Vt.	Mrs. Francis H. Vail	do. do.
Nathan Marble	Port Byron, N. Y.	Mrs. F. W. Griswold	Oakville, Conn.
Mrs. C. A. Gorham	Boston, Mass.	Troy City Bank	Troy, N. Y.
John Bradford	Milwaukee, Wis.	O. Wooster	Middlebury,Vt.
S. S Daggett	do. do.	John W. Paine	Troy, N. Y.
J. H. Van Dyke	do. do.	Mrs. Mary R. Hale	St. Paul, Minn.
Asa Sprague	Rochester, N. Y.	Mrs. Harriet F. Buck	Lockport, N. Y.
Hannah F. Sherwin	Lowell, Mass.	B. Pierce	Chester'Fy, N.H.
W. R. Sill	Portage, Wis.	R. H. Hopkins	do. do.
F. N. Wilson	Catskill, N. Y.	B. F. Bowles	Springfield, Mass
Eliza M. Wilson	do. do.	C. D. Nash	Milwaukee, Wis.
V. Cooke	do. do.	W. W. Bacon	New Haven, Ct.
W. W. Cornell	Troy, do.	Henry C. Lockwood	Troy, N. Y.
Mary Abbie Todd	Conway, Mass.	John Plankinton	Milwaukee, Wis.
Samuel Root	Brattleboro', Vt.	Edwin Knowlton	Mansfield, Ct.
Royal Woodward	Albany, N. Y.	Daniel Humphrey	Maromania,Wis.
Otis Woodward	Mansfield, Conn.	W. Haile	Hinsdale, N. H.
Willard Gay	Troy, do.	Elisa H. Dewey	Williams'n, Ms.
John S. Ganson	Buffalo, do.	Jane R. Wilder	Brattleboro', Vt.
Edward Pierson	do. do.	Susan B. Salisbury	do. do.
Charles Allen	Boston, Mass.	George Chamberlain	Chesterfield, N H
Tracy Taylor	Troy, N. Y.	David Smith	Perrisburg, Vt.
W. A. Young	Albany, do.	C. F. Dana	Boston, Mass.
E. A. Birchard	Boston, Mass.	Elisa A. Blake	New York, N. Y.
John A. Griswold	Brattleboro', Vt.	H. Leach	Troy, N. Y.
W. C. Simonds	Shoreham, Vt.	Mrs. E. D. Mather	Cleveland, O.
James Voorhees	Pittsford, N. Y.	Juliette D. Hubbell	Troy, N Y
Thomas White	Troy, do.	Electa K. Buell	New York, do.
Abraham Wing	Glenn's Falls, do.	Elizabeth W. Allen	Boston, Mass.
A. Van Schoonhoven	Pittsford, Vt.	Edward Hubbell	Gambier, O.
	Brattleboro', do.	Sarah G. Buil	Brattleboro', Vt.
	nfield,Mass.	Harriet G. Holbrook	do. do.
	Vt.	Mary Ann Cune	do. do.
		Francis Goodhue	do. do.
		W. P. Cune, Trustee	Rochester, N. Y.
		Miss Susan J. Potter	Racine, Wis.
		Sherwin	Racine, Wis.

Milwaukee Bank
July 5. 1865

National Exchange Bank of Milwaukee,

UNITED STATES DESIGNATED DEPOSITORY.

Milwaukee, July 5th. 1865.

Dear Sir,

Herewith please find Draft on Mercantile National Bank, $ 165———, being 5 per cent. Dividend, free from Government Tax on your Stock in this Bank, declared payable on and after the 5th inst.

Very Respectfully,

C. D. NASH, Pres't.

RESOURCES.

Notes and Bills Discounted,	$282,175 54
Overdrafts,	805 00
Real Estate and Office Furniture,	22,181 23
Premium on U. S. Bonds,	1,300 00
Remittances and other Cash Items,	777 40
Due from National Banks,	61,145 72
Due from other Banks and Bankers,	16,171 42
U. S. Bonds Deposited with S. T. Treasurer to secure Circulating Notes,	50,000 00
U. S. Bonds Deposited with U. S. Treasurer to secure Deposits,	100,000 00
Other U. S. Securities,	5,000 00
Revenue Stamps,	5,562 65
Wisconsin State Sixes,	187 50
Minnesota State Sevens,	56,000 00
Specie,	5,000 00
Cash on hand in Circulating Notes, State Banks,	8,075 00
Other Lawful Money,	924 55
	115,307 00
	$755,198 67

LIABILITIES.

Capital Stock,	$200,000 00
Circulating Notes Received from Comptroller,	79,450 00
" Bank of Milwaukee, outstanding,	7,000 00
Individual Deposits,	345,043 42
United States Deposit,	33,404 80
Due National Banks,	53,145 08
Due State Banks,	22,516 77
Profits after Dividend this day paid,	2,519 70
	$755,198 67

C. D. NASH,
President.

JOHN BRADFORD,
Vice President.

W. G. FITCH,
Cashier.

DAY, ALLEN & CO.
Wholesale Grocers and Tea Dealers,
NO. 69 SOUTH WATER ST.,

L. C. DAY,
W. T. ALLEN,
S. P. FARRINGTON.

CHICAGO, ILL.

List of ILLINOIS BANKS rejected Nov. 20, 1860.

American Exchange Bank, Raleigh.
Bank of Aurora.
Bank of the Commonwealth.
Bank of Raleigh.
Corn Exchange Bank,

Grayville Bank.
National Bank, Equality.
State Bank of Illinois, Shawneetown
Southern Bank of Illinois, Grayville.

The following ILLINOIS BANKS were rejected by the Bankers of Chicago, Monday, April 1, 1861, consequently are not received as Currency.

Bank of Albion.
Bank of Chester.
Bank of Carmi.
Bank of Pike County.
Bank of Quincy.
Bank of the Republic.
Bank of Southern Illinois, Bolton.
Bank of the Federal Union.
Belvidere Bank.
Canal Bank, Thebes.
Citizen's Bank.
Commercial Bank, New Haven.
Continental Bank.
Corn Planters' Bank.
Edgar County Bank.

Farmers' and Traders' Bank.
Farmers' Bank, Metropolis.
Farmers' Bank, New Canton.
Frontier Bank.
Grand Prairie Bank.
Illinois State Bank, New Haven.
Merchants' and Drovers' Bank.
Mississippi River Bank.
Morgan County Bank.
New Market Bank-
Railroad Bank.
Shawanese Bank.
Prairie State Bank.
Union County Bank.

All WISCONSIN BANKS are rejected here, but are Par at Milwaukee, except the following:

Arctic Bank.
Bank of Appleton.
Bank of Albany.
Bank of Eau Claire.
Beloit Savings Bank.
Chippewa Bank.
Clark County Bank.
Citizens' Bank.
Farmers' Bank.
Hall & Bro's Bank.
Katayan Bank.
Koshkonong Bank.

Laborers' Bank.
Mechanics' Bank.
Northwestern Bank.
Osborn Bank.
Portage County Bank.
Reedsburgh Bank.
State Stock Bank.
St. Croix River Bank.
Tradesmens' Bank.
Wood County Bank.
Oconto County Bank.

All other Wisconsin Bank Notes, if remitted to us, we will send to Milwaukee on your account and credit you with proceeds.

DAY, ALLEN & CO.

Chicago, April 17, 1861.

TERRITORIAL SCRIP

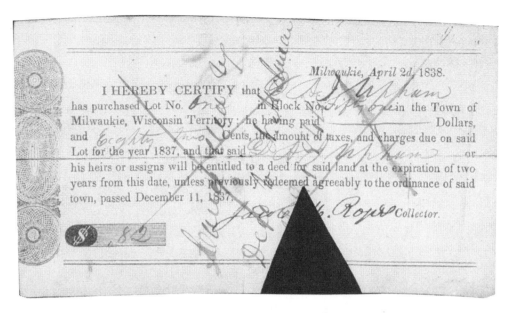

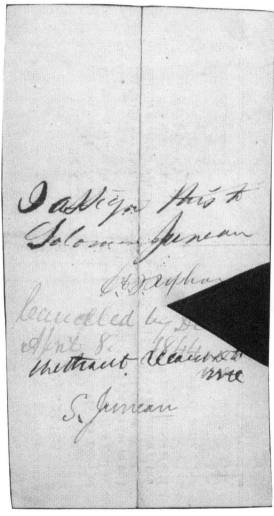

Tax receipt. Included here only because of its makers: Don A.J. Upham and S. (Soloman) Juneau. Juneau arrived in 1818 and was the first white settler in what is now the greater Milwaukee area, and remained the only white man as late as 1833. In 1835 a post office was established in Milwaukee and he became the first postmaster. He became the city's first mayor in 1846. Upham became U.S. Attorney for the district of Wisconsin.

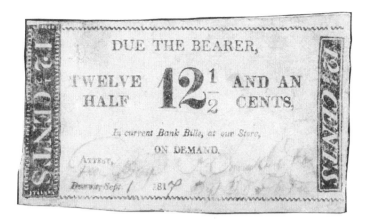

Wisconsin earliest scrip. Dated Sept. 1, 1871 with the city of Detroit crossed out and Green Bay written in. It would have been the only 12-1/2¢ denomination known. It arose from one-eighth of a Spanish Real. Also the value of a British Shilling.

A most difficult document to read but probably five dollars paid for a bond for Geo. P. Delaplaine, auditor. Reverse is signed by J. Larkin Jr. Treasurer W.T.

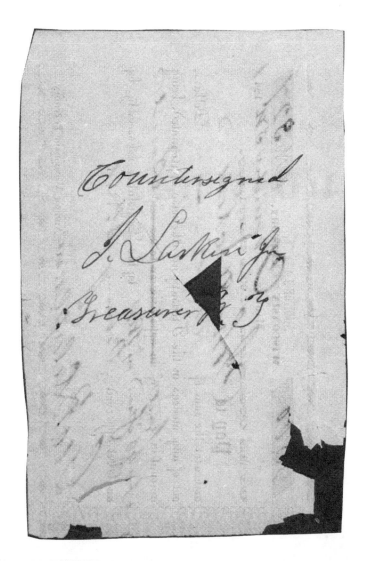

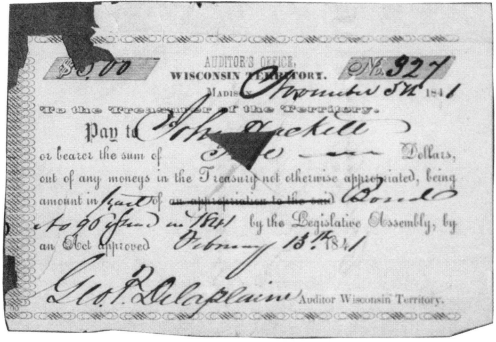

A piece of scrip used to disperse funds from the Legislative Assembly raised from the bond issue of February 13, 1841.

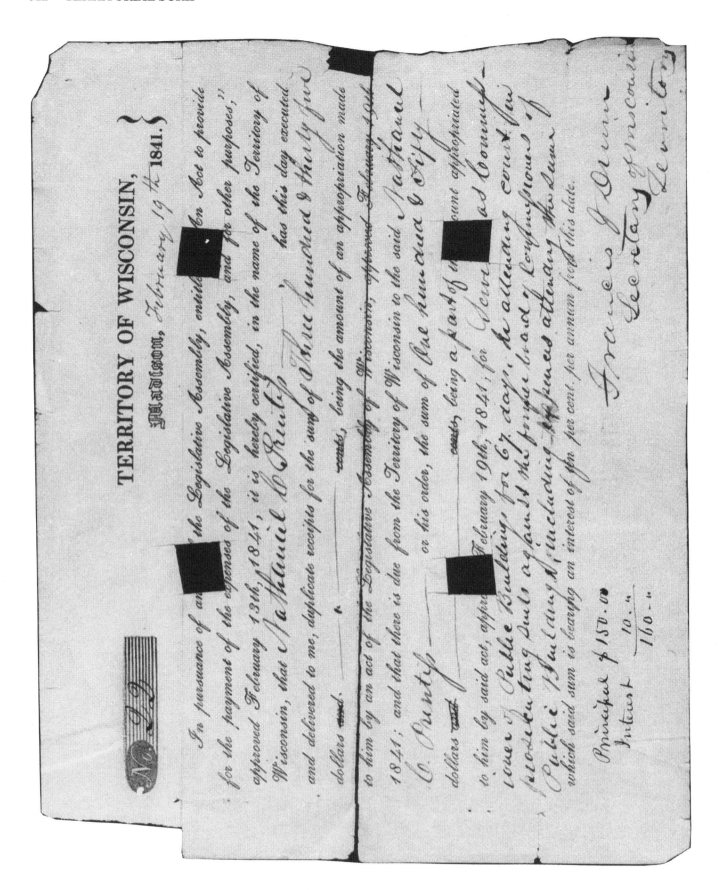

An interest bearing note issued February 19, 1841 (issued) to Nathaniel C. Pruitys for $335.00 and $150.00 due him for "services as commissioner of Public Buildings for 67 days. In attending court in prosecuting suits against the former board of commissioners of Public Buildings including attending the same."

Territorial bond: Issued under the Act of February 19, 1841. Several of these unissued bonds have been seen but an issued one has never surfaced. Remember this falls within the Jacksonian period — 1832-1844 — also known as the "Hard Times" period. Thus money and wealth were scarce and those issues were most probably redeemed as well.

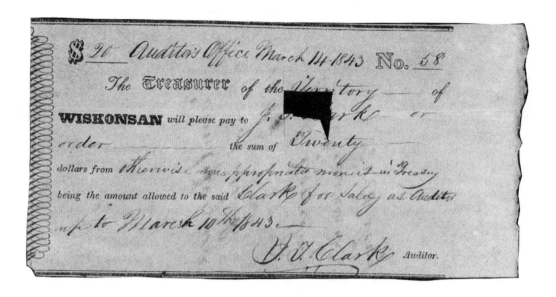

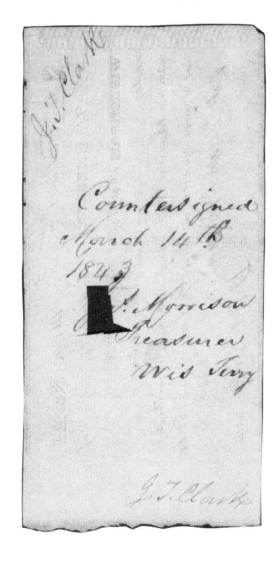

Auditor's office — R-7
(Note spelling of Wiskonsin. This could be a typesetting error or an alternate way of spelling. Early Wisconsin maps use yet a different spelling, such as Wiskonsan). Apparently auditors issued scrip, the treasurer redeemed it.

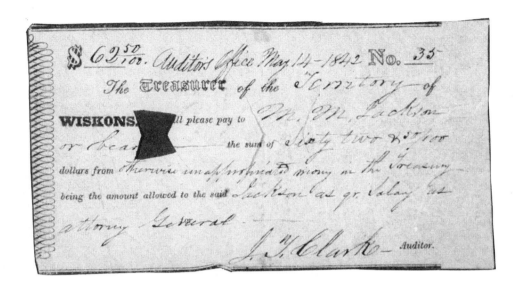

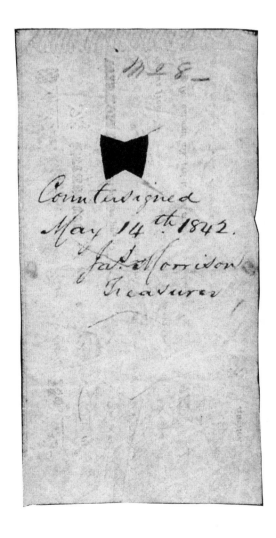

Check paid to M. M. Jackson for $62.50 as gross salary as Attorney General, May 14, 1842. (Note spelling of Wiskonsin). This is the earliest known use of this spelling as it had been spelled Wisconsin on all earlier currency. (Could have been a printer's error). Endorsed on back by Jas. Morrison Treasurer W.T.

The next six notes are commonly referred to as the 1942 Scrip. All are dated February 19, 1942. They were printed by Charles Sholes of Racine, father of Christopher Sholes, the inventor of the typewriter. Like the other scrip shown, here a new Legislature had no money, thus it had no choice to print scrip. Hand written denominations are for amounts under $20. While it hasn't been seen lately, there is a printed $100 been reported several years ago.

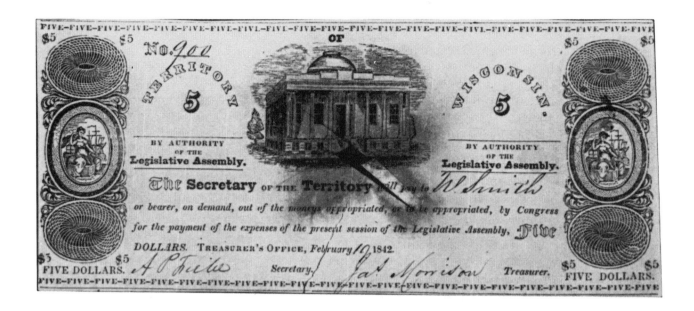

$5   Will pay to _____ or bearer   R-5

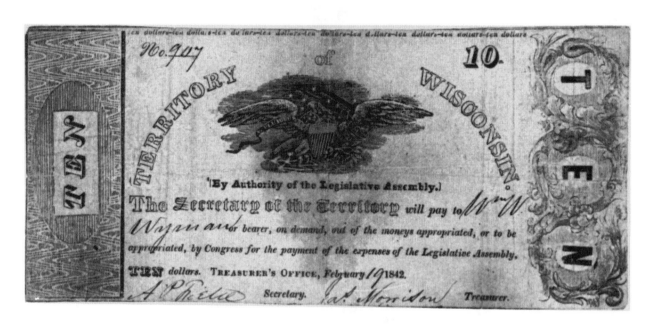

$10

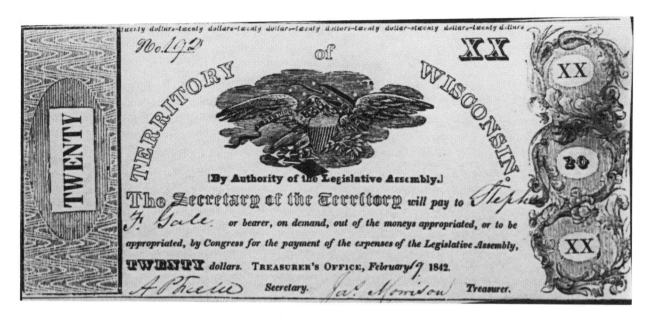

$20

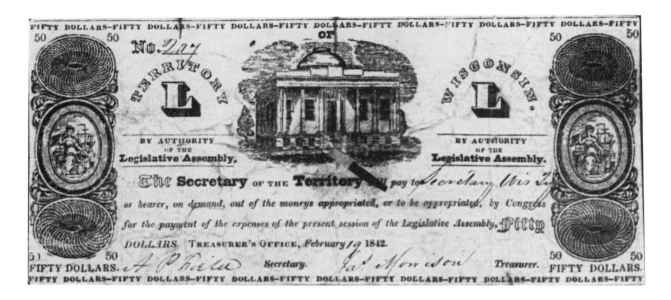

$50   R-7

$100   R-7

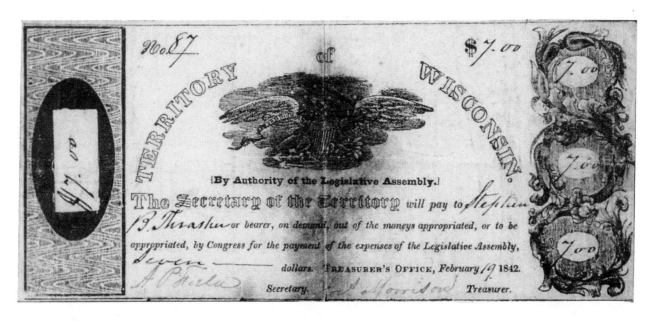

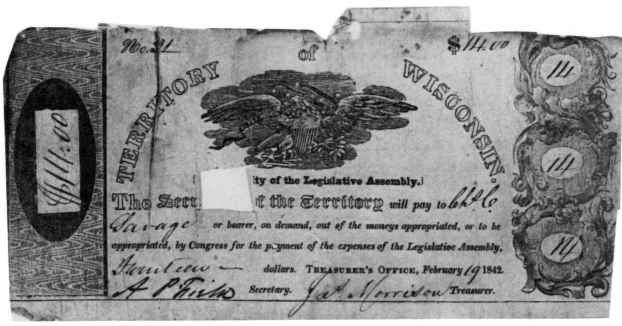

Handwritten denominations

R-5

Auditor's office — R-7
As above. Is actually a check as they were cashed the same day they were made. In this case monies paid
were for transporting witnesses in governmental suits.

Constitutional Congress warrant. Wisconsin tried without success to become a state in 1846, the year Iowa succeeded in doing so. The delegates reached an impass on two issues. Free banking was in effect from 1836 to 1839 and then suspended. It was not reinstated until 1851. Also canals. These were at odd from Sturgeon Bay to Lake Michigan, Green Bay to Portage via the Fox River, and one from Milwaukee West to the Rock River.

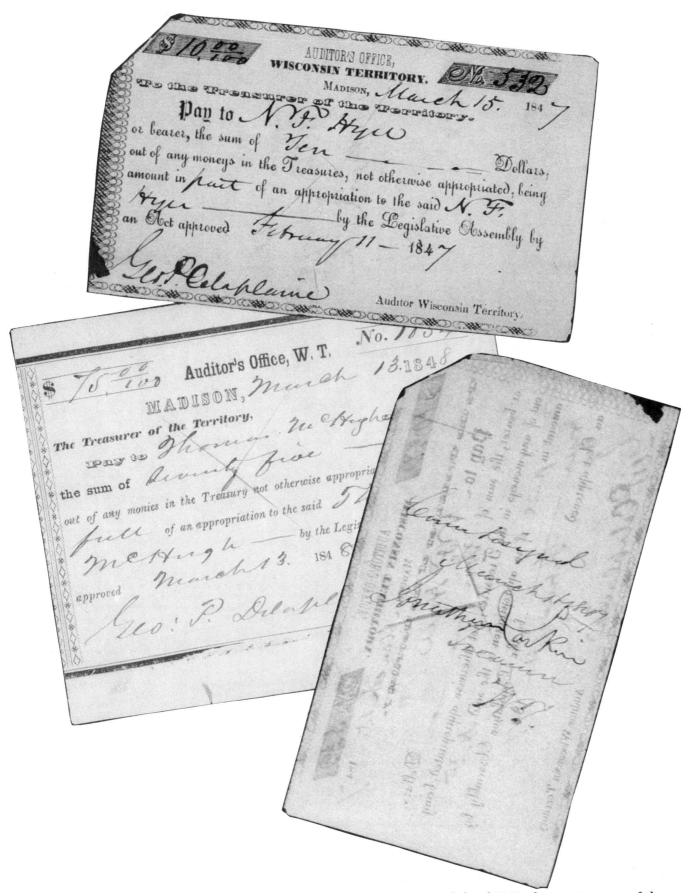

Auditor's office, March 5, 1847. R-7. As Wisconsin became a state in July of 1848, these notes some of the last issue as a Territory. Legislation granting free banking was passed in late 1851, three years after becoming a state. Yet the first bank to issue currency did not do so until 1853. Fiscal documents from 1848 to 1853 are unknown to this author.

CANAL BONDS

Fox & Wisconsin Improvement Corp. Scrip

Dated at Oshkosh. August 13, 1851. Signed by Nelson Dewey, Governor. Payee: Morgan L. Martin (prominent city of Green Bay). Interest rate of 12% per annum. M. L. Martin signature on verso. Actual size 14-1/4 x 8-3/4 white bond paper, real overprint.

Fox & Wisconsin Improvement Scrip

Dated at Oshkosh. May 15, 1852. Signed by the Sec. of State, November 30, 1851, by the Act of Legislature, March 11, 1851. Payee: Morgan L. Martin for work on the lower Fox River, i.e. between Lake Winnebago & Green Bay. Actual size 16-1/4 x 12. Blue paper. M.L. Martin signature on verso.

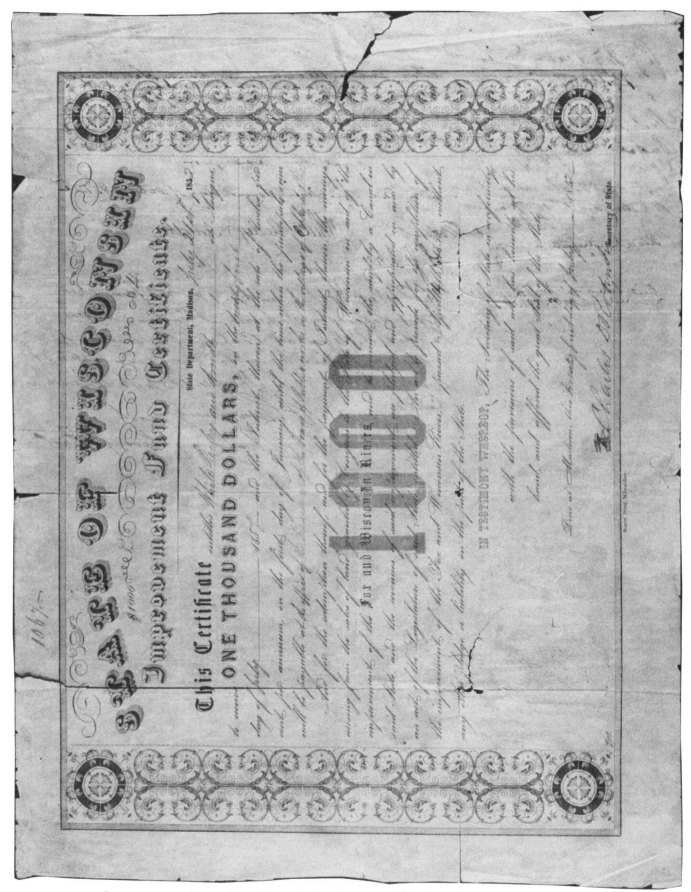

Improvement Fund Certificate for the Fox and Wisconsin Rivers

Dated and issued at Madison July 21, 1852. 12% per annum. This certificate included the connection of the two rivers by a canal. Actual size 14 x 11-1/8. Blue paper.

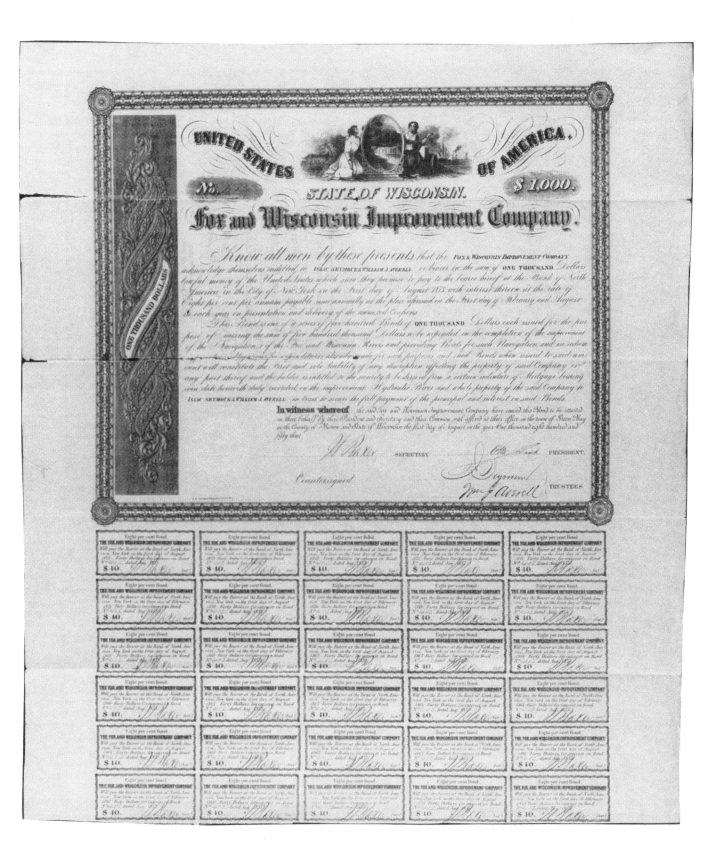

Fox & Wisconsin Improvement Company

Payees: Isaac Seymour & William J. Averrel. $1000. 8% per annum. In addition to improvements this bond also includes expenditures for boats dated at Green Bay August 1, 1853. Signed by Otto Tank, I. Seymour and Wm. J. Averill. This is a first mortgage bond indicating they had privately invested in the canal.

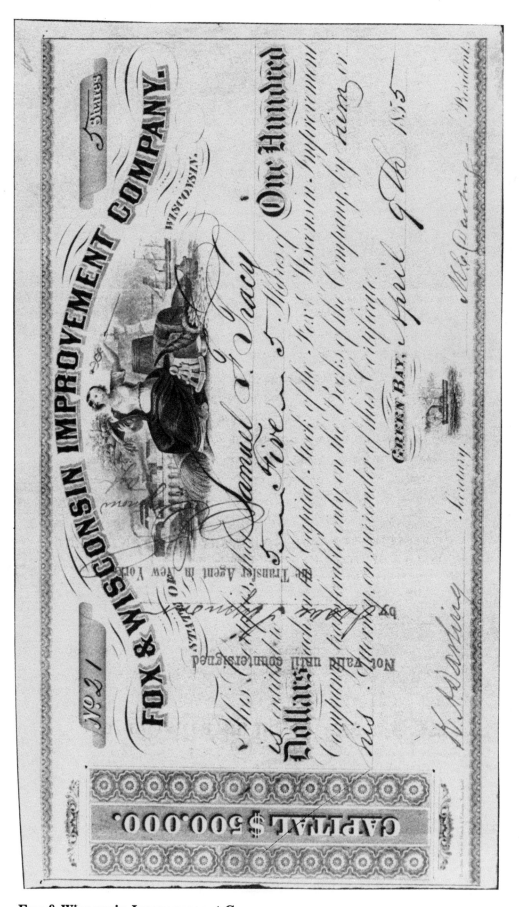

Fox & Wisconsin Improvement Company

5 shares, $100 par value. April 9, 1855.

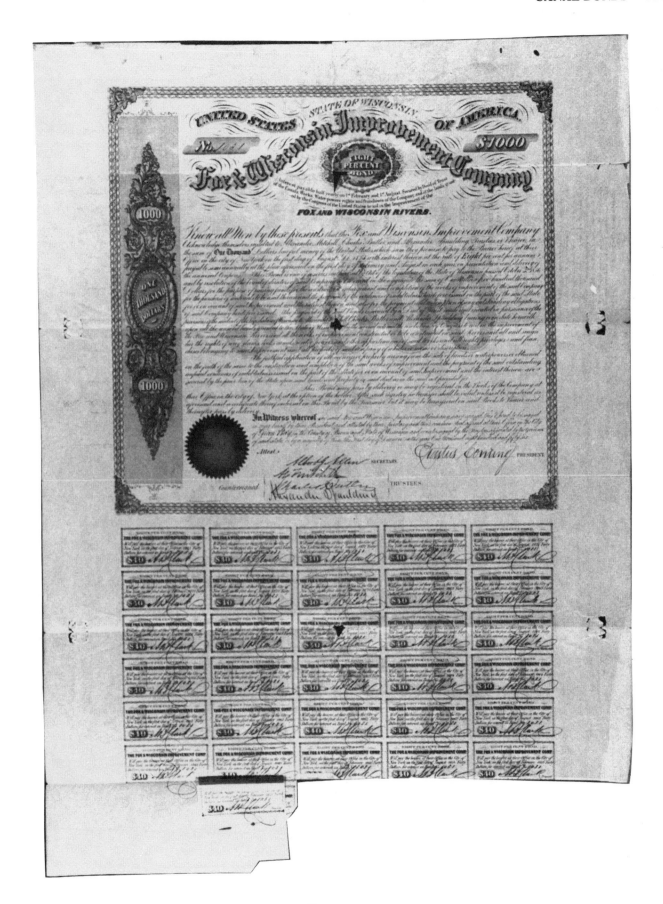

Fox & Wisconsin Improvement Company

$1000, 8%, December 1, 1856. Alexander Mitchell, Charles Butler & Alexander Spaulding, trustees. White bond paper, 14 x 23-1/2. Red overprint.

Sturgeon Bay and Lake Michigan

Ship Canal and Harbor Company. $1000, 7% per annum. Moses L. Scudder Jr. of Chicago, Ill. trustee or bearer. May 1, 1874. White bond paper, green ink. 16 x 18. Gold overprint.